CRITICAL THINKING

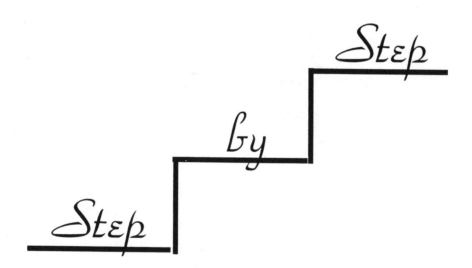

Step by Step

Robert Cogan

University Press of America,® Inc.
Lanham • New York • Oxford

Copyright © 1998
University Press of America,® Inc.
4720 Boston Way
Lanham, Maryland 20706

12 Hid's Copse Rd.
Cummor Hill, Oxford OX2 9JJ

Library of Congress Cataloging-in-Publication Data

Cogan, Robert.
Critical thinking : step by step / Robert Cogan.
p.   cm.
l. Reasoning. 2. Critical thinking.   I. Title.
BC177.C64   1998   160 —dc21   98-5370 CIP

ISBN 0-7618-1067-6 (pbk: alk. ppr.)

TABLE OF CONTENTS

PREFACE
TO THE CORRECTED 1ST EDITION

Richard Paul defines critical thinking as disciplined, self-directed thinking which exemplifies the perfections of thinking appropriate to a particular mode or domain of thought (Paul, 1990, p. 51.) Some of the perfections are clarity, precision, accuracy, relevance, consistency, and logicalness. To do justice to this richly detailed definition would require many books. Stephen Thomas once gave a briefer, narrower definition which describes what this book is about. *Critical thinking is the reliable, reasoned determination of whether to believe, disbelieve or suspend judgment about the truth of any statement.* Corrections to this printing are minor to give more emphasis to the Correspondence Theory of Truth, to improve wording of the explanations of deductive and inductive validity, and to make more comprehensive the treatment of degrees of support reasons give to conclusions.

Critical thinking values **skepticism** (doubt, slowness to believe, free questioning) over its' opposites gullibility and dogmatism (easy, firm belief in claims which are unsupported or improbable.) It values **realism** as opposed to idealism, **rational hope** as opposed to wishful thinking, **self-understanding** as opposed to self-deception. It values **reason,** as opposed to faith, **science,** as opposed to pseudoscience, **true democracy** and **social justice,** not government by special interest, and an active search for **happiness.**

For skeptics and humanists out of school, the text provides coverage of a recent advance in argument analysis (arrow diagraming), and a very new, great expansion in syllogistic logic. It also contains a discussion of justification, the leading recent topic in theory of knowledge, and a compact, cultural literacy review of basic schools, fields and problems in philosophy.

But I wrote this book primarily for two groups of people: students like my own and other teachers of critical thinking. My students are incoming freshmen in our basic critical thinking course, one of two taken before Introduction to Philosophy. I teach in an open admissions state university. Many of my students want to learn the truth about the real world, as well as have some fun and get a good job. However, they went to schools whose curricula and teaching methods did not inspire their best efforts. Many performed in the middle, fourth or fifth quintiles of their high school graduating classes. They were not equipped with factual knowledge, learning skills and enthusiasm for academic work matching their desire to learn.

For such students I have written a text "shaped" like a pyramid. It starts with sharply-pointed, narrow, formal, noncontroversial material. Essentially it is on reading comprehension of reasoning by arrow diagraming. It then broadens out somewhat to deal with the fundamental concepts of evaluating statements and reasoning such as truth, validity and soundness. For teachers, almost every skill in the book is taught with some new wrinkle, born of my determination to develop the skills of students like my own to the point where their exercise and test answers converge on those given by highly skilled students. An example would be my adaptation of Bruce Thompson's system of Expanded Syllogistic Logic (Thompson, 1992) to the "Cross Hatch Method" which is in Chapter Six. This system is applicable to 10 categorical statement forms and 4,000 argument forms. I hope these wrinkles will help you help other students.

I have long held the belief that we can not really teach students to think critically by giving them merely formal tools while not acquainting them with some of the negative facts and realities about which to be critical. Therefore in Part Three this book broadens out into a wide base of critical material about philosophical theories like Dualism, religion and science, pseudoscience and the United States and the global corporate economy. I actually use the same book for Basic Critical Thinking, Chapters 1 through 5 and 11 through 15, and Chapters 5 through 10 and supplementary materials for our next level Beginning Logic course.

Wishful thinking and fantasy are fun. Critical thinking is sometimes fun, but deflating wishful thinking and fantasy is no fun. So I have a critical thinking character in a number of drawings, a nerdy, lab-coated, pen pocket protector wearing Dr. No Phun.

If my money debts were as great as my debt to others for ideas and facts, I would be just about broke. I am indebted to Richard Double, Nancy Folbre, Terrence Hines, David Korten, Charles Mercer, James Munro, Richard Paul, Lawrence Persinger, Kathy Johnson Plaza, Carl Sagan, Wesley Salmon, Steven Thomas, and Bruce Thompson, from whose works and conversations I have drawn much material. I learned a great deal in a Regional Institute on Critical Thinking run by the Foundation for Critical Thinking and thank Edinboro University for funding my attendance. I like working with serious students. Kathy is an art education major at my university. She did the wonderful drawings which grace my often artless writing. I am also indebted to many other authors mostly of books published by Prometheus Books and articles from *The Skeptical Inquirer,* and *Skeptic Magazine.* Errors are, of course, my own. I would be grateful for constructive criticism of this book. I need also to thank my wife Ruth and children Sam and Marin, from whom many valuable days were stolen writing this book. Thanks are also due to Ian Phillips and Paul Tarasovitch for producing excellent camera ready copy.

Department of Philosophy,
Edinboro University of Pennsylvania
August, 1998

ACKNOWLEDGEMENTS

Chapter Two, Section 4 and Exercise 7C, Problem 14.: From *An Essay Concerning the True Original, Extent and End of Civil Government*, Chapters 9, and 1 by John Locke. Reprinted by permission of Blackwell Publishers from The Second Treatise of Government, edited by J. W. Gough, Barnes and Noble, 1996.

Exercise 7C, Problems 2, 4 and 7 from *How to Keep your VCR Alive*, second edition, Copyright 1990, by Steve Thomas, reprinted by permission of Worthington Publishing Company, Tampa, Florida.

Exercise 7C, Problem 8 from Meditations on First Philosophy by Rene Descartes, tr. by Lawrence J. La Fleur. Copyright 1951, renewed 1979. Problem 9 from Descartes Selections, ed. Ralph M. Eaton, copyright 1927. Both reprinted by permission of MacMillan Co.

Exercise 7C, Problem 15: *"Antimony of Pure Reason: Third Conflict of Transcendental Ideas"* from Emmanuel Kant, Critique of Pure Reason. Copyright 1952, 1990, reprinted by permission of Encyclopedia Britannica, Inc. from Great Books of the Western World.

Part One

ANALYSIS OF REASONING

SHORT, SIMPLE REASONING

I

SECTION I.I: RECOGNITION OF REASONING

A group of sentences is called a *"discourse."* When reading a group of sentences in a novel, textbook or other source, or when hearing a group of sentences, we are seeing or hearing a discourse. There are different kinds of discourse. Reasoning is one kind. Narration or story telling is another. Description is a third kind. Imperative discourse, which tells how to do something, is a fourth kind. Often the four kinds are mixed together. But there are important differences between them. Different kinds of things are important in different kinds of discourses. In this book, we will be concerned with what is important in reasoning discourse. *Reasoning* **is discourse in which some statements are set forth as supporting, justifying belief in, or explaining some other statement or statements.**

Sometimes a person reasons to extend his or her own knowledge. Many times reasoning is done to persuade or convince another person of something. Sometimes it is done to explain some statement. One of the most important things in reasoning discourse is getting the point. Logicians, people who study reasoning, call the point or points of reasoning its' "conclusion" or "conclusions." *Conclusions* **are statements which are supported, for which evidence is given, the ones justified or explained.** *Reasons* **are statements which are given to support, justify or provide evidence for conclusions.** It is quite easy to learn how to tell what the conclusion of a piece of reasoning is, or what point is being made. The first step is to learn how to recognize reasoning at all.

The presence of certain words helps to identify reasoning rather than some other form of discourse. **An** *inference* **is a step of reasoning.** There are two kinds of words people use to indicate that they are taking a step of reasoning. They are called *inference* **indicators.** Some are conclusion indicators; others are reason indicators. The following is a list of some Conclusion Indicators. When part of a sentence, they usually mean that the statement following them is a conclusion of some reasoning: *so, thus, therefore, hence, whence, accordingly,* and *consequently.* Here is an example. "Sam just got back, so it is after 3 pm." The "so" indicates that "it is after 3 pm" is the conclusion.

The following words are reason indicators. Anytime they are part of a sentence, what follows them is being offered as a reason: *because, since, for,* and *as.* Here is another example: "It must be after 3 pm. because Sam just got back." The word "because" indicates that "Sam just got back" is being offered as a reason. Other words and phrases can serve as indicators, too. So, it is important to read carefully and think about whether any statements are being used to support others or not.

Inference indicator phrases relate two complete or easily completed *thoughts*, or *claims*. If there are not two complete or easily completed claims on either side of a phrase, then there is not reasoning. What must a sentence contain to be counted as expressing a complete claim? It must have a word or phrase answering the question "What action is happening?" or the question "What state of being is described?" This is the verb. It becomes at least part of the predicate of the sentence. It must also have a word or phrase which answers to the question "What is being talked about here?" This is a noun. It becomes the most important part of the subject. A little further along we will learn how to make brackets "<" and ">" to analyze reasoning into reasons and conclusions. These simple questions from grammar are very important to remember to use as tests of whether we have made our marks correctly. Other words are important to reasoning but are not indicators. Certain helping words sometimes signal that a conclusion is being stated. These words include "must," "must not," "should," "should not," "ought," "ought not," "can," "cannot," "necessarily," and "impossible." *When a critical thinker sees or hears these words, she asks "why" of the claim. "Why?" calls for the reasons.* But caution must be used with these words. Many times they are used in other ways. Often they are used to express judgments of right and wrong, or legal requirements, or what can or can't be done physically.

Certain other words are called *"connectives"* because they connect or relate statements to each other. They are very important, but are not inference indicators. They include the word "not" itself. They include the words "if" and "then" in conditional sentences like "If you go, then we will go." *Such words are connectives, not inference indicators.* The same goes for *disjunctions* like "or." *Conjunctions* like "and," "additionally," "also," "besides," "moreover," "but," "however," "nevertheless" are not indicators. The first five of them often tell us that two statements have the same function. Maybe they are both reasons. Maybe they are both conclusions. Words like "and" often tell us where one reason or conclusion ends and another one begins.

Below can be found a pretty complete list of reason and conclusion indicators. Learn whole indicator phrases exactly as they are in the list to avoid confusion. Only when found exactly as they are, are they likely to be functioning as indicators. *In deciding whether a phrase is functioning as an indicator, ask two questions. First, are there at least two separate claims in this discourse? Second, does this phrase have the same use as "so" or "because?"* If it does, then the phrase is very likely to be functioning as an indicator. If it doesn't, then the phrase is very likely not functioning as an indicator.

How is it possible to tell whether a phrase has the same use as "so" or "because?" Simply read the discourse with "so" or "because" in place of the phrase in question. If it makes good sense with one of them, then the phrase probably is functioning as an indicator. If it does not, then the phrase is probably not functioning as an indicator. Here are some examples to illustrate these points. Separation of words will show some errors in indicator recognition and cases of correct recognition.

WRONG: After three months   I concluded that   I wasn't cut out for college. "After three months" is only a fragment, not a complete or easily completed thought, so "I concluded that" is not functioning as an indicator.

RIGHT: After being bored and doing poorly,   I concluded that   I wasn't cut out for college. "I was bored and did poorly" are two reasons giving evidence for not being cut out for college.

This example shows one way indicators appear. A claim is made, then there is an indicator and then another claim: <Claim,> indicator <claim.> Here the indicator indicates a conclusion. However, in other cases it could be a reason indicator, as in <Claim,> because <claim.>

WRONG: "As the years have gone by,   much has happened to change MTV for the better." (Rapping, 1993). "As" here is just an adverb of time.

RIGHT: As women began demanding more videos by and about them, the network had to respond with women-identified, even feminist messages in a context of extreme sexism and conservatism. (Rapping, 1993 paraphrased). Here "as" indicates a reason. This shows the other way reason indicators only appear: Indicator <claim,> <claim.>

Table One: INFERENCE INDICATORS

UNDERLINE THESE - DRAW ONE ARROW FOR EACH - BRACKET BOTH CLAIMS

<u>Indicator Phrase</u> \<Claim\> \<Claim\> or \<Claim\> <u>Indicator Phrase</u> \<Claim\>

CONCLUSION INDICATORS	REASON INDICATORS
so	because (and because of)
thus (exceptions)	since (exceptions)
therefore	for (exceptions)
hence	as (exceptions)
whence	being as
consequently	inasmuch as
accordingly	firstly, secondly
then (without "if")	on the grounds that
indicates that	as indicated by
allow us to infer that	may be inferred from
it follows that	follows from
you see that	seeing that
we can deduce that	may be deduced from
we can derive that	may be derived from
demonstrates that	in light of the fact that
proves that	on the assumption that
entails that	on the supposition that
implies that	is implied by the view that
for this reason	for the reasons that
that's why	in view of the fact that
bears out the point that	whereas
leads me to believe that	

FREQUENT CONCLUSION SIGNALS DO NOT UNDERLINE THESE. MAKE ARROWS ONLY WHEN CLAIMS ARE CONCLUSIONS.	IMPORTANT NON-INDICATORS DO NOT UNDERLINE THESE. DO NOT MAKE ARROWS. THESE WORDS APPEAR AROUND OR BETWEEN CLAIMS.
should, should not	Connectives like "and", "or"
can, cannot	"not", "If...then.."
must, must not	\<Claim P and/or claim Q\>
ought, ought not	\<If claim P, then, claim Q\>
necessarily	QUANTIFIERS "all", "some", "no"
impossible	"that", "by" "from", "of"

Notice how similar some of these are, like the conclusion indicator "for this reason" and the reason indicator "for the reasons that." The moral is: *learn these phrases exactly, not just the root words in them. The student should now do Exercise 1 on Indicator sorting. The ability to recognize and sort indicators will be tested.*

SECTION 1.2:   DIAGRAMING REASONING

"Analyzing" means breaking something down into its' parts. Use underlining to mark indicators. Use *"angle brackets"* to mark off reasons and conclusions. Angle brackets look like this: "<" and ">." Underline the whole of every indicator word or phrase found. **Brackets should go, so far as possible, around complete thoughts starting with a noun subject and containing a verb predicate.** Place a pair of angle brackets around the whole of each reason and conclusion found in discourse. A bracket will be placed in front of the first word of the claim, and one will be placed after the last word of the claim. Number the statements as they are read. Always number the first claim "1," the second "2," and so on. Then make diagrams of the reasoning, putting the numbers of the indicated reasons up above and the numbers of the indicated conclusions down below. Last, draw an arrow pointing downwards from the number or numbers for the reason to the number or numbers for the conclusion or conclusions. (There may be one or more reasons and conclusions.) The arrow will represent the claim that in this passage the above numbered statements are offered to support the statements numbered below the arrow. Such diagrams are called "Arrow Diagrams."

A general diagram of how to represent reasoning is printed below. When making such a diagram, we are claiming that the statement up above and the statement down below actually have some indicator phrase between them or in front of both. Or, we may be claiming instead that one statement is, in fact, reason for the other, even though the speaker or writer did not explicitly say or write an indicator phrase. We can always read the arrow as "so" or any conclusion indicator.

THE BASIC ARROW DIAGRAM

REASONS (above)

CONCLUSIONS (below)

HOW TO MAKE ARROW DIAGRAMS

1.   UNDERLINE ALL INDICATORS. UNDERLINE THE WHOLE INDICATOR. IF IT INDICATES A REASON, LABEL IT "R." IF IT INDICATES A CONCLUSION, LABEL IT "C."

A. Because he tripped, he fell.   ^R <u>Because</u> he tripped, he fell.

B. She ran fast, because of the cold.   She ran fast,   ^R <u>because of</u> the cold.

C. It's hot, so let's go swimming. It's hot, ^C <u>so</u> let's go swimming.

2. PUT ANGLE BRACKETS < > AROUND EACH COMPLETE OR EASILY COMPLETED CLAIM. EXAMPLE: <THE COLD> IN B = IT WAS COLD.

   A. Because he tripped, he fell. [R] <u>Because</u> < he tripped,> < he fell.>

   B. She ran fast, because of the cold. <She ran fast,> [R] <u>because of</u> <the cold.>

   C. It's hot, so let's go swimming. <It's hot,>[C] <u>so</u> < let's go swimming.>

3. ALWAYS NUMBER THE FIRST CLAIM "1" AND THE SECOND "2", A THIRD "3" AND SO ON. DO NOT LOOK FOR THE CONCLUSION AND NUMBER IT "1". PUT THE NUMBERS ABOVE THE LEFT BRACKET.

   A. Because he tripped, he fell. [R] <u>Because</u> [1]<he tripped,> [2]< he fell.>

   D. [1]<Calculus shouldn't be required,> [R] <u>since</u> [2]<it isn't widely needed,> and [R] <u>because of</u> [3]<its' extreme difficulty.>

4. DRAW AT THE RIGHT AN ARROW POINTING DOWN. A NUMBER ABOVE IT REPRESENTS THE REASON AND A NUMBER BELOW IT REPRESENTS THE CONCLUSION.

Number of Reason

↓

Number of Conclusion

5. IF THE INDICATOR IS A REASON, PUT THE NUMBER OF THE INDICATED REASON ABOVE THE ARROW. THEN PUT THE NUMBER OF THE OTHER CLAIM BELOW THE ARROW.

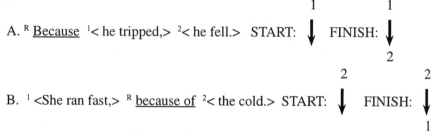

A. [R] <u>Because</u> [1]< he tripped,> [2]< he fell.> START: ↓ FINISH: ↓

B. [1] <She ran fast,> [R] <u>because of</u> [2]< the cold.> START: ↓ FINISH: ↓

6. IF THE INDICATOR IS A CONCLUSION, PUT THE NUMBER OF THE INDICATED CONCLUSION BELOW THE ARROW. THEN PUT THE NUMBER FOR THE OTHER CLAIM ABOVE THE ARROW.

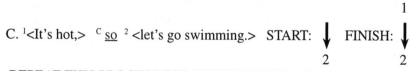

C. [1]<It's hot,> [C] <u>so</u> [2] <let's go swimming.> START: ↓ FINISH: ↓

7. REPEAT THIS PROCESS FOR EVERY INDICATOR.

   D. [1]<Calculus shouldn't be required> [R] <u>since</u> [2]<it isn't widely needed> and [R] <u>because of</u> [3] <its' extreme difficulty.>

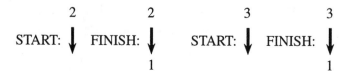

SECTION 1.3: BRACKETING INCOMPLETE THOUGHTS

"Its' extreme difficulty" does not express a complete thought. It lacks a verb. It is, however, an easily completed thought. It means "It is extremely difficult." Make it complete by simply adding the verb "to be". Another example of making an incomplete thought into a complete one is the use of "because of." With this phrase, what comes after it is a participial phrase which can easily be completed. For example:

Because of feeling too hot, he took off his jacket.
becomes

[He felt]
Because of ¹<feeling too hot,> ²<he took off his jacket.>

"Feeling too hot" is not a complete thought. Complete it by adding the understood subject and changing the form of the verb.

Another kind of case is unessential or non-restrictive clauses. Here is an example: "The Hispanic squad leader, who was the bravest of them all, led the charge." Here two separate claims are made, <The Hispanic squad leader led the charge> and <The Hispanic squad leader was the bravest of all.> This would be bracketed as follows:

¹<The Hispanic squad leader, ²<who was the bravest of them all,> led the charge.>

A third kind of case arises because sometimes people use nothing more than a noun phrase to stand for a whole statement. Sometimes they use only a pronoun as short as the word "this" or even "it." In such a case, bracket the pronoun and *give it the same number as the number of the statement it stands for.* Consider, for example, this dialogue. Two detectives on the anti-terrorist squad, Mohammed and Sarah, are talking. Mohammed says, "There were no signs of forced entry into the crime scene." SARAH asks, "So what does that tell you?" Mohammed replies, "It tells me that this crime was an 'inside job'." Mohammed's remarks contain an argument which should be bracketed as follows.

¹ <There were no signs of forced entry into the crime scene.> ¹<It> <u>tells me that</u> ² <this crime was an 'inside job'.>

So read very carefully. Always ask exactly what pronouns mean. Pronouns will usually mean some subject already named or described. When it is not clear which, take it as standing for the last mentioned subject, unless this doesn't make sense. When people say "this" or "it," they usually have their last subject in mind.

Never bracket off the statements between "If" and "then" or after "then" in An "If...,then..." or so called "conditional" statement. *The words "if" and "then" in "If...,then..." sentences are not inference indicators. They should never be underlined. The statement parts after them should not be bracketed off separately.* Consider, for example, the conditional sentence:

If you go, then we will go.

This does not assert or imply that you go. It does not assert or imply that we will go. "You go" provides no reason to support "We will go" as a conclusion. This sentence expresses a possible connection of future events made by our will. It does not express any evidence for the part after either "if" or "then". "If you go" and "then we will go" are sentence fragments which need each other to make a complete thought. So they should not be bracketed separately. There is only one correct way of bracketing any conditional sentence. Put one set of brackets around the whole sentence.

WRONG: If [1] <you go,> then [2] <we will go.>

WRONG: [1] <If you go,> [2] <then we will go.>

THE ONLY RIGHT WAY: [1] <If you go, then we will go.>

Punctuation is a valuable aid to bracketing correctly. Punctuation marks come in "strengths." By "strength" is meant how much a form of punctuation demands bracketing. End punctuation marks (periods, exclamation points, and question marks ending rhetorical questions) are super strong. *Almost always put a bracket after the end punctuation of a sentence :* !> and ?> and .>. Semicolons (";") are pretty strong, too. They often mark the end of a complete thought. Full colons (":") are weaker. They often separate a phrase from a list which should not be bracketed off. For example: "<This computer system includes: CPU, monitor, disk drives, printer, DOS and manuals.>" It wouldn't be right to bracket off "This computer system includes" without the object of "includes," nor, probably, to bracket off each of the phrases "CPU," "monitor," and so on, even though the commas do mean "and." This may be unnecessary: <This computer system includes CPU> <monitor> <disk drives> and <manual.>

Whenever there is reasoning discourse with "since" or "because" as the indicator, there is a compound sentence containing both a reason statement and a conclusion statement in the same sentence. So the most common punctuation clue to help bracket is the comma which appears or should appear at the end of the first complete thought. Here are some examples:

[R] Because [1]<we are going to the game, > [2]<we had better dress warmly.>

[1]<He pulled over at the rest stop, > [R] since [2]<he was very tired.>

Suppose the commas are in a series which separate members of a list of subjects or predicate words all in one place. Suppose it makes no difference to the strength of the reasoning whether they are bracketed separately or not. Then they should not be used to make brackets. For example, "Carol, Alice, Bill, and Ted all had an excellent adventure" strictly is a conjunction. It says "Carol had an excellent adventure, and Alice had an excellent adventure..." and so on. It may be unnecessary to the strength of a piece of reasoning to bracket this sentence as follows: <Carol,> <Alice,> <Bill,> and <Ted all had an excellent adventure> just like it may be wrong to bracket "CPU," "monitor," and so on.

One more point on bracketing thoughts. The kind of thoughts to be bracketed are *assertions.* An assertion is a claim put forth in speech or writing as true rather than false. Assertions are directly expressed in indicative (declarative) sentences. Ordinarily such sentences are **used** to make claims. Sometimes the same sentence can be used to make different claims. For example, the sentence "I am over 6' tall" can be used by different people and in each such use it makes a different claim. Also, different sentences in different or even the same language can express the same claim. For example, "Es regnet," "Il pleut," and "it is raining" all make the same claim. "It is raining hard" and "It is pouring" can also be used to make the same claim. In textbooks however, examples like these sentences are being **mentioned,** not used. *When sentences are merely mentioned, not used, many like these examples can be generally understood, but they are neither true nor false. They should still, however, be bracketed.*

The student should now do Exercise 2 on diagraming the simplest possible reasoning discourses and Exercise 3 on making arrow diagrams where you have only "condensed forms," indicators and numbers without statements.

SECTION 1.4: BRACKETING QUESTIONS AND COMMANDS

Sometimes people use questions or commands to actually make a claim. When this happens, transform the sentences from interrogative and imperative forms to indicative ones. For example, suppose, after you arrive home late from a date, Mom and Dad are really ticked-off. They yell: "Your grades are lousy. Your room is a pig sty. You don't do your chores. And you worry us to death by not paying any attention to your curfew! When are you going to grow up?" They don't really mean to be asking a question. In addition to expressing anger, they are making a point. They are giving reasons for the conclusion [You are not grown up]. The kind of question in which somebody is really making a statement is called a "rhetorical question." Transform it from a question to a statement by switching the word order from verb-subject "When are you... to subject-verb "You are not...."

Imperatives can also be easily transformed. Consider, for example, the line "Don't worry, 'cause the brothers on the street gonna work it out" from Public Enemy's album <u>Fear of a Black Planet</u>. The subject, "you" is understood. Simply write the subject and a modal word like "should" which may be necessary to make a grammatical indicative sentence. This becomes "You should not worry." We will use square brackets to enclose anything any time we change wording to indicate that we are doing so. We do this because sometimes it might not be so easy to get the author's exact meaning right. In some cases this can be very important, such as in legal contracts or treaties or negotiations.

TRANSFORMATIONS OF EASILY COMPLETED
TO ACTUALLY COMPLETE THOUGHTS

I.   COMPLETIONS - CLARIFY BY PUTTING IN AN UNDERSTOOD SUBJECT

EXAMPLE: PARTICIPIAL PHRASE
Change "feeling" to "He felt"

[He felt]
<u>Because of</u>   [1]<feeling pain,>   [2]< he moaned.>

EXAMPLE: PREPOSITIONAL PHRASE
Change "to" to "Raising tuition will"

[1]<We have to raise tuition>   <u>in order to</u>   [2]<offset increased costs.>

[Raising tuition will]
[1]<We have to raise tuition>   [2]< offset increased costs.>

2. CHANGE OF WORD ORDER

Type of Sentence	Punctuation	Function	Grammar
Declarative	.	make claim	Subject, verb
Interrogative	?	ask for info.	Verb, subject
Imperative	!	give command	Verb, subject
Exclamation	!	express self	Subject, verb

EXAMPLES:
Rhetorical Questions: When are you going to grow up?
Transformation: You are not grown up. Verb, subject to Subject, verb
Imperatives: Don't worry!
Transformation: [You should] not worry. Add subject and helping word "should."

SECTION 1.5: ELEMENTS OF SUCCESSFUL REASONING: ARGUMENTS AND EXPLANATIONS

There are many difficulties of applying Arrow Diagraming to discourse in any natural language. People are very irregular in the way they write and speak natural languages. People sometimes use interrogatives and imperatives to make claims. They use shortening devices such as noun phrases and pronouns like "it" to stand for whole statements. Furthermore, a discourse may or may not contain one or more pieces of reasoning. *No reasoning indicators may be present and there may still be reasoning.* Read carefully and ask if any attempt is being made to explain or persuade the reader of any point. For example, suppose someone said: "The sky is full of dark clouds. It's going to rain." She could be just making two separate observations. But the two sentences could be read with either the word "so" or the word "because" between them, and the compound sentence would make sense.

Elements of Successful Reasoning: "The sky is full of dark clouds, so it's going to rain" is an argument. "The sky is full of dark clouds because it's going to rain" is an explanation. Arguments and explanations are two different forms of reasoning. What's the difference? In what circumstances do we need to make arguments? We need arguments *when somebody does not accept a claim we make.* We make a claim. They reject it or ask the critical thinking question "Why do you think that?" Then we make an argument. By an argument, we do not mean a fight or dispute.

An argument is a group of statements in which reason(s) are set forth to persuade someone of the conclusion(s.) The ones set forth to persuade are called the "premises." The ones that they are set forth to convince us of are conclusions. An argument in this sense is not a fight, dispute or disagreement. There may be a contradiction in a fight, dispute or disagreement. There should be no contradiction in an argument in the sense just defined. If there was, the argument could not serve one of its most common functions: to help settle disputes. In an argument, in our sense, usually indicator words do the setting forth. The purpose of an argument is to persuade the person argued to that the conclusion is true. So to be successful, an argument must go from *more evident reasons, to less evident conclusions.* What If its reasons are less evident than its conclusion? Then the person argued to will simply say "Well, I didn't accept your original statement and now I don't see your reasons either."

To be persuasive, a person making an argument may need to have knowledge of three things. The first is the *subject* about which she is arguing. The second is something about the *audience* to whom the argument is being made. For example, suppose Mary believes that prayer should be kept out of the local public school, as it has in the recent past. John believes it should be reintroduced. Mary is not likely to persuade John by arguments about there being a constitutional "wall of separation" between church and state. John will probably reject Mary's reasons, saying that America is a Christian nation. But suppose Mary knows that John believes strongly in the Bible.

Suppose further that Mary knows her Bible well, or looks into it. She can quote to John the following passage from Matthew, Chapter 6, verses 5 and 6 where Jesus says, "And when thou prayest, thou shalt not be as the hypocrites are: for they love to pray standing in the synagogues and in the corners of the streets, that they be seen of men. Verily I say unto you, They have their reward. But thou, when thou prayest, enter into thy closet, and when thou hast shut thy door, pray to thy Father which is in secret; and thy Father which seeth in secret shall reward thee openly." This argument is much more likely to persuade John, or at least give him difficulty in trying to make his case. He must now explain why this passage does not clearly mean that Jesus was plainly against public prayer. Mary supports the claim that public prayer is Non-scriptural, or Unchristian.

The third thing a person needs to know to reason successfully is the *forms of arguments*. There are two kinds of forms, "valid" and "invalid." This distinction will be explained later. Generally speaking, *valid forms both are and ought to be much more persuasive than invalid forms.* Therefore we will study valid forms in detail and certain "formal fallacies," which are forms of argument which look very similar to valid forms, but which are not, in fact, valid.

The purpose of explanation is different. An explanation attempts to produce understanding of some evident datum (a given fact) often by some less evident, or less observable point. For example, "Grass is green because it contains chlorophyll" is an explanation. Nobody needs to be persuaded that grass is green. This explanation cites a less observable technical fact to explain it. Another example would be that we explain people's actions by mental states. For example, we might say: "He gave her flowers (action) <u>because</u> he loves her (mental state)." But we argue from action to mental states when we say "He gave her flowers (action), <u>so</u> he must love her (mental state)."

Two Kinds of Reasoning: Arguments and Explanations

		MORE EVIDENT	LESS EVIDENT
Purpose			
OF ARGUMENTS:	*to persuade*	*reasons*	*conclusions*
OF EXPLANATIONS:	*to help us understand*	*conclusions*	*reasons*

SECTION 1.6: ORDER IN REASONING

How do we decide, when there are NO indicators present whether there is reasoning present? How do we decide whether it is argument or explanation? Also, how do we decide which are the reasons and which the conclusions? These are three extremely important questions of reading comprehension. We can answer all three by means of a principle called *"The Principle of Charity,"* and a test of order in reasoning. We introduced this test earlier in substituting "so" and "because" for phrases we thought might be inference indicators. *The Principle of Charity* **says: "We should interpret everything we read or hear in such a way as to make the most sense out of it."** We don't adopt this principle out of Christian charity particularly. We don't adopt it to be nice guys. Reading is work, often hard work. It would just be dumb to do hard work and not get as much out of it as we can! And this principle does not mean making sense out of total nonsense.

There are rules and limits to making sense. There are standard and deviant interpretations. The Principle of Charity applied here is that *if there are no indicators present, treat the passage as containing reasoning only if, when you read a pair of statements in it with "so" and "because" between them, they seem to make sense (with at least one of these words) and to make at least moderately strong reasoning.*

This is also the way to test the order of reasoning. The order of reasoning is which statement(s) are the reasons and which are the conclusions. The test is called *"The So/Because Test."*

The So/Because Test: To get the conclusion when the indicators are not present between sentences S_1 and S_2, read them twice, once with "so" and once with "because" between them. Ask, "Does either of these make sense and make reasoning that is at least moderately strong?" If the answer is "yes," then the indicator ("so" or "because") in the one which makes the most sense, the strongest reasoning, tells which statement is the reason and which is the conclusion.

Let us apply this test to several examples. Suppose a Midwestern farmer, speaking to his friend, says: "Been rainin' for weeks. We'll have floods by Spring." Is there reasoning in this discourse or not?

"It's been raining for weeks

so

we'll have floods by Spring"
makes sense.

"It's been raining for weeks

because

we'll have floods by Spring"
does not make sense.

So by the Principle of Charity, we do not interpret the farmer as reasoning this second way. We interpret "It's been raining for weeks" as his reason and "We'll have floods by spring" as his conclusion.

What about the chlorophyll example? Read the sentences "Grass is green. It contains chlorophyll" aloud once with "so" and once with "because" between them. One way should makes somewhat more sense than the other.

"Grass is green <u>because</u> it contains chlorophyll" makes a fair amount of sense.

"Grass is green <u>so</u> it contains chlorophyll" makes a little less sense unless other unstated reasons are added.

One needs to consider that grass is a plant and the greenness of plants is explained by their containing chlorophyll. The indicator "because" tells us that "It contains chlorophyll" is being offered as the reason explaining why grass is green.

What about this discourse?

"He has blue eyes. He weighs over 180 lbs."
"He has blue eyes <u>so</u> he weighs over 180 lbs." doesn't make sense.

Nor does "He has blue eyes <u>because</u> he weighs over 180 lbs." make sense. So the Principle of Charity would say, do not assume that the author of the discourse is reasoning, instead the author is only describing a subject.

Finally, let us consider our example: "The sky is full of dark clouds. It's going to rain."

(1) "The sky is full of dark clouds, <u>so</u> It's going to rain" makes sense.

(2) "The sky is full of dark clouds, <u>because</u> It's going to rain" makes about equal sense. (1) goes from a present fact evident to sight to a less evident prediction about the future. So it is an argument. (2) reasons to a conclusion of the present fact evident to the senses. The conclusion is like "Grass is green;" nobody needs to be persuaded of it. So (2) must be an explanation.

Let's summarize our applications of the So/Because test in four cases: A, arguments; B, explanations; C, No reasoning and D Exceptional or Bilateral cases. We will use the lower case "s/b" between the two statements to stand for "so or because". We'll underline the "s" or "b" to indicate that, after reading the sentences twice, this is the indicator, if any, which we think makes sense and at least moderately strong reasoning. We will also use brackets in those cases where we do find reasoning and make a diagram. But no brackets and diagram will be made where we do not find reasoning.

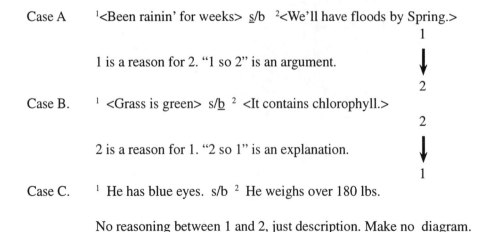

Case A   ¹<Been rainin' for weeks> <u>s</u>/b ²<We'll have floods by Spring.>

1 is a reason for 2. "1 so 2" is an argument.

1
↓
2

Case B.   ¹ <Grass is green> s/<u>b</u> ² <It contains chlorophyll.>

2 is a reason for 1. "2 so 1" is an explanation.

2
↓
1

Case C.   ¹ He has blue eyes. s/b ² He weighs over 180 lbs.

No reasoning between 1 and 2, just description. Make no diagram.

Case D.   [1] <The sky is full of dark clouds> <u>s/b</u> [2] <It's going to rain.>

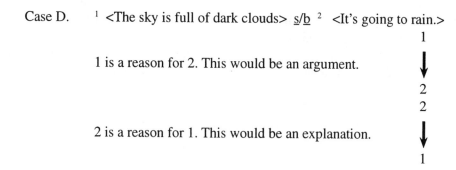

1 is a reason for 2. This would be an argument.

2 is a reason for 1. This would be an explanation.

There is probably a lot more descriptive and story telling and other kinds of discourse than reasoning discourse. So for any two sentences with no indicators between two sentences, it is most likely that they are of case C. But reasoning discourses are very important especially in mathematics, science, technology, philosophy and law. They are also important in politics, advertising and news media editorials, and opinion articles. They are also found in tests like college and graduate school entrance exams. When reading these kinds of discourses, *failure to apply the So/Because test can cause the test-taker to miss reasoning and fail to get the point.* In these kinds of discourses, Case A, arguments, are probably most common, with explanations; Case B, very prominent in the sciences. There is a little problem about Case D, the exceptional case. How do you diagram it? *For the purposes of this book, always diagram such bilateral cases as arguments, not explanations. That means: take the more evident statement to be the reason.* A table is given below showing which types of statements are more and which are less evident.

Now we can summarize the types of *contents* needed in reasons to make generally persuasive arguments for conclusions. The table below also, looked at from right to left, gives a list of the typical contents of reasons in explanations.

MORE AND LESS EVIDENT STATEMENT CONTENTS

<u>MORE EVIDENT</u>	<u>LESS EVIDENT</u>
the Present	the Past and Future
behavior	state of mind
facts	theories
facts	evaluations, judgments
evaluations, judgments	recommendations for action
symptoms	diagnosis
diagnosis	treatment
ends (goals, purposes)	means (action, tools)

In other words, if required to persuade someone of a conclusion about the past or future, to be successful, the reasons will be about things in the present. To convince someone of a conclusion about someone's state of mind, reasons are needed about his or her behavior. To get someone to accept a theory or an evaluation, facts must be presented. To get someone to accept a diagnosis, convince them with statements about symptoms. Then, to get them to undertake a certain treatment, refer them to the diagnosis of the problem. To be successful at persuading someone to use a certain means, give them reasons dealing with a desirable goal or purpose.

In an exceptional case like our clouds and rain example, which makes sense either way, try to classify one statement as about the present and another as about the past or future. If so, diagram it with the one about the present as the reason. If that doesn't work, see if one is about some person's state of mind and the other about her behavior. If so, make the one about her behavior the reason, and so on.

But what if someone says or writes a discourse without indicators in a way where you know *some* people take it to be acceptable reasoning but *others* think it is terrible or no reasoning at all? Suppose Bubba says to Maybelle:

> "They were colored in a white neighborhood after dark. We beat them up real bad."

Is there reasoning there? Bubba and Maybelle may think it is acceptable reasoning with "so," while Jamal and LaTonya think it is terrible or no reasoning at all. If the reader were there, he or she could probably easily tell from the context whether the person was trying to reason or not. Out of context, in a critical thinking textbook, one should treat such terrible arguments as cases as reasoning *so that they can be critically evaluated as reasoning.*

The student should now do Exercise 4 on Testing Evidence Relations with the So/Because Test.

2 LONGER, MORE COMPLEX DISCOURSES

SECTION 2.1: BASIC REASONS, INTERMEDIATE AND FINAL CONCLUSIONS

The So/Because test explained in the last chapter can be generalized to cases of three or more statements. Several paragraphs will be needed to explain this for two reasons. First, reasoning comes in different *architectures*, just like there are different kinds of houses. There are ranch, colonial, Cape Cod, brownstone, row-type, Native American hogan, and other kinds of houses. The student needs to learn the different types or architectures of reasoning. Then he or she can learn how to connect partial diagrams to make diagrams of larger structures, just like house builders connect frames, joists, rafters and so on. Second, the process of connecting partial diagrams of the sort we will start with is an algorithmic process. "Algorithm" (AHL go rih thum) is just a fancy word for a precise, step by step method for doing something. An algorithm is like a recipe. Grasping this will be very useful for putting together or analyzing structures in any level of critical thinking, logic or mathematics. It is a major form of sequencing, putting things in order.

A *basic reason* is a statement which is used to justify or explain other statements but which is not itself justified or explained by other statements in reasoning. We will use the word "support" as short for "justify or explain." A basic reason is a starting point. Every piece of reasoning must have one or more basic reasons. These are the statements the reasoner thought to be evident enough to stand on their own. Otherwise the reasoning would go on forever. **An *intermediate conclusion* is a statement which is supported by another statement or statements and which is used to support a further statement or statements. A *final conclusion* is a statement which is supported by other statements, but which is not used to support further statements.** It is "the point" of the argument or the point being explained. And a complex argument can have many basic reasons, intermediate and final conclusions.

Consider this specific case to which the method is applied. Suppose our flooded-out American farmer had said (without the numbers added): 1. "These crops will be ruined." 2. "It's been raining for weeks." 3. "We'll have floods by Spring." Everybody has some degree of a natural sense of order in reasoning. However, if help is needed, read each pair first with "so" and then with "because" between them.

A. "These crops will be ruined, so It's been raining for weeks?" No.

B. "These crops will be ruined, because It's been raining for weeks?"
   This makes better sense but the connection may not be entirely clear.
   This shows that 2 is a fair reason for 1.

C . "These crops will be ruined, so We'll have floods by Spring?" No.
This doesn't seem to make sense.

D. "These crops will be ruined, because we'll have floods by Spring?" Yes. This makes sense
and shows that 3 is a reason for 1.

Now what about the relation between 2 and 3?

"Its been raining for weeks, so We'll have floods by Spring?" Yes.
This makes good sense and a moderately strong causal (KAW-zal) argument.

However "Its been raining for weeks, because We'll have floods by Spring" seems to put the cart
before the horse.

So 2 is a fairly strong reason for 3 and 3 is a reason for 1. Therefore 2 is the basic reason, 3 is the
intermediate conclusion, and 1 is the final conclusion. This is an argument going from an evident basic
reason: that it has been raining for weeks. This supports an intermediate conclusion: a prediction of
floods. That in turn supports a final conclusion which is a prediction or evaluation about other effects.

It should be fairly easy to see how to extend the system of Arrow Diagraming to cover cases like this.
Consider this example: "Rosa got all that work done on time, so she's very reliable, so we ought to
promote her." If we draw an arrow down from ¹<Rosa got all that work done on time> to <she's very
reliable> then *we can simply draw a further arrow down from 2 to* ³<We ought to promote her.> 1 with
an arrow down to 2, and 2 with an arrow down to 3 are called "**partial diagrams**" of the whole piece of
reasoning.

Connecting partial diagrams is very important to extending our system of arrow diagraming. Here
is a little form which will be used to diagram such "serial" reasoning and to do exercises. The blank in
front of the statement is to be filled in last with the letters "BR" for "basic reason" or "IC" for "intermediate
conclusion", or "FC" for "final conclusion." To the right, under "FINAL FORM" are three spaces with
the abbreviations "B.R. No.," "I.C. No.,"   and "F.C. No." These indicate that next to last, after working
through the two lines below the form, fill in the number of the basic reason in the top space. The number
of the intermediate conclusion goes in the middle space. The number of the final conclusion goes in the
bottom space. Between the top and middle space draw the downward arrow. Do this also between the
middle and bottom space.

Beneath each set of three statements are the two lines that must be worked with right after reading the
three statements. The first line, "Forms, Read, underline S or B," gives, systematically, all three cases to
which the So/Because test must be applied. "1 s/b 2 " means read the first statement with the second. "1
s/b 3" means read the first statement with the third, and "2 s/b 3" means read the second with the third.
Always ask, does each pair makes sense and make at least moderately strong reasoning? If it does, then
underline the letter "s" or "b" which makes the strongest argument to mark the direction of the reasoning.
If it doesn't make sense, put an "x" beneath the "s" or "b."

The direction of reasoning is simply which statement is the reason and which the conclusion in a piece
of reasoning. The next line "Diagrams based on reading;" directs us, immediately after trying the "so /
because" test, to make the partial diagram of that piece of reasoning, if it makes sense and at least moderately
strong reasoning. After doing this it will be only a matter of putting two of the three partial diagrams
together. Here is the form of our exercises.

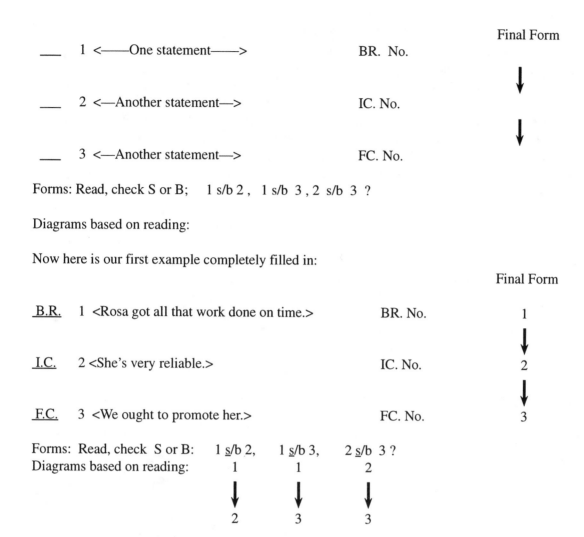

___   1 <——One statement——>   BR. No.   Final Form

___   2 <—Another statement—>   IC. No.

___   3 <—Another statement—>   FC. No.

Forms: Read, check S or B;   1 s/b 2 ,   1 s/b 3 , 2 s/b 3 ?

Diagrams based on reading:

Now here is our first example completely filled in:

                                                                      Final Form

<u>B.R.</u>   1 <Rosa got all that work done on time.>   BR. No.   1

<u>I.C.</u>   2 <She's very reliable.>   IC. No.   2

<u>F.C.</u>   3 <We ought to promote her.>   FC. No.   3

Forms: Read, check S or B: 1 <u>s</u>/b 2,   1 <u>s</u>/b 3,   2 <u>s</u>/b 3 ?
Diagrams based on reading: 1   1   2

                                  2   3   3

What about those blanks in front of and the spaces after the statements? How are they filled in? How are partial diagrams connected when the basic reason is not stated first? Here it looks like 1 makes sense with 2 both ways. But "2 so 1" would be an explanation, not an argument. How do we know which to use? It is not really that difficult. The definition of a basic reason was a statement which is used to support other statements but which is not itself supported by other statements. The arrow means that the statement above supports the statement below. So a basic reason will have an arrow coming down out of it, but no arrow going into it from above. The definition of an intermediate conclusion, (both supporting other statements and being supported by other statements) means that an intermediate conclusion will have an arrow going down into it and an arrow coming down out of it. A final conclusion, (a statement which is supported by another but which is a stopping point) will have an arrow going down into it but none coming down out of it. They will look like this:

                                                    Final Form

Basic Reason Number:

Intermediate Conclusion Number:

Final Conclusion Number:

With this information we can just look at the (usually) three partial diagrams and locate which numbered statement, if any, has an arrow going down into it and an arrow coming down out of it in another partial diagram. *This statement will have to be the intermediate conclusion.* The partial diagram with this number at the bottom will be the *upper half* of the completed diagram. The partial diagram with this number at the top will be the *lower half* of the completed diagram. If this sounds confusing, imagine having two partial diagrams with a common number as the top of one and the bottom of the other diagram. Imagine simply picking up the one with the common number on the bottom and laying it with the common number right on top of the same number in the other diagram. For example, if in reading " 1 so/because 2 " we decide that "because" makes more sense and underline "b," then "1 because 2" is diagramed as :

In cases where all three claims make sense with "so" and "because," reading each pair of statements twice will produce 3 such arrow diagrams such as:

If there is any case in which there is an intermediate conclusion, (the reason of one diagram and the conclusion of another) then connect the two diagrams by placing the one in which that statement is the reason right below the one in which it is the conclusion. For example, since 2 is an intermediate conclusion here, move

Dr. No Phun

to create the connected diagram:

Fill in the spaces in the final diagram form with the right numbers. Then fill in the blanks in front of the statements with the letters "BR," "IC," or "FC" according to the completed diagram. The statement whose number has been filled into the top blank should be labeled "BR." The one in the middle, label "IC." The one in the bottom blank label "FC." In cases where only two of the statements make reasoning, fill in the number of the basic reason in the top blank and the final conclusion in the bottom blank. Where a statement is not involved in reasoning, write the letters "NR" for "not in reasoning" in the space to its' left and in the middle blank in the final form. There are cases like this Rosa problem, where a pair of statements (1 and 2 here) make sense both ways. In such cases an additional decision must be made as to which way it is an argument and which way an explanation. Then use diagram for the argument. Since 1 expresses an evident fact and 2 "She's very reliable," represents a less evident judgment, "1 so 2" is the argument. It is the one used to identify statement 2 as the intermediate conclusion here. Most problems are simpler than this. They will not have any pair of statements which make sense both ways. Now let us look at the rain example completely filled out:

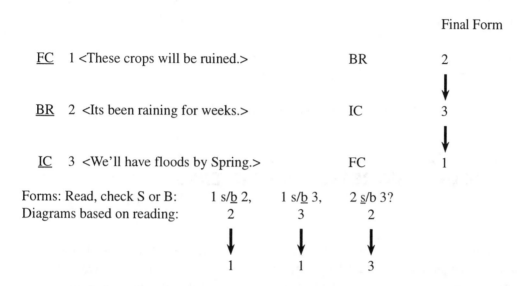

There are cases where only two of three statements are involved in reasoning. There are also cases where none of the statements supports any other. The statements are all description or narration. Let's conclude by looking at an example of each of these. Suppose someone says: "I bought it for her. It's very pretty. It cost $55.39." Is there reasoning here among any of these statements? Let's number these statements "4," "5," and "6" in order not to confuse them with the earlier ones. Here is the answer which the reader should check for him or herself.

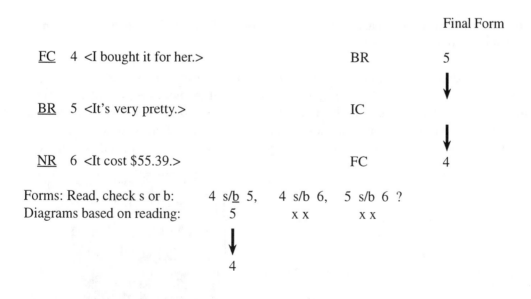

Notice an example like the case of mere description with the sentences "He has blue eyes. He weighs over 180 lbs.," where there is no reasoning among any of the statements.

Final Form

<u>NR</u>   7   <It is used..>   BR   NR

↓

<u>NR</u>   8   <It'is cream colored.>   IC   NR

↓

<u>NR</u>   9   <It has four drawers.>   FC   NR

Forms: Read, check s or b: 7 s/b 8,   7 s/b 9,   8 s/b 9?
Diagrams based on reading: x x   x x   x x

The student should now do Exercise 5 on serial reasoning.

SECTION 2.2: FOUR BASIC REASONING PATTERNS

The form of reasoning we have been talking about is called *serial* reasoning. When people reason in discourses using three claims, there are four basic patterns that their reasoning takes. We call them *"serial," "divergent," "linked"*, and *"convergent"* reasoning. In serial reasoning the argument or explanation goes from only one statement to support a second, which supports a third and so on. **In serial reasoning,** single statements operate as both conclusions from other statements and as reasons for other statements. For example, suppose two girls in a dormitory share clothes. One might say to the other: "You can't borrow my brown velvet pants tonight, because I want to wear them with my new top, since I'm going out with this real cute guy I met." Underlining indicators, bracketing and numbering would give us this:

¹ <You can't borrow my brown velvet pants tonight, > <u>because</u> ² <I want to wear them with my new top,> <u>since</u>   ³ <I'm going out with this real cute guy I met.>

This contains two partial diagrams. In condensed form, leaving the indicators underlined but only the numbers of the statements, we have this: " 1 <u>because</u> 2, <u>since</u> 3 **It is always a good idea to write down these condensed forms and then to make partial diagrams based on them before making a completed diagram.** The partial diagrams for these condensed forms are 2 arrow down to 1, and 3 arrow down to 2. Putting them together, then, the whole explanation would be diagramed as follows:

³ <I'm going out with this real cute guy I met.>

↓

² <I want to wear them [my brown velvet pants] with my new top>

↓

¹ <You can't borrow my brown velvet pants tonight.>

In **divergent reasoning** the same reason is given as supporting two or more different conclusions which are not reasons for one another. This situation will be represented by two or more arrows going downward in different directions from the reason to the conclusions. Here is an example. "Mom's gone for the evening. Therefore the kids won't get their homework done. Also, the dishes won't get done."

[1] <Mom's gone for the evening.>   <u>Therefore</u> [2] <The kids won't get their homework done.> Also [3] <The dishes won't get done.>

Here we have the condensed form "1 <u>therefore</u> 2," which becomes 1 arrow down to 2. What about the word "also?" Why wasn't it underlined? It wasn't underlined because it is not an indicator. It means "and," not "so." It wasn't included in the bracket, because it is no part of the claim that the dishes won't get done. "Also" is one of those words which are important to the structure of reasoning discourses. But it is neither a reason nor conclusion indicator. It is a **connective,** specifically a conjunction. Other conjunctions are: "and," "additionally," "moreover," "but," "yet," "however," and "nevertheless." *Conjunctions tell you that the two statements on either side of them have the same status.* They are both reasons or, in this case, both conclusions. So as soon as we have made the little arrow diagram for "1 <u>therefore</u> 2" and seen "Also 3 <...>," we can make the partial diagram connecting 1 as a reason to 3, 1 arrow down to 3. But neither of these conclusions is a reason for the other. It is not serial reasoning. So put the number of the reason up above and two separate arrows to the two separate conclusions below, like this:

[1] <Mom's gone for the evening.>

[2] <The kids won't get their homework done.> [3] <The dishes won't get done either.>

Another example would be "School starts tomorrow; accordingly, I'll have less free time, but I'll be earning money from my college work-study job." The "but" coordinates two independent conclusions.

[1] <School starts tomorrow.>

[2] <I'll have less free time.>   [3] <I'll be earning money from my work-study job.>

An argument is said to have a **linked** pattern of reasoning when it involves several reasons *each of which is helped by, and has to be helped by the others to support the conclusion.* **This kind of diagram should be made for all standard deductive and inductive types of arguments.** What "deductive" and "inductive" mean will be explained later. For now, make a note of this, because *failure to diagram standard deductive and inductive arguments as linked may be disastrous to performance on exercises and tests.* In linked reasoning, the reasons depend on each other. They need each other to support the conclusion. To show the dependency between reasons in a linked argument we put a plus sign, "**+**," between reasons. Draw a line under all of the reasons and just one arrow from the line to the conclusion.

There are two kinds of reasoning which are very common. They are very widely used in logic books, in everyday reasoning, and on college and graduate school entrance tests. They both have some deductively valid forms and other forms which look like valid forms but are not valid. *Both should always be diagramed as linked.* Both have what may be called loosely a "linking middle idea." But it is a different sort of idea in the two cases. The first type of reasoning is called a "**categorical syllogism**" (see Chapter Six.) Here is a classic example correctly bracketed.

[1] <All men are animals> and [2] < all animals are mortal,> <u>so</u> [3] <all men are mortal.>

LINKING MIDDLE IDEA: animals

Here the linking middle idea, "animals," called specifically a "middle term," connects the two end terms, the subject and predicate of the conclusion, "men" and "mortal." Neither of these reasons alone provides any support, all by itself, for the conclusion. "All men are animals" provides no support for "All men are mortal" because it doesn't mention mortality. "All animals are mortal," all by itself, provides no support whatever for the conclusion either, because it doesn't even mention "men." So it would not be right to draw an arrow from each of these reasons to the conclusion, for *the arrow means that what is above, all by itself, provides some evidence for the statement below.* Notice also how certain it is that if these two reasons are linked together, the two "no-supports" equal 100% support. If these two reasons are true, then this conclusion must be true. This is a quality of deductively valid reasoning which inductive reasoning lacks. So when we run into such an example, our condensed version will contain the numbers linked and a plus sign is used to symbolize this relation among reasons, here "1 + 2."

^{1} <All men are animals> + ^{2} <All animals are mortal>

$\downarrow$

3 <All men are mortal>

The second kind of reasoning which is extremely common is called **"conditional reasoning"** (see Chapter Seven.) This is because it always involves a conditional sentence, that is, a sentence like "If you go, then we will go." Here is an example of conditional reasoning.

^{1} <You go.> and ^{2} <If you go, then we will go,> so ^{3} <We will go.>

The part after the "If" and up to the "then" in a conditional sentence is called the "*antecedent.*" The part after the word "then" is called the "*consequent.*" Remember from before that *a conditional sentence does not claim that its antecedent or consequent is categorically true.* **The truth of a conditional all by itself does not support the truth of either its antecedent or its consequent.** The conditional sentence is a linking thought. It needs to hook up with a "categorical" sentence like "You go" to provide evidence for some conclusion. As with the syllogism, neither the categorical assertion "You go," nor the hypothetical or conditional sentence provides any support, all by itself, for the conclusion that you will go also. So it would be wrong to diagram this with two separate arrows, one from each reason to the conclusion. The only right way to diagram conditional reasoning , whether valid or not, is as linked. The condensed version of the reasons is again 1 + 2 and of the conclusion, "so we will go," the partial diagram would be an arrow down to 3. Putting these together gives us this:

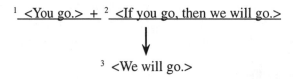

^{1} <You go.> + ^{2} <If you go, then we will go.>

$\downarrow$

^{3} <We will go.>

To conclude looking at linked reasoning, let us examine one more type. This is an example of *inductive* reasoning. The distinction between deductive and inductive reasoning will be defined later. For now, note this. When making a generalization from examples, we are reasoning inductively. The specific examples need each other to support a general conclusion. Here is an example about a college student learning how to drink (or not to drink). He goes to the bar one night and drinks 6 vodkas and gets sick. Not being a critical thinker, he explains "It must be from impurities in this booze." So he goes the second night and downs 6 Zimas, and gets sick. The next night he is still pushing his limit with 6 beers, but gets sick

again. He continues this process, always getting the same results ,"hurling" after 6 drinks and having a hangover the next morning (as well as flunking out). Now he is developing evidence for the conclusion that *always, after 6 drinks, I get sick.* Such an argument will be diagramed as linked.

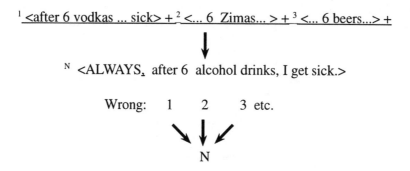

Do not draw one separate arrow from each little reason to the conclusion. None of them all by itself provides moderately strong support for the conclusion. They need each other and so should be linked. Notice how, in this inductive argument, the word "always" makes the claim in the conclusion go beyond information given in the reasons? This was not true in the cases of the syllogism and the conditional argument example given above. Their conclusions did not go beyond the information in the reasons. This is why, in deductively valid reasoning, if the reasons are true, then the conclusion must be true. It is why some deductively valid arguments establish their conclusions "with necessity" or certainty, *if* their reasons are known to be true. But in inductive cases like this, the conclusion claims more than the reasons. So it is possible that the reasons are all true and the conclusion is false. He could still find some sort of booze that he could drink 6 of without getting sick. That's why inductive arguments only establish a probability that their conclusions are true. That is also why inductive arguments are not simply valid or invalid but stronger or weaker. The more cases the reasons are based on, the stronger is the argument. The fewer cases they are based on, the weaker is the argument.

Convergent reasoning is reasoning in which two or more reasons support a conclusion *separately* and *independently* of each other. In such cases, use a separate arrow from each reason to the conclusion. Suppose it's winter and snowing very hard and the reader has made plans to drive into town to go to a movie. He or she might reason as follows: "It's snowing very hard. The show isn't supposed to be very good anyway. So I guess I'll stay home." Giving these two independent reasons for a conclusion would be diagramed this way.

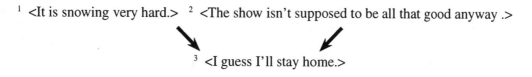

Again, suppose somebody says "Smoking is bad for you in several ways. It costs a lot of money. It's very unhealthy." There are no indicators here. But when the So/because test is applied, it can be seen that the second and third statements are good, independent reasons for the first. The diagram for this would be:

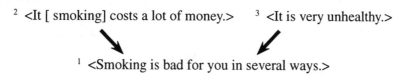

By comparison and thinking about what is actually claimed in them, it should be possible to see that syllogisms and conditional arguments cannot be properly diagramed this way. Remember that when an arrow is drawn, this represents the claim that what is above the arrow, *by itself*, supports or provides at least moderately strong evidence for the statement below.

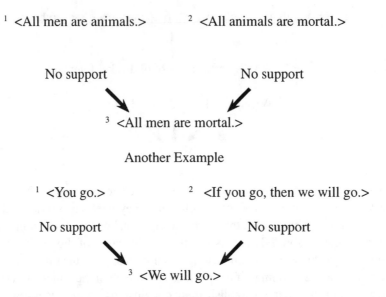

How does one tell whether one has linked or convergent reasoning? Sometimes it is difficult and there can be borderline or unclear cases. Such cases have been avoided in the exercises. If one is really unsure about a case, write out the reasons on a line above, the conclusion below, without any pluses, arrows or lines. Then cover one reason, or all but one with fingers or a piece of paper and use the "So" part of the So/because test all by itself. If the reasoning passes the "So" test, then that reason can have an arrow of its own. But try each of the other reasons alone also. It can happen that it sounds like one reason can stand alone, but later we discover that another needs it. In such cases, diagram them as linked. There is much more linked reasoning than convergent reasoning in most logic and critical thinking texts, on tests and in everyday life, so when in doubt, diagram as linked.

The commonest error in diagraming is mistaking linked, particularly deductively valid arguments for serial ones. Here is an example of a categorical syllogism. It also illustrates how to deal with what may be called the doubled indicator structure." Once in a while we see someone write "so since" or "thus because." "Every horse is a mammal, <u>so</u> <u>since</u> every mammal has a heart, every horse has a heart." There is no such thing as an indicator which is both a reason and a conclusion indicator. So each indicator should be underlined separately. This means:

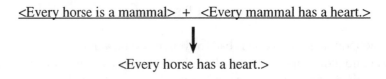

In a doubled indicator structure ¹< >, C. I., R. I., ²< >, ³< > *the last statement is almost always the final conclusion.*

THIS ARGUMENT IS NOT SERIAL:

^{1} <Every horse is a mammal>

↓

^{2} <Every mammal has a heart.>

↓

^{3} <Every horse has a heart.>

Ask yourself about the reasons: Do the two of them fit, either way into the pattern 1 s/b 2 ? The answer should be clearly "no." Cases of doubled indicators like this or "1, thus because 2, 3" are not uncommon, and the third statement in them is often a final conclusion from two linked reasons.

Syllogistic and conditional arguments like these examples must be diagramed as linked, not serial or convergent! Such arguments are much more common than convergent, serial, or divergent reasoning. Many more of the linked type will appear on exercises and tests and in reasoning in everyday life. If one doesn't diagram them correctly, one is likely to make diagrams where the correct evaluation for what has been diagramed wrongly is **nil.** At the same time one may rightly judge the argument to be deductively valid. The previous two examples show what a royal screw-up occurs if this is not learned and deductively valid linked arguments are diagramed as convergent. First, there are two arrows where there should only be one. Second, neither of the reasons all by themselves, provides any support for the conclusion. If these were accurate diagrams, the words "No support" would have to be written twice to give an accurate evaluation. But making such a diagram would violate the Principle of Charity which says: "Do not find reasoning when there is no indicator between statements and it would be very bad reasoning." Yet at the same time, it is probably correct to judge that there is only one step of inference in such cases. So remember the rule: *Diagram all standard form deductive (syllogistic and conditional) arguments and inductive arguments as linked!*

Below is a summary of correct and incorrect forms. In it only the letter "S" is used for the various statements. Any use of numbers or alphabet subscripts might mislead the reader into thinking that there is some necessary order to the statements as they appear in a diagram. There isn't. For example, serial reasoning can have 2, 3 or any number of statements in it. That is why it is illustrated with two diagrams. And in a three-statement serial diagram as shown first, the order of the statements from basic reason to final conclusion could be any one of the following: 1,2,3; 1,3,2; 2,1,3; 2,3,1; 3,1,2; or 3,2,1.

Summary of Correct Forms

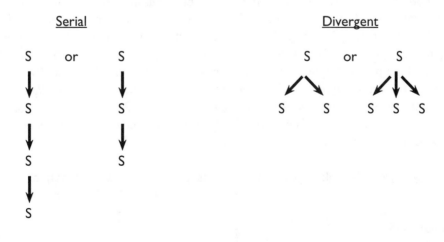

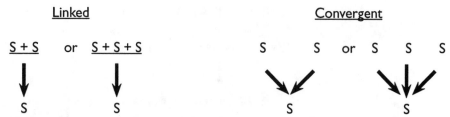

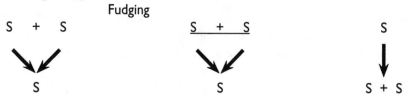

INCORRECT FORMS - Only reasons can be linked. Don't make diagrams "fudging" linked and convergent! Also, the mark for a link, "+," does not represent a statement, so there should never be an arrow drawn to a plus sign.

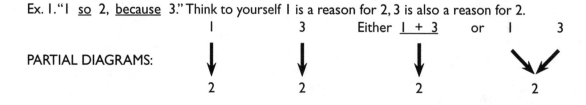

SECTION 2.3: CONNECTIVE WORDS VERSUS INDICATORS

When we have reasoning with three or more statements, connective words become very important to grasping structure. When conjunctions like "and," "also," "besides," "additionally," and "moreover" appear between two reasons or conclusions, the two statements should almost always be bracketed separately: <Statement 1> AND <statement 2.> So when an "and" is spotted between claims, place a bracket in front of it and one just after it like this: > and <. Then go looking for where the corresponding left and right brackets should be. *Every right bracket has to be matched with a left and every left with a right.* Correct: < > Incorrect: > or just <. Other connectives like "if - then" require that we keep the statements in the same bracket, like this: <If statement 1, then statement 2>, for "if" is not a reason indicator and "then" is not a conclusion indicator. *Remember: connective words like "and, " "or," "if-then" should not be underlined, nor should arrows be drawn between statements they connect!*

To diagram reasoning with three or more statements, we will replace whole statements with just numbers which stand for them. Such symbols containing indicators and sometimes connectives and numbers for statements are **condensed forms**. Next are some condensed forms and how to think about them. We will look at how to make partial diagrams of them first. Then we will see how to put the partial diagrams together. Think of statements joined by indicators or connectives as like atoms, Lincoln Logs or Leggos. Connecting partial diagrams is like connecting the logs or Leggos. Students who don't bother to learn this often skip making partial diagrams and end up making many errors. There are two keys to making partial diagrams: 1) *An indicator phrase almost always ties the two statements immediately on either side of it. It rarely jumps over and ties the first statement to the third.* 2) The student should join partial diagrams *at the common number, whether or not it is a basic reason, and intermediate or a final conclusion.* Now let's look at some examples.

Ex. 1. "1 <u>so</u> 2, <u>because</u> 3." Think to yourself 1 is a reason for 2, 3 is also a reason for 2.

PARTIAL DIAGRAMS:

These two partial diagrams mean that 1 and 3 are both reasons for 2. They would be diagramed as convergent or linked. Without actual statements the "So/because" test cannot be practiced. So we cannot tell which it should be. For exercises on making complete diagrams out of partial ones when only condensed forms are given, the book will give instruction on how to diagram it. If it instructs us to diagram the problem as linked, the partial diagram of the reasons is made by putting a plus between the numbers for the reasons. Then put a line under all of them like this: 1 + 3. Last, draw an arrow down from the line to the number for the other statement. If they are convergent, just leave the 2 arrows originally drawn alone and join the two partial diagrams at the common number, in this case the final conclusion 2.

Ex. 2. " Since 1 and 2, therefore 3. Suppose they are linked. Make the partial diagrams 1 + 2 and arrow 3 and attach the arrow 3 under the line.

Ex. 3. " Because of 1, 2 and also 3." Think: 1 is a reason for 2; 1 is also a reason for 3. Make the partial diagrams 1 arrow 2 and 1 arrow 3. Then join at the common basic reason 1.

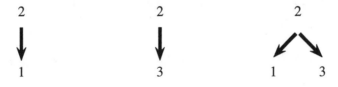

Ex. 4. "1, because of 2, therefore 3. " Think: 2 is a reason for 1, and also for 3. Make the partial diagrams 2 arrow 1 and 2 arrow 3. Then join them at the common basic reason 2.

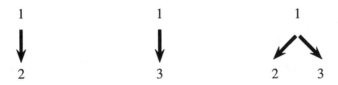

Ex. 5. " 1, because 2, as 3 "Think: 2 is a reason for 1, 3 is a reason for 2. Make partial arrow diagrams 2 arrow 1 and 3 arrow 2. Then join them at the common intermediate conclusion 2.

Ex. 6. "1, <u>so</u> 2, <u>therefore</u> 3." Think: 1 is a reason for 2, 2 is a reason for 3. Make partial diagrams 1 arrow 2 and 2 arrow 3. Join them at the intermediate conclusion 2.

Examples like 2 and 3 show the importance of conjunctions. Words like "and," "also," "additionally," "moreover," "besides which," and sometimes "but" alone mean that two statements have the same status. They may both be reasons for the same conclusion. Otherwise, they may both be conclusions from the same reason. Therefore, one should *never see a conjunction alone and draw an arrow to replace it between two statements.* The arrow would indicate one was a reason while the other was a conclusion from it. Use the arrow only when an indicator is present or the so/because test shows that conjunctions cannot be mechanically translated into pluses ("+"). When they appear between reasons the reasons may or may not be linked. Conclusions are very rarely linked.

The student should now do Exercise 6 on connecting Partial Diagrams and then Exercise 7 on Diagraming the Four Basic Argument Structures.

SECTION 2.4:   DEALING WITH LONG SENTENCES OR PASSAGES WITH OLD OR TECHNICAL WORDS.

Analysis and diagraming of reasoning will be concluded by showing how it can be applied to longer and more complex passages. Most reasoning occurs in short bursts of no more than one reason and one conclusion or in the serial, divergent, linked and convergent forms. But there are more complex pieces of reasoning, in science and law and other areas of life. Subjects are sometimes complex and require more extended reasoning. There is no mechanical way of doing such passages. A person must pay attention to the meanings of the sentences. But it will helpful to follow the basic procedure set out before. With more complex reasoning, always do the following things. A. Underline indicators. B. Supply and underline indicators which have been left out but which the application of the So/because test indicates should be there. C. Angle bracket and number the separate statements. D. Make partial diagrams. Lastly, E. Put partial diagrams into an all - inclusive argument diagram.

First, note that sentences can be long and compound. They can contain several claims. Still, for the purpose of analysis, much of this complexity can be ignored and not bracketed off into separate claims. Here is an interesting example from Paul Krassner (1986.)

[1]<After James Huberty killed 22 people at a MacDonald's in California, his wife sued MacDonald's for millions of dollars, claiming that the MSG MacDonald's used in their food drove him crazy and got him killed in return.> [2] < MacDonald's was just getting what it deserved,> <u>because</u> 3 <MacDonald's was and still is one of the biggest sponsors of violence on TV.>

There are four to six claims in the first sentence. But they all function as one unit in this argument. It is a simple linked argument with a diagram like this.

Here is an example from business. "The deal needs to be closed this week: if it isn't, then the cost of borrowing money will make it impossible for us. The Federal Reserve is tightening up the money supply in such a way as to increase interest rates, and inflation will also push rates up. Moreover, since our competitors will soon have financing to make a better offer, we have to act as soon as possible.

Here we have to use the So/because test. There are several places where it works. "Because" fits at the colon between "week" and "if." It also works between the end of the first long sentence and the word "The" at the beginning of the second. The second sentence is a conjunction. It appears to give two reasons why the cost of borrowing money will make the deal impossible for us. "Moreover" tells us that the third sentence will be doing the same sort of thing that the last one was. So it will be giving a reason for the first sentence.

We have to note in this and many other cases that the first sentence is compound and contains two claims. One claim is about the deal. The other is about the cost of borrowing money. So we have to decide whether the third sentence relates to the need to close the deal this week, or to the cost of money. It seems clearly to relate to the need to close the deal. Finally we note that "since" means that the third sentence is also a compound one which contains a reason and a conclusion. So we look carefully and see that the reason ends at the comma. We put closing and opening brackets between "offer" and "we." The bracketing and numbering of separate claims looks like this:

[1] <The deal needs to be closed this week:> [because] [2] <if it isn't, then the cost of borrowing money will make the deal impossible for us.> [because] [3] <The Federal Reserve is tightening the money supply in such a way as to raise interest rates> and [4]<inflation will also push rates up.> Moreover, since [5]<our competitors will soon have financing to make a better offer,> [6] <we have to act as soon as possible.>

Now think a little about what these statements mean. This should enable the reader to complete the diagram. "1 because 2" becomes 2 arrow 1. Statement 2 makes a conditional claim that if we wait longer than this week, the cost of money will be too high for us. "2 because 3 and 4" tells us that 3 and 4 are reasons to be placed above 2. Statements 3 and 4 seem to be linked evidence that the cost of money will be too high. And "since 5, 6", or 5 arrow 6, seems to be evidence to support the other part of the first claim that we must close the deal this week. This, then, converges on statement 1.

Our final completed diagram would look like this.

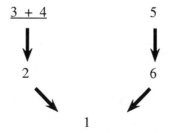

Notice in this passage how the first, or topic sentence is the conclusion. *People often start with their conclusions.* Do not confuse the fact that we represent reasoning with the conclusions always at the bottom with the fact that people sometimes start with their conclusions or put them in the middle or at the end.

Now here is a long passage which was written by the English philosopher John Locke in 1690 at the beginning of Chapter Nine of his *Second Treatise of Civil Government*. Locke's ideas were adopted by the founding fathers of the United States in the Declaration of Independence and the Constitution. If these ideas are not understood, it will not be possible to understand the role of the police, the National Guard in riots, taxes, or the court system. It will not be possible to understand why the government will react in a certain way to any "revolution" which would really redistribute the wealth in America. But the passage illustrates the difficulties of very long sentences and old uses of words.

It will help to understand the passage to know that before Locke, there was a philosopher named Thomas Hobbes. Hobbes had argued the following: Once upon a time, before people developed civil society and government, they lived in a "State of Nature." The State of Nature, for Hobbes, was a wild state. It was a state in which each person had absolute freedom. There was no government, no laws, no police. Hurrah for freedom! But people are greedy and want other people's stuff. So it was also, therefore, a state in which all people were always at war with all other people. Some people would use force or fraud to get what they wanted. So everybody would have to defend themselves and their own family members and stuff. If somebody got mad at you, or wanted your mate or your daughter or your stuff, he could kill you, or kidnap and rape them, or rip you off. There were no laws and cops to stop or deter him! You would similarly be able to rip off others, but you alone would have to defend yourself against murder, kidnap, rape, robbery or whatever.

The lines of the passage have been numbered for easy reference.

L.1.   "If man in the state of Nature be so free as has been said, if he
L.2.   be absolute lord of his own person and possessions, equal to the
L.3.   greatest and subject to nobody, why will he part with his freedom,
L.4.   this empire, and subject himself to the dominion and control of any
L.5.   other power? To which it is obvious to answer, that though in the
L.6.   state of Nature he hath such a right, yet the enjoyment of it is very
L.7.   uncertain and constantly exposed to the invasion of others; for all
L.8.   being kings as much as he, every man his equal, and the greater part
L.9.   no strict observers of equity and justice, the enjoyment of the
L.10.   property he has in this state is very unsafe, very insecure. This
L.11.   makes him willing to quit this condition which, however free, is full
L.12.   of fears and continual dangers; and it is not without reason that he
L.13.   seeks out and is willing to join in society with others who are
L.14.   already united, or have a mind to unite for the mutual preservation
L.15.   of their lives, liberties, and estates, which I call by the general
L.16.   name - property.
L.17.   The great and chief end, therefore, of men uniting into
L.18.   commonwealths, and putting themselves under government, is the
L.19.   preservation of their property; to which in the state of Nature there
L.20.   are many things wanting.
L.21.   Firstly, there wants an established, settled, known law,
L.22.   received and allowed by common consent to be the standard of right
L.23.   and wrong, and the common measure to decide all controversies
L.24.   between them. For though the law of Nature be plain and intelligible

L.25.   to all rational creatures, yet men, being biased by their interest, as
L.26.   well as ignorant for want of study of it, are not apt to allow of it as
L.27.   a law binding to them in the application of it to their particular
L.28.   cases.
L.29.   Secondly, in the state of Nature there wants a known and
L.30.   indifferent judge, with authority to determine all differences
L.31.   according to the established law. For every one in that state being
L.32.   both judge and executioner of the law of Nature, men being partial to
L.33.   themselves, passion and revenge is very apt to carry them too far,
L.34.   and with too much heat in their own cases, as well as negligence and
L.35.   unconcernedness, make them too remiss in other men's.
L.36.   Thirdly, in the state of Nature there often wants power to back
L.37.   and support the sentence when right, and to give it due execution.
L.38.   They who by any injustice offended will seldom fail where they are
L.39.   able by force to make good their injustice. Such resistance many
L.40.   times makes the punishment dangerous, and frequently destructive
L.41.   to those who attempt it.
L.42.   Thus mankind, notwithstanding all the privileges of the state
L.43.   of Nature,being but in an ill condition while they remain in it are
L.44.   quickly driven into society. Hence it comes to pass, that we seldom
L.45.   find any number of men live any time together in this state."
J. W. Gough, ed. (1966)

With a passage this long, *first, read the whole passage through, noticing which type of sentence each sentence is: indicative, interrogative, imperative or exclamatory.* The reader is not likely to have to bracket and number real questions, commands, and exclamations. *Second, underline each inference indicator, and bracket the statements which it seems to relate.* Locke uses reason indicators at the start of the third, fourth and fifth paragraphs. Look for others in lines 7, 17, 24, 31, 42 and 44.

A serious problem for most students in understanding a passage like this is that Locke writes enormously long sentences. He packs in unnecessary words. He sometimes puts several complete thoughts into non-restrictive clauses in a sentence. So a good *third step is to pay careful attention to commas which may mark off non-restrictive clauses that make complete claims within a sentence. (See Chapter 1, Section 3 on non-restrictive clauses.) Also, in long sentences it may be necessary to ask, "What is the main subject?" and "What is the main verb?" At the same time, a Fourth step is to eliminate words, phrases and whole sentences that are unnecessary to the meaning of the claims in the reasoning.*

Applying the first step, we can drop the whole first sentence (lines 1-5) since it is a question. We can also drop the beginning words of the next sentence "To which it is obvious to answer that". Even the next part of that sentence up to the word "yet" is only necessary to understand what the pronoun "it" at the end of line 6 refers to. This suggests a *Fifth step. While reading, be sure to understand what each pronoun refers to. Write the noun it refers to in square brackets in the margin or wherever notes are taken.* Usually the pronoun will refer to the last noun phrase mentioned, or one of the last few. In line 6, "it" refers to [Man's right to control himself and his possessions]. We should now bracket and number [1]<the enjoyment of [Man's right to control himself and his possessions] is very uncertain and constantly exposed to the invasion of others;> since the next word is the reason indicator "for", and bracket what comes after it. It seems that Locke gives three reasons for this conclusion; [2] <all being kings as much as he, > [3] <every man his equal> and [4]<the greater part no strict observers of equity and justice>. All who? What's this use of "being"? *Step Six: fill in left out subjects and understood verbs.* [2] <all [people] [are] kings as much as he, > [3] <every man [is] his equal> and [4] <the greater part [the majority of people are] no strict observers of equity and justice.>

A good *Seventh* step can be illustrated by this last sentence. When uncertain about the meaning of a sentence, *try to paraphrase the sentence,* following the Principle of Charity. That is, if there are two or more interpretations of a statement, choose the one which makes the most sense, or seems most obviously true, or which will make the argument valid. 4 seems to mean something like "Most people [at least in a State of Nature] don't behave very justly."

Now we come to a dilemma. The next claim, [5] <the enjoyment of the property he has in this state is very unsafe, very insecure> sounds a lot like what we have numbered 1, and it looks like a conclusion from the same reasons. Since 1 comes before the reason indicator "for," and seems to refer to both himself and his possessions, while 5 refers only to his property, this author interprets 1 as being the conclusion from 2, 3 and 4, and takes 5 as a conclusion from 1. This seems to follow the flow of the paragraph, which is toward the last word, "property." Also, it follows the Principle of Charity. It seems stronger to argue that what applies to person *and* possessions applies to property, than to argue that what applies to property applies to possessions *and* persons. This is true at least until one reaches the last sentence of the paragraph in which Locke explicitly includes lives in "property." But this gives no reason to change the diagraming.

Sentence 5 is linked to the next sentence, 6, by the subject [insecurity] which is left out of 6 - so supply it. Also, the phrase "however free" is unnecessary. Finally, there is a long phrase in it functioning as a conclusion indicator. Spot what it is and bracket the conclusion. It is the phrase: "it is not without reason that." After underlining this we have to bracket [7]<he seeks out...> to "estates" in line 15. Notice how an important definition or spelling out of what makes up property, "lives, liberty, and estates," is left by Locke in a relative clause at the tail end of the paragraph.

So why did Locke write so badly? He didn't! He wrote quite clearly for his time. Writing styles change with the times. If all we have ever had a chance to read is "dumbed down" textbooks with very short, stubby "See Spot run" - type sentences, we would think he wrote poorly. The logical structure of the rest of the passage should be somewhat clearer to us. The second paragraph begins with claim [8] <The great and chief end ...of men uniting ... is the preservation of their property>. Another parenthetical phrase "and putting themselves under government" comes between the subject and the verb and so has been left out. The indicator "therefore" tells us this is a conclusion from the last statement of the first paragraph.

Another difficulty relates to the fact that the next three paragraphs all begin with the reason indicators "Firstly," Secondly," "Thirdly." Also, these are all related to the clause in lines 19 to 20, "to which in the state of Nature there are many things wanting." This seems like almost an afterthought of Locke's, until we read further. That is why we cannot always diagram a passage without reading the whole thing through first. These all relate because each of the sentences after these indicators contains the word "want." So we need to bracket and number [9] <to which in the state of Nature there are many things wanting>.

What does Locke mean by"*things* wanting?" *Eighth step: when trying to paraphrase,* **there is no substitute for looking up words in the dictionary.** "Wanting," in this context, means "absent," "missing" or "lacking." Only with this meaning will we think to ask what is the real subject. Lacking to what? - to the preservation of men's property. So 9 means "In the state of Nature there are many things [lacking] [to the preservation of men's property] ". Most of the rest of the reasoning in the whole passage consists of reasons for this conclusion! In the next paragraph, after "Firstly," we number "10" the sentence <"there [is lacking] a...law..." and we can bracket the whole thing right to the period as one unit. Then in line 23 we have the reason indicator "For" again, so we must bracket and number [11] <"Though the law...be plain..." all the way to the end of the sentence. Remember, neither of the two occurrences of 'as' in "as well as" are indicators.

In the next paragraph, after underlining "Secondly" in line 29, we number and bracket [12]<"In the state of nature there [is lacking] a known... judge..." to the period. Next in line 31 comes "For" again, indicating that we should number and bracket as [13]<"everyone in that state... " and so forth. Again, it is possible to break this sentence up into two between "Nature" and "men" on line 32, but it seems not necessary to do so. Look up "remiss" if necessary, to find out that Locke means that peoples' negligence and unconcernedness about justice for other people makes them [lax in seeking justice for] other men.

In the fifth paragraph, after underlining "Thirdly," number [14] <"in the state of nature there often [lacks] power..." to the period. If we try the So/Because test between 14 and the next two sentences, we will see that each of them is a reason for 14. So Number and bracket [15] <"They who by any injustice [are] offended will..." to the period. Number and bracket the next whole sentence as [16]<"Such resistance..." to the period. 15 and 16 seem to be linked reasons for 14.

In the last paragraph, after underlining "Thus," number and bracket the sentence beginning [17]<Mankind...are quickly driven into society.> All the earlier part of the sentence is really a repetition of what was said in detail earlier and can be left out. Finally, underlining "Hence," number "18" and bracket the next sentence leaving out the unnecessary phrase "it comes to pass, that" [18]<we seldom find any number of men live at any time together in that state.>

Now we see that there are two large sub-arguments in this passage. One is to the final conclusion that [8] <The great ... end of men uniting into commonwealths... is the preservation of their property>. The other is to 9 that there are many things lacking to the preservation of men's property in the State of Nature. These two are linked reasons for 17 which is indicated to be a reason for the final conclusion[18] <we seldom find any number of men live any time together in this state.> So here is what the passage looks like with irrelevant parts left out, numbered and bracketed. Remember, everything up to line 6 is not part of the argument.

[1]<the enjoyment of [Man's right to control himself and his possessions] is very uncertain and constantly exposed to the invasion of others;> for [2] <all[are] kings as much as he,> [3]< every man [is] his equal,> and [4]<the greater part [of people are] no strict observers of equity and justice> [5] <the enjoyment of the property he has in this state is very unsafe, very insecure.>

[6] <This [insecurity] makes him willing to quit this condition which... is full of fears and continual dangers;> and it is not without reason that [7] <he seeks out and is willing to join in society with others who are already united, or have a mind to unite for the mutual preservation of their lives, liberties, and estates,> which I call by the general name - property.

[8] <The great and chief end, therefore, of men uniting into commonwealths, and putting themselves under government, is the preservation of their property;> [9] <to which In the state of Nature there are many things wanting [lacking to the preservation of men's property].>

Firstly, [10] <there [is lacking] an established, settled, known law, received and allowed by common consent to be the standard of right and wrong, and the common measure to decide all controversies between them.> For [11] <though the law of Nature be plain and intelligible to all rational creatures, yet men, being biased by their interest, as well as ignorant for want of study of it, are not apt to allow of it as a law binding to them in the application of it to their particular cases.>

Secondly, [12] <in the state of Nature there [is lacking] a known and indifferent judge, with authority to determine all differences according to the established law.> For [13] <every one in that state being both judge and executioner of the law of Nature, men [are] partial to themselves, passion and revenge is very apt to carry them too far, and with too much heat in their own cases, as well as negligence and unconcernedness, make them too remiss in other men's.>

Thirdly, [14] <in the state of Nature there often [lacks] power to back and support the sentence when right, and to give it due execution. > [because] [15] <They who by any injustice [are] offended will seldom fail where they are able by force to make good their injustice.> [and because][16] < Such resistance many times makes the punishment dangerous, and frequently destructive to those who attempt it.>

Thus [17] < mankind ... are quickly driven into society.> Hence [18] <it comes to pass, that we seldom find any number of men live any time together in this state.>

Here is what a completed diagram of the whole passage looks like.

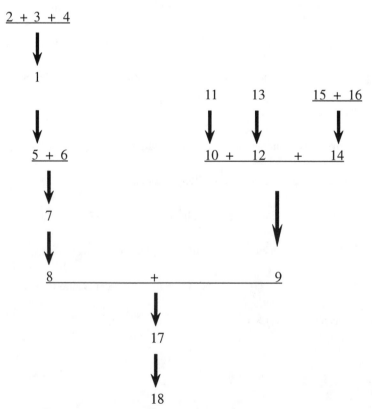

The student should now do Exercise 7C on Diagraming Longer Passages.

Part Two

EVALUATION OF REASONING

3

BASIC CONCEPTS OF EVALUATION

SECTION 3.1: THE VALUES OF CRITICAL THINKING

What is the value of critical thinking? When someone else writes or speaks a piece of reasoning, they are trying to persuade us of something. Persuasion is an attempt to get us to believe something. People want us to believe things so that we will act in certain ways. Action requires some effort. There are choices involved. We could be doing something else. Because of this, it is very useful to be able to evaluate reasoning, for some pieces of reasoning should be accepted while others should not be accepted.

If persuasion occurs in advertising, we could be doing many other things with our money. Take buying a car, for example. A lot of money can be involved, so what kind of car to buy can be a pretty big decision. Whether to marry a certain person or which of a couple of job offers to take are still bigger decisions. Almost every reader will eventually get some serious illness. There may be several different treatments available. One's comfort, health, even one's life may depend on the decision as to which treatment to undertake. To make these decisions well, we will need to gather our own reasons to support various alternative conclusions. At that time, we could make an irrational decision, or a sheep-like decision to follow some other person's advice. Even doctors have been known to have limited knowledge and to make bad decisions! So we had better prepare now to evaluate arguments for one decision or another. For an excellent treatment of this subject, see Thomas (1993.)

The values of critical thinking, specifically how to recognize and evaluate reasoning, are the following: **1) It helps us arrive at true conclusions, and therefore 2) it increases our knowledge. 3) It should help us make better decisions. 4) It should help us persuade others and 5) explain truths to them.** We need the cooperation of others. We will need to persuade employers to hire us rather than someone else. Car and home purchases are negotiations with no fixed prices. We will need to persuade the seller to accept our price or pay hundreds to thousands of dollars more than we need to pay. These examples show that making better decisions and being able to persuade others should **6) contribute to a happier life.**

SECTION 3.2: SOUNDNESS, TRUTH, AND VALIDITY

The kind of reasoning which we should be persuaded by and which we should always seek to present to others is called logically **"sound reasoning."** Its opposite is **"logically unsound"** reasoning.

Definition: Logically sound reasoning is reasoning in which: 1) all the reasons are true and 2) the reasoning is valid.

Later we will define a weaker sense called "epistemic soundness." Since "premises" is another word for "reasons," we can write this formula:

$$\textbf{SOUNDNESS}_{\text{of reasoning}} = \textbf{TRUTH}_{\text{of premises}} + \textbf{VALIDITY}_{\text{of argument.}}$$

$$S_R = T_P + V_A$$

This formula is read as "S sub r equals T sub p plus V sub a." It is in some ways like an addition problem, $5 = 3 + 2$. Can we have 5 things without at least 3 things and 2 more things? No. Similarly, reasoning must have all true reasons to be sound. Also it *must* be valid in order to be sound. Reasoning can have all true reasons and not be valid and therefore be unsound. Also, reasoning can be valid and not have all true reasons so that it is again unsound.

Definitions like this are rules. Rules have implications. If we want to learn how to play chess and win, we have to learn how the pieces move. If we don't, then we will have to either leave them alone, be crippled by not being able to use them, or we will make illegal moves and be disqualified. The same is true here. This definition implies that: 1) all sound reasoning is valid. 2) Some valid reasoning is unsound (that which has false reasons.) 3) All sound reasoning always has all true reasons. 4) Some reasoning with all true reasons is unsound (that which is invalid.)

Truth and validity are different from and independent of one another. Truth and falsehood are relations between individual statements and the world. Validity and invalidity are relations between statements and other statements in pieces of reasoning. No reasoning can *make* (force, compel, cause) a statement be true (or false.) No true statements can *make* a bad argument valid. No false ones can *make* it invalid. Both validity and truth are necessary for soundness and for probable or necessary truth of a conclusion. Even then, they don't cause truth of a conclusion. They at most justifiably persuade us of its truth.

The Correspondence Theory of Truth: What makes many statements true is that they correspond to reality, to the facts. False ones do not correspond to the facts.

An affirmative claim says some subject has some predicate, e.g., "$2 + 2 = 4$." A negative claim such as "$2 + 2 \neq 4$" says some subject does *not* have some predicate. An affirmative and negative claim with the same subjects and predicates like these two are called **negations, contradictories,** or **denials** of one another. Most critical thinking proceeds by a principle called **The Law of the Excluded Middle.** This law says *Every real, precise, unambiguous claim made by a person in some circumstances is either true or false. If it is true, then its' negation is false. If it is false, then its' negation is true.* There is no middle ground between truth and falsity. In the circumstances shown in the picture "The cat is on the mat" is true and its denial "The cat is not on the mat" is false.

A statement can be true even if no one has any support for it at all. So the conclusion of a piece of reasoning can be true even if the reasoning is invalid or the reasons false. The conclusion can also be false even if the reasoning is valid. Do not get the false impression that if a statement is only weakly supported or not supported at all, that it is probably false.

Many truths and falsehoods are objective matters. They have nothing to do with whether anybody sees or believes the fact or has any reasons to support a claim that it is a fact. Correspondence can be direct, as in the drawing, or indirect. Even if the cat is unobserved, the statement "The cat is on the mat" would correspond to the fact and be true. The young man in the cartoon has been passively reading about how much "support" reasons give to conclusions. Whether a statement is true or false often depends on facts. Reasoning has to do with coming to know facts or explaining or persuading others of them.

The following three definitions must be memorized word for word.   **"Valid" reasoning in general is reasoning in which if all its' reasons were true, then its' conclusion either would have to be true or would very probably be true.** "Its' " refers to the reasoning.

The important elements of these definitions are: 1) their conditional form, 2) their making claims about truth or falsehood of reasons and conclusions and 3) their use of the subjunctive "were" and "would be." 1) The "If... then..." form does not imply that either its "If..." part or its "then..." part alone is true. So it is possible for reasoning to be valid even if some or all statements in it are actually false! Under this definition it is possible for all the reasons of valid reasoning to be true and the conclusion still to be false (This will be in rare cases of inductive reasoning where the conclusion, although very probable, is in fact false.)

"Deductively valid" reasoning is reasoning in which if all its' reasons were true, then its conclusion would have to be true.
"Inductively valid" reasoning is reasoning in which if all its' reasons were true, then its conclusion would very probably be true.

2) The sense of "were true" in our definitions is not the sense of "was true in the past." It is the sense of "*supposing* that these reasons are true, then this conclusion would have to be, or very probably is true." 3) It is individual reasons and conclusions which are supposed to be true.

For many cases, the difference between deductively valid and deductively **in**valid reasoning can be explained this way. In deductively valid reasoning, its form guarantees that its reasons already claim to be true all of the information which is going to be claimed true in the conclusion. In deductively invalid reasoning, the form allows the conclusion to claim information to be true which is not already claimed to be true in the reasons. But in **in**ductively **valid** reasoning truth of the information in the reasons makes highly probable the truths of the conclusion.

Reasoning

Valid {	Deductively valid: The information claimed true in the reasons contains all the information claimed true in the conclusion.
	Inductively valid: The information claimed to be true in the reasons does not contain all the information claimed to be true in the conclusion, but makes it highly probably true.
Invalid	The information claimed true in the reasons neither contains nor makes highly probably true the information claimed true in the conclusion.

Here are two examples of very simple, deductively valid arguments.

No men are adults. -FALSE   No men are women. -TRUE

No adults are men. -FALSE   No women are men. -TRUE

Suppose we use the letter "F" to represent the subject class and the letter "G" to represent the predicate class. These two arguments have the same form.

No F's are G's

No G' s are F's

There are an infinite number of valid and invalid deductive arguments. So we can not teach how to evaluate them just by making a list of all the valid and invalid ones. This is where **form** and **variables** like "F" and "G" are needed. That does not mean that critical thinking or logic is mathematics. Nothing in this book will require more than addition. Variables are a shortening and generalizing tool. **If a form is deductively valid, every argument of that form is valid. If a form is invalid, every argument of that form is invalid.** The form above is deductively valid. If any reason of its form is true, then the conclusion of the form "No G's are F" must be true. A deductively valid form is one in which, if it is filled in exactly, there can be no cases where all its premises are true and its conclusion false.

Truth and falsehood apply to one sort of piece of language, while validity and invalidity apply to another sort. Truth and falsehood apply at first to simple indicative sentences, "SIS's" for short. Validity and invalidity apply to reasoning discourses "RD's," or groups of SIS's. Below is a table which makes a clear division between SIS's and RD's. It tells which adjectives apply to SIS's and which to RD's. It does not make sense to say the same sorts of things about simple indicative statements and about reasoning discourse.

Mistakes can be made in reasoning from classes to individuals. For example, "Men are numerous. Socrates is a man, so Socrates is numerous." The two reasons make sense and are true, but the conclusion does not even make sense. "Numerous" is an adjective applying only to a class, not an individual. "Native Americans are rapidly disappearing. That man is a Native American. Therefore, that man is rapidly disappearing." Again, the conclusion does not make sense. "Rapidly disappearing" applies only to a class, not to an individual. Note which nouns in the top of the table have the same meanings. Note what adjectives make or do not make sense with them. This will become clearer as one learns how to evaluate reasoning. Avoid the pronoun "it." Don't say "It" is true or false, valid or invalid. Instead, say "The statement that so-and-so is true or false" or "The argument such-and-such is valid (or invalid), sound or unsound."

Simple Indicative Statements (SIS's)	versus	Reasoning Discourse (R.D.)

Claims, assertions, propositions, truths, falsehoods, statements, reasons and conclusions, assumptions, suppositions, are all directly expressed in **simple indicative sentences.**	Arguments, explanations, demonstrations, proofs, deductions, inductions, reasonings are all directly expressed **in reasoning discourses.**
Statements, etc., are individuals.	Reasonings are **groups**, **sequences** of statements.

Individuals are concrete unities. Groups are abstract pluralities. It doesn't make sense to say the same things of individuals as of groups.

"All men are mortal" is a S.I.S. "Socrates is a man" is another S.I.S. "Socrates is mortal" is a 3rd. S.I.S.	"All men are mortal. Socrates is a man. So Socrates is mortal" is a **RD, a series of SIS's** in which the word "so" makes a claim that the reasons support the conclusion.

SIS's ARE True or False Warranted or not Warranted Probable or Improbable Proved or Unproved	**RD's ARE NOT** True or False Warranted or not Warranted Probable or Improbable Proved or Unproved
SIS's ARE NOT Deductively Valid or Invalid Deductive or Inductive Sound or Unsound Strong, Moderate, Weak, Nil	**RD's ARE** Deductively Valid or Invalid Deductive or Inductive Sound or Unsound Strong, Moderate, Weak, Nil

Using wrong adjectives with these nouns is like lack of agreement:
"That's a *true* (or '*false*') argument" is like   "They   goes to the store."
      Singular adjective - Plural noun.   Plural Pronoun - Sing. verb.

"That's a *valid* (or '*invalid* ') statement" is like "He   *go* to the store."
      Plural Adjective-Sing. Noun.   Sing. Pro. - Plural verb.

The student should now do Exercise 8 on Evaluation Adjectives.

Unsound reasoning is not necessarily all bad. We will see in the next chapter that unsound reasoning can vary in strength. Sometimes we can have reasoning which provides moderate support for its conclusion even though it does not guarantee that the conclusion must be true. Sometimes strong or moderate reasoning is the best we can get and still keep all true reasons. Sometimes reasons provide only weak support for a conclusion, and sometimes no support at all.

"Valid" means "logical," in a narrow sense, not "true." "Invalid" means "illogical," not "false." *Validity* is a relationship between or among statements. The wording of the first definition explains validity in general. It is intended to cover strong inductive arguments as well as deductively valid arguments. Strong inductive arguments are ones in which if all the reasons were true, then the conclusion would be established as *very likely* to be true. Another way to say this is to say that "the conclusion is established as highly probably true." Natural logicians think we run into many more, and many more interesting and important inductive than deductive arguments in everyday life.

A concept like validity is needed for an important reason. Our explanation of validity implies that **valid reasoning is RELIABLE.** *It will be reasoning in which we are able to know, without first knowing that the reasons are, in fact, true, that if they are true, then the conclusion will have to be true, or is very probably true.* The discovery and development of the idea of validity and showing it in argument forms enable us to judge whether our reasoning is *reliable* even where we are not certain that our reasons are true. Deductive validity means *absolute* reliability, while the reliability of inductive reasoning varies by degrees. Because valid reasoning is reliable as a source of true conclusions when it has true reasons, it is a major source of justification for believing statements which one had no reason to believe before the presentation of the argument.

Why are some arguments valid? There are several different reasons. In some cases, reasoning is deductively valid because all of the information made explicit in the conclusion was already present in the reasons. It will be helpful to see a couple of examples of this to get a grip on this idea that, in deductively valid reasoning, if all the reasons were true, then the conclusion would have to be true. These examples will illustrate also that we cannot tell simply by looking to see whether the reason statement(s) contain the exact same statement parts as the conclusion. We have to think whether if the reason were true, the conclusion would have to be true also. Here is an example from William Earle (1992), which illustrates this point:

I kissed her in New Jersey.   (IF TRUE)

I kissed her
in New Jersey.

 Deductively valid

I kissed her.   (MUST BE TRUE)

I kissed her.

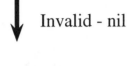
I kissed her in dream.　　　(IF TRUE)

I kissed her in a dream.

↓ Invalid - nil

I kissed her.　　　(COULD BE FALSE)

Did I really kiss her?

One degree of support (DOS) phrase like "deductively valid," "invalid," "strong," "moderate," "weak," or "nil" will be written beside, that is, just to the right of each arrow to show that we understand that we are judging reliability of reasoning and not truth. We see from this example that, even though the "subclaim" conclusion "I kissed her" is, indeed, included exactly in the reason, the reasoning is not valid, *because the reason could be true and the conclusion false.*

Although it may seem confusing, to get an understanding of validity, it will be useful for us to consider the same two statements twice, once with one as the reason and the other as the conclusion and then the other way around. That is, we will take the reason of the first argument and consider it as a conclusion and see if the conclusion of the first argument makes a good reason for it. This will rarely be the case! We will call this "reversing" the reason and conclusion.

Suppose the reason and conclusion of the first argument were reversed.

I kissed her.　　　(IF TRUE)

I kissed her.

↓ Invalid - Nil

I kissed her in New Jersey. (COULD BE FALSE)　　　**???**

Here is another example:

I am over 7 feet tall.   (IF TRUE)

↓   Deductively valid

I am over 5 feet tall.   (MUST BE TRUE)

But again suppose the reason and conclusion were reversed:

I am over 5 feet tall.   (IF TRUE)

↓   Invalid - Nil

I am over 7 feet tall.   (COULD BE FALSE)

The reader does not know who "I" or "she" stands for. So she cannot judge these statements to be true or false. Therefore she cannot judge these arguments to be sound or unsound. These examples illustrate the idea that what makes some arguments valid is that all of the information made explicit in the conclusion was already contained in the reasons. The picture of the reasons contains the picture of the conclusion. This is the sort of thing we can know by understanding the statements without knowing their actual truth or falsehood. However, the invalid examples show clearly the limitation of this thinking. They show that we cannot just look and see if the same "sub statement" parts are contained in both the reason and the conclusion to see if an argument is valid! Also, we cannot make clear pictures to represent very many deductively valid inferences, like the following examples.

He will never drive drunk again.   (IF TRUE)

↓ VALID   ↓

He will not drive drunk next week.   (MUST BE TRUE)

Again, suppose the reason and conclusion were reversed:

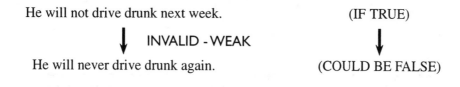

He will not drive drunk next week.   (IF TRUE)

⬇ INVALID - WEAK   ⬇

He will never drive drunk again.   (COULD BE FALSE)

And consider this argument closely related to the first:

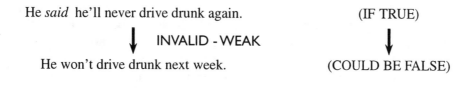

He *said* he'll never drive drunk again.   (IF TRUE)

⬇ INVALID - WEAK   ⬇

He won't drive drunk next week.   (COULD BE FALSE)

Here are two more to illustrate the difference.

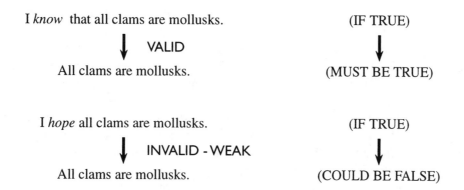

I *know* that all clams are mollusks.   (IF TRUE)

⬇ VALID   ⬇

All clams are mollusks.   (MUST BE TRUE)

I *hope* all clams are mollusks.   (IF TRUE)

⬇ INVALID - WEAK   ⬇

All clams are mollusks.   (COULD BE FALSE)

These examples were chosen to show two things. They show that the validity or invalidity of a piece of reasoning can rest on the use of just one word like "know" or "hope." Do not confuse truly knowing with falsely claiming to know. A person can falsely believe and claim that he or she knows. But we are to suppose it is really true that I *know* that all clams are mollusks. Let "S" be any name or personal pronoun and "P" be any statement. "S *knows* that P, so P" is always deductively valid. But "S 'says,' 'thinks,' 'believes,' 'opines,' 'guesses,' 'predicts,' 'wishes,' 'hopes,' 'desires,' or 'dreams' that P," without any other reason, is always a *weak* argument to "P" as a conclusion. This is a consequence of the way we use words. When we say we "know" something and are later proven wrong, we take it back. We correct ourselves and say only that we *thought* or *believed* it to be true. Thinking, believing and so on can't usually make something true.

These examples also illustrate that we have to be very careful not to confuse reason and conclusion indicators. If we do, then we will make wrong diagrams. They show that *to evaluate reasoning, we have to read like a lawyer!* A lawyer has to read every word of a proposed contract or testimony very carefully. Reasoning which is deductively valid with one statement taken as the reason and another as the conclusion is often invalid if we mistake the reason to be the conclusion and the conclusion for the reason.

There are deductively valid arguments to which the explanation of validity given so far does not apply. Here is one by Willard Quine, recalled to the author by Steven Thomas: "All circles are figures. Therefore all (persons) who draw circles draw figures." Such examples show that we cannot avoid making our general definition of deductive validity in terms of the idea that *if* all the reasons of an argument were true, then the conclusion would have to be true.

SECTION 3.3: ANALOGIES, PATTERNS AND COUNTER-EXAMPLES

The argument about no men being women shows that there can be deductively valid reasoning from all true reasons to a true conclusion. The example about no men being adults shows that there can be valid reasoning from all false reasons to a false conclusion. There can also be deductively valid reasoning from false reasons to a true conclusion. For example, suppose some ancient Greek or medieval person did not know that unicorns do not exist. She thought that horses were a type of unicorn with very short or missing horns. She might have reasoned like this:

"All horses are unicorns and all unicorns are mammals, so all horses are mammals."

According to our definition of "validity," she would have reasoned validly, although not soundly.

The one combination of truth and falsehood there cannot be is deductively valid reasoning from all true reasons to a conclusion that turns out to be false. This is a consequence of the definition given of deductive validity. It is exactly what is meant by saying that these valid forms are reliable.

If we can have a valid argument with all false statements in it; what use can it be to know which arguments are valid? There are a couple of analogies which can help to understand this. An analogy is a comparison between something unfamiliar and something familiar. It is made to help a person understand the unfamiliar thing by saying what it is like. *Deductively valid patterns of reasoning are like sets of directions for the mind to follow in reasoning.* They are "truth tracking" and *guarantee* that *if* one starts off on truths, *then* the steps that one takes will end up on truths. Deductively invalid patterns of reasoning range from strong to no support at all. They are like anything from having a map to *random walking*. **Fallacies** are common forms of reasoning which provide weak or no support for their conclusions. Reasoning fallaciously is like random walking. If one starts out on truths and reason fallaciously, the steps that one takes are as likely to end up on falsehoods as on truths.

Validity is truth-preserving or truth tracking. Invalidity is not truth preserving or truth tracking. Deductive validity is always truth preserving. When steps of reasoning are deductively valid, truth becomes an hereditary property. It is passed from the reason statements to the conclusion statements. *Strong inductive arguments are frequently, but not always truth preserving also.* One purpose of reasoning is to extend our knowledge, to go from things that one already knows to things that one doesn't yet know. One can't actually know something if it is false. Therefore, it is very important that we learn these sets of directions for reliably extending our knowledge. There are also a few closely similar ways of reasoning which do not reliably extend knowledge. These are called "formal fallacies." This book will discuss them, because we should not be fooled by patterns which are similar to valid ones, but which are unreliable.

Valid patterns are like sets of directions, fallacies like random walking.

VALID

INVALID: Weak to Nil

No S is P ➡ No P is S

All S is P ➡?➡ All P is S

A VALID PATTERN
All A's are B's
<u>All B's are C's</u>
So all A's are C's

AN INVALID PATTERN
<u>All A's are B's</u>
So all B's are A's?

People who start out on truths and reason validly never lose truth and end up on falsehoods.

Another analogy to validity can be given. One could say that *validity is like a well-functioning freezer.* A well-functioning freezer is one which can keep the same low temperature all the time. Suppose one puts fresh meat into it. When one takes it out, the meat will still be fresh. It may suffer a little change in quality known as freezer burn. But basically it will be all right to eat. Invalidity, particularly fallacy, is like a poorly functioning freezer. It may keep a steady temperature over a period of time or not. If one puts fresh meat into it, then one *might* get fresh meat back when one takes it out later. But suppose the freezer went off for a long period of time while the person was gone. The meat *might* not be fresh any longer. Validity preserves truth like a well functioning freezer preserves freshness.

This analogy is a little misleading. One takes out exactly the same size and shape pieces of meat from the freezer that one wrapped and put away in the first place. But people rarely reason out exactly the same conclusion as their reason. To do so would be to commit the fallacy called "Begging the Question." An example of this would be to reason as follows: "No cats are pets, so no cats are pets." It is obviously wrong somehow to try to persuade someone of a conclusion by stating the exact same point as a reason. They didn't find it evident as an unsupported claim. So they should not be persuaded by this kind of reasoning. But notice that this argument is perfectly *valid* by our definition. *If* the reason were true, *then* the conclusion would have to be true! If we are going to call such an argument by the nice sounding term "valid," then we have to have other words to say what is wrong with it also.

Examples like this are described using the distinction between sound and unsound arguments. With it, we can say: "This argument is valid but unsound, because the reason is false." Such an argument is "formally valid" and, at the same time, it is "informally fallacious." In most deductively valid reasoning, the conclusion that is said to "follow from" the reasons is likely to contain only a part of the information in the reasons (or none of it in invalid reasoning.) This would be like putting packages of meat into the freezer and somehow the meat comes out cut into smaller pieces and wrapped differently. And in inductive reasoning, the conclusion expresses information going beyond that in the reasons. This would be like somehow getting not only differently packaged but more meat out of the freezer! So only the idea of preservation of truth or freshness is the accurate general point of this analogy.

Logic is a part of critical thinking which deals with facts as to which patterns of reasoning are valid or reliable and which are not. Here are examples of patterns or forms of reasoning using variables to stand for phrases as before. This is an example of a valid, reliable form:

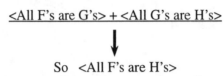

<All F's are G's> + <All G's are H's>

So   <All F's are H's>

No one can know that there is any truth here. That is because there can be no truth in mere *statement forms* like these making up an *argument form*. "All F's are G's" is neither true nor false. But suppose one believes that the so-called "greenhouse effect" is real. That is, we believe that gasses given off in the manufacture or use of certain products are dangerously increasing the atmosphere's capacity to heat up the earth. Suppose, also, we learn that a corporation plans to build a plant in your area that will produce trichloromonoflouromethanes. We can hardly say the word, much less know right offhand whether such a plant is OK with us, or whether we should oppose it because it adds to the greenhouse effect. Let's say we are not chemists and so we can't directly investigate this. Our knowledge that the above pattern of reasoning is valid could help us. Suppose we did a little book research and found out that all trichloromonofluoromethanes are chlorofluorocarbons and that all chlorofluorocarbons are Greenhouse gasses. Our knowledge that the pattern of reasoning just given is valid now enables us to conclude with certainty that all trichloromonofluouromethanes are greenhouse gasses.

Now compare the form just discussed with a related but unreliable, invalid form.

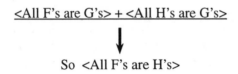

<All F's are G's> + <All H's are G's>

So <All F's are H's>

Suppose we were students in a grade school biology class. The teacher had made "All clams are mollusks" a true - false question on a quiz and many of the class got it wrong. The teacher became angry. He said he would put the question on the final exam and make it worth a lot of points. Nevertheless, we did not remember to look this up. Minutes before the test, we recall that this will be on it and worth a lot of points. We ask a friend who comes up whether he studied and if he knows whether all clams are mollusks or not. We know he is a poor student and he admits he did not study. But he says, "All clams are water dwelling animals. All mollusks are water dwelling animals. So all clams are mollusks" Both of his reasons are true and his conclusion is, in fact, true also. But his conclusion *does not follow logically from* his reasons. It is more like a lucky guess that this conclusion is true. The reasons are, in fact, relevant to the conclusion. But they don't establish it with certainty. If you were not convinced that all clams were mollusks before, you should not be convinced by this reasoning.

One thing which shows that such reasoning is invalid or unreliable is that there can be counter-examples to it. A *counter-example* in this case would be a piece of reasoning which has the same form as another, yet in which the reasons are known to be true and the conclusion is known to be false. Here is a counter-example to this piece of reasoning. It is like arguing "All cats are animals. All dogs are animals. So all cats are dogs." This counter-example shows that reasoning in this form randomly leads from truths to falsehoods just as it sometimes randomly leads from truths to truths. Counter examples in this sense are used in a method of showing reasoning to be invalid called "Refutation by Logical Analogy."

Using variables and forms offers us a short way to determine that a very large number of arguments are valid or invalid. Suppose we look at two forms. One is valid, having arguments A_1, A_2, A_3, A_4 of that form. Another is invalid and has arguments A_5, A_6, A_7, A_8 of that different form. Here is a diagram to illustrate this situation.

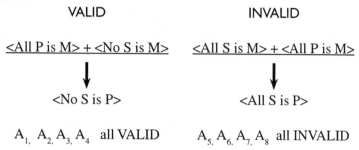

VALID	INVALID

<All P is M> + <No S is M>   <All S is M> + <All P is M>

<No S is P>   <All S is P>

A_1, A_2, A_3, A_4 all VALID A_5, A_6, A_7, A_8 all INVALID

This is the basis of the method of Refutation by Logical Analogy which will be explained in more detail later. The central idea is this: Suppose we get an argument that we suspect to be invalid. Try to find another argument having the same form which has clearly true reasons and a false conclusion. If such an argument can be found, this shows that the *form* of the suspected argument is not valid. That shows that the suspected argument itself is not valid.

Here is another example of going to the form of an argument to see its weakness. It is an advertisement also cited in Thomas (1993): "The oil filter protects the engine. So if the engine is the most important part of the car, then the oil filter is the second most important part." This is weak reasoning. When students are given this problem, they sometimes protest: "How can I be expected to judge the validity or degree of support reasons give to conclusions in cases like this, if I have no knowledge of the subject matter?" There is a 5 part answer to this. 1) Many cases of validity depend largely on *form*, not subject matter. 2) A few valid and invalid forms can be learned. 3) Many valid forms are rules of logical thinking which have already been learned and are now used, even if they have not been learned explicitly. (That is why they seem familiar, obvious or trivial when seen explicitly.) 4) This book will teach a general method of judging the degree of support reasons give to a conclusion called the "Truth Pretense Method." A general question called "The Magic Question" of reasoning evaluation will be included. This question can be used on *any* piece of reasoning to evaluate it without knowing specific forms. 5) This book will also teach two specific methods of showing arguments to be invalid: Refutation by Logical Analogy, and what the author calls "the Inconsistency Method." For now, suppose we replace the nouns "oil filter," "engine" and "car" with the variable letters "A," "B," and "C." We now have the form:

The A protects the B

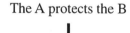

If the B is the most important part of the C, then the A is the second most important part.

After some thought, the reader should be able to come up with examples of this form where the reason is true and the conclusion false. Here is one: Let "A" be the Secret Service, B = the President of the United States, and C = the Executive branch of the government. The Secret Service protects the President of the United States. But it is not true that if the President is the most important member of the Executive branch of the government, then the Secret Service is the second most important part. Most people would say that the Vice President and other persons who would take over the President's job, if he or she were to die, were certainly more important than the Secret Service.

Let's conclude this section with an illustration to sum up the relations among soundness, truth, and deductive validity. The support which a sound deductively valid argument gives to its conclusion may be pictured as a strong column with the conclusion on top. The non-support of arguments in which the reasoning is 1) invalid or 2) one or more reasons is false, or 3) both 1 and 2, is represented by three low ground areas beside the column. Always remember that we are interested in judging whether argumentative reasoning contains true reasons and whether it is valid so that we can go on to make a decision on whether it is sound (that is, supports its conclusion) *in order to at last decide whether to accept its conclusion as true or to continue to suspend judgment on it.*

Sound and Unsound Reasoning

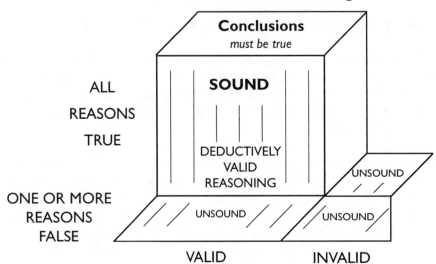

4 DEGREES OF SUPPORT REASONS GIVE TO CONCLUSIONS

SECTION 4.1 DEDUCTION, INDUCTION AND DEGREES OF SUPPORT

The questions we are now going to deal with could be shown in an arrow diagram with "Y/N" standing for "Is the answer 'Yes', or 'No' ?"

If this reason (or these reasons) were true, then

would this conclusion have to be true? Y/N

"Yes" = argument is deductively valid. "No" = ask next question down.

would the conclusion be made extremely probable? Y/N

"Yes" = argument is strong. "No" = ask next question down.

would it be made significantly more probable than not? Y/N

"Yes" = argument is moderate. "No" = ask next question down.

would it be made slightly probable? Y/N

"Yes" = argument is weak. "No" = ask next question down.

does the reason give equal probability to the conclusion and to its negation? Y/N

"Yes" = argument is nil. "No" = ask next question down.

does the reason give more probability to the negation of the conclusion than to the conclusion itself? Y/N

"Yes" = argument is self-defeating. "No" = ask next question down

would this conclusion have to be false? Y/N

"Yes" = argument is antilogical.

Conclusion

Reasons can give an infinite number of **degrees of support** to different conclusions. To make things simpler, we crunch these degrees of support down into seven kinds: Deductive validity, Strong support, Moderate, Weak, Nil, (a Latin word meaning no support at all.), Self-defeating, and antilogical. We are using the expression "degree of support" like the word "validity." *In this sense, reasons can provide "degrees of support" for conclusions even if we don't know whether they are true and even if they are false!* The diagram is a waterfall of questions. If the answer to the top question "Would the conclusion have to be true?" is "Yes", then the argument is **deductively valid.** If it is "No", then the student should ask the next question down and so on.

Deductive Validity: We need to support a claim with argument when there is a dispute or disagreement. Suppose we state the claim, and someone else does not accept it. It would be great if we could find some other statements which he does accept and which, unknown to him, are related to the claim he is presently denying in such a way that, if they are true, then the claim he doubts must be true. Rarely, such reasons can be found. In such a case, suppose we stated those reasons to him. Then we ask him if he accepts each of these reasons as true. He says he does. Then there is a sense in which he simply has to accept the conclusion. In a deductively valid argument it is *logically impossible* for the reasons to be true and the conclusion false. This means that for him to accept the reason(s) and continue to deny the conclusion would be to contradict himself. For example, to say "All men are animals and all animals are mortal, but some men are not mortal" would be a contradiction. To say "You go and If you go, then we will go, but we won't go" would again be a contradiction. In such cases, it is impossible to explain how all the reasons can be true and the conclusion false.

In strong arguments, if the reasons were true, then the conclusion would very probably be true. Let's illustrate deductive validity versus strong support by comparing a deductively valid syllogism with a strong inductive argument to the same conclusion.

A deductively valid syllogism   *A strong inductive argument*

All horses are mammals. +   All horses ever observed had hearts.
All mammals have hearts.

So all horses have hearts.   So all horses have hearts.

Differences

1. The information claimed true in the reasons contains all the information claimed true in the conclusion.	1'. The information claimed true in the reasons does not contain all the information claimed true in the conclusion, but makes it highly probably true.
2. THAT'S WHY, if all the reasons were true, then the conclusion would have to be true.	2'. THAT'S WHY if all the reasons are true, the conclusion is at best PROBABLY true.
3. THAT'S WHY the argument is deductively valid or not. There are no degrees of deductive validity.	3'. THAT'S WHY there are degrees of strength. The more evidence in the reasons, the stronger, the less, the weaker.

It used to be said that the difference between deductive and inductive arguments is that all deductive arguments go from the general to the particular while all inductive ones go from the particular to the general. *These examples show that this is not true*! The same conclusion could not be both particular and general. Counter examples have been found showing this old definition to be wrong. The difference marked off by point 1 applies only to certain deductive arguments. The other two differences are differences between all deductively valid and inductive arguments.

With this contrast we can separate out and explain what is meant by a deductive argument in general. It is one in which the author's *intent* is to argue in a way having the qualities 2 and 3 listed under the deductively valid argument above. A similar definition is all right for an inductive argument with points 2' and 3'. An author sometimes shows her intent. She does this by choosing to write the argument in one of the common forms of deductive argument like the syllogistic or conditional forms. But often an author has no clear intent to argue in either general type of way.

Some of the forms of deductive argument are deductively *valid* and others are not. "Deductive" and "Inductive" are descriptive words. But "Deductively valid", like "strong", is a success-word or phrase. It means an achievement of something. So do not lazily cut "-ly valid" off of "deductively valid" and write "deductive" when you mean "deductively valid"! *Many deductive arguments are not deductively valid!*

To classify as strong, the truth of the reasons must enable us to be *certain beyond a reasonable doubt that the conclusion is true*. We could also say the reasons must make the conclusion *likely enough on which to bet something of great value*. They must make it probable enough *to act when there is a lot at stake*. In such cases it may be very difficult to explain how all reasons could be true and the conclusion could be false.

Probabilities are measured in fractions, decimals or percents. In the fraction form, the top part is the number of cases one is looking for, while the bottom part is the total number of cases. The probability of a coin flip coming out heads is 1/2 or .5 or 50%. The probability that "The coin comes out heads" and its contradictory "The coin does not come out heads" are also .5. Deductively valid arguments give a 1.0 probability, certainty, that if the reasons are true then the conclusion is true. At .5 reasons give no more support to a conclusion than to its contradictory. Here are examples to contrast the difference between deductively valid and strong support. Assume that the percentages mean "exactly this percent and no more."

<u><100% of black Americans are of West African ancestry. > + <Jamal is a black American.></u>

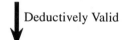
Deductively Valid

So Jamal is of west African ancestry.

These reasons, if true, confer a probability of 1.0 on the conclusion, certainty that it is true.

<u><99% of black Americans are of West African ancestry.> + <Jamal is a black American>.</u>

Strong

So Jamal is of West African ancestry.

If these reasons were true, then the probability that Jamal was of West African ancestry would be .99 and the probability that he was not would be .01. But you might be able to explain that these reasons can be true and it can also be true that Jamal's ancestors came from Kenya or some other part of Africa.

The induction in the horses example is "induction by enumeration", or counting. It may look very strong partly because of unstated extra reasons. But it is not the only kind of induction. Nor is it always strong. Suppose that at one time people had only seen white swans. They would have concluded that all swans were white. At a later time they would notice that most species show differences of color. This would be called a "higher level induction." By this induction they might correct their view and come to believe only that most swans are white. The examples using 100% and 99% are called "statistical syllogisms." Reasons like these are established by sampling and making simpler inductive generalization arguments from a form like the following.

<u>X% of sample S of population P have quality Q</u>

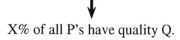

X% of all P's have quality Q.

The strength of such generalization arguments can vary greatly. With inductive arguments, it will be useful to know *alternatives* to the conclusion in order to explain how the reasons could all be true and the conclusion false. In generalization arguments, the sample was perhaps selected in some way so that it is unrepresentative of all P's. A second alternative is that the sample was so small that the X% in it was just a coincidence.

Explanations can also be of different strengths. The subject of explaining action is complex. For present purposes, the *best available folk explanation* of action (one in terms of reasons and desires) can be classified as strong. Less good explanations should be classified as weaker (but see Chapter 11, section 1, Chapter 12, Section 2.)

For example, suppose Jesus (say "HAY soos") tells Lupe ("Loo pay"): "Yesterday, when I came to school, I found my lock, locked, on another kid's locker. Some kid in this school is a thief." Lupe knows that Jesus is careless. She asks: "Is anything missing?" "Nope." "More likely you just left it open and some jerk came along and pranked you," Lupe explains. Lupe's explanation is stronger because it is more probable. When faced with a situation calling for explanation, consider whether there are any other possible explanations which are more probable.

Moderate Support: An argument presents moderate support for its conclusion when truth of the reasons is a passable, defensible ground for believing the conclusion, one which makes it considerably more than .5 probable. More evidence would be necessary before one would be justified in believing in the conclusion beyond a reasonable doubt. Here it is easier to explain how reasons could be true and the conclusion false. We can take as our example the same type of statistical syllogism with a lowered percentage in the first reason.

<75% of black Americans are of West African ancestry.> +< Jamal is a black American.>

 Moderate

So Jamal is of West African ancestry.

Many arguments given in everyday life only provide moderate support, such as a probability of .75 for their conclusions. It may well be all right to accept such arguments when not much is at stake.

Weak Support means an argument's reasons provide very little support for its conclusion. Here it should be easy to explain how all reasons could be true and the conclusion false. Most informal fallacies are of this degree of support. The following would be a weak argument:

<65 % of black Americans are of West African ancestry.> + <Jamal is a black American.>

 Weak

So Jamal is of West African ancestry.

Little support is not no support. Nor does the weakness of any one argument for a conclusion have any tendency to show that the conclusion is false. Remember, the truth of many conclusions depends on their correspondence with fact. This can very well exist in cases where we have only weak or no support for the statement as a conclusion.

<50% of black Americans are of West African ancestry.> +< Jamal is a black American.>

 Nil

So Jamal is of West African ancestry.

Nil Support: "Nil" means "no support". Here the truth of the reasons gives no more probability to the conclusion than to its contradictory "Jamal is not of West African ancestry."

If exactly 30% and no more are of West African ancestry, then this reasoning is self-defeating.

<u><30% of Black Americans are of West African ancestry.>+ <Jamal is a black American. ></u>

↓ Self-defeating

So Jamal is of West African ancestry.

An antilogism is, in a loose sense, a set of statements such that the truth of one or more imply with deductive validity, that another (the conclusion here) is false. So we will call this degree of support "antilogical."

<u><No Black Americans are of West African ancestry.>+ <Jamal is a black American. ></u>

↓ Antilogical

So Jamal is of West African ancestry.

Let's sum up how we are using our terms in a diagram which we will call a "Validometer," like a thermometer.

The Validometer

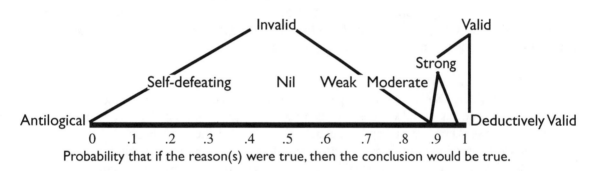

Probability that if the reason(s) were true, then the conclusion would be true.

SECTION 4.2 THE TRUTH PRETENSE METHOD OF JUDGING DEGREE OF SUPPORT

There is a method which can always be used to help decide whether a piece of reasoning is deductively valid or not; and if not, how much support its reasons give to its conclusion.

Step 1: Disregard your own personal opinions on whether the reasons are true or not and pretend that all the reasons are true.

Step 2: Ask: "If this reason (or these reasons) were true, would this conclusion have to be true?" Thomas (1991) calls this "the Magic Question" of argument evaluation. A "Yes" answer means the argument is deductively valid. This question works, because in a deductively valid argument, if the reason(s) were true, then the conclusion would have to be true. So if the conclusion can be false at the same time that the reasons are all true, then the reasoning is not deductively valid.

If the right answer is "yes", then the argument is deductively valid. If the right answer is "no", then the argument has a lower degree of support. We are not asking whether the reasons or conclusion are, in fact, true. Instead, we are asking whether it is logically possible that the reasons could be true and the conclusion false at the same time. We are asking whether the situation of the reasons being true and the conclusion being false at the same time is consistent.

Step 3: If the answer is "yes," then estimate the probability of the circumstances under which all the reasons can be true and the conclusion false at the same time.

The more improbable the circumstances, the stronger the argument. The more probable the circumstances, the weaker is the argument. This method may be applied in two questions, 1) "Can it be that these reasons are all true and this conclusion is, at the same time, false?" and 2) "How probable is it that this can be?" If the right answer to 1) is "no," then one should write "This argument is deductively valid" and the answer to 2) is "it is impossible". If the right answer is "yes," then the argument has a lower degree of support than deductive validity. A specific explanation of how these reasons can be true and the conclusion false needs to be given. Question 2) will need to be answered with an estimate of probability.

In many cases readers can not precisely estimate probabilities. Consider this argument. "Genesis 1 and Genesis 2 contradict each other on whether men or the birds were created first. It is improbable that one author would contradict himself in neighboring verses. It is improbable that editors, regarding two verses as each possibly the Holy Word of God, but not knowing which is which, would take the chance of leaving out the one which was truly it. Therefore, it is probable that Genesis 1 and Genesis 2 were written by different authors." Here we can only say that "improbable" means below .5.

Suppose, however, we had this argument. "Barnes jumped toward the edge of the top floor of the Empire State Building. So Barnes hit the pavement 1,000 feet below with fatal force." This reason can be true and this conclusion false. Here we can rank - order the probability of circumstances which would allow the reason to be true and the conclusion false. It is quite probable that there is a wall or fence in place for suicide prevention. Slightly improbable would be that he landed on a ledge or an awning. More improbable: He was hang gliding, wearing a bunji cord, or parachute. Still more improbable: firemen with an inflatable mattress saved him. Even more improbable: as he is about to hit, an air compressor exploded and slowed his fall to a gentle landing.

To use this "Truth Pretense Method" we must learn to form the "negation" of a conclusion. A statement like "15 times 15 equals 225" is called an "affirmative" statement. The negation of a statement is formed by inserting "not" into it, such as "15 times 15 is not 225." Starting in the late 1950's a psychologist named Peter Wason showed that people have more difficulty understanding negations than affirmations. An example is this. What is the negation of "All cats are nice"? People often say "All cats are not nice." This is an unclear form which should never be used. The negation of a statement is also called its' "denial" or "contradictory." The exact contradictory of "All cats are nice" is "Some cats are not nice." **Generally, If a statement is true, its negation is false. If it is false, then its negation is true.** An affirmative statement is also called the denial of its negation statement. When one person makes a claim and another asserts its negation, they contradict each other. They do not "refute" each other. To refute is to disprove, not just to contradict.

For our Truth Pretense Method contrary statements to a conclusion can also be used. Contrary statements can't both be true, but can both be false. Here are examples. The contrary of "All cats are nice" is "No cats are nice." Another example is "Julio is taller than Jesus" and "Jesus is taller than Julio." Both are false if they are of the same height.

On the next page is a table of contraries and contradictories, by Bruce Thompson. Use it to form contradictories of conclusions. Letters are short for statement types. Solid lines represent contradictories, dotted ones are contraries.

Table of Contraries and Contradictories

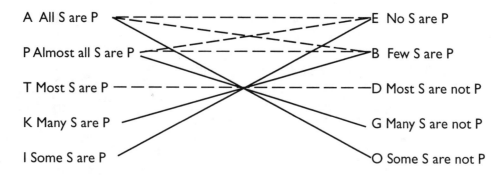

Contraries and contradictories are called "inconsistent." It should be obvious from these examples that *inconsistent statements can't both be true.*

Conditional arguments contain "If- then-" statements. The contradictory of the conditional statement "If you go, then we will go" is "You go and we do not go." The form of a conditional statement is pictured by using the variable letters "P", for the part after "if" and "Q" for the part after "then" like this: "If P, then Q." To contradict such a statement, then, you must say "P and not-Q."

Let's apply the Magic Question to the kissing examples. The Magic question for "I kissed her in New Jersey, so I kissed her" is: "Can it be true that I kissed her in New Jersey and, at the same time, that I did not kiss her at all? How can this be?" Clearly, the answer is "No, it can't be. This argument is deductively valid. This is not even possible."

The Magic Question for "I kissed her in a dream, so I kissed her" is "Can it be true that I kissed her in a dream and at the same time, that I did not kiss her at all?" Here the answer is clearly "Yes, so this is not a deductively valid argument. How? A person can dream of doing many things he does not actually do."

The Magic question for "I kissed her, so I kissed her in New Jersey" is: "Can it be true that I kissed her and, at the same time, that I did not kiss her in New Jersey?" The answer is "Yes, so the argument is not deductively valid." How? I could have kissed her in many other states or countries.

Do not get the false impression that logical evaluation requires us to pretend forever that false reasons are true! This method requires us to temporarily pretend that the reasons are true. To judge whether an argument is sound, we also have to evaluate whether each reason is actually true or not. An argument which has a false reason is unsound, but not necessarily invalid. We have seen valid arguments with all false reasons.

Be careful not to confuse three different things: 1) explaining how all the reasons, without self-contradiction, can be true and the conclusion can still be false, 2) arguing that a reason is, in fact, false and 3) arguing that the conclusion is, in fact, false. 1) is not easy but is, in fact, your task in dealing with validity. Showing a reason or even the conclusion to be actually false does not show the argument containing it to be invalid! It shows the argument to be unsound. When using the Truth Pretense Method, avoid this confusion by pretending that the reasons are, in fact, true! Any text or teacher of critical thinking will give examples which deliberately have reasons or conclusions with which readers are going to disagree. But they will be valid. This will be done to see if the reader understands the idea that validity is independent of truth. Here are three examples to illustrate this. Are the following arguments valid?

A.   [1] <All vegetables are plants> and [2] <no dogs are plants,> <u>so</u> [3] <no dogs are vegetables.>

B.   [1]<Music is a combination of sounds pleasing to the human ear,> and [2] <Heavy Metal is not pleasing to the human ear,> <u>so</u> [3]<Heavy Metal is not music!>

In B. we have to interpret how many are meant because the statements do not say. The first looks like a definition, so we will take it to mean "All music." The second similarly seems to express disapproval of all Heavy Metal, so we will take it to mean "No Heavy Metal is pleasing to the human ear." Then the conclusion drawn seems to be that No Heavy Metal is music.

Some confused student will say "No, this is not valid because lots of kids like Heavy Metal." The teacher will mark the answer down and reply, "You are arguing that a reason, 2, IS false instead of explaining how all the reasons CAN BE true and the conclusion CAN still be false at the same time. The question is 'Can it be true that All music is a combination of sounds pleasing to the human ear and that No Heavy Metal is pleasing to the human ear and, at the same time, that All Heavy Metal is music?' Answer: No! If the second reason is not true, the argument is unsound. However, it is valid." Consider a third example. The argument is:

C.   [1] <All responsible drivers get lower insurance rates.> [2]<No teenagers get lower insurance rates.> <u>So</u> [3]<No teenagers are responsible drivers.>

Again some students judge this to be invalid. An incorrect comment would be: "This argument is invalid. Lots of teenagers are responsible drivers." The teacher's comment might be: "Maybe so, but you are confusing arguing that the conclusion IS FALSE with explaining HOW the reasons COULD all be true and the conclusion COULD still be false. The question here is 'Can it be true that all responsible drivers get lower rates and that no teenagers get lower rates and yet some teenagers are responsible drivers?' There is no way this could be. So this argument is deductively valid. If we want to criticize it, we may add that 'It is unsound, owing to a false reason.'"

All three of these arguments have exactly the same form:

[1] <u>< All P is M> +</u> [2] <u>< No S is M></u>

[3] <No S is P>

So they must *all* be deductively valid or not deductively valid! Keep the Magic Question in mind and ask it of every example given.

The stronger arguement is, if the answer to the Magic Question is "yes," then the more improbable it is that all the reasons can be true and the conclusion false at the same time. The more probable the circumstances are under which all the reasons can be true and the conclusion false, the weaker the argument. It is worth illustrating this and the degrees of support with one more example.

If it would take unusual or abnormal, but not extremely improbable events to make it possible for reasons of an argument to be true and a conclusion false, then the argument is only moderate in support.

Sometimes it is necessary to weigh improbabilities against one another. Here is an example. A car comes over the top of a hill. It slowly drifts across the center line of a two-way road. An oncoming driver flashes his lights, pulls to the right, slows to a stop, beeps his horn. He is still hit, hard, on the driver's side, while his car is against a guard rail. Luckily, no one is injured. The driver who hit the car smells of alcohol. The victim concludes the driver was drunk. But the other driver points to a flat tire on his car. He claims his tire blew out as he came over the top of the hill. The tire looks bald. It is improbable that the man was driving drunk. Most people don't. It was also improbable that the tire blew out just at the instant necessary to let the driver escape blame for the accident. But tires do blow out even at such times. Lying also is somewhat improbable. An investigating police officer has to weigh the improbabilities of drunk driving against the tire blowing out at the time alleged and the improbability that the driver who hit the car has a blood alcohol level high enough to arrest him for driving under the influence.

The student should now write out answers to the Diagnostic Test in the Appendix, then check answers against the Summary of Evaluation Concepts and correct wrong answers.

SECTION 4.3: FORMAL METHODS OF SHOWING ARGUMENTS TO BE INVALID

Sometimes it is difficult to think up a specific explanation of how reasons can be true and a conclusion false. If so, this can be done by one of two formal methods. **The Inconsistency Method** is based on this idea that in a deductively valid argument, the truth of the reasons excludes all possibility that the conclusion will be false. A pair of statements is inconsistent if and only if they can't both be true (at the same place and time and of the same subject and for the same person.) Statements are consistent if they can both be true at the same time. contraries and contradictories are two kinds of inconsistent statements. The examples given earlier of types of negations, contraries and contradictories or other inconsistent statements can be used to form some statement (let's call it "CB" for "connection breaker") which is consistent with the reasons but inconsistent with the conclusion. Any such statement will express a possibility that the conclusion is false which is not excluded by the truth of the reasons. For example:

Here is a model which Correctly Explains this type. The reason, "He threatened to kill her" can be true and it can be true that she's not even dead, in which case the conclusion "He killed her" would be false.

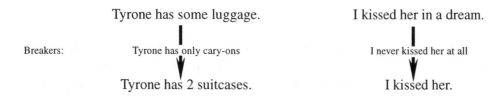

MODEL EXPLANATIONS: "Tyrone has some luggage" can be true and it can be true that he only has carry-ons, which would mean that "He has two suitcases" is false.

It could be true that I kissed her in a dream and also true that I never kissed her at all, so "I kissed her" could be false.

In cases where there are two or more reasons, it gets a little more complex. But for syllogisms, first try to identify a contrary or contradictory of the conclusion. Then ask: Does the truth of these two reasons make it impossible that this contrary or contradictory statement is true? If not, use that contrary or contradictory in the explanation, as in the following examples.

<u>All clams live in water. + All mollusks live in water.</u>

Breaker: some clams are not mollusks

All clams are mollusks.

Model correct explanation: "Some clams are not mollusks" is the contradictory of "All clams are mollusks." The two reasons could be true and it could still be true that Some clams are not mollusks, in which case, the conclusion would be false.

<u>Most owls are birds that hunt at night + Most birds that eat mice are owls</u>

Breaker: Most birds that eat mice are not birds that hunt at night.

Most birds that eat mice are birds that hunt at night.

Model explanation: It could be true that most owls hunt at night and also that most of the mice eating birds are owls, but it could still be true that most of the mice eating birds are not ones that hunt at night. In this case, the conclusion could be false, even if the reasons are true.

Conditional reasoning also often has two reasons, but careful thought about the situations the statements describe should allow you in invalid cases to find a contrary or contradictory of the conclusion whose truth is not excluded by the truth of the reasons.

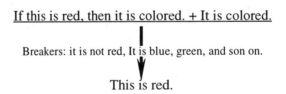

<u>If this is red, then it is colored. + It is colored.</u>

Breakers: it is not red, It is blue, green, and son on.

This is red.

Summary of the Inconsistency Method: 1) Form a statement "CB" which is inconsistent with the conclusion. 2) Think hard and decide whether CB is consistent with the truth of the reasons. If it is, write an explanation in the following form: "These reasons are consistent with CB (write out CB) and if CB is true, then C (the conclusion) would be false." If no such statement CB exists, then the argument is valid.

THE METHOD OF REFUTATION BY LOGICAL ANALOGY: In a deductively valid argument "A", if all the reasons are true, then the conclusion must be true. So finding another argument, "LA," for "logical analogy," which has the same form as A, but which has reasons known to be true and a conclusion known to be false, is sufficient to show that A is not of a deductively valid form.

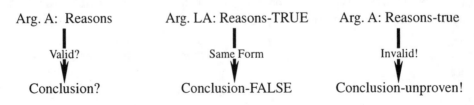

Arg. A: Reasons   Arg. LA: Reasons-TRUE   Arg. A: Reasons-true

Valid?   Same Form   Invalid!

Conclusion?   Conclusion-FALSE   Conclusion-unproven!

Example 1. God created us of 2 different sexes, so He didn't intend for us to love people of our own sex.

God created us (of 2 different sexes).

He didn't intend for us to (love people of our own sex).

FORM: God created us X.

He didn't intend for us to Y.

LOGICAL ANALOGY: God created us to be born naked. -TRUE

He didn't intend for us to wear clothes. -FALSE

MODEL EXPLANATION: "This is like arguing that God created us to be born naked, so He didn't intend for us to wear clothes; or God created us without wings, so He didn't intend for us to fly."

By the way, it would be totally against the type of mental attitude critical thinking tries to teach, to jump to the conclusion that an author's criticism of one argument on a certain subject is an attack on or support for the subject as a whole. It would be an example of jumping to a conclusion. It would be a fallacy of hasty generalization.

Example 2. Most heroin users previously smoked marijuana, so marijuana smoking leads to heroin use.

Most (heroin users) previously (smoked marijuana).

(Marijuana smoking) leads to (heroin use).

FORM: Most X users previously Y-ed.

Y-ing leads to X.

LOGICAL ANALOGY: <u>Most cigarette smokers previously drank milk</u>. -TRUE

Milk drinking leads to cigarette smoking. -FALSE

MODEL EXPLANATION: "That's like arguing: Most cigarette smokers previously drank milk, so milk drinking leads to cigarette smoking."

The student should now do Exercise 9: Judging the Degree of Support Reasons give to Conclusions.

SECTION 4.4: REASONING OF SPECIAL KINDS

Linking conditional arguments come in valid and invalid forms. If...then..." statements are so important that we will devote a whole short chapter to them. Syllogistic arguments involving quantifier words will also be examined. First, let us look at certain common kinds of arguments which differ basically in content.

Some words are *increasers* of information content when added to claims and others are *decreasers*. Some are quantifier words and others are qualifier words. Examples of qualifier increasers are "certainly," "exactly," "necessarily," "highly," and "very." Examples of qualifier decreasers are "probably," "presumably," "roughly," and "generally." Suppose we have the reason "He is very fussy" as a reason for three different conclusions: 1. No woman ever pleases him. 2. Few women ever please him and 3. Many women please him. This reason provides strongest support for "Few women ever please him" and weaker support for the other conclusions. So reasoning really does come in degrees of support, not a cut - and - dried difference of kind between deductively valid reasoning and reasoning which is not deductively valid and therefore worthless. Such an example show again that we need to read like a lawyer; read every word of a piece of reasoning carefully. Each word can have an effect on the degree of support reasons give to conclusions.

Causal (KAW-zahl) arguments are inductive arguments about what event(s) cause(s) what others. Such arguments are very common. They can be stronger or weaker. By a "cause" we will mean the total set of events and conditions necessary for an event "e" to occur. Taken together these are sufficient to make e occur. The paradigm (clearest example) of causality is one billiard ball, the "cue ball," hitting another, the "object ball," and making it start to move. This way of speaking describes only two events which are parts of the full cause and effect.

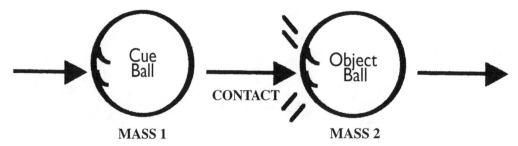

ACCELERATION 1 x MASS 1 = FORCE, CAUSES ACCELERATION 2

However partial our description, note three fundamental points about cause and effect events. *1. Causes always come before their effects. 2. Causes have to happen where their effects happen.* If the cue ball does not make contact with the object ball, the object ball does not move. Finally, *3. Causes make their effects happen.*

Since causes always come before effects, *it is impossible for anyone to see an event (an effect) before it happens.* It may be possible to predict events, but clairvoyant or precognitive seeing of an event before it happens at all is not possible. The laws of the universe do not fit certain people's fantasies. Second, because causes have to happen where their effects happen, there can be no instantaneous action at a distance. It would be impossible for anyone to think a thought and have some telepath elsewhere instantly know that thought. If a thought is something natural, like the firing of bundles of neurons in the brain, the fastest anything natural can go is the speed of light.

It is essential in determining whether one event causes another to determine whether they are even uniformly correlated. People have a bias toward looking at confirmatory instances and avoiding non-confirmatory ones. The science - minded philosopher Bacon was once shown a painting of people who had prayed and been saved from drowning as "evidence" that prayer was effective. He replied by asking "Where are those depicted who prayed and were not saved?" Unless we know their number in a population, we have no idea whether prayer is positively correlated with being saved. Whenever it is claimed that X is correlated with or causes Y, four cases need to be considered: X and Y both happening, X but not Y happening, X not happening but Y happening anyway, and neither X nor Y happening.

CORRELATION TABLE

	Y Happens	**Y Does not happen**
X Happens	a	b
X Does not happen	c	d

Bacon was, in effect, arguing that there may be more cases in cell "b" where prayer goes unanswered than in "a" where it is answered. That alone would make causal connection unwarranted. More cases in cell c than a, where people saved themselves or were coincidentally saved without praying, would also cast doubt on the efficacy of prayer.

Sometimes we reason from effect to cause. "the object ball is moving, so the cue ball hit it." Other times we argue from cause to effect. "The cue ball hit the object ball, so the object ball moves." However, the form of a causal argument of interest now is this:

<u><Event or property C is correlated with event or property e.></u>

$$\downarrow$$

C causes e.

"Correlated" means that whenever C occurs, then e occurs. Explanations of how this type of reason can be true and this type of conclusion false are tied up with alternatives to the conclusion. If no timing of C and e is mentioned, it could be that e causes C. It could be that something else, B, causes both a and e.

It could be that something else, D, causes e. Finally, it could be that the correlation between C and e is just coincidence.

John Stuart Mill made clear methods used in scientific reasoning to find causes and stronger argument forms. The first of his methods, the Method of Agreement, was based on the principle that if two or more cases in which an event "e" occurs have only one earlier event in common, then that earlier event is probably at least part of the cause of e. Let $C_1, C_2, C_3,... C_n$ stand for earlier events.

$\underline{<C_1, C_2, C_3, C_4 \text{ happened before e.}> + <C_1, C_5, C_6, C_7 \text{ happened before e.}>}$

C_1 is probably at least part of the cause of e.

Consider the following example. Suppose people all over the United States become ill with a very serious and infectious disease. They all exhibit similar symptoms. The disease detectives at the Center for Disease Control in Atlanta try to see whether they had something in common. Perhaps they discover that the people were all on flight with one passenger who came from the "Hot Zone" of Zaire where they have the disease Ebola. (This is not realistic. Ebola, fortunately, is not that contagious.)

Mill's second method, the Method of Difference, is based on this principle. If a case in which e happens and a case in which e doesn't happen are alike in all earlier events except one, say C_1, which occurs when e happens and does not when e doesn't happen, then that one is probably at least part of the cause of e.

$\underline{<C_1, C_2, C_3, C_4 \text{ happened before e.}> + <C_2, C_3, C_4 \text{ happened and e did not.}>}$

C_1 is probably at least part of the cause of e.

This time, imagine a group of people eating a meal after which some get very ill. Ask what each person ate and keep a record. Perhaps you will find that all the sick ones ate one particular item, C_1, while none of the well ones ate that item. Then you will be able to concentrate analysis for poisons on that item. When these methods are used together we get a powerful form of causal argument.

$\underline{<C_1, C_2, C_3, C_4 \text{ came before } e_1.> + <C_1, C_5, C_6, C_7 \text{ came before } e_2> + <C_2, C_3, C_4 \text{ happened and e did not.}>}$

C_1 is probably at least part of the cause of e.

Mill's Method of Residues (leftovers) is based on the principle that if we take away from any any event "e" all parts known by earlier investigation to be caused by any causes, then the rest of e is caused by the remaining earlier events. Lets call parts of e, "$e_a, e_b, e_c, e_d.$"

$\underline{<C_1, C_2, C_3, C_4 \text{ cause } e_a, e_b, e_c, e_d.> + <C_1, C_2, C_3, \text{ cause } e_a, e_b, e_c>}$

C_4 is probably at least part of the cause of e_d.

This method works sometimes when some event varies in quantity and we know that other parts of the quantity are explained by other causes. Mill also developed a Method of Co-variation. The principle is this: If an event e varies in some way whenever another event C varies in the same way, then the variation in C is probably part of the cause of the variation in e. Let us use a superscript $+$ or $-$ for variation in both cause and effect.

$$<C_1, C_2, C_3 \text{ cause } e_a, e_b, e_c> + <C_1^+, C_2, C_3 \text{ cause } e_a^+ e_b, e_c> + <C_1^-, C_2, C_3 \text{ cause } e_a^- e_b, e_c>$$

The variation in C_1 is probably the cause of variation in e_a.

Analogical argument is argument based on a likening as a reason. An analogy is a likening or comparison of one thing to another. Analogical arguments come in two forms. Letting "O" stand for an object and "P" for some property, in the simple form someone tries to persuade us that an object O_2 has a property P_1 because it is like some other object, O_1, which also has that property. In the complex form, someone tries to convince us that an object O_n has a property P_n because a number of objects including O_n all have several properties in common, and all the others have the property P_n as well, so probably O_n has it too.

ANALOGICAL ARGUMENT: Simple form $^1 <O_1 \text{ is like } O_2> + {}^2 <O_1 \text{ has } P_1.>$

$^3 <O_2 \text{ has } P_1>$

COMPLEX FORM $^1 <O_1, O_2...O_m, O_n \text{ have } P_1, P_2,...P_m> + {}^2 <O_1, O_2...O_m \text{ have } P_n>$

$^3 <O_n \text{ has } P_n.>$

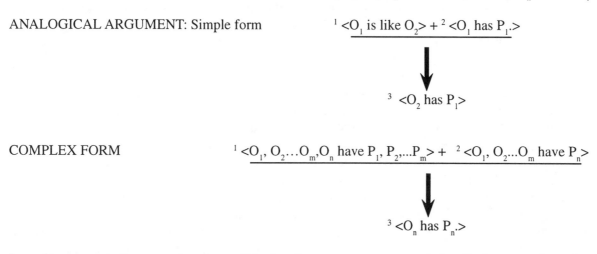

In such arguments it seems always possible that the reasons are true and that O_n does not have the property P_n. The main reason for this alternative is that the properties chosen in the comparison may be relevant to the property we are drawing a conclusion about, or not relevant to that property. When they are not relevant, then the argument is weak to nil.

For an example of the simple form, consider the following: "<The computer I want to buy has the same type of central processing unit as yours,> <the same expansion capabilities as yours,> and <about the same amount of random access memory.> <Yours runs software QRZ.> <So probably mine will get run QRZ.>" This is pretty strong reasoning. That is because these properties of a computer are related to running software. But using other properties in reasons would yield a weak argument such as this: "<The computer I want to buy is made by the same company as yours,> <comes with the same peripheral devices,> and <is about the same price.> <Yours runs QRZ.> So probably <mine will run QRZ.>" Sameness of manufacturer, and price and peripheral devices are less relevant to whether the computer will run QRZ software.

The complex form is shown by this example, famous in philosophy. The universe is like a watch. The universe and a manufactured object like a watch are both made of different materials, they have separate parts made of these materials, the parts interact with each other, and they engage in regular motions. A manufactured object like a watch had a designer. So the universe must have had a designer and creator." The degree of strength of this argument, called "The Design Argument," is quite controversial.

MORAL REASONING is giving reasons for actions. Some philosophers have argued that any statement about what ought to be done cannot be deduced from any statements about what is the case. Others have disagreed. Those who disagreed first put forth a form of argument called "the Practical Syllogism."

<If condition C is the case, then action A ought to be done.> + < Condition C is the case.>

So action A ought to be done.

This is deductively valid. Those who emphasize that you can't deduce any "ought" from "is" point out that the conjunction of an "Is" statement and the contradictory of an "Ought" statement seems never contradictory. They find counterexamples where the conditional is falsified by circumstances in which the antecedent is true and the consequent is false. For example, consider the statement: "If a baby is crying because it needs to be held by its' mother, then its' mother ought to pick it up." Even if the baby was actually crying for that reason, it would still not be right for mother to pick it up if the evil enemy soldiers had placed the baby on a pressure sensitive land mine. The mine will blow it to bits if the baby is lifted off the mine's detonator plate.

In real life we do sometimes have to deal with moral disagreements. Part of what we mean by calling something a "moral" problem is that we feel it is an *important* problem. So let's look at the kinds of reasons given for conclusions of the form "Agent P (some person) ought to do action A." These will be useful in a moral disagreement when persuasion is needed. Everybody is thought to have certain rights and duties. Rights to life and liberty are unconditional claims on others' acts, also called "duties." If Mary has a right to liberty, Sal has duties not to stalk or kidnap her. A first sort of reason that P ought to do A is that it is P's duty to do so. Circumstances can make for counterexamples. However, usually we can find some over-riding "categorical" duty. For example, it is a general duty to tell the truth. But suppose a person is hiding an innocent, abused woman from her violent husband. He comes to the door, enraged and asking if she is there. The duty to protect innocent human life is an over-riding duty.

A second sort of reason why P ought to do A is that A has the best consequences. But, best for whom? *Ethical Egoism* argues that people are naturally selfish. They can only act for their own self-interest. Furthermore, "ought" implies "can." A person can only be obliged to do (ought to do) what he or she can do. Since we can only act on our own self-interest, the argument goes, we can only be obliged to do what is in our own self-interest. We ought, this theory says, to do what is best for us personally. This theory is not likely to be persuasive. A person might hold it for himself. He won't be likely to persuade someone else to accept, as right, his own self-interested acts.

"*Utilitarianism*" holds that we ought to do those actions which have the greatest "utility," or usefulness. This means the best consequences for the total happiness of all people. The reasoning: "A promotes the greatest total happiness, therefore person P ought to do A" will generally be good, persuasive reasoning. But even it won't work in cases where the action called for seems to unjustly sacrifice too much of one party for the sake of others. For example, suppose five different patients in a hospital need heart, lung, liver, kidney, and cornea transplants. It would contribute to the total happiness to grab one healthy person and transplant all these organs from him to them. However, nobody would think that fair or just.

A third kind of reason is that action A reflects certain *virtues.* Virtues are good qualities of character. The virtues have opposite vices. Examples of virtues and their opposite vices are: honesty - dishonesty, justice - injustice, truthfulness - untruthfulness, charity - stinginess, and so on. So one can reason, "I ought to do A because it is the honest, (or just or truthful) thing to do," or "I ought not to do A because it is dishonest (and so forth)."

A fourth kind of reason is that doing or avoiding A is following some *moral rule.* The 10 Commandments or the Golden Rule are examples of *moral rules.* Suppose it is the first week of college. Students have bought their books. But often they have not yet put their names in them. Ellen and Rachel find an unmarked text for a course Ellen is taking. She hasn't bought the book for the course yet. She proposes to just take it. Rachel might argue, "You shouldn't take that book because it's stealing and stealing violates one of the Commandments."

A fifth kind of moral reason comes from Emmanuel Kant. Kant had an idea that right actions are in some sense "*universalizable.*" His supreme moral rule, the Categorical Imperative, has been popularized into two ideas. One is the question "What would happen if everybody acted like that?" If we think a proposed action is wrong, ask the person who proposes it this question. If the act is wrong, probably if everyone did it, the act itself would cease to serve its purpose. For example, suppose all people who wanted to buy things when they didn't have the money were to write bad checks. They are falsely promising to pay money they don't have. Eventually stores wouldn't take checks anymore. Kant's other idea was that it is not right to just use people. People ought to be treated the way they would want to be treated if they were perfectly rational beings. So one can argue that an action ought to be avoided because it involves just using someone.

Why be moral? Wouldn't it be a difficult to always do right? Plato thought that if we look carefully at the vices, we see that they are kinds of *emotional illness.* The kleptomaniac takes big risks to steal little items he could easily buy. The person who always lies to make him or herself look better is called a "pathological liar." Some vices seem to be addictions, which we know are illnesses, such as alcoholism, drug abuse, gluttony (food addiction), the sex addiction of "studs" and "nymphos." All these vices seem to involve normal desires which have gotten out of the person's control. The desires now control the person. If so, then we should always avoid immoral actions because doing them again and again increases the strength of the desire until it does get out of control. Asking "Why should a person be moral?" becomes like asking "Why should a person do things which keep her healthy?" Morality, like health, would be intrinsically good (good in itself.)

Five more reasons can be given for always being moral. The first is that morality includes personal self-interest. We have duties to ourselves. Morality is not all self-sacrifice! Second, if we do wrong and are caught, those we harm can retaliate. Third, morality is often backed by social and/or legal punishments. Act immorally, get caught and we are likely to suffer at least loss of respect and trust. Fourth, being moral lets us feel good about ourselves. It lets us have high self-esteem. Immoral people often have low self-esteem. Evil people often don't feel very good about themselves, no matter how much money and power they have. Movies and TV shows only make it look like they never feel guilty. Finally, fifth, if you believe in a God who wants people to be good and has made moral rules for us obey which are written in a Bible, that becomes another reason to give for always being moral.

5 CRITICAL LIFE DECISIONS: COMPLETE EVALUATION OF REASONING

SECTION 5.1: JUDGMENTS ON STATEMENTS AND EPISTEMIC SOUNDNESS

Critical Life Decisions are ones which require al lot of our resources and will affect our lives in major ways. They require complete evalution of arguments for alternatives. It will be useful at this time to go over an eight step method for complete evaluation of a piece of reasoning. More details on how to perform some of the steps will be found in later chapters. For now, the method will be summarized and the instructor or student herself can decide which subjects to pursue further. Some of these topics are also taught in informal fallacies and formal logic courses.

Earlier we defined a logically sound argument as one in which a) all of the reasons are true, and b) the reasoning is valid. The purposes of reasoning are: to extend our own knowledge, to persuade ourselves or others to believe a conclusion to be true or to explain why it is true. To make a complete evaluation of a piece of reasoning, then, we must judge not only the validity of the reasoning but also the truth of the reasons. For this purpose we will use the following categories. **A statement is either 1) definitely true (so far as we know), or 2) probably true (so far as we know), or 3) we don't know whether it is true (we are uncertain) or 4) probably false or 5) definitely false (so far as we know.)** For now, these judgments may vary greatly among students. Part Three will give background helpful to make these judgments on statements more uniform.

Two observations are necessary. First, for now at least, "I don't know" or "I am uncertain" are not bad answers. They can reflect intellectual honesty. They reflect critical self-assessment. They are the sort of answer Socrates often gave. In particular, *if a statement refers to people, places or things unknown to the student, he or she should judge the statement by responding "I don't know" or "I am uncertain."* On the other hand, there is certain basic information which everyone in a culture or country above a certain age is supposed to have. The student is expected to use that fund of knowledge to judge statements and not rely on "I don't know" when the matter should be known to everyone. Also, *if students do not know the meanings of words in statements, it is expected that they look the words up in a dictionary before making a judgment.* If after doing and showing this work and trying to write a paraphrase, they still do not understand the statement, then it is acceptable to answer "I do not understand" or "I do not know."

Second, we can now define a concept of "epistemic soundness."

Epistemic soundness is soundness with respect to adding to our knowledge. It is that level of confidence we can have in some arguments which allows us to accept their conclusions. After background knowledge, the student will be expected to judge statements as definitely true or false, or probably true or false, or still uncertain. However, for the purpose of making judgments of epistemic soundness, we can lump together "don't know," "uncertain," "probably false" and "definitely false" as all cases of **unwarranted** statements. Definitely true and probably true statements are "warranted." **An argument is epistemically sound if and only if all of its reasons are warranted and every step of reasoning in it is at least strong.**

SECTION 5.2: AMBIGUITY AND VAGUENESS

There are other problems with evaluating reasoning than the ones already discussed. Some of them arise because of difficulties with language. These difficulties affect our judgment as to the truth or falsehood of the reasons. They can also affect the extent to which reasons support a conclusion. An example is ambiguity. A word or phrase is *ambiguous* when it has two or more different meanings. A statement which can be true in one sense of an ambiguous phrase, can be false in another. Or in one sense it can be very supportive of a conclusion, while in another it can give much less support. Stephen Thomas gives an example like this. How much support does the reason give to its conclusion?

Professor Cogan gives objective tests.

 ?

Professor Cogan gives fair tests.

"Objective," in one sense, means unbiased. In another sense here, it could also mean "multiple choice." However, multiple choice tests are not necessarily fair. Suppose Professor Cogan gave multiple choice tests on material he did not cover or even assign students to read. The reason could be true in the sense of "objective," meaning "multiple choice," and the conclusion could be false.

First - decide whether each of the basic reasons is definitely or probably true or unwarranted and write "T" for "true" or ""U" for "unwarranted" beside each of them. Where this is not possible because of ambiguity, go to step 2. Where it is not known whether a basic reason is true or false, judge it to be *unwarranted.* (To do this in detail, one will need to read Part Three, Evaluation of Unsupported Claims.)

Second - use semantic clarification, where necessary, to determine truth or warrant of ambiguous statements. Write "T" for "definitely or probably true" or "U" for "unwarranted" beside each clarified statement. Semantic clarification is the process of fixing the meaning of vague or ambiguous words. This is done by either drawing a *distinction* between the meanings of word or giving a *definition*. A *distinction* is a sentence in which someone says that a word or phrase has two or more uses, or that a general class has two or more subclasses called species. A *definition* is a sentence which gives some words having the same meaning as a given word.

There are several kinds of definitions which can be important in reasoning. The most common sort is called a "lexical" definition. This is the sort of definition which attempts to state the most frequent use of a word. The reasoning "Professor Cogan gives objective tests, so his tests are fair" *has no degree of support at all* until we have drawn the distinction between the meanings of "objective' and substituted one of them for the ambiguous word itself. If this ambiguity of the words "objective test" is not apparent, it is possible to accept the reason by interpreting it as meaning multiple choice tests, and then fail to notice that this is no evidence at all that his tests are fair!

SECTION 5.3: CRITICAL THINKING AND DEFINITION

Definition is important in a few of the most controversial, "life and death" issues. For example, in the issues of abortion and mercy killing the definition of "human life" is criticallly important. Another example would be the issue of "Holocaust Revisionism." A Holocaust Revisionist claims that "The so-called 'Holocaust' never occurred." Others become enraged. A critical thinker's reaction is to ask both sides "What do you mean by 'The Holocaust?'" Shermer (1993, p. 33-34) defines "The Holocaust" as the intentional or functional near-destruction of an entire people based primarily on race." He gives a definition of 'holocaust' with a small "h" with the same words except adding that the destruction may be based on *race, religion, ethnicity, land, and/or property and wealth.* By his definitions only what happened to European Jews constitutes "the Holocaust." What whites did to Native Americans and Africans in colonization and slavery, killing up to 1 and 10 million, religious war in Bosnia, and the Hutu murders of 500,000 Tutsi's in Ruwanda are small "h" holocausts.

Only with definitions like these are we able to ask the right questions, such as "How many Jews were there in Europe before WWII?" "How many were alive after it?" "How did the non living die?" "Were gas chambers and crematoria used to engage in mass extermination?" "Is there good evidence that it was Hitler's intention to exterminate, rather than deport the Jews?" "Did the Nazi government carry out a coordinated plan to exterminate the Jews?" (This author's acquaintence with convergent evidence strongly suggests the answer to the last three questions is "yes.")

In reading, *always look up* unknown words in a dictionary! Words express ideas. A person of few words is one of few ideas, one who can not think interesting or powerful thoughts. A definition should state important, universal features of something, not less important ones. Wrong: "Man is a featherless biped." Better: "Man is a rational animal." One way of defining a common noun is to state a genus (animal), such that every member of the species (man) is a member of it, and also a difference (rational). which marks off men from the other animals. Such a definition should be neither too narrow nor too broad. Too narrow: "A chair is a 4 legged wooden piece of furniture for sitting on." Too broad: " A chair is anything that can be sat upon." A definition should not be vague or use analogies or wording more unfamiliar than the word being defined. Avoid overly general words like "some-" or "any-" thing, body, one, and obscure words, if possible. A definition should not be negative as in "vague" means "not precise."

Another way of defining is to give a synonym. Be careful, however, to find an exact synonym or add words to avoid excess broadness or narrowness. A definition should be a complete sentence. It should reflect the word's part of speech. Do not use a form for verbs when the word is a noun or adjective. Wrong: "A rock is to...." "Rock" is a common noun, not "to" do anything. To define is to explain the meaning of a word. This can not be done using the word or a related word in the definition itself. That is called "circular definition." A person who does not know what Socratic Method is gets no information out of being told "Socratic Method is the method used by Socrates." A definition must be relevant to the field in which it is requested. For example: In philosophy "argument" means a group of statements made to persuade. It would not probably not be acceptable to give as an answer, on a philosophy test, a dictionary definition synonym that "argument" means a fight, dispute or disagreement.

A disagreement can sometimes be settled by either giving a dictionary definition or by parties stipulating (agreeing to) a meaning for a word. But in the philosophical sense of argument, any argument in which there was a disagreement (inconsistency) between any or the reasons would automatically be an unsound argument. Most arguments are certainly not unsound for this reason.

Consider the following illustration of the substitution process to clarify the degree of support, using "gives objective tests," as short for the reason, and "gives fair tests," as short for the conclusion. Note that the ambiguous word is underlined and its substitute meanings are italicized.

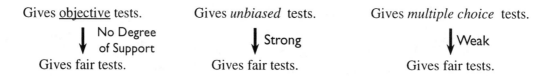

A word or phrase is vague when it has no clear boundaries of meaning. When it is not certain whether word applies to some object or not, then the word is vague. For example, color words are vague. Trying to match a very dark piece of cloth for sewing can demonstrate this point. It may not be clear whether the dark cloth is "black" or "dark blue" or a color in between called "navy". There are no precise standards for the use of such words. But vagueness is widespread and can be important.

In a Pennsylvania town, a paralyzed man in a motorized wheel chair could not go on the sidewalk under a bridge. There was a pile of debris blocking his way. So he went out into the middle lane of a three lane road. On the other side of the bridge, a police officer gave him a ticket. The man in the wheelchair had to go to court. It had not yet been decided in local law whether a motorized wheelchair was a "motor vehicle." The vagueness of "motor vehicle" was important to him in this case. Suppose motorized wheelchairs were made much heavier to protect their users. They might now and then run over and hurt people walking. For someone who might get struck by one, this vagueness might become important in determining an insurance settlement. A precise definition is needed to clear up a matter like this.

Another example of how to fix vagueness in an argument could be:

David had 6 bookcases at home.

↓ ?

He must keep some books there.

This is a pretty strong looking argument. However, both the words "some" and "there" are vague. Remember that one way of judging the degree of support reasons give to a conclusion is to consider how willing the reader or listener would be to bet something of great value on the truth of the conclusion, given the truth of the reasons.

Suppose there was someone, Ms. Confirmation, who had a lot of money and was not interested in trying to trick anybody. She goes around telling people that certain statements are true. Then she tells them another statement, a possible conclusion. Then she offers them a chance to place an "even money" bet, given the truth of the earlier statements, on the truth of the conclusion. If she told Gary that it is true that David has 6 bookcases at home and Gary had a total of $100,000 life savings, would he bet $10,000 on the truth of "David must keep some books there?" How about the whole bundle, all $100,000? Before Gary bets, it would be wise to come to agreements with her on three things.

First, Gary would want her to agree that "must" is only an inessential conclusion signal. That is, that it does not mean that David is *required* in some way to keep books there. This fixes an ambiguity in "must." Second, how much is "some?" Third, what, exactly, is included in "there?" If "some" meant "two or more," then Gary would lose if David had only one book. If it meant "at least one," then Gary would win even if David had only one book. If "there" meant "on his bookshelves," then Gary would lose if David had books in the house but not on the bookshelves. Gary would rather that "there" meant "anywhere in the house." In this specific meaning, Gary would win even if David had no books on any of his 6 bookcases.

In both ambiguity and vagueness, what is fundamentally wrong is that the meaning of the statement is not clear. Therefore it is not clear exactly what the statement claims. Therefore it is not clear how much support it gives to a conclusion. It may also not be clear whether it is true or false. Vague and ambiguous statements will be classified as unwarranted until clarified. More information on this is to be found in Part Three.

The student should now do Exercise 10 on Semantic Clarification.

SECTION 5.4: DRAWING CONCLUSIONS AND FINDING MISSING ASSUMPTIONS

Third - One form of the Principle of Charity says: make an argument as strong as possible before evaluating it. Consider whether there is any definitely or probably true statement the maker of the argument did not state which would raise the degree of support the reasons give to the conclusion. If so, add these omitted truths. We are not talking any longer about just evaluating somebody else's argument. We are talking about using argument *to get at the truth for ourselves* and others. This is much more what fair minded critical thinking is all about (Paul, 1996, p. 32.)

Sometimes people leave out statements which seem to them so obvious that they don't need to say them. Sometimes they seem obvious because they are parts of patterns of valid reasoning which are particularly simple and clear to most people. These omitted statements are either conclusions or reasons. In case they are conclusions, filling in missing statements is called "drawing one's own conclusions." In case they are reasons, it is called "bringing out the unstated assumptions" of the argument. Everyone has a natural sense, more or less developed, of patterns of valid reasoning. This sense can be aided by being taught certain valid patterns.

Here is how to draw conclusions: Ask, "If these reasons are true, then what conclusion must be true?" Say aloud the reasons of the argument in question. Then say "SO.....", in a leading way, and then go on to fill in the missing statement. Try it with the following examples. They were picked from advertisements by Thomas (1993), probably because most readers would be familiar with the conclusions they imply. Try to be specific and get the exact conclusion.

EXAMPLE 1. "The more carefully brewed a beer, the better it tastes; and Budweiser is the most carefully brewed beer in the world. *so…* <........>."

Did the reader remember or understand the conclusion the advertisers wanted us to get from this commercial? It is that Budweiser is the best tasting beer in the world. Here is another example from commercials.

EXAMPLE 2. "The bigger the burger, the better the burger; and Burger King's burgers are bigger, *so…*

<.........>."

Did the reader draw the conclusion that Burger King's burgers are better? That is what the advertisers wanted us to understand. The argument to this conclusion is valid. When doing this, *stick to the wording of the reasons.* Arguments to conclusions less similarly worded to the way the reasons are stated are weaker.

Remember also the two common types of linked reasoning from Part One: syllogistic reasoning and conditional reasoning. Try to do this syllogistic example before reading the answer.

EXAMPLE 3: "All horses are mammals and no mammals are cold-blooded. *so* …<.............>."

Did the reader reason out the conclusion that no horses are cold-blooded? Consider the following example of conditional reasoning.

EXAMPLE 4. "If this object is red, then it has some color. But it has no color. *so*…<............>"
Did you correctly deduce that "it is not red?"

Here is how to deal with missing reasons. Say aloud the reasons given. Then say "so" and the conclusion. Then say *"because"* in a leading way, and go on and complete the sentence with the missing reason.

EXAMPLE 5: "All men are mortal, so Socrates is mortal *because*…<.............>"
Did you get the missing assumption that Socrates is a man?

EXAMPLE 6: "If you go, then we will go. So we will go" *because*…<............>.
Here the missing reason is "You go."

Step Four: *Make each step of inference in an argument as strong as possible before evaluating it.* This is one of the things that the Principle of Charity says we should do. However, there are limits to how far we should carry that. Any inductive argument can be made into a deductively valid one by adding certain reasons. But sometimes to do this, we would need to add reasons which are obviously false. For example, we could make our strong inductive argument, "All horses ever observed have hearts, so all horses have hearts", valid by adding to the reason the claim: "We have observed all horses." But this reason is definitely false.

Suppose we are trying to make an argument as strong as possible. We find that the only way we can make it deductively valid is to add some assumption like this which "blows up in our face." When we uncover it, it is an assumption we immediately realize to be false. Such an assumption is called a "land mine assumption." In that case, the argument can not be deductively valid.

Step Five: a **Principle of Total Available Evidence** must also be followed. This principle says we must take into consideration all available evidence including reasons against a conclusion. To be sure, to reach a conclusion reliably, we should *add* any true or warranted statements which *lower* the degree of support. Suppose, for example, a woman is considering whether to marry someone. She may think "He's good looking. He's fun to be with. I'm attracted to him. He has a good job. He's generous with his money. He loves me. So I should marry him." Suppose it is also true that he has slapped her around a couple of times. Also, he has been arrested for assault. She had better add this information in reasoning about the conclusion unless she wants to risk ending up a battered or murdered woman. By writing the reasoning out, we could just write these statements down with dotted line arrows to the conclusion, or with the words "reasons against" beside the arrow. The dotted line arrows could represent reasons *against* a conclusion. These reasons would greatly lower the degree of support the woman has for the conclusion that she ought to marry him.

An argument justifies its conclusion if and only if all its basic reasons are true, or at least warranted, and every step of inference is at least strong, if not deductively valid. Here is a possible picture of the whole reasoning on marrying the man.

<u>He's good looking. + fun + sexy + good job + generous + loves me.</u>
<u>He slapped me around. + He was arrested for assault.</u>
↘   ↗ Reasons Against
I should marry him.

Sixth, rejudge the degree of support for each step of inference and write one degree of support phrase beside each arrow.

When it comes to complete evaluation of reasoning, we need to understand the *Weakest Link of the Chain Principle*. A chain is only as strong as its weakest link. Similarly, *an argument is only as strong as its most doubtful necessary basic reason and its weakest step of inference*. If presented with an argument with seven necessary basic reasons, and six are definitely or probably true while one is unwarranted, the whole set must be evaluated as unwarranted. If there are five necessary steps of inference and four are deductively valid while one is only moderate, evaluate the whole set of inferences as only moderate. This principle is illustrated in the diagrams below.

Suppose we have an argument in which statement 1 is claimed to support 2 while 2 is claimed to support 3 and 3 and 4 are linked and claimed to support 5. In such a case we always have 2 questions of evaluation to deal with: A. How strong are the inferences? and B. Are all the basic reasons true? Suppose further that when we make our preliminary evaluation, we judge the following.

```
1               2               3 + 4
| Moderate      | Moderate       | Strong
2               3               5
```

Here is an example of a preliminary diagram of a piece of reasoning before clarifying and adding missing statements, along with what it might look like after clarifying and adding assumptions which make it as strong as possible. The ideal is to be able, as in this example, to find sufficient unstated but true assumptions which will make the every step of inference deductively valid. In the diagrams notice what effect this has on the questions of evaluation. However, it is often the case that we can not find such statements and this does not prevent an argument from being a strong inductive one.

BEFORE

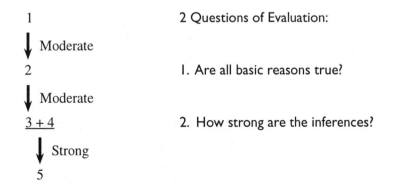

```
1
| Moderate
2
| Moderate
3 + 4
| Strong
5
```

2 Questions of Evaluation:

I. Are all basic reasons true?

2. How strong are the inferences?

AFTER

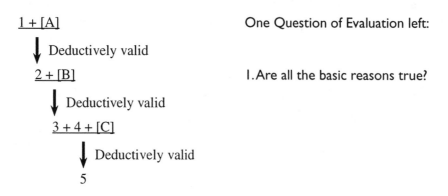

1 + [A]

Deductively valid

2 + [B]

Deductively valid

3 + 4 + [C]

Deductively valid

5

One Question of Evaluation left:

1. Are all the basic reasons true?

SECTION 5.5:   SOUNDNESS VERDICTS ON REASONING FINAL EVALUATION OF CONCLUSIONS

The seventh step of our method is to *judge the epistemic soundness of the argument* in question. Based on the definitions above, we will judge arguments to be either "epistemically sound", for which we will use the letter "S", "probably epistemically sound", symbolized by "PS" or "unsound," indicated by a "U." *Any argument which is logically sound should be epistemically sound.* This means that it is one on the basis of which we may include the conclusion in our beliefs. The eighth step is *to make the final judgment on whether or not to accept the conclusion and add it to our stock of beliefs.* If the argument is epistemically sound or probably sound, then judge the conclusion as definitely or probably true; believe it; rely on it. If it is unsound, judge the conclusion as unwarranted, unproven by this argument. Do not yet add it to your stock of beliefs. Do not rely on it.

There will be times in life when it will be helpful to arrive at a final verdict on the soundness of an argument and then use that verdict to accept a conclusion or continue to suspend judgment on it. These times are when critical life decisions must be made. **Critical life decisions** *are situations in which one has to make a choice which will involve a lot of one's resources and affect one's life and happiness for a long time.* Critical thinkers make such decisions by completely evaluating arguments for the choices they have. Critical life decisions include whether to go to war or to college, what to study, whether to leave one job and home for another, whom to marry or partner with, whether to have a child, and what course of treatment to undertake for a serious illness. Almost everybody has to make some of these decisons. So critical thinking is useful for almost everybody.

In order to judge an argument to be sound, judge the degree of support the reasons give to the conclusion at every step of inference. Judge also whether each basic reason is definitely or probably true (warranted) or unknown, probably or definitely false (unwarranted.) The distinction among true, warranted, unwarranted and false statements will be explained in Part Three.   But it is desirable here to illustrate the final steps of evaluating argument.

The purpose of logic and critical thinking is to seek reliable patterns of reasoning. These are ones which enable us to be certain, or as near to certain of our conclusions as possible. So we are conservative in our evaluations. We apply the **Weakest Link of the Chain Principle** to statements as well as to steps of inference. *The group of all the basic reasons has, as a whole, the value of the least warranted statement which is necessary to argue for the conclusion.* Again, if there are seven necessary basic reasons, and six are known to you to be definitely true, but the seventh is probably untrue, then they are *probably untrue as a whole*. This does not prove that the conclusion is false! All this shows is that the present reasoning for it is unsound. There may be other true or warranted basic reasons which could be relied upon to prove the truth of the conclusion. The Principle of Charity suggests that we look for them.

When evaluating long, complex pieces of reasoning, write degree of support judgments beside each arrow. After clarification, if necessary, write judgments of definite or probable truth or unwarrantedness beside each statement. Next, write the label "Final Verdict" and either "sound" or "probably sound" or "unsound" for the argument as a whole. If the argument is sound, then we know we can have a very high level of confidence in the (definite) truth of the conclusion. If it is probably sound, then we will say we should treat the conclusion as probably true. If it is unsound, then treat the conclusion as unwarranted, at least by this argument. Here is a table of final verdicts on reasoning. It is a simplification because "don't know", "probably false" and "definitely false" have all been collapsed in meaning into "unwarranted". An argument with any necessary unwarranted basic reasons is unsound. Its conclusion, like bad meat, is unfit for (epistemic) consumption.

Table of Final Verdicts

DEFINITE OR PROBABLE TRUTH OR FALSEHOOD OF STATEMENTS	DEGREE OF SUPPORT				
	DED. VALID	STRONG	MODERATE	WEAK	NIL
DEFINITELY TRUE	S	PS	U	U	U
PROBABLY TRUE	PS	PS	U	U	U
UNWARRANTED INCLUDES DON'T KNOW, PROBABLY AND DEFINITELY FALSE	U	U	U	U	U

Final Verdicts: S = epistemically sound argument, conclusion very probably true.
  PS = probably sound, conclusion probably true.
  U = unsound, conclusion unproven by this argument.

When a person goes through the eight step process with many long, complex decision problems like the career change example mentioned above, he or she will find that at first there are one or more unwarranted reasons. So the reasoning appears unsound. This should motivate the individual to do sufficient research so that a decision can be made strictly on warranted reasons, and at least strong, if not deductively valid, reasoning. Warrantedness is not exactly an hereditary property of statements like truth is under deductive validity. However, if a statement is originally unwarranted to the reader and she comes up with a sound or probably sound argument for it, then she should upgrade it in her thinking to warranted.

Here are a few examples showing how to make final judgments of soundness and warrant of conclusions.

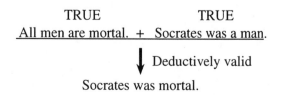

TRUE   TRUE
All men are mortal. + Socrates was a man.

↓ Deductively valid

Socrates was mortal.

Final Verdict: This argument is sound, so the conclusion is true.

TRUE   FALSE
<u>All gods are immortal. +   Socrates was a god.</u>

$\downarrow$ Deductively valid

Socrates is immortal.

Final Verdict: This argument is unsound due to a false reason, so it's conclusion is unwarranted.

TRUE   TRUE
<u>All clams live in water. + All mollusks live in water.</u>

$\downarrow$ Weak

All clams are mollusks.

Final Verdict: This argument is unsound due to weak reasoning, so it's conclusion is unwarranted (by this argument.)

Now let's look at a complex case of a sort young students may frequently face. A young woman comes to the guidance counselor and says the following. "I'm doing poorly in most of my courses, because I watch too much TV, the daytime 'soaps.' Then there's my job: I work 20 hours a week at MacDonald's. That takes time from school work. So does my sorority. We have at least one major drinking party every weekend, and I'm wrecked the next day. I don't want to flunk out, so I've got to do something! Joe, my boyfriend, wants to get married. I could drop out and get married. This would mean that I'd end up a homemaker dependent on my husband for an acceptable income. That's a bad idea in this day and age, because 1 in 2 marriages end in divorce and lots of men don't pay child support, leaving the woman stuck with kids and poverty. So I shouldn't drop out and get married. T.V. is addictive to me, so I probably can't cut back there. I could quit my job, because I don't really need the money for school expenses. But I do really need it for the nice clothes girls in the sorority are expected to wear. I could stop going to sorority parties, but that would mean that they would probably drop me from the pledge class." Let's bracket, number and diagram this passage, picking out her alternatives as we go.

 [1] <I'm doing poorly in most of my courses,> <u>because</u> [2] <I watch too much TV, the daytime 'soaps'.> [3] <Then there's my job: I work 20 hours a week at Mac Donald's.> [4] <That takes time from school work.> [5]<So does my sorority.>

Note that "So" is not functioning as an indicator here, but like "also". [6] <We have at least one major drinking party every weekend,> and [7] <I'm wrecked the next day.> [8]<I don't want to flunk out,> <u>so</u> [9] <I've got to do something!> [10] <Joe, my boyfriend, wants to get married.> ALTERNATIVE: [11] <I could drop out and get married.> [11] <This> <u>would entail that</u> [12] <I'd end up a homemaker dependent on my husband for an acceptable income.> Number 11, dropping out and getting married, is referred to by the pronoun "this," so the pronoun alone is bracketed and gets the same number as the statement it refers to. [13] <Much as I love and trust Joe, that's a bad idea in this day and age,> <u>because</u> [14] <one in two marriages end in divorce> and [15] <lots of men don't pay child support, leaving the woman stuck with kids and poverty.> <u>So</u> [16] <I shouldn't drop out and get married.> [17] <T.V. is addictive to me,> <u>so</u> ALTERNATIVE: [18] <I probably can't cut back there.> ALTERNATIVE: [19] <I could quit my job,> <u>because</u> [20] <I don't really need the money for school expenses.> [21] <But I do really need it for the nice clothes girls in the sorority are expected to wear.> ALTERNATIVE: [22] <I could stop going to sorority parties,> but <u>that would mean that</u> [23] <they would probably drop me from the pledge class.>

The discourse has the statements about TV, the job, and the sorority as converging reasons which explain doing poorly. Doing poorly, linked with not wanting to flunk out, support the conclusion of having to do something. Joe wanting to get married and her being able to do this support the conclusion that she'd end up a dependent homemaker. My judgment is that they provide strong support for this conclusion. The statistics on divorce and child support provide strong support for the conclusion that dropping out is a bad idea, which supports the conclusion that she shouldn't do it. But the statement that TV is addictive is only warranted, not definitely true. Also, the step to "so it can't be cut back" is, at best, only moderate and so that inference is unsound.

The passage also illustrates how deliberation may include reasoning which weakens other reasoning. The reasoning from needing the money for nice clothes for the sorority weakens the argument that she doesn't really need the money for school expenses, so she could quit her job. But it is doubtful that it makes it less than a strong argument. Finally, the argument that her stopping going to the sorority parties would mean that they would drop her is less than strong. It is at best moderate. So it looks like TV could be controlled somewhat. She could quit or cut back on her job hours, and might even explain that she needed to stop going to the parties for a while, so that she could stay in school. The reasoning would then look like this, with all judgments of warrant, degree of support and final soundness judgments in place.

We will use "true" for "definitely true" and "warranted" for "probably true" here.

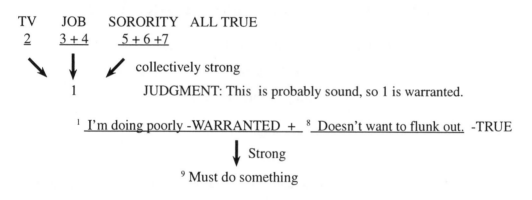

JUDGMENT: This argument is probably sound, so 9 is warranted.

> [10] Joe wants to marry -WARRANTED + [11] I can drop out and marry -WARRANTED

⬇ Strong

[12] I'd become dependent homemaker.

JUDGMENT: This argument is probably sound, so 12 is warranted.

> [14] 1/2 end divorce. -WARRANTED*.[15] Many men don't support kids. - TRUE

⬇ Strong

[13] Being dependent is bad idea

* 14 is commonly believed, but may be a significant exaggeration.

JUDGMENT: This argument is probably sound, so 13 is warranted.

[12] <u>I'd be dependent -WARRANTED +</u> [13] <u>Dependency is a bad idea.</u> -WARRANTED

↓ Strong

[16] I shouldn't drop and marry.

JUDGEMENT: This argument is probably sound, so 16 is warranted.

[17] TV is addictive. -WARRANTED

↓ Moderate

[18] I can't cut TV.

JUDGMENT: This argument is unsound, so 18 is unwarranted.

[20] Don't need school $ -WARRANTED   [21] Need clothes $ -WARRANTED.

↘   ↗ Reason Against

[19] Could quit job

JUDGMENT: The argument 20 —> 19 is probably sound despite 21, so 19 is warranted.

[22] I could stop going to parties. -WARRANTED.

↓ Moderate

[23] The sorority will probably drop me.

JUDGMENT: This argument is unsound, so 23 is unwarranted.

More examples of such decision problems can be found in more advanced textbooks of direct natural logic, such as Thomas (1993.)

6 SYLLOGISTIC LOGIC

SECTION 6.1: CATEGORICAL STATEMENTS

A *syllogism* is any reasoning having exactly two reasons and one conclusion. A *categorical syllogism* is a syllogism having two categorical reasons and one categorical conclusion. A *categorical statement* is a statement which affirms or denies that the members of one class are included in another class, in whole or in part. A categorical statement has a certain *quantity* and a *quality*. Its quantity is how many of the subject class it talks about. This is usually expressed by a quantifier like "all" or "some." Its quality is either *affirmative* or *negative*. Classes are expressed by *terms*.

Term means a noun phrase which stands for a class. Each class has an opposite class within a *universe of discourse* (such a universe is also called a "parameter.") A universe of discourse is a larger class into which all terms in a statement or syllogism fall. Each term has a *complement* which refers to members of the opposite class. If A is a term, we express its complement as "non A." For example, the complement of "dogs" is "non dogs." Between them, they exhaust the universe of discourse "animals." People frequently use prefixes "un-," "in-," and "dis" in ways that we can express as complements without doing violence to an argument. For example, "effective" and "ineffective" form a term and its complement with the parameter "acts." The complementary terms are "effective acts" and "ineffective acts." Other examples would be "sympathetic" and "unsympathetic," "honest" and 'dishonest" in the universe of discourse "people."

There is a standard form for a categorical statement. It begins with a quantifier. It then has a subject term, the verb "to be," and a predicate term. It may have the word "not" between the verb and the predicate term. Here is the standard form of a categorical statement.

Quantifiers	Subject	to be	not (maybe)	Predicate.
All, No or Some	F	is/are	not	G.

The words "affirms," "denies," "in whole," and "in part" set up types of categorical statements. The letters "F," "G," and "H" will be used as variables to stand for different classes. The quantifiers listed in the form above are called the classical *universal* quantifiers: "all," and "no," and the *particular* quantifier "some." They are not the only quantifiers.

SECTION 6.2:   MARKING TERMS AND THEIR POSITIONS

Affirmative categorical statements say that one or more of a subject class is *included* in the predicate class. Negative ones say that one or more of the subject class is *excluded* from the predicate class. Many statements which do not appear to be categorical can easily be put into categorical form. A verb ordinarily marks the break between the subject and the predicate of a statement. The verb answers the question "What action or state of being is described here?" The subject answers the question "Who or what is doing the action or is in the state of being?" *First, begin to put a statement into categorical form by finding this subject - verb break.* The verb is often not "to be." *Second, if the verb is not "to be", then fix this by inserting between the subject and verb "are," a plural noun for the type of things being talked about by both the subject and predicate, and relative pronoun like "that,' "who," or "which."* The verb "to be" is called the copula (KOH puh la). The plural noun for the type of thing being talked about is called a "parameter." Examples of typical parameters are "people," and "things." For example, "All young colts love to run" must be put into this form: "All young colts *are animals that* love to run." Do not throw a parameter into a subject which is already a plural noun. Wrong: "All *animals that are* young colts are animals that love to run."

Categorical statements can have short subjects and predicates or long ones like this: "All members of the Catholic Church who are preparing to go into the priesthood of the Catholic church are persons who should be prepared for the frustrations of a celibate life." *Third, automatically put parentheses around the whole subject noun phrase after the quantifier and up to the verb "are."* "Put another set around the whole predicate term after "are" or "not" to the end of the sentence.* All (members of the Catholic Church who are preparing to go into the priesthood of the Catholic church) are (persons who should be prepared for the frustrations of a celibate life.) These are the subject and predicate terms of this statement. Failure to do this correctly can prevent one from evaluating a syllogism correctly.

Syllogisms all have a linking *middle term* which appears once in each reason. It links, or appears to link, the subject of the conclusion and the predicate of the conclusion. The subject and predicate *of the conclusion* are called the *end terms.* The subject of the conclusion is called the *minor term.* The reason containing it is called the *minor premise.* The predicate of the conclusion is called the *major term.* The reason containing this term is called the *major premise.* One reason ties the subject to the middle term. The other ties the middle to the predicate. The conclusion contains the subject and the predicate with the middle term left out. The major premise is always listed first, then the minor premise and finally the conclusion. Each statement has a single letter abbreviation (such as A, E, I or O.) The *mood* of a syllogism is represented by 3 of these letters for the major premise, minor premise and conclusion respectively, e.g. EIO. E is the major premise, O the conclusion.

The letters "S," "M," and "P" will stand for the *Subject of the conclusion*, the *Middle term of the syllogism* and the *Predicate of the conclusion.* There are four different possible ways the subject, predicate and middle terms can appear in syllogisms. A row of letters "S," "M" and "P" will stand for each statement. Here are the four possible positions of the middle term. The word *figure* is used to denote these four possible positions of the middle term. They make up what are called "the four figures of the syllogism."

	1st. Fig	2nd. Fig	3rd. Fig	4th. Fig
Reason 1	M - P	P - M	M - P	P - M
Reason 2	S - M	S - M	M - S	M - S
Conclusion	S - P	S - P	S - P	S - P

The standard form of a categorical syllogism has its major premise listed first or on top, its minor premise second and its conclusion last. The major premise is the one containing the major term, "P," the predicate of the conclusion. The minor premise is the one containing the minor term, "S," the subject of the conclusion.

Each statement in a standard form syllogism can be either an A, E, I or O, so there are at least 4 x 4 x 4 types of syllogisms. But the middle term could be in any one of the 4 positions. So there are 4 x 4 x 4 x 4 or 256 possible types of syllogisms. Under Aristotelian rules of validity, 24 forms are valid. Under Boolean rules, only 15 are valid.

SECTION 6.3: DISTRIBUTION

The concept of distribution deals with the number of items in a class which the quantifier refers to in the subject or predicate. Universal quantifiers distribute their meaning maximally, i.e., to all members of a subject class. Particular quantifiers distribute minimally to at least one of the subject members. Affirmative statements distribute their import minimally to some of the predicate class. Negative statements distribute maximally to all of the predicate. We will use subscript distribution index numbers, "5" for maximal distribution and "1" for minimal distribution under the term letter to indicate how much the term is distributed. This gives us the following table.

SYLLOGISTIC DISTRIBUTION TABLE

QUALITY

	AFFIRMATIVE	NEGATIVE
	A: All F_5 are G_1	E: No F_5 are G_5
QUANTITY		
	I: Some F_1 are G_1	O: Some F_1 are not G_5

This pattern of distribution can be summarized in a handy little rule abbreviated as USNP. *Universal statements (A and E) maximally distribute their Subject terms; Negative ones (E, O) maximally distribute their Predicates, and all others are minimally distributed.*

SECTION 6.4: A COMPARISON OF ARISTOTELIAN AND BOOLEAN RULES

A statement has "existential import" provided that it implies the existence of some objects. Aristotelian rules assume that all four types of statements have existential import; Boolean ones that only particular statements do. Boolean rules were written to avoid inferences to the existence of things we do not think to exist. For example, when we say "All trespassers will be shot," we do not imply that there are trespassers. Boole's interpretation said this means: "If anything is a trespasser, then it will be shot."

Aristotelian Rules are the following: A standard form categorical syllogism is valid if and only if: *Rule 1: The middle term must be maximally distributed at least once. Rule 2: If an end term is maximally distributed in the conclusion, then it must be maximally distributed in the premises. Rule 3: The number of negative reasons equals the number of negative conclusions.*

Boolean Rules are the following: *Rule 1: The middle term must be maximally distributed exactly once. Rule 2: No end term is maximally distributed only once. Rule 3: The number of negative reasons equals the number of negative conclusions.*

Boolean Rule #1 is narrower than Aristotelian Rule #1. AR#1 allows syllogisms with M distributed twice to be valid; BR #1 does not. Similarly, BR #2 is narrower than AR #2. AR #2 allows an end term to be distributed in a reason and not in the conclusion. BR # 2 does not allow this. The result is that 9 of the 24 syllogistic forms which are valid by Aristotelian rules are not valid by Boolean Rules. The totality of all valid forms by Aristotelian rules are shown below. Those not valid by Boolean rules are marked with asterisks.

FIRST FIGURE	SECOND FIGURE	THIRD FIGURE	FOURTH FIGURE
AAA	AEE	AAI*	AAI*
AAI*	AEO*	AII	AEE
AII	AOO	EAO*	AEO*
EAE	EAE	EIO	EAO*
EAO*	EAO*	IAI	EIO
EIO	EIO	OAO	IAI

Boole's interpretation removes existential import from universal statements but leaves it for particular statements. A valid argument can have no information in the conclusion which was not already contained in the reasons. So those syllogisms valid on Aristotelian rules, but not on Boolean ones, are those which involve trying to draw a particular conclusion with existential import from two universal premises (the ones with asterisks.)

An extended syllogistic like that in Thompson (1992) has 5 levels of quantifiers: Universal (all-no), Predominant (almost all - few), Majority (most - most are not), Common (many - many are not) and Particular (some-some are not.) In such a system, we assign subscripts for intermediate quantities of distribution. If universal quantification is represented by 5, predominant would be 4, majority 3, common 2, and particular 1. Predicates of affirmatives would get distribution 1 and of negatives 5. Here is a Distribution Table for this.

QUALITY

AFFIRMATIVE	NEGATIVE
A: All F_5 are G_1	E: No F_5 are G_5
P: Almost all F_4 are G_1	B: Few F_4 are G_5
T: Most F_3 are G_1	D: Most F_3 are not G_5
K: Many F_2 are G_1	G: Many F_2 are not G_5
I: Some F_1 are G_1	O: Some F_1 are not G_5

Notice the regularity of the statements and distributions of the table. It should be fairly easy to memorize quantifiers in order. The standard quantifiers on affirmative statements are "all," "almost all," "most," "many," and "some." The ones on negative statements are "no," "few," "most - are not, "many - are not," and "some - are not." One could memorize the letters which stand for the statements with phrases like "All Poisons Taken Kill Internally" and "Every Boy Deserves Good Oranges." One could also just memorize a nonsense pronunciation of the letters. It is better in applying the third rule of validity to learn a phrase or pronunciation for EBDGO. Say "EHBD," as in "the tide ebbed," and "GO" (The water went away.) For APTKI one could say "AHPT" as in "He was apt," meaning good at doing something, "Kuh" for "K," and "EYE" for the last letter "I." Then all one needs to remember is that the distribution numbers for subject and predicate start with 51 for A, and go down ten for each affirmative statement and 55 for E and down 10 for each statement.

A: All 51	E: No 55
P: Almost all 41	B: Few 45
T: Most 31	D: Most-are not 35
K: Many F 21	G: Many-are not 25
I: Some 11	O: Some-are not 15

This yields 4,000 syllogistic forms, of which 105 are valid by Thompson's rules. Thompson's rules for validity are these: An extended form syllogism is valid if, and only if,

Rule 1. The value of the middle terms added together is more than 5. The values under the two "M's" must add up to 6 or more.

Rule 2. No end term may have a greater value in the conclusion than in a reason. The value of "S" in the conclusion must be less than or equal to its value in the reason. The value of "P" in the conclusion must be less than or equal to its value in the reason.

Rule 3. The number of negative reasons equals the number of negative conclusions. If there is no negative conclusion, there can be no negative reason. If there is a negative conclusion, there must be exactly one negative reason. No syllogism is valid with two negative reasons. A syllogism with no negative reasons and no negative conclusion satisfies the rule. Zero negative reasons equals zero negative conclusions.

Why are these rules of *validity?* In a valid categorical syllogism all of the information presented in the conclusion must already have been contained in the reasons. Distribution, making reference to members of classes, is information. Rule 3 is a rule of validity because any negative information of exclusion in a conclusion could only be supported by some negative information of exclusion in a reason, but two reasons of exclusion do not contain enough information to support any claim about the relations of the end terms. Rule 2 is a rule of validity because if an end term was more distributed in the conclusion than in a reason, this would mean that the conclusion claimed information not claimed in the reasons. Rule 1 is a rule of validity because, if the information in the reasons does not refer to some M's twice, it would be possible that "S's" are related to some "M's" and "P's" are related to other "M's" so that the reasons claim no information about the relation of "S's" and "P's."

To be a valid syllogism, an argument must have two reasons and one conclusion containing *exactly three terms total.* The S and P end terms each occur twice, once in a reason and once in the conclusion. The M term occurs once in each reason and not in the conclusion. A term can be expressed by different words such as synonyms. For example, if one statement had "attorneys" in it and another had "lawyers," the student would be expected to count them as one term, pick one of them and substitute it for the other to reduce the number of terms to exactly three.

Students are also expected to recognize "equivocation," using the same word in two or more different meanings. For example, "Love is blind. God is love. So God is blind." Each reason seems true. However, the conclusion is nonsense. The reason is that "love" is used differently in the two statements. The two uses of "love" are not really the same middle term. The student is expected to be able to understand that in such a case there are really four (4) terms. The argument can not be a valid syllogism because it does not have exactly three terms. **Look out for occasional equivocation.** *In that case write: "This syllogism cannot be valid. The term 'T' has two meanings." The student should be able to state the different meanings.*

Here are our three examples from Chapter Four with quantifiers, what are called "parameters" and standard plural copulas put in to clearly show their form. "All vegetables are plants and no dogs are plants, so no dogs are vegetables." " (All) (pieces of) music are combinations of sounds pleasing to the human ear, and (No) (pieces of) Heavy Metal (music) are (combinations of sounds) pleasing to the human ear, so No (pieces of) Heavy Metal (music) are (pieces of) music." and "All responsible drivers (are) (people who) get lower insurance rates. No teenagers (are) (people who) get lower insurance rates, so no teenagers are responsible drivers." These all have the following form and distributions.

$$\underline{\text{All } P_5 \text{ are } M_1} + \underline{\text{ No } S_5 \text{ are } M_5}$$
$$\downarrow$$
$$\text{No } S_5 \text{ are } P_5.$$

This form obeys Rule 1, because the "5" under one M and the "1" under the other add up to more than 5. It obeys Rule 2, because the "5" under each of the "S" and "P" in the conclusion is not greater than the "5" under the corresponding "S" and "P" in the reasons. It obeys Rule 3 because 1 negative reason equals 1 negative conclusion. So all of these arguments are deductively valid.

This example points out something else. One may not be able to prove that Bigfoot, flying saucers or ESP do not exist. However, one can "prove a negative," in some forms of syllogistic argument.

SECTION 6.5: DETERMINING VALIDITY OF SYLLOGISMS

Cross Hatch Method of Determining Validity

Step 1: Identify the conclusion by reason and conclusion indicator words.

Step 2: Make a Cross Hatch or Tic Tac Toe Design.

Step 3: Write the letters "S" and "P" in the lowest left and right spaces respectively.

Step 4: In the argument, put parenthesis around the subject term in the conclusion and label it "S". Do the same for the predicate term and label it "P".

Step 5: In the middle column spaces, put the letters representing which type of categorical statement (A, E, etc.) each statement of the argument is. This column represents the mood. The left column represents the subject position of all 3 statements and the right represents the predicate position.

Step 6: (a) Look at the reasons of the argument to see where the subject and predicate terms occur. Put parentheses around them and label them "S" and "P".
(b) Place the letters "S" and "P" in the corresponding subject and predicate position outer column spaces in the cross hatch.

P	E	
	I	S
S	O	P

Step 7: Put the letter "M" in the two remaining spaces to represent the position of the middle term.

P	E	M
M	I	S
S	O	P

Step 8: Use the distribution table to write subscript 5's, 4's, 3's, 2's or 1's under the letters S, M and P. Put 5 under the S, M or P in the subject position of an A or E, 4 under a P or B, 3 for a T or D, 2 for a K or G, 1 for an I or O. If the statement is an APTK or I, put 1 under its predicate. If it is an EBDG or O, put a 5 under its predicate.

P_5	E	M_5
M_1	I	S_1
S_1	O	P_5

A SYLLOGISM IS VALID IF AND ONLY IF ALL RULES ARE SATISFIED.
To say that a rule "is satisfied" is to say that the cross hatch contains marks which conform to the rule.

FOR ARISTOTELIAN SYLLOGISTIC RULES IT IS VALID IF AND ONLY IF
Rule 1: There is a "5" under at least one "M."
Rule 2: If there is a "5" under "S" or "P" in the conclusion, then there must be a "5" under it in the reason.
Rule 3: If the conclusion is "E" or "O", then there is exactly one "E" or "O" reason. Also, no syllogism with EE, EO, OE, or OO reasons is valid.

FOR BOOLEAN SYLLOGISTIC RULES IT IS VALID IF AND ONLY IF
Rule 1: There is a "5" under one "M" and not the other.
Rule 2: If there is a "5" under either "S" or "P" then there must be a "5" under the other "S" or "P" respectively.
Rule 3: Same as R3 above.

FOR THOMPSON'S EXTENDED RULES IT IS VALID IF AN ONLY IF
Rule 1: The sum of the values under the "M"'s is greater than 5.
Rule 2: The value under "S" and "P" in the conclusion must be equal to or less than that in the reason.
Rule 3: If the conclusion is an "E", "B", "D", "G" or "O", then there is exactly one "E", "B", "D", "G" or "O" reason. Also no syllogism with two "E's", "B's", "D's", "G's" or "O's" or any combination of them as reasons is valid.

Here is an example from the Extended System:

P_4	P	M_1
M_5	E	S_5
S_3	D	P_5

Almost all A are B

No B are E

Most E are not A

Extended Rules:

R1 satisfied 5+1>5

R2 violated for P

R3 satisfied

invalid

SECTION 6.6: WAYS OF EXPRESSING QUANTIFICATION

We have five levels of quantification. Their names, together with the standard quantifiers which express them are: Universal ("all" or "no," meaning "absolutely every one"); Predominant ("almost all," "few,") meaning "more than a majority, but less than all"; Majority ("most," "most are not," meaning "more than half"); Common "(many," "many are not," meaning "more than one") and Particular ("some," "some are not," meaning "at least one"). Each can be expressed in many ways. I am grateful to Bruce Thompson (1992) for having gathered them most systematically. Among these ways are the use of synonyms, adverbial forms, numbers, and alterations of other quantifiers. Also, a statement can express a quantificational attitude (universal, etc.) without any explicit quantifier on it.

Universal quantification: First note some synonyms for "all." The universal affirmative words "any," "any one of the," "every," "every one of the," "each," and "each one of the" F's are G's and "the only F's are G's." should be translated into "All F's are G's." The same is true of compounds like "everybody" or "anybody" or "everyone" or "everything." This is also true for words like "wherever" and "whenever." When these words are found we can add a parameter like "places" or "times" to a quantifier to make a noun phrase. "Wherever" means something like "all places." "Whenever" means "all times."

Universal quantification can also be expressed this way: F's are always G's (or never G's.) *Notice that "universal" is not equivalent to affirmative in meaning!* "F's are never G's" means "No F's are G's." In Chapter 4 we dealt with the syllogism "Music is a combination of sounds pleasing to the human ear and Heavy Metal is not pleasing to the human ear, so Heavy Metal is not music." Such statements are probably intended to be universal. But while the first means "*All* music..." the second and third are properly translated into universal negatives: "No Heavy Metal is a combination of sounds pleasing to the human ear" and "No Heavy Metal is music."   Only in the Extended System could we show this argument invalid by interpreting it as saying "Most music is pleasing to the human ear."

Note also that "All S is not P" is not a standard form. *Never translate any statement into this form!* To put the music syllogism into standard form we have to do something unusual, add a pluralizing parameter to the subject to make it plural as well as to the predicate. Music comes in pieces. So we can translate it as "All *pieces* of music are combinations of sounds pleasing to the human ear and no *pieces of* Heavy Metal *music* are combinations of sounds pleasing to the human ear, so no *pieces of* Heavy Metal music are *pieces of* music."

With numbers, universal quantification is expressed when one says both of the F's are G's or each or all of the n F's are G's, where "n" is a number. That is, "Each of the 17 F's is a G" should be translated into "All F's are G's." Numbers are relative to context. "Each of the 37 billion inhabitants of the planet Crude-O watched the televised executions" simply means "all inhabitants watched them."

There are also "negative exceptive quantifiers" which should be translated as universal. In "Only F's are G's," *the word "only" functions to reverse the subject and predicate.* To understand this, consider 1. "Only women are nuns" and 2. "Only nuns are women." 1 is true and 2 is false. 3, "All women are nuns" is false, while 4, "All nuns are women" is true. For one statement to be a correct translation of another, it must have the same truth value, true or false, as the other. Since 1 has the same truth value as 4, not 3, 4 is the correct translation of 1. This is always the case. "Only F's are G's" equals "All **G**'s are **F**'s." Never translate it as "All F's are G's," even if it sounds false when translated. We do not employ a Principle of Charity when translating fixed meaning words like "only." "Just F's are G's," "None but F's are G's," and "None except F's are G's" are also translated as "All G's are F's."

Cases where articles "a," "an," "the," "these," or "those" are followed by a term should frequently be translated as universal. For example, "a" or "the bat is a mammal" means "All bats are mammals." However, take care when there is no quantifier at all. "Crows are birds" should be translated as "All crows are birds." "Crows are eating my corn," however, should be translated as "Some crows are eating my corn." Again, the point is that the student must ask him or herself: "Is this statement universal, predominant, majority, common or particular?"

Proper names, abstract nouns, descriptions like "the so and so," "these so and so's" should be translated using universal quantification. Treat proper names like "Socrates" as standing for a class with only one member. Use a parameter like "people." Construct a universally quantified phrase like "All people identical with Socrates" or "No people identical with Socrates." "Socrates is a philosopher," would become "All people identical with Socrates are philosophers." "Socrates is not a philosopher" would be "No people identical with Socrates are philosophers." "The red roses are wilting" becomes "All roses identical to the red roses are wilting flowers."

Nouns with articles, mass nouns, even abstract nouns in front can and should be translated as having universal quantification. This enables us to translate into standard categorical statement form any phrase standing for an individual. We can translate into universal statements not only any statements about "this car," or "that lake," but also about "metal," or "liquids," and even "justice," "truth," and so on. "This car failed to stop" would be "All cars identical with this car are cars which failed to stop." "That lake has no fish" would be "No lakes identical with that lake are lakes with fish in them."

Abstract singular nouns like "justice" or "truth" sometimes need to have a parameter added in the subject to put the statement into standard form. We saw this in the music example. Another example is this. "All justice is loved by God" might be translated as "All just *acts* are acts loved by God." "There has never been a good war or a bad peace" means "No *times of* war are *good times* and no *times of* peace are *bad times*," or "No *periods of* war are *good periods* ...." To determine the proper parameter for a whole syllogism, ask "What is it about?" "Terms 'S,' 'M,' and 'P,' are all kinds of ___" (fill in the blank.) Common parameters needed largely for predicates are "people," "things," "places," and "times." Sometimes a parameter must itself be quite abstract like "cases," "instances," "items," or "principles."

Predominant quantification is frequently expressed by putting a modifier in front of a universal quantifier. So "nearly," "practically," "almost," "just about," in front of "all," "every," "any," or "the only F's are G's," should all be translated as "Almost all F's are G's." For example, "Nearly any F is a G" = "Almost all F's are G's." Negative predominant quantification is expressed with the same modifiers in front of "no." "Nearly," "practically," "almost," "just about," No F's are G's and also "scarcely," "hardly," any F's are G's should all be translated into "Few F's are G's." Adverbs following "is" are also to be translated into predominant quantification. "F is *almost, or nearly, or practically or just about* always G" should also be translated as "Almost all F's are G's." Similarly, "F's are *almost, or nearly, or practically or just about* never G's" all should be translated as "Few F's are G's."

Certain adverbs of time also express negative predominant quantification. "F is *seldom, rarely, or not often* G" should be translated as "Few F's are G's." "Only" or "Just" *some, a few, or a couple* F's are G's also means "Few F's are G's." There are negations which mean the same thing. "Not *many, a lot, more than a few, more than a couple* F's are G's also mean "Few F's are G's." Finally, quantifiers using many of these adjectives to modify a number should be translated into "Few F's are G's." Only *just, not more than, not over, fewer than, less than, at most, barely* n F's are G's all express the attitude that "Few F's are G's." This can be true even when "n" seems to be a large number. This depends on context. The student needs to understand that when a chemist says, "At most, a billion chlorine atoms are in this pool," or a member of Congress says, "Only a billion dollars is unaccounted for in the Defense Budget" they mean "Few chlorine atoms" and "Few dollars."

Majority quantification is standardly expressed using "most." *The majority of, more than half of, over half of* F's are G's mean "Most F's are G's." A lot of adverbs also express majority quantification. "F is *primarily, mainly, usually, principally, chiefly or generally* G," all should be translated as "Most F's are G's." *For the most part , and By and large,* F's are G's also say "Most F's are G's."

Common quantification has "many" as its standard quantifier. It means a significant number less than half. So "*A lot of,*" "*Quite a few,*" and "*Quite a lot of* F's are G's" all should be translated as "Many F's are G's." Adverbs after "is" which express common quantification are the following. F *is often, quite often, frequently, quite frequently, commonly, quite commonly* G. These should all be translated as "Many F's are G's." Alteration on other quantifiers, which make common quantification, include "*More than a few*" and "*More than a couple* F's are G's," both of which should be rewritten as "Many F's are G's." Negations of "only" or "just" in front of particular quantifications make common quantification. "*Not only,*" or "*Not just some, a few or a couple* F's are G's" mean "Many F's are G's." Finally, modifiers on numbers can make for this level of quantification. "*More than n,*" "*Over n,*" "*At least n,*" "*No*" or "*Not fewer than*" or "*Not less than n*" F's are G's should be translated as "Many F's are G's."

Particular quantification is standardly expressed by the word "some." We take a minimal interpretation of all affirmative quantifiers. That is, "Q F's are G's" is interpreted as true if *at least* Q F's are, in fact, G's. "Some F's are G's" is interpreted as true even if only one F is a G. "A few," "a couple," "several" F's are G's should be translated as "Some F's are G's." F is *sometimes*, or *occasionally* G should also be translated as "Some F's are G's." So should other preceding phrases like *"From time to time"* and *"Once in a while"* F is G. Negations which translate into "Some F's are G's" include "Not all F's are G's" and "Not every F is a G." Note that the addition of a little word like "a" in front of "few" changes the level of quantification from predominant to particular. "Few F's are G's" is a predominant negative. "A few F's are G's" means "some F's are G's." *The student will have to read very carefully to get the right quantificational attitude.*

Negative exceptive quantifiers like "Not only" or "Not Just F's are G's" are tricky as usual. Since "Only" or "just F's are G's" means all G's are F's, we have to apply negation to this statement. A negation of a statement produces its contradictory (see below.) The contradictory of "all G's are F's" is "Some G's are not F's." So "Not only" or "Not Just F's are G's" mean "some G's are not F's." When you have plain numbers unqualified in any way, it is particular quantification. "N F's are G's" means "some F's are G's." Numbers out of context are neither small nor large. In a swimming pool there may be quintillions or more atoms. So "1 billion chlorine atoms are in this pool" is to be translated as "Some chlorine atoms are in this pool." Finally, the indefinite article "a" should sometimes be translated as "some" rather than "all." To repeat, in "A crow is a bird" it means "all," but "A crow is in the field" should be translated as "Some crow is in the field."

The student should now do Exercise 11A on translating into standard form.

SECTION 6.7: THE SQUARE OF OPPOSITION

A **Square of Opposition** is a kind of table which shows logical relations among categorical statements. Logical relations are relations between the truth or falsehood of one statement and that of another. Contradiction, Contrariety (say KON TRA r eye eh tee), sub-contrariety and implication are logical relations between statements.

Contradictories are pairs of statements which can not both be true and can not both be false. If one of them is true, then the other must be false. Any pair of statements having the same subject and predicate where one is of the form "All F's are G's" and the other is "Some F's are not G's", are contradictories. So are "No F's are G's" and "Some F's are G's". The contradictory of a statement is also called its negation or denial. Note that all one needs to say to contradict or deny a universal statement is to claim that there is one F which is or is not a G. Thus A and O, E and I type statements contradict each other.

Contraries are a pair of statements which can not both be true but can both be false. Statements of the form "All F's are G's" and No F's are G's" are contraries. They can not both be true. However, they can both be false. This will happen when some F's are G's and other F's are not G's. For example, "All calculators are complicated to use" and "No calculators are complicated to use" cannot both be true. However, both are false, since some calculators are complicated to use and others are not. A and E statements are contraries.

Sub-contraries are pairs of statements which can not both be false but can both be true. "Some F's are G's" and "Some F's are not G's" are sub-contraries. If "Some whales are mammals" was false then "Some whales are not mammals" would have to be true. I and O-type statements are sub-contraries.

Implication: To say that one statement A *implies another,* B, is to say if A were true, then B would have to be true. "Implies" here means that B follows with deductive validity from A. It means "A -> B" is a deductively valid argument. "All F's are G's" implies every less general affirmative type of statement. If "All F's are G's" is true, then "Almost all F's are G's," "Most F's are G's," "Many F's are G's," and "Some F's are G's" are also true. They are less informative, but still true because we interpret quantifiers below the universal minimally, as meaning "at least Q." We have plenty of use in real life for conservative generalizations when we are not justified in making universal ones. What is true of A implying P, T, K, I (and all top - down combinations like A implying T, P implying K) is also true for the negative statements. "No F's are G's" implies "Few F's are G's" and so forth. We sum up the relations of implication and contradiction up in a Square of opposition. Arrows show implications, diagonal lines show contradictions, dashes show contraries, and dots show subcontraries.

SQUARE OF OPPOSITION FOR THOMPSON'S EXTENDED SYLLOGISTIC LOGIC

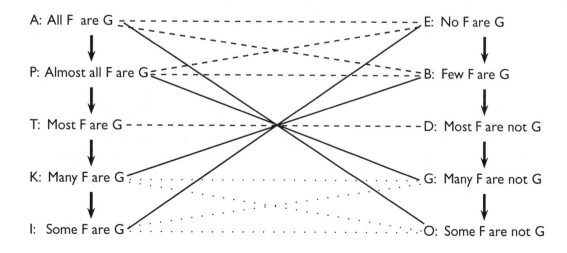

The student should study the diagonal relations of contradiction in particular. *They are essential to transforming denials into standard form.* Knowing that "Almost all F's are G's " contradicts "Many F's are not G's" enables the student to translate *"It is not the case that* Almost all F's are G's" or *"It is false that* Almost all F's are G's" into "Many F's are not G's." *No standard form has a denial at the beginning. All denials must be translated into their contradictories, driving the negation into the statement, to get standard forms.*

How to Rewrite Negations according to the Square of Opposition

Universal:	Not All S are P -> Some S are not P
	Not No S are P -> Some S are P
Predominant:	Not almost all S are P ->Many S are not P
	Not few S are P-> Many S are P
Common:	Not many S are P ->Few S are P
	Not many S are not P->Almost all S are P
Particular:	Not Some S are P -> No S are P
	Not Some S are not P -> All S are P

SECTION 6.8: IMMEDIATE INFERENCES

An immediate inference is a valid argument from just one reason to one conclusion. Implications like "A implies P," shown in the Square of Opposition, are immediate inferences. Syllogisms and any multi-premise arguments are mediate inferences. There are three types of immediate inferences which are particularly useful for translating syllogisms into standard form. They are called "Conversion," Contraposition" and "Obversion." They are most usefully described as translation operations on statements. They produce equivalent statements, cases where each statement validly implies the other, so one can be rewritten as the other.

Conversion is the operation of exchanging the subject and predicate. It is valid only for E and I-type statements. We can rewrite "No F's are "G's" as "No G's are F's" and vice versa. We can also rewrite "Some F's are G's" as "Some G's are F's" and vice versa. Conversion leaves a statement of the same type. E-type statements remain E's, and I's remain I's. *Conversion is not valid for any other type of categorical statement.* Never convert an A, P, T, K, B, D, G, or O-type statement. In such cases, the reason could be true and the conclusion false. Neither term, nor both terms may validly be turned into their complements. A helpful symbol for remembering conversion is: For E and I only, [S - P] exchanges with [P - S.]

Contraposition replaces both terms with their complements and exchanges these complements. It is valid only for A and O-type statements. We can rewrite "All F's are G's" as "All non G's are non F's" and vice versa. We can rewrite "Some F's are not G's" as "Some non G's are not non F's" and vice versa. It too leaves statements of the same type. Contraposition is valid only for A and O-type statements. Never use it on the other types of statements. Both terms must be made into complements. A symbolism for contraposition is: For A and O only, [S-P] exchanges with [non P-non S.]

Obversion is first changing the quality of a statement and then replacing the predicate with its complement. It is valid for all 10 forms. For example, if "*No* F's are G's" is true, then "*All* F's are *non* G's" must be true and vice versa. Note that both the quality (affirmative to negative or negative to affirmative) must be changed, *and* the predicate *only* must be turned into its complement. Universal and Predominant quantification change quality by changing the quantifier, but Majority, Common and Particular change quality by putting in or taking out the "not" after the copula. "*Almost all* F's are G's" and "*Few* F's are *non* G's" are obverses. However, "*Most* F's are G's" and "*Most* F's are *not non* G's" are the obverses on the majority level. "Not" *must* be put in when obverting a T, K or I to a D, G or O, and dropped when obverting a D, G, or O to a T, K or I. Do not confuse it with "non" or a "not" inside a predicate. A symbolism for obversion is: For all types of statements [(Qual) S-P] exchanges with [Non (Qual) S - non P]. Some syllogisms are not in standard form because they contain terms and their complements. They thus contain four or more terms. Valid reduction leaves valid arguments valid and invalid ones invalid. These operations are used to reduce the number of terms to three when complements are present so that our rules of validity can be used.

The student should now do Exercise 11B, C, D on Immediate Inferences.

SECTION 6.9: REDUCING TERMS IN A SYLLOGISM

Sometimes it looks like there are more than three terms, so an argument is not a syllogism. However, if there are only slight variations of wording, synonyms or complements, it is possible to put the argument into standard form. Here is a strategy for reducing to three terms. *First, count the number of terms.* If it is only three, nothing below needs to be done. If it is 4, 5 or 6, then, second, if any terms can be made the same by just change of word order, do so. For example, one statement might contain the phrase "all of the members" and the other just "members." Just cross out "of the." If any terms are synonyms, pick one of the synonyms and substitute it for the other. This can be done for 1, 2 or 3 pairs of synonyms, reducing to only 3 terms. Third, note if any terms have complements in the statements.

Complements appear as contrary words or prefixes. Words like "high," "low;" "good," "bad," can often be treated this way: "low" as "non high;" "bad" as "non good." Prefixes like "un," "in," or "dis" can be treated similarly. "Unjust," "just;" "adequate," "inadequate;" "honest" and 'dishonest" are complements. Put parentheses around each term. Label each with a capital e.g., the first letter of an important word in the term. Complements are labeled with "non" in front of the letter.

Contraposition allows a person to change 2 terms into their complements, obversion only 1 and conversion none. So if there are 4 or 5 terms and the 4th. or 4th. and 5th. are both predicates, use obversion on the statements containing them to get rid of the complements. If there are 6 terms, then using contraposition on a statement with a 5th. and 6th. term will reduce to a syllogism containing only 4 terms. Cases where a complement is a subject may require two operations. Usually one is conversion of an E or O to get a term in the predicate so that obversion can then be used on it. In some cases it may require two operations on one statement and one or even three or four total, but no more. In Aristotelian logic one can always reduce a syllogism containing up to six terms and complements to three. However, this is not always possible in the extended system. For example, any syllogism with premises such as "Most M are P and Most non M are S" will not be reducible, because conversion and contraposition are not valid forms of inference for these types of statements. (I'm again grateful to Bruce Thompson for this observation.)

Let us apply this strategy to examples. First, an apparent 4-term syllogism: "No cult leaders are moral and Herff Applewhite was a cult leader, so Herff Applewhite was immoral." Recall that singular statements about named people must be treated as universals and that a parameter is needed to make "immoral" into a noun phrase. So first, it is "No cult leaders are moral people and *All people identical with* Herff Applewhite are cult leaders, so *all people identical with Herff Applewhite* are immoral *people.*" It seems that "cult leaders," "moral people," "people identical with Herff Applewhite," and "immoral people" are 4 terms.   However, obversion of "no cult leaders are moral people" to "all cult leaders are immoral people" leaves us with just three terms. So would obversion of the conclusion. An example with 5 terms, showing that valid reduction of an invalid argument will leave an invalid 3-term syllogism is this. "All females are non sexists and all high school boys are males, so all high school boys are sexists." "Females," "non sexists," "high school boys," "males," and "sexists" look like 5 terms. However, we can force this into standard form by treating "females" and "males" as complements without doing violence to the illogic of the argument. Contraposition on "All females are non sexists" gives us "All sexists are non females" (that is, 'males'.)

Finally, consider a 6-term case suggested by one in Copi (1962) "No non members are golfers. All non golfers are non club users. So all club users are members." With the terms counted, it looks like this.

R1 No non members[1] are golfers[2].
<u>R2 All non golfers[3] are non club users[4].</u>
So all club users[5] are members.[6]

It does not matter what number we use for which term, so long as we do not mix them up. So suppose we decide to keep "club users" and "members" in the conclusion fixed. Taking the contrapositive of R2, [S-P] to [nonP-nonS], makes it "All club users are golfers." This reduces from 6 to 4 terms. Converting R1 [S-P] to [P-S] makes it "No golfers are non members." Now we can obvert this [(Qual) S-P] to [Non(Qual) S - nonP]. That is, "No golfers are non members" becomes "All golfers are members."

All golfers[1] are members[2].
<u>All club users[3] are golfers[1].</u>
All club users[3] are members[2].

Do not reduce statements and then go back and use the original, unreduced statements. This leads to wrong cross hatches. Also note that *there are cases where a syllogism has more than three terms and can not be reduced by valid inferences to any valid syllogistic form.* In a case like this, write out attempts to reduce the syllogism to three terms. If it is possible to do so, this should be done and a cross hatch made. If it is not, the syllogism should be written up as "invalid because it contains more than three terms."

SECTION 6.10: OTHER TRANSLATION PROBLEMS

It is not difficult to determine whether a syllogism is valid, *if its' statements are in standard form.* Standard form *must* begin with a standard quantifier, its subject *must* be a noun phrase, its' verb must be "are," and it *must* end with a predicate noun phrase. Recall that "not" between "are" and the predicate is an essential part of the form of D's, G's and O's. One must get each statement into one of these forms:

Standard quantifiers	subject noun	TO BE	NOT(in D,G, O)	predicate noun.
All, Almost all, Most, Many, Some	F's	are		G's.
No, Few, Most, Many, Some	F's	are	not	G's.

In some cases it is difficult just
phrase is a word or phrase which
what is doing the action or in the
sentence?" A phrase which
sentence is not a noun phrase.
this phrase be a subject?"
words like "justice" or
categorical statement need help
Here are several examples:
good" might be translated as "all
of knowledge are intrinsically
to add the plural-making noun
the parameter "things" to the

Translation: "The Devil is in the details."

to create noun phrases. A noun
answers the question "Who or
state of being described in the
cannot be the subject of a
Therefore, always ask "Can
Sometimes abstract singular
"knowledge" used in a
from an unusual parameter.
"knowledge is intrinsically
items of knowledge" or "*pieces*
good things." Notice the need
"item" to the subject as well as
predicate. "Justice" might

need to be made into "*principles of* justice" or "*just acts.*" A word like "disease" might need a parameter like "case" or "instances" or "*types of* disease."

Statements can be very long and contain unnecessary words like "it is true that," "it is obvious that," and so on. They should be eliminated. The student would do well to find the break between the subject and the verb. Whenever the verb is not "to be," it will have to be put in, and the verb presently there will usually become an important part of the predicate term. Here is a general method for translating non standard syllogisms.

A. Identify the conclusion by underlining indicator words and noting premise connectives.
B. Bracket and number the statements.
C. Inside the brackets cross out unnecessary words (e.g., "it is true that," but never negations like "it is false that").
D. Starting with the conclusion, identify the terms:
1. Find the break between the subject and the verb.
2. Make a left parenthesis just in front of the first word of the subject, excluding any quantifier. Put the right parenthesis between the last word of the subject and the verb. Write "S" for subject above it and "P" above the predicate. If exactly the same terms occur elsewhere, mark them "S" and "P" also. Start parentheses for predicates after "not." Label the middle term "M."
3a. If the verb is "to be," put a left parenthesis after it unless there is a "not" right after it. In that case, put the left parenthesis after the "not." Close the parenthesis at the end of the thought. Change singular terms to plural and "is" to "are" if necessary.
3b. If the verb is not "to be," insert "are" and put the left parenthesis to start the predicate term between the last word of the subject and the verb so that the verb is included in the second term.
   Example of 2 and 3a: "Many a bird is migratory" becomes
                Many (birds) are (migratory)
   Example of 2 and 3b: "Few men gave blood that day" becomes
                Few (men) are (gave blood that day.)
4a. Check if there are exactly three different parenthesized noun phrases. If not, because one or more is not a noun phrase, insert a parameter. Ask, "What is the universe of discourse in this statement or syllogism?" "What is it about?" Frequently, the appropriate parameter is used at least once in a syllogism. *Use the same parameter wherever necessary to make predicate noun phrases.*
   Examples: Many (birds) are (migratory *animals*)
                Few (men) are (*people who* gave blood that day.)
4b. If there are not exactly three terms because of synonyms, then reduce to three by substitution.
4c. If there are not exactly three terms because of complements, reduce to three by obversion, conversion or contraposition.

5. If there are any pronouns for terms, replace the pronouns with the terms.
6. Make a key which shows what noun phrase is the subject of the conclusion, the predicate of the conclusion and the middle term as follows: S= , M= , P= .
7. Make quantifiers standard. This includes transforming any negations at the start by *writing out the contradictory, not the contrary of a statement!* For example: "Not every S is P" equals "Not all S are P" which equals "Some S are not P." It does not equal "No S are P." While doing this, it is a good idea to write the letter for the type of statement which each categorical statement is above the verb "are."

Finally, make a cross hatch, transfer the letters to it, and determine validity. When in serious doubt about translation, follow the Principle of Charity: If an argument "feels valid," see if it can be translated into a valid standard form. Here is a simple example without complements. "Most of the older teachers do not believe in 'social promotion', so no older teachers are members of the administrative staff, since almost all of the administrative staff believe in 'social promotion'." Here the unnecessary words "of the" and "members of the" are deleted.

Steps A, B, C: <¹Most older teachers do not believe in 'social promotion',> so <² no older teachers are administrative staff,> since <³ almost all administrative staff believe in 'social promotion.>

                        S   M
Step D: <¹Most (older teachers) do not (believe in 'social promotion'),>
                        S   P
    so <² no (older teachers) are (administrative staff),>
                              P   M
    since <³ almost all (administrative staff) (believe in 'social promotion.)>

Step D3b: there is a "not" after "do" in the first statement. So we must insert "are" in place of "do," and put the parenthesis after the "not."
                        S   M
    <¹Most (older teachers) are not (believe in 'social promotion'),>
                        S   P
    so <² no (older teachers) are (administrative staff),>
                              P   M
    since <³ almost all (administrative staff) are (believe in 'social promotion.)>

Step 4a: We need to make the middle term into a noun phrase. This can be done simply by adding "rs" to "believe": "believers in 'social promotion.'"
                        S   M
    <¹Most (older teachers) are not (believers in 'social promotion'),>
                        S   P
    so <² no (older teachers) are (administrative staff),>
                              P   M
    since <³ almost all (administrative staff) are (believers in 'social promotion.)>

Step 5: There are no pronouns, so no action is needed. Step 6: The key is S= older teachers, P= administrative staff, and M= believers in 'social promotion.' Step 7: No action is necessary on making quantifiers standard. The types of the statements, D, E and P should be put above "are" in each statement.

Step 7: Here is our cross hatch with the major premise on the top.

P	P	M
S	D	M
S	E	P

The student should now do Exercise 12A on determining validity of syllogisms.

SECTION 6.11: SUPPLYING MISSING REASONS AND CONCLUSIONS

An "enthymeme" is a valid argument which is missing a reason or conclusion. In Chapter Four we presented an intuitive way of guessing at a missing statement in a classical two-quantifier syllogistic system. It is possible to give a specific recipe for doing this for the extended 5-level system. First, note whether the missing statement is a premise or conclusion. Second, write down exactly which terms are missing in alphabetical order. Third, determine what quality (affirmative or negative) the missing statement must have to make a valid syllogism. (If neither or both of the given statements are negative, then the missing statement must be affirmative. If one is negative, then the missing one must be negative.) Fourth, assign distributing index values to the statements given. (This requires remembering A_{51}, P_{41}, T_{31}, K_{21}, I_{11} and E_{55}, B_{45}, D_{35}, G_{25}, O_{15}.) If the missing statement is a premise, determine the *minimum* distribution for each term necessary to make the argument valid. The reason for this is that one wants to assume, under the Principle of Charity, as little as possible to make the argument valid. (This requires recalling the rules that the sum of the distribution indexes for M must be greater than 5 and for S and P less than or equal to that in the conclusion.)

Sixth, if the missing statement is the conclusion, determine the *maximum* distribution indexes for the terms in the conclusion which satisfy the rule that the value of S and P in the conclusion must be less than or equal to the distribution index in the reason. The reason for this is again, the Principle of Charity: we want make arguments as strong as possible, to learn as much, as highly general a conclusion, as follows validly from the reasons. Seventh, use the quality determination (Step 3) to consult A_{51}, P_{41}, T_{31}, K_{21}, I_{11} and E_{55}, B_{45}, D_{35}, G_{25}, O_{15} to determine which term is the subject and which the predicate. All pairs of distribution indexes together with qualities and figures have uniquely determined term orders.

Here are some examples from condensed forms of syllogisms using letters standing for actual terms.

Many F are not G.
> Missing term letters F, H. Statement must be affirmative

So some H are not G.

Put in the distribution values:

> Many F_2 are not G_5.

> So some H_1 are not G_5.

A missing reason to make a valid argument must have the other middle term "F," with at least a distribution of 4 (2+4) needed to be more than 5. It should also have the minimum value which will make the argument valid which is also 4. The term H must have distribution value of at least 1. Since this is also the minimum value we should accept, we assign 1 to H. Since this is an affirmative statement, its predicate must be the term with 1. (All predicates in affirmative statements have distribution 1). Therefore the order of the terms and distributions is F_4 - H_1. This must, therefore, be a P-type statement. The missing reason is therefore "Almost all F's are H's."

Second example:

All E are F

      Missing term letters D, F. Statement must be negative.

So some D are not E.

Putting in distribution values give this:

     All E_5 are F_1

     So some D_1 are not E_5.

In this case, since the conclusion is negative, the missing reason must be also to satisfy the third rule of validity. The term "D" must have at least distribution "1" which is also the minimum needed to validly deduce the conclusion. "F," on the other hand, requires a distribution of 5 to satisfy the middle term rule. The only type of negative statement with this distribution is an O-type of statement with "D" as its subject and "F" as its predicate: "Some D_1 are not F_5."

Here is an example with a missing conclusion.

   Almost all J are K.
   No K are L.
   So   Missing terms J, L. Statement is negative.

Putting in distribution values gives us this.

   Almost all J_4 are K_1.
   No K_5 are L_5.
   So

Since the distribution index of the terms in the conclusion must be less than or equal to those in the reasons, and those of J and L in the reasons are 4 and 5; they must be 4 and 5 in the conclusion also. With a negative statement with indexes of 4 and 5, it can only be a B-type statement: Few J_4 are L_5.

The student should now do Exercise 12B on Drawing Conclusions and Supplying Missing Reasons.

7

REASONING WITH STATEMENTS

SECTION 7.1: CONDITIONAL STATEMENTS

Inside the American Family Publishers envelope is a piece of paper which says "If you have and return the winning entry, we'll say ...

Robert Cogan, You've finally made it —
You're set for life with $11,000,000 guaranteed!"

I don't jump for joy because I understand that this does not assert or imply that I have actually made it, that I will receive $11,000,000. Yet people who read other such "If ... , then ... " statements frequently mistakenly clip off the "If" part and think they imply the "then" part.

Statements of the form, "If P, then Q" are called "conditional" statements. A *conditional statement* is a compound statement. Its standard form begins with "If". It then contains a statement. It continues with "then", and goes on with another statement. The part after the "if" up to the "then" is called "the *antecedent*." It will be labeled "P." (The student will use capital letters which are "statement constants." That is, "P," "Q," are short names for the statements. In stating valid rules we will also use these letters for variables. Lower case "P" and "Q" are confusingly similar.) The part after the "then" is called "the *consequent*." It will be labeled "Q." It does not matter which part is stated first. In "We will go, if you go", "You go" is the antecedent, P. "We will go" is the consequent, Q. This is exactly as if it had been written "If you go, then we will go." *Conditional statements are extremely important in many sorts of reasoning. They are also important in contracts and promises.* So it is important that you understand exactly what a conditional statement says and implies and what it does not say or imply.

The conditional form can be used to express many connections. In "If this object is red, then it has some color" the conditional expresses a necessary connection, because red is a color. In "If Lone Eagle inhales adenovirus, then he will get a cold" it expresses a causal connection. In "If you go, then we will go" it expresses a decision. The common minimum meaning all conditionals have is this. ***In case** the situation described by the antecedent exists, the situation described by the consequent exists or will exist **also**.* So the conditional does not make one simple claim. It does *not* validly imply that its antecedent alone is true, or that its consequent alone is true. It is *not* a conjunction claiming that both its antecedent and consequent are true. Yet it is all one claim.

Perhaps what a conditional claim is can best be seen by considering what it takes to *negate* or contradict it. To do this, you have to say that the antecedent is true *and* the consequent is false. The contradictory of our first example is "I have and return the winning entry *and* they do *not* say I have finally made it, etc.." The contradictory of the second is "This object is red *and* it has *no* color." The contradictory of the third is "Lone Eagle inhales adenovirus *and* he does *not* get a cold." The contradictory of the fourth is "You go *and* we do *not* go."

Suppose I have a pack of cards. Each has a letter on one side and a number on the other. I lay out four cards which have on their exposed sides E, T, 4 and 7. Consider this rule: "If a card has a vowel on it, then it has an even number on the other side." Which cards need to be turned over to decide if this rule is true or false? Warning: Most people give stubbornly wrong answers. This problem is called "the Selection Task." It was invented by Peter Wason. People often think either the vowel card E alone or the E and the 4 must be selected. You must, indeed, select the E, because if it has an odd number, then the rule is false. But selecting the 4 is a waste. The rule does not validly imply that "If the card has an even on one side, then it has a vowel on the other." So neither even/vowel nor even/consonant shows the rule true or false. But you must select the 7, because if it has a vowel, this again shows the rule false. What falsifies, contradicts, negates "If P (vowel), then Q (even)" is " P (vowel) and not-Q (odd)" or its equivalent "Not-Q (odd) and P (vowel)."

Our method of analyzing such statements is this. Put angle brackets around the *complete* conditional statement thus: <If P then Q> and give the whole statement, from "if" through the period, just one number. Then put regular parentheses around the antecedent and consequent. Label the antecedent "P" and the consequent "Q" even if they are negative statements.

$$\begin{array}{cc} P & Q \\ <\text{If}(\text{---}) \text{ then}(\text{---}).> \end{array}$$

SECTION 7.2 SYMBOLIZING CONDITIONAL ARGUMENTS

In the simplest kinds of conditional arguments you have a conditional statement as a reason and another conditional with the same antecedent and consequent or their negations as the conclusion. In the next simplest kind you have a conditional reason and a categorical (non-conditional) reason which is the antecedent, the consequent or the negation of one of these statements alone, (P, Q, NOT-P or NOT-Q) and then the conclusion is again either the antecedent, consequent or the negation of one of these.

This may seem very confusing at first. That is for several reasons. First, people do not, in everyday life, often make arguments with exactly contradictory statements appearing once alone, categorically, and another time as an antecedent or consequent of a conditional. Such arguments look repetitious and trivial. Please recall that the essence of validity lies, for many arguments, in precisely this: that all the information claimed in the conclusion is already claimed in the reasons.

Second, people have been taught to vary the wording of their statements so as not to bore readers or hearers. But repetition, as exact as possible, is a good quality in the teaching of these forms and the making of such arguments. Such repetition makes the forms clearer and more obviously valid or invalid.

Recall for a moment affirmative and negative statements and negations. A statement which says some subject has some property or relation is affirmative. A statement which denies that some subject has some property or relation is said to be negative. Thus, "This object is colored" and "Lake Erie is in North America" are affirmative. "This object is not colored" and "Lake Erie is not in North America" are negative. Also, "This object is colored" and "This object is *not* colored" are negations of one another. Consequently if "P" is used to stand for "This object is colored", then "NOT-P" will stand for its negation "This object is not colored". Similarly, if "P" stands for "This object is not colored", then "NOT-P" will stand for its negation "This object is colored."

When dealing with a conditional argument, first number the statements. Second, put parentheses around and carefully label the antecedent of the conditional "P", and the consequent "Q." Use these letters even if the antecedent or consequent is a negative statement. Third, put parentheses around the antecedents and consequents (inside the brackets) in the other statements of the argument. Fourth, carefully label these statements "P", if it is the antecedent again, "Q" if it is the consequent again, "NOT-P", if it is the negation of the antecedent, or "NOT-Q" if it is the negation of the consequent.

Read carefully: Notice "Not!"

One must be *extremely careful* to label the same statement with the same letter used before and not to ignore "not." The same statement can be expressed in slightly different words, such as "This object is red" and "It is red." But if there are significant differences of words, as between "this object is red" and "This object is colored", then you have different statements which need different letters.

Example 1: "If this object is red, then it is colored. This object is red. So it is colored." becomes

$$^1\underline{<\text{If (this object is red) then (it is colored).}>} + \ ^2\underline{<\text{(This object is red).}>}$$

$$\downarrow$$

$$^3 <\text{(It is colored.)}>$$

P = This object is red and Q = It is colored.
The form here is:

$$^1\underline{<\text{If P, then Q}>} + \ ^2\underline{< P >}$$

$$\downarrow$$

$$^3< Q >$$

Example 2: "This is colored, if it is red. It is not red. So it is not colored." becomes

$$^1\underline{<\text{If (It is red) then (this is colored.)}>} + \quad ^2\underline{<\text{(It is not red.)}>}$$

$$\downarrow$$

$$^3 <\text{(It is not colored.)}>$$

Notice that we are using the same letter to stand for the same statement whether the pronoun standing for the subject is "this" or "it" and whether the word "object" is there or not. To repeat, you have to be *extremely careful* to always use the same letter for the same statement even if statements are quite close in wording. The form here is:

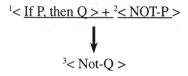

$$^1< \underline{\text{If P, then Q}} > + \ ^2< \underline{\text{NOT-P}} >$$

$$\downarrow$$

$$^3< \text{Not-Q} >$$

SECTION 7.3 SOME VALID AND INVALID PATTERNS

THE VALID PATTERN TRANSPOSITION

<If (this is red,) then (it is colored.)>

$$\downarrow$$

<If (this is not colored,) then (it is not red.)>

< If P, then Q >   (IF TRUE)

$$\downarrow$$

< If not- Q, then not- P >   (MUST BE TRUE)

THE INVALID PATTERN CONVERSION

<If (this is red,) then (it is colored)>

$$\downarrow$$

<If (this is colored,), then (it is red)>

< If P, then Q >   (IF TRUE)

$$\downarrow$$

< If Q, then P >   (COULD BE FALSE)

THE INVALID PATTERN NEGATING THE CONDITIONAL

If this object is red, then it has some color.

$$\downarrow$$

If this object is not red, then it does not have some color.

< If P, then Q >   (IF TRUE)

$$\downarrow$$

< If NOT-P, then NOT-Q >   (COULD BE FALSE)

Students often mistake negating the conditional for a valid form for one of two reasons. One is a failure of imagination to think about other conditions, antecedents, under which the consequent might exist or occur. The second is that they have in mind examples like "If you go, then we will go." In such cases the promiser frequently has in mind that the antecedent is the only condition under which the consequent will exist or occur. *But the "if -- then --" sentence does **not** assert that the antecedent is the only condition under which the consequent is true.* It only asserts that the antecedent is *one* condition under which it is true.

Suppose that there are a different kind of viruses called "rhinoviruses" which cause colds as much as adenoviruses. Then it can easily be true that "If Lone Eagle inhales adenovirus, then he gets a cold" and, at the same time, false that if he does not inhale adenovirus, then he does not get a cold, because he could get a cold from inhaling rhinovirus. In the current example, "if this object is red, then it has some color" certainly does not say that *only if* it is red, does it have some color. So the reason could be true and "If it is not red, then it has no color" will be false when the object is not red but has some other color.

This is the place to explain the use of "only." It reverses the order of an antecedent and consequent, just as it does a subject and predicate. The form "P, only if Q" or "Only if Q, P" means "If **P**, then Q." To see that this is true consider the following statements.

1. If this object is red, then it has some color. - TRUE
2. Only if this object is red, has it some color. - FALSE
3. This object has some color, only if it is red. - FALSE

The equal falsehood of 2 and 3 show that they mean the falsehood: "If this object has some color, then it is red." *Remember that the part after "only if" is the consequent of a conditional.* So "P if, and only if Q" means "P, if Q and P only if Q." Since "P only if Q" means "If **P**, then Q," and the part "P, if Q" means "If Q, then P," the whole, "P, if and only if Q," means this: "If Q, then P and If P, then Q." "If P, then Q" is usually put first.

VALID PATTERNS WITH TWO REASONS
AFFIRMING THE ANTECEDENT

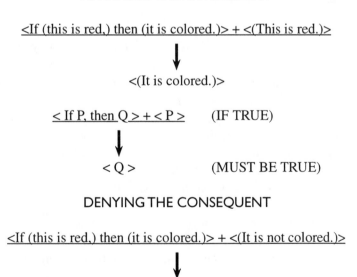

<If (this is red,) then (it is colored.)> + <(This is red.)>

↓

<(It is colored.)>

< If P, then Q > + < P >   (IF TRUE)

↓

< Q >   (MUST BE TRUE)

DENYING THE CONSEQUENT

<If (this is red,) then (it is colored.)> + <(It is not colored.)>

↓

<(This is not red.)>

Warning: Memorize this form below and that it is valid! Wason's research showed more mistakes are made thinking that arguments of this form are invalid than mistakes about Affirming the Antecedent, Affirming the Consequent or Denying the Antecedent.

FORM OF DENYING THE CONSEQUENT

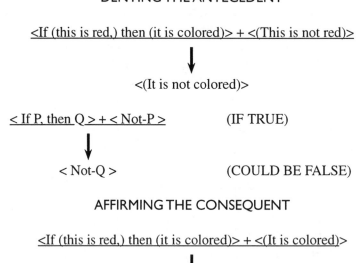

$\leq$ If P, then Q> + < NOT-Q >   (IF TRUE)

↓ Deductively valid

< NOT-P >   (MUST BE TRUE)

SIMILAR BUT **INVALID** PATTERNS

DENYING THE ANTECEDENT

<If (this is red,) then (it is colored)> + <(This is not red)>

↓

<(It is not colored)>

$\leq$ If P, then Q > + < Not-P >   (IF TRUE)

↓

< Not-Q >   (COULD BE FALSE)

AFFIRMING THE CONSEQUENT

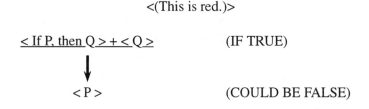

<If (this is red,) then (it is colored)> + <(It is colored)>

↓

<(This is red.)>

$\leq$ If P, then Q > + < Q >   (IF TRUE)

↓

< P >   (COULD BE FALSE)

Pieces of reasoning can be long and complex and contradictories need to be recognized even when not expressed in exactly contradictory form. Consider this argument. "If (the brain can transmit information all by itself to a specific external point in space, say another brain) 'P', then (it must have a directional antenna much longer than the wavelength of the energy needed to transmit the information) 'Q'. No one has ever reported seeing such an antenna in any of the hundreds of human brains which have been dissected. So telepathy is not possible." The sentence "No one has ever reported..." contradicts Q and should be symbolized as Not-Q. The conclusion should be translated as Not-P.

A couple of points should be made before closing on conditional reasoning. First, although Affirming the Consequent is not deductively valid, it is related to inductive forms often used in everyday life and science and comes in varying degrees of strength. We will go into this in more detail in Chapter Ten.

Second, two forms of argument, called "Reduction to Absurdity," are often-used extensions of Denying the Consequent. In the simple form to prove a statement P, we assume its exact contradictory, NOT-P. If we can validly deduce a false statement from this assumption, that proves that the assumption itself was false. (That's what Denying the Consequent tells us.) But if NOT-P is false, then p must be true. Here is one example, in brief and simplified form, from Emmanuel Kant's Critique of Pure Reason. Thesis: (P) The world has a beginning in time ... Proof: Granted, that the world has no beginning in time, [NOT-P.] [so] up to every given moment in time there must have passed away an infinite series of conditions or states of things in the world. But an infinite series can never be completed. It follows that an infinite series already elapsed is impossible and that consequently the world must have a beginning in time. [This is P again.]

The more complex, common form involves adding other statements accepted as true, deducing a false conclusion, and then concluding that the original assumption was false. A simple example is Socrates first criticism of a wrong definition of "right" or justice in Plato's *Republic*. The definition is that "right" means "what is in the interest of the stronger party." Socrates gets the definer to accept that athletes are stronger than couch potatoes and that it is right for athletes to eat a lot of meat. He then draws the conclusion that eating a lot of meat must be right for couch potatoes too. The definer must agree that this is a false implication and concludes that since the other reasons are undoubtedly true, the definition must be wrong. (To be fair, we must admit that the definer claims that Socrates took "stronger" in the wrong sense.)

REDUCTION TO ABSURDITY, COMMON FORM

ASSUME P: <If P + Q + R + S, then T> + <Q> + <R> + <S> + NOT-T

$$\downarrow$$

NOT-P

The student should now do Exercise 13 on Determining the Forms of Conditional Arguments.

SECTION 7.4 SUPPLYING MISSING REASONS AND CONCLUSIONS

Now that we have the forms, it should be easy to see how to draw valid conclusions following the patterns of Affirming the Antecedent and Denying the Consequent. Drawing conclusions is called "deduction." It is nothing more than recognizing partial patterns as the top parts of valid forms and completing the pattern by filling in the missing bottom parts, the conclusions. For example, if you are given a conditional statement "If P, then Q" and its antecedent, "P", as a separate unconditional statement, then you can go on and draw the conclusion "Q."

"If it is snowing, then the streets will soon become wet. It is snowing, so...." What conclusion can be drawn? We have <If P, then Q> and P. Q completes the valid pattern Affirming the Antecedent: <If P, then Q> and <P>, —> Q, so I can deduce Q, "The streets will soon become wet."

On the other hand, if given the conditional and the negation of the consequent, NOT-Q, then one can draw the conclusion that NOT-P. "If it is snowing, then the streets will soon become wet. The streets will not soon become wet, SO..." Here I have <If P, then Q> and NOT-Q. This is the top part of the pattern Denying the Consequent: <If P, then Q> and NOT-Q, ——>NOT-P. I can validly deduce that it is not snowing.

Don't forget also the pattern of Transposition in which one conditional statement follows from another. Given "If it is snowing, then the streets will soon become wet", <If P, then Q>, you can draw the conclusion <If NOT-Q, then NOT-P>, that "If the streets will not soon become wet, then it is not snowing."

Supplying missing assumptions is not much harder. Suppose you are missing the conditional statement itself. You can construct it simply by taking the reason, or the conjunction of all the reasons as the antecedent and the conclusion or conjunction of all the conclusions as the consequent. This has been called "the lazy man's way" of making any argument deductively valid. Suppose we have the semantic argument: "This is red. So it is colored". We take "This is red" as the antecedent and "It is colored" as the consequent. We simply write out the reason "*If* this is red, *then* it is colored". By "conjunction" of reasons or conclusions I mean simply all of them with the word "and" between each pair. If we have reasons R_1 R_2, R_3 and on through R_n for conclusion C, we add the conditional "If R_1 and R_2 and R_3...,and R_n, then C."

If the conditional reason and the conclusion are present, put parentheses around the statements so that you determine which categorical statement the conclusion is. It can only be P, NOT-P, Q, or NOT-Q. Only Affirming the Antecedent, with Q as the conclusion, and Denying the Consequent with NOT-P, are valid. So if you have "If P, then Q", and "Q" as the conclusion, you know from the form of Affirming the Antecedent that the missing reason must be P.

"If this is tiresome, then you will soon quit. Therefore you will soon quit, BECAUSE... Let's see. <If P, then Q>, so Q. This fits only one valid pattern I know, <If P, then Q> and <P>, so <Q>. Therefore the missing the missing reason is P, "This is tiresome."

On the other hand, if you have the conditional statement, "If P, then Q," and the conclusion "NOT-P," then Denying the Consequent requires that the missing reason to be filled in must be NOT-Q. For example, what is the missing assumption here?   "If this is red, then it is colored. So it is not red, BECAUSE..." Here I have <If P, then Q> so NOT-P. These two only fit the pattern of Denying the Consequent: <If P, then Q> and <NOT-Q>, so <NOT-P>. Thus the missing reason must be <NOT-Q>, "it is not colored."

Now do Exercises 14 and 15 on Missing Reasons and Conclusions.

SECTION 7.5 NON-CONDITIONAL VALID PATTERNS

A compound statement of the form "P or Q" is called "a disjunction." "Inclusive" disjunctive claims seem true if and only if either one of their disjuncts is true or both are true. For example, "This object is red or They drink tea in China" is true if and only if either "This object is red" is true or "They drink tea in China" is true or both. "Exclusive" disjunctions can be defined in terms of this sense and conjunction. "Rolls or salad" on the menu means "one or the other, and not both." But we have no simple way of restricting the contents of "P" and "Q." So this definition allows the following two valid inference patterns to be stated.

THE VALID FORM ADDITION

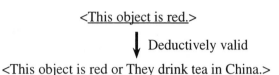

<u><This object is red.></u>

↓ Deductively valid

<This object is red or They drink tea in China.>

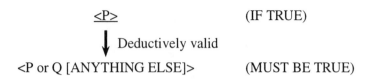

<u><P></u>   (IF TRUE)

↓ Deductively valid

<P or Q [ANYTHING ELSE]>   (MUST BE TRUE)

Example: < This object is red,> so <This object is red or They drink tea in China.>

THE VALID FORM DISJUNCTIVE SYLLOGISM

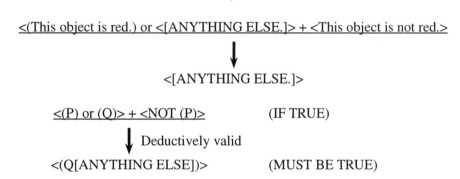

<u><(This object is red.) or <[ANYTHING ELSE.]> + <This object is not red.></u>

↓

<[ANYTHING ELSE.]>

<u><(P) or (Q)> + <NOT (P)></u>   (IF TRUE)

↓ Deductively valid

<(Q[ANYTHING ELSE])>   (MUST BE TRUE)

Some logicians are troubled that the definitions of truth and falsehood of compounds allows us to put together compounds and draw inferences with irrelevant statements. This has yielded attempts to restrict conditional statements and inference patterns as well as Disjunction and Conjunction. These attempts leave systems of logic more complex or weaker. They are weaker in the sense that some inferences we now think are valid no longer remain so.

We want simple, powerful rules for an introductory text. We also keep the standard rules because they yield a strong reason to be consistent in our beliefs. Given Addition and Disjunctive Syllogism, if a person accepts inconsistent beliefs "P" and "NOT-P," it can be validly deduced that he ought to accept *any* conclusion "Q." By Addition, if "P" is true, then "P or Q" is true. But if "NOT-P" is also true, then, by Disjunctive Syllogism, we can infer that 'Q" is not true, no matter what "Q" may be. So if you accept these rules of this logic *and* also accept any inconsistent statements, then you are justified by valid deduction in believing *any* and every statement. To do that would be the opposite of being a critical thinker.

8

MODERATE TO FALLACIOUS ARGUMENTS

SECTION 8.1: PRESUMPTION IN DIALOGUE AND PLAUSIBLE REASONING

So far this text has dealt with arguments as if they were isolated monologues. However, many occur as part of dialogues or open discussions. Discussion normally occurs according to unspoken principles of "conversational cooperation." These principles permit participants to draw inferences which are neither deductively valid nor very strong. However, they may still be quite correct inferences. Grice (1975) formulated these principles as follows. 1. Provide as much information as will be useful and appropriate. 2. Take care not to say false things. 3. Be relevant (stick to the topic, etc.) 4. Be perspicuous (clear, orderly, brief, and so on.) These rules are unilaterally suspended without warning in advertising, negotiations, debates and confrontations of critical thinkers with con artists, frauds and pseudo scientists.

Examples of such conversational "implicatures" operating in normal conditions can be drawn from Haugeland (1987). Mary asks Peter: "Where's Paul?" Peter replies: "He's in one of the Dakotas." Mary infers that Peter does not know which Dakota. A son says to his father "I wish I had money for a movie." The father replies "The lawn needs to be mowed." The son infers that if he mows the lawn, his father will pay him some money.

A lot of dialogue is goal-directed information seeking or critical discussion of conflicts of opinion (Walton, 1996, passim.) It involves practical reasoning about what to do. It also involves presumptions. Arguments in it should be evaluated as good (correct or reasonable) to the extent they contribute to the goal of the discussion. They are bad (incorrect, fallacious) to the extent that they block the goal of the dialogue (Walton, p. 1.)

Presumption and conflict of information have been dealt with by Rescher (1976.) Presumptions are frequently unstated prima facie justified statements. They are not held because they are more probable than their contradictories. Presumptions are pretenders to truth like eldest sons of kings were pretenders to thrones. We give them some credit sufficient to call forth efforts to dislodge them. The introduction of a presumption into an argument by a party in a dialogue shifts the burden of argument in the dialogue to the other party. This burden can be met by appropriate critical questions concerning the argument.

There is a standing presumption in favor of the normal, usual, customary course of things. Presumptions are based on such things as conventional wisdom, customs, fashions, cooperation, politeness and routine ways of doing things. Presumptive inferences are at best moderate arguments, subject to provisions, defeat and withdrawal or rebuttal. Nevertheless, they are capable of non fallacious use and shifting the burden of argument. Here is an example of a presumptive argument by Walton. "The prisoner confessed to the crime. Therefore he is guilty." This presumes that a person knows whether he did an act or not. The inference is not strong. One can easily think of conditions under which the reason is true and the conclusion false. One can even think how the presumptive generalization might be false in a specific case. However, the argument is not necessarily fallacious.

Rescher argues that the notion of plausibility can serve to determine where presumption lies. His work on plausible reasoning is aimed at the open ended situation of real life in which we have to weigh conflicting information. He suggests that we try to rank the reliability of sources of information and use that ranking to derive plausibility values from the reliability of sources and deductive logic. Sources which can be ranked by reliability include: 1) persons who make claims (eyewitnesses, trained observers, contemporaries who kept diaries) 2) historical sources like newspaper accounts, oral tradition, common knowledge, rumor; 3) our own senses and memories, 4) intellectual resources like conjecture, assumption, hypothesis formation and 5) claim-authorizing principles like simplicity (Ockham's Razor) and uniformity.

Suppose we let 1 equal maximal reliability, the data of a 1-grade source being virtually or effectively certain. We use fractions with 1= n/n to represent less than total reliability. The lower grades of reliability would be represented by n-1/n, n-2/n, n-3/n and so on. This will produce decimals such as .9, .65, etc. A plausible proposition, then, is one vouched for by a source of at least 1/n reliability. This is *not* the same use of decimals as in probability theory employed in Chapter Four. Plausibility theory is useful for dealing with contradictory statements in a set of data *vouched for by one or more sources.* It does not have a negation rule and is not consistent with probability theory. A source of low reliability is still a source of some plausibility.

Perhaps we could roughly rank probabilities as "bound to be" = 1.0, "highly probable" = .9 or better, "middling probable" = somewhere from .89 toward .5, "improbable"= below .5 to "bound not to be" = 0.0. However, a statement can have a low probability and a high plausibility. Consider that a regular die is tossed. An unreliable source reports P, "The toss result was a number different from 1." P has a high probability but a low plausibility. Probability is internal likelihood, plausibility is an external status changing feature. There are many arguments to which we can assign no probability of truth of the conclusion. In some such cases plausibility considerations may help in evaluation.

Sources of plausibility can be qualities of the source like established fact, expert witness, personal witness, trained observation, or status in a body of statements like being a definition, foundational principle, well supported thesis, or modalities like being necessary, contingent or at least possible, or even psychological states like certainty or reasonable certainty.

The basic principles of Rescher's theory are these. First, the plausibility of a statement derives from its most reliable source. Second, the plausibility of a conclusion reflects the least plausible of its premises. Third, in restoring consistency always retain the more plausible statement. We made use of the second principle in the Weakest Link of the Chain Principle in Chapter Five. We can illustrate how the second can be applied in evaluating information in a dialogue. Suppose the body of a wealthy woman has been found in ambiguous circumstances. Did she die of natural causes, was she a suicide or was she murdered? A representative of the prosecutor's office "P" calls a conference with the local coroner (LC), and an outside expert consultant (EC,) both men of few words.

P: "How did she die?"

LC: "Murder or suicide ....Not suicide." M or S, Not-S

EC: "Not Murder!" Not-M

Here "M or S" and "Not-S" validly imply M by disjunctive syllogism. This is inconsistent with EC's claim that Not-M. Suppose we can assign a reliability index of .85 to LC and .95 to EC. The first principle dictates that "Not-M" gets a plausibility index of .95. The second dictates that "M" gets one of .85. The third dictates that the prosecutor treat M, murder, as the most plausible thesis on this information. There is always a positive presumption in favor of the most plausible claim among available alternatives. This presumption remains until set aside by something more plausible or direct evidence contrary to it.

SECTION 8.2: FALLACY AND PROCEDURE

Given the above considerations, arguments which used to be classified as "fallacious" are now seen as not always so. All fallacies are weak to nil arguments. However, not all moderate or weak arguments are fallacies. A **fallacy** is a weak to nil argument which obscures truth rather than reveals it, which leads astray, retards rather than advances progress toward satisfactory closure of a dialogue. It may be a trick but is not necessarily one. The student must consider carefully these questions. *Who is making the argument? What is his, her, or it's final conclusion? What are their intermediate conclusions and basic reasons? What conclusions and assumptions have been left unstated?* The Principle of Charity to make an argument as strong as possible before evaluating it should not be used at this point. Rather, a more descriptive principle should be followed. Unstated presumptions actually relied on should be spelled out so that good evaluations can be made.

The best procedure will be to distinguish several broad, general families of moderate to weak arguments and consider when they step over the bounds into fallacy. For each type of argument the English name will be given. Then there will be a definition or generalized description of it. An example or two of it will be given. An arrow diagram will show its *general* kind of content. A couple of test questions will be given to test if the passage really does contain that type of argument. Finally, in some cases, critical discussion-advancing questions will be listed. With problems, the task will be to say what kind of argument is found in a discourse, to explain why the argument is at best only moderate in degree of support and to evaluate whether it is a fallacy.

Passages or dialogues can be on a wide variety of topics and embody the same type of argument. It is a matter of correctly interpreting a passage as containing a sort of argument. The test questions are given to avoid a sort of "Fallacy Name Guessing" game which a lot of students play with other texts. If the student cannot answer the test questions set forth, then the passage almost certainly does not contain the type of argument for which these are test questions. Also, if the critical discussion - advancing, or evaluation questions do not seem appropriate, then probably the passage contains another type of argument. *Work by process of elimination.* Make an arrow diagram. Compare the problem to examples and forms given. Ask the test questions. Rule out forms whose questions can not be answered.

SECTION 8.3: THE AUTHORITY FAMILY OF ARGUMENTS

Appeal to Authority: This is a family of arguments in which an arguer offers as the explicit reason for a conclusion that some expert asserts the conclusion, or it is widely believed or based on some popular value or traditional wisdom. There are presumptions in favor of each of these things, but those presumptions are questionable. We present a form for each type of presumption.

ARROW DIAGRAM FOR AUTHORITY:

Authority A asserts statement "P".

So "P" is true.

Presumably authorities are in a position to know. Suppose that Dr. No Phun is a leading AIDS researcher who has addressed a conference of the worlds' leading experts on AIDS. He has said that abstinence from sex with multiple partners remains the safest way to limit the sexual transmission of AIDS. This statement has been integrated into an approved conference press release. Citing Dr. Phun's remark to argue for abstinence is no fallacy but a legitimate use of authority.

 However, sometimes experts disagree. Other times examination shows that the claimed expert is not really an expert on the subject of the conclusion. In such cases reasoning of this form is fallacious. Suppose someone argues as follows. "Dr. No Phun says that sex outside of marriage, especially homosexuality, is morally wrong, and he is the world's leading AIDS researcher." This hints at connections which do exist between sexual activity and AIDS. However, that is not what is offered as a reason for the conclusion. The subject of this conclusion is morality, a matter in which ministers, priests, ethical philosophers and law makers, more than doctors, are supposed to be the experts.

Test questions for Appeal to Authority are " Sez who?, Who is the supposed authority appealed to?" "What claim is advanced as that of some authority?" Critical evaluation questions for the respondent to ask to shift the burden of argument back include "What field is the authority an authority in?" "What are the authority's qualifications?" "Did the authority really make exactly this claim?" and "Is the conclusion really in this person or group's field of expertise?" "Is it consistent with what other experts in the field say and with other evidence in the field?"

The popularity form of authority argument occurs when an arguer offers as an explicit reason for a conclusion some appeal to widely held values, beliefs, actions or choices. Presumably their popularity is some ground for having similar values, beliefs, choices, etc. The form is this.

ARROW DIAGRAM FOR POPULARITY:

<u>Many people value, buy, do, use or think X.</u>
or
<u>Valuing, buying, doing, using or thinking X will get you sex, money, security...</u>

So you ought to value, buy, do, use or think X.

Consider an example: "You ought to buy a Ford Taurus for your next car. They are the biggest selling car in America." Presumably this is not for nothing, nor basically for irrational reasons like extreme advertising. The most popular family sedan has probably gotten a good rating from critical sources like *Consumer Reports*. Purchase of it will probably ensure easy availability of spare parts and mechanics who know how to repair them years down the road.

Advertisers often use Appeal to Popularity in a form more likely to be fallacious. They argue that you should buy their product because it will get you sex, companionship, security, money or the admiration of other people. The fallacy arises because there is no causal connection between purchase of the product or service and getting the desired value.

Test questions for this form of argument are: What is the popular belief, value, or choice appealed to in this argument? How does this argument involve appeal to a large number of people doing or believing something? Critical evaluation questions for the respondent include: "Do many people really value, etc. this?" "Do they do so for good reason?" "Is there a causal connection between valuing, etc. this and getting the desired good?"

Traditional Wisdom: This is a type of argument in which one offers as an explicit reason for a conclusion that the conclusion represents the way people have generally thought or acted in the past. Presumably long established usages have some merit or they would not have remained long in place. Also, established usages form a network so that nonconformity to one may involve misunderstandings or difficulties with others. An example would be the argument "You should send a 'Thank You' card for that gift. It's customary." This is not a fallacy. A person who has sent a gift and not received such a card may wonder whether the gift arrived or infer that it had and was not appreciated or that the receiver is rude.

ARROW DIAGRAM FOR TRADITIONAL WISDOM

So "P" is true, OK, right, etc.

On the other hand, consider "No society has ever legalized same sex marriage, so our society should not do so." No society has ever extended purely civil rights as far as ours has either. Unless one assumes that this tendency in civil rights is wrong, this is a bad argument. A test question for the presence of this argument type is: What claim is made here about how things have always been or how people have always thought? The line into fallacy is crossed in this form precisely when the traditional wisdom has been questioned on good grounds, or values and circumstances have changed. So a critical evaluation, burden-shifting question would be: "Is this 'traditional wisdom' true in the light of current knowledge, values and circumstances?"

SECTION 8.4: APPEALS TO IGNORANCE

An Argument from Ignorance is given when someone argues that a conclusion must be true because no one has ever proven it false, or false because no one has ever proven it true. There are a lot of subtypes of this argument (Walton, p. 121) The following can sum them up.

ARROW DIAGRAM FOR ARGUMENT FROM IGNORANCE

So C is false (or true.)

This sort of argument is not fallacious when a knowledge base is closed. For example, suppose you were looking at a current airline route map and were asked whether this airline has flights from Chicago stopping at Kansas City on the way to Los Angeles. The map has dots on various cities and lines from one to another. It shows a route marked from Chicago to L. A. which does not go over Kansas City and there is no dot marking Kansas City as any end point of any flight. Your argument is "There's no evidence that this airline has flights from Chicago stopping at Kansas City on the way to Los Angeles, so it doesn't have such flights."

Another sort of non fallacious use of argument from ignorance is that in which a lot of research has been done already. It is not fallacious to argue like this. "None of the over 3,000 experiments attempting to demonstrate ESP has scientifically proven it to exist, therefore it does not exist." Such an argument is only moderate, subject to defeat, but gets stronger with each further set of experiments which either fail or are shown to have involved poor methodology, falsification of data, etc. It gets stronger also by addition of other sorts of evidence, such as the idea of ESP being based on doubtful theories like dualism and lacking any physically explicable way of happening.

Argument from ignorance becomes fallacious when it is used to try to shift a burden of argument from a proponent of a statement to a denying respondent. It also becomes a fallacy when not enough research has been done. An example of the first case would be this. Mulder says to Scully "Let's go. We have a murderous ghost in a farm house outside of Ida, Oregon." Scully: "I don't think so." Mulder: "Then when we get there, you can prove to me that there isn't a ghost there." The challenge is: you will not find evidence that there is no ghost, so there is one. An example of the second type is this. Fifteen subjects have been treated with drug X. No evidence of harmful effects have been found. The tester argues "There is no evidence that drug X has harmful effects, so it does not have harmful effects."

Test questions for this fallacy are: Who first introduced a claim needing proof? What was the claim? Did the claimant try to shift the burden of argument rather than carry it? Are words like "proved," "demonstrated," or "evidence" used in this argument? What is the claim alleged to be true or false? What words are used in the reason claiming that this conclusion has never been proved? Evaluation questions would include these. Has positive evidence been presented for a claim? What is that evidence? Is it sufficient for proof? How many attempts have been made to prove this true (or false?) Have these attempts exhausted all means? Have they been conducted scientifically?

SECTION 8.5: ARGUMENT AND THE MAN

Arguments "against (or to) the man" occur when an arguer offers as an explicit reason for acceptance of a conclusion some claim which seems to have more to do with the respondent or some other person than to be evidence for the conclusion. It has two varieties, "circumstantial" and "abusive." The circumstantial type involves an appeal to consistency or self interest. A positive form for it is this.

ARROW DIAGRAM FOR ARGUMENT TO THE MAN CIRCUMSTANTIAL

<A holds theory T or is in group G> + <Statement "P" is implied by T or is in the interest of G's.>

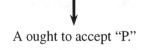

A ought to accept "P."

Presumably a person who holds a theory accepts its implications. Also, one in a certain group finds that what is in the group's interest is in his or her own. Suppose a woman is a college professor nearly 65 and needing to continue to work. The American Association of University Professors takes the position that mandatory retirement for university professors should be abolished. She is not on bad grounds, on learning of this, in accepting the proposition. However, this moderate to weak form of argument goes over into fallacy if the arguer insists that P is certainly true on just the reasons given in the form.

A form for the abusive type of Argument Against the Man is this.

ARROW DIAGRAM FOR ABUSIVE ARGUMENT AGAINST THE MAN

<u><A asserts "P"> + <A is a liar, bad, stupid, irresponsible..></u>

↓

So "P" is false, bad, stupid, irresponsible...

More arguments of this form are fallacious than merely moderate or weak. Still, it has acceptable uses. The new duty officer comes up to the Chief and says: "Chief, I've got a Mr. Mulder out here and he says he wants to report being abducted by some aliens." The Chief truthfully replies: "This Mulder has made 5 reports of wacky things in the last year. Not one of 'em checked out with any other witnesses or evidence. So be polite, take his report. But don't assign anyone to investigate." The Chief's argument is like that in which an attorney destroys the general credibility of a witness to cast doubt on the truth of his specific testimony.

Suppose one student said to another "You don't buy that argument Professor Jackson was offering in Sociology class about why homosexual marriages ought to be legal and they ought to have the same rights as everybody else, do you? After all, He's a queer himself!" Here the abusive form has gone over into fallacy. The professor's sexual orientation may have something to do with the *cause* of why he advances his argument. However, causes are not always reasons. He may have good or bad reasons.

Abusive Argument Against the Man is sometimes called "poisoning the well." Arousing feelings of anger and hurt is sometimes persuasive or at least distracting. The hurt feelings and anger cover up the lack of argument. It poisons the well-springs of further discussion. The best response is to keep one's cool. Stick to the position. Point out that name calling does not disprove one's point. Some people are always persuaded by the loudest mouth and the sharpest tongue. They are stupid people. If one doesn't persuade them, one hasn't lost the debate, those people have lost the truth!

Test questions for Circumstantial Argument To the Man are the following. Who or what group is claimed to hold a theory? What is the theory, position or group which they are claimed to hold? What statement is claimed to be implied by T in G's interest? To justify that an argument is a case Against the Man ask "Is someone being attacked personally here?" "Is there name calling or some appeal to irrelevant personal circumstances to explain what caused someone to hold a position?"

Test questions for the Abusive Variety are: Is some individual or group called bad names here or unfavorably described? What are the negative terms used? What is the individual or group's described position? Is the conclusion that position "P" is bad, stupid or irresponsible?

Critical questions which can shift the burden of argument back are these. Is A really a member of G? Does A really assert P, or hold theory T? Is P really implied by T or in G's interest, or specifically in A's interest? Is there any other evidence that P is true or false beyond what has been supplied so far? Is A really a liar, bad, stupid or irresponsible?

SECTION 8.6: GENERALIZATION ARGUMENTS

Indefinite generalizations are a serious problem for evaluation. So Chapter 4 gave an example of a precise form of generalization argument. Examples of arguments of the 5 degrees of support were precise by involving percents: "100%," "99%," etc. Chapter 6 presented a syllogistic logic to determine validity using quantifiers less precisely expressed, such as "almost all," "most," and "many." That system is expandable to a logic with an infinite number of forms (Thompson, 1992, Ch. 10 - 12) We can substitute "100%" for "all," and "no," and "over 50%" for "most," and agree that "almost all" and "few" mean "90% or more." However, beyond this, logic meets with a level of vagueness and incompleteness in language which gives rise to problematical kinds of statements and arguments which trail off from moderate to fallacious.

Some people speak or write in abstractions such as 'Man is...' this or that, "Religion holds..." "Society makes ..." Science asserts..." "Those people..." We shall call such indefinite statements "sophomoric generalizations." "Sophomoric" (say SAW foe more ik) means self assured and opinionated, as college sophomores often are. The root of the word is related to sophistry, which is loosely the use of verbal tricks in reasoning. Sophomoric generalizations are vague because they lack quantifiers. Generalizations with no quantifiers at all can not be verified or falsified unless one can pin their authors down to a quantifier. A critical thinker's response to such a generalization should be "What men? Which religions?" "What social groups do you mean? " "Which science and at what time?" "Exactly what people are you talking about?" Critical thinkers have a right to reject such claims if their authors never make their sophomoric generalizations clear and specific.

There are two kinds of imprecise moderate to weak generalization arguments, one inductive and statistical going from cases to generalizations. This "Sample to Class" form of argument goes as follows:

ARROW DIAGRAM FOR SAMPLE TO CLASS ARGUMENT

<u><Members of class A have property U.)></u>

↓

So A's are U.

Snowflakes I have observed have had regular patterns before melting, so I conclude that snowflakes have regular patterns. This form of argument goes over the boundary into fallacy when the sample a person chooses is either too small to sustain a conclusion on some high level of generalization or the sample is unrepresentative of the population. (These are called the fallacies of "Small Sample" and "Unrepresentative Sample," both lumped under "Hasty Generalization.") Here is an example of both sorts. "There were three Puerto Rican kids in our high school class. They all got in trouble with the law. Those people have poor impulse control." The concluding generalization that "Those people," presumably Puerto Rican Americans, all or in general have "poor impulse control," is drawn from far too few cases and from cases which are exceptions.

Test questions for this fallacy would be these. What words tell you some sample has been considered? What is the class claimed to be the one from which the sample was drawn? What is the generalization drawn? Discussion advancing questions include: How large was the sample? What exactly is the generality level of the conclusion? (universal, predominant, etc.) Is the sample big enough for this level? Was the sample taken in any non-random way? Is there anything atypical, unusual, abnormal about the cases the generalization is based on?

A second type of generalization argument goes from applying general reasons to cases to draw particular conclusions. Problems arise in such arguments because of another feature of ordinary language use. This is that generalizations are often stated without all the qualifications which apply to them. H. W. B. Joseph gave this classic example. "Water boils at 212^0 Fahrenheit, therefore boiling water will be hot enough to cook an egg hard in 5 minutes." (Impurities may change boiling points.) The problem is that the generalization is stated without qualifications or boundary conditions. The time it will take water to heat enough to cook an egg hard varies with air pressure and hence altitude. Adding "at sea level" to the generalization would take care of this incompleteness.

Incompleteness of this sort does not make a generalization sophomoric. When one makes a generalization there is a presumption that it is said to be true under normal conditions, in most cases, or something like this. Arguments like the boiling egg one are enthymemes. Their strength or weakness is only shown when qualifications are added, including those pertaining to the case being argued about. If we add "at sea level" to the generalization and try to make the argument in Denver Colorado's Mile High Stadium, then the argument passes over into a Fallacy of Ignoring Qualifications.

Critical questions for this type of argument involve asking "Under what conditions is this generalization true?" "Does the case in the conclusion fall under these conditions?"

SECTION 8.7: SLIPPERY SLOPES

Slippery Slope is a family of arguments which, according to Walton, has causal, principle and incremental (that is, adding on) forms. In the causal form an arguer advances against an idea, policy or action A, basic

reasons including the claim that A will lead to B, C, D and so on. B, C, D and so on are less desirable until we reach something very undesirable or wrong. The conclusion is that the original idea A was wrong or bad. In the principle form P is claimed to justify a certain questionable action A_1. So it would justify A_2, A_3, A_4 and so on, where these other actions are more clearly wrong. In the incremental form it is argued that since A_1 is an F, where F is something vague, $A_2 A_3, A_4$ and so on must also be F. The causal form is diagramed as follows.

ARROW DIAGRAM FOR CAUSAL SLIPPERY SLOPE
<u><A leads to B, C, D.> + <B, C, D are bad (or getting worse.)></u>

So A is bad.

It used to be argued by so-called "doves" on war that failure of the nuclear nations to reach agreements on disarmament would lead to medium sized nations getting them. This would in turn cause "terrorist" groups struggling against governments to seek to buy nuclear weapons. The world would become a much more dangerous place. Events seem to have borne this out.

The argument goes over into fallacy when it is claimed that A *inevitably* leads to B, etc., when there is no clear causal connection. The Reverend Donald Wildmon's American Family Association, in a full page advertisement objecting to "NYPD Blue" even before the first pilot aired, Wildmon's association argued as follows. "After the Networks begin showing soft core pornography on 'R-rated' programs, the next step is hardcore pornography on 'X-rated' programs. The time to stand up against the filth on television is now" (Erie Times News, 7/18/93.)

ARROW DIAGRAM FOR PRINCIPLE SLIPPERY SLOPE

$$\underline{\text{<Principle P justifies action } A_1 \text{>}}_+ \underline{\text{<}A_2, A_3, A_4 \text{ etc., are very similar to } A_1 \text{>}}$$

$$\downarrow$$

$$\text{So P justifies } A_2, A_3, A_4.$$

An example of this type is given by Walton. The principle that Congress shall make no law prohibiting the free exercise of religion is claimed to justify giving fundamentalist students the right to use school classrooms for after school Bible Study. Then it is concluded that it would be necessary to grant this right to Jewish students, Muslims, Hindu's, Buddhists and even Satanists.

The incremental (additive, by small steps) form goes like this.

INCREMENTAL SLIPPERY SLOPE

$$\underline{\text{<}A_1 \text{ is an F> + < }A_2 A_3, A_4 \text{ are very similar to } A_1 \text{>}}$$

$$\downarrow$$

$$\text{So } A_2 A_3, A_4 \text{ are also F.}$$

An example might be this. A fetus just before it is born (A_1) is a person with rights. A fetus a few days before then (A_2) has all the same organs, capacity to feel, and so on. However, a few days before that it is indistinguishable from its current state. So one should grant it rights at that time also, and so on. There is no point at which one can legitimately draw a line.

These forms cross over into fallacy when it is claimed without further evidence that one event *inevitably* leads to another or that cases *necessarily* fall under the same principle or that cases far apart must have the same properties. This sort of argument is used against almost every type of social change, activity of youth, or science. Examples revolve around basic reasons like smoking marijuana inevitably leads to becoming a junkie, premarital sex leads to infidelity and divorce, abortion to mercy killing and selective breeding. Selective breeding or behavior modification or genetic engineering or cloning, or psychosurgery, or nationalization or resources, or progressive taxation or deficit spending or inflation or sexual liberation are claimed to inevitably lead to some sort of highly class - divided dictatorship.

One problem with such arguments is that we already have a highly class-divided society, along lines of how much wealth people have. That doesn't make it a dictatorship. It isn't. None of these arguments shows such connection to be *inevitable*.

Test questions for this form of argument are: "What idea, policy, or action A is supposed to lead to others?" "What other ideas, B, C, D are mentioned as consequences of A?" "What words are used to claim how these consequences will be bad?" "What principle is cited and what actions is it claimed to justify? "What wrong action or consequence is claimed to be justified by it?" "What is the dimension that can be increased or decreased (like time in the example?)" Discussions advance by investigating whether A inevitably causes B, C, D. It also advances by insisting that a principle which applies to one sort of case does not apply to others and adding appropriate qualifications to it. In the incremental form, one may point out that when differences of degree become sufficiently great, they become differences of kind. Over sufficient time or space differences of degree become differences of kind.

SECTION 8.8: QUESTIONABLE ANALOGIES AND CAUSES

One of the Slippery Slopes above has a causal premise. Two involve analogical premises. Analogical and causal arguments are so common their forms and sources of possible weakness were dealt with under Reasoning of Special Kinds in Chapter 4, Section 3. All that needs to be done now is to state the test and critical questions for these sorts of arguments.

Analogical arguments claim that one object is like another and has a certain property, so the other has the property also. Test questions for analogical argument are these. "What two objects are claimed to be alike here?" "In what ways are they claimed to be alike?" "What property of one or a group is inferred to belong to another thing?" Such arguments become fallacious when the objects are really very different or the property inferred is not relevant to the other similarities between things. Good critical questions to judge the strength of the argument and perhaps shift the burden back include: Is this object really similar to the other one? Does the object the conclusion is drawn about really have the same properties as the others? Are there serious relevant differences which weaken the analogy?

Causal arguments go from premises about correlations between events A and B to conclusions about causal relations between them. They can go wrong when someone simply infers that A causes B because A comes before B. They can also go wrong when they conclude that A causes B when, in fact, something else causes B, or causes both A and B or B causes A. The only needed test question here is, "What event is said to cause what other event?" Good critical questions to ask are: "In how many cases has A been observed to be correlated with B? Has A always been present before B? Are there cases where A occurs and B does not? Is there any other factor always present with A and B? If A and B vary in quantity, do they vary in any regular, predictable way? Is there any theory which would explain why A's variation with B is other than a coincidence?"

SECTION 8.9: QUESTION BEGGING

Question begging is pure presumption. The term "Begging the Question" covers two related fallacies. The simple form occurs when an arguer advances as a basic reason for a conclusion a statement which is just another way of saying the same thing as the conclusion. He presumes that his respondent accepts the point. Such an example *must* be deductively valid, for if the reason is true, then the conclusion must be true. Yet there is obviously something wrong with such an argument. If the conclusion was not evident to the respondent, then the reason should not be any more evident, since it says the same thing.

ARROW DIAGRAM FOR BEGGING THE QUESTION

SIMPLE FORM: P   COMPLEX FORM: Q (denied)

↓   ↓

P   P

Paraphrasing something one has said may help another to *understand* it better. However without some linking middle idea, or the following of some pattern of reasoning like inductive generalization, rephrasing alone should not provide any *evidence* or support for a statement. Here is an example. Suppose Dominic says "None of our Edinboro University students are really stupid." Mary replies, "Why do you think that?" Dominic says, "Because all of them are at least moderately intelligent." Because such examples are deductively valid, not formally fallacious, logicians created the term "informal fallacies." Mary should reply: "But that *begs the question* of whether any of them are really stupid."

The complex form of Begging the Question occurs when an arguer presumes acceptance of a basic reason which is denied by the person argued to. The claim may be true and the argument even sound, but it should not be persuasive. Suppose Latoya says, "Clinton's right. The government ought to see to it that there's enough doctors, health insurance and low enough doctor's fees so everybody can get adequate health care." Leona replies in a horrified tone: "But that would be socialized medicine!" Leona has presumed that LaToya is against 'socialized medicine.' Latoya may reply: "So what? You beg the question by *assuming* that socialized medicine is bad. I think it would be a good idea for this part of the economy to be socialized." Test questions for the presence of these forms are as follows. "Do a reason and conclusion say the same thing in different words?" "Is a reason relied on here which the person argued to would not accept?" Discussion advancing questions revolve around showing that the reason and conclusion really mean the same thing or that the respondent simply does not accept the premise in the complex form.

SECTION 8.10: OUTRIGHT FALLACIES

The remaining cases are more or less always fallacies. They may be persuasive sometimes for psychological reasons. They are at best, however, always very weak to nil as arguments. Therefore only test questions for detection will be given. Once detected, these forms of argument can be labeled, explained to any audience and dismissed.

Two Wrongs Make a Right: this is the fallacy committed when an arguer reasons to the conclusion that some act is not wrong for "our side" to do, because "the other side" has committed the same or similar acts before. This is used to try to excuse wrong behavior. Test questions for this type of argument are: "What are the two wrongs here? What action is supposed to excuse what other action?"

Two wrongs make a right...

ARROW DIAGRAM FOR TWO WRONGS

Person A (not myself) also did this, or did it first, or did wrong.

↓ Weak

So it is not wrong (or it is excusable) for me to do this.

Irrelevant Reason is the fallacy committed when an arguer is unable to prove the conclusion she desires to prove. So instead she gives reasons for a different but somehow related conclusion. The arguer herself may confuse the two conclusions. But perhaps she just hopes that the person argued to will not notice the difference.

The classic example of this is the prosecutor in court who can't actually prove that the defendant is the specific party guilty of the crime. Let's say it was a particularly horrible crime like the murder, mutilation and cannibalism of Jeffrey Dahmer. The evidence the prosecutor may have are things like the battered head, torso, feet and hands nibbled and gnawed away. Perhaps she just has pictures of these things. She gets up at the beginning of the trial and says that "the state will prove that this defendant is a horrible, awful *murderer* and ought to pay for this crime". But suppose she doesn't have evidence to actually prove this. She may use the evidence to prove the related but different conclusion "This was a horrible, awful *murder* and *somebody* ought to pay for this crime." Notice how closely related the stated conclusion is to the conclusion for which she actually gives evidence. By giving evidence for this conclusion she may stir up the emotions of the jury. She may make them angry to the point where their anger over the terribleness of the crime, and their desire to do something about it may make them confuse the two conclusions and convict the defendant.

It is especially important not to let this fallacy become a grab - bag. Ask the following test questions. Did the arguer change the subject here? From what to what? Are these reasons actually for the stated conclusion, or do they prove some other related conclusion? What is that conclusion?

For the general arrow diagram here we will use "R1", "R2", etc. for "Reason 1", "Reason 2", and "C1" for the stated conclusion. "C2" will be used for the actually proved conclusion which will be in square brackets because it is unstated. We will use an equals sign, "=" with a slant line through it indicating inequality to symbolize the idea that C_1 and C_2 are not the same statement.

ARROW DIAGRAM FOR IRRELEVANT REASON

$$\underline{R1 + R2 + R3 + ...}$$

$$C_1 \text{ (stated)} \neq [C_2 \text{ (actually proved)}]$$

Appeal to Force is a fallacy committed when an arguer advances as the sole or most important reason for accepting a conclusion some threat or not relevant consideration of power. An old sexist example is the guy who drives a date to a lonely lovers' lane parking area. He parks, and asks her "Do you believe in the here-after?" She says "What do you mean?" He replies: "If you're not here after what I'm here after, you'll be here after I'm gone!" The conclusion of this jerk's argument is that she had better make out with him, because if she doesn't, then he will leave her there.

Appeal to Force.

A threat, physical, financial, etc. may be a good reason for acting as if one believed something, but never a good reason for actually believing its' truth or justice. Test questions for the presence of this fallacy are: "What threat is being made here?" "What consideration about the power of the parties to this argument is being introduced as a reason?"

ARROW DIAGRAM FOR APPEAL TO FORCE

<u>Accept conclusion C or else ... THREAT!</u>

↓ Weak

So C is true.

Tokenism is committed when an arguer exaggerates or minimizes the importance of some action to conclude that it was adequate or inadequate to deal with some situation. Tokenism is often practiced in politics. One side will say "We spent a whopping $4 billion on this problem." The other side will say "They only spent a tiny 1 tenth of 1 percent of the budget on that problem." To resolve whether tokenism is being committed, ask these test questions. What is being exaggerated or minimized here? What words say it was too much" or "too little?"

ARROW DIAGRAM FOR TOKENISM

<u>Action A was too little (or too much).</u>

↓ Weak

So A was wrong, shows misplaced values, etc.

Ambiguity or Equivocation is a fallacy arising from using a word in more than one meaning. It requires semantic clarification to show this fallacy. Ambiguity has two forms. In one form an arguer uses an apparent linking middle term which really has two senses. The term must be taken in those different senses in order for both reasons to be accepted as true. But when this is done, it turns out that there really is no linking idea. Here is an example by Copi (1961.) "A college student who likes poetry is *abnormal$_1$.* *Abnormal$_2$* people are to be pitied. So college students who like poetry are to be pitied." The word "abnormal" must be interpreted as meaning "unusual" to make the first reason true. But in the second, that interpretation would not be regarded as making it true. Most people wouldn't agree that "Unusual people are to be pitied." To make the second statement true, "abnormal" must be interpreted as something more like "handicapped." However, when one semantically clarifies this one sees that there is not a single linking middle idea.

The second form of the fallacy occurs when the ambiguous term appears in a reason so that it can be interpreted in one way to get one conclusion and in a different way to get a different conclusion. A trick I learned from another author is this. When a student writes me to complain of a bad grade during the summer months, I scribble the following on a post card. "Thanks for your letter, I'll lose no time in reading it." The student interprets "I'll lose no time in reading it" as meaning a second reason like "He'll read it right away" and draws the conclusion "He'll review my grade and maybe raise it." Lazy me, I can do this if I want, but *I* interpret "I'll lose no time in reading it" as meaning a second reason that I'll do it if and when feel like it. So I draw the conclusion that I don't have to review and raise his grade. Test questions for ambiguity are: "What is the ambiguous word or phrase here?" "What, exactly, are its two different meanings?" Unless there are two or more clearly different meanings, this fallacy is not committed.

ARROW DIAGRAM FOR AMBIGUITY FIRST FORM

<u><S is M$_1$> + <M$_2$ is P></u>

↓ Weak

S is P

SECOND FORM

$$\underline{A \text{ is } B \text{ (ambiguous term>} + <B_1 \text{ yields Conclusion } C_1> \text{ OR } + <B_2 \text{ yields } C_2>}$$

$$\downarrow \text{Weak} \quad \downarrow \text{Weak}$$

$$C_1 \quad \text{or} \quad C_2 ?$$

"Lose no time in reading it" is the ambiguous term in the above example.

Suppressed Evidence is a large category of fallacies. They are hard to spot. One has to recognize that the conventions of conversational cooperation may be suspended. Also, one needs to have some *knowledge* of the subject to detect it. This fallacy occurs when an arguer knows of or should know of evidence against his conclusion but deliberately leaves it out of the argument. Such arguments are weak, because on doing a complete evaluation of them, we find that they leave out the step of supplying total available evidence.

Much advertising and selling engages in suppression of evidence. It always tells you what is good about a candidate or product and not what is bad. Test questions for suppressed evidence would be these. "What negative facts about this conclusion, person, candidate, product or situation are being left out?" "Do alternative conclusions, persons, candidates or products have equally good features or better ones?"

ARROW DIAGRAM FOR SUPPRESSED EVIDENCE

$$\underline{<R_1> + <R_2> + ..<R_m> \text{ FOR A CONCLUSION}} \quad [<R_n> + <R_o> +... \text{ AGAINST}]$$

$$\searrow \qquad \swarrow$$

CONCLUSION

Straw Man is a particularly dishonest fallacy. It amounts to distorting or lying about someone else's position. Straw Man is the fallacy committed when an arguer introduces a distorted version of an opponent's position in order to conclude that the opponent or the opponent's position is wrong, stupid, or irresponsible. Politicians use it to argue that an opponent is not to be believed or voted for, or that she holds an extremist position. The distorted position is the "straw man," a scarecrow.

During the presidential campaign of 1964, the Republican candidate Barry Goldwater said "Extremism in the defense of liberty is no vice." The Democrats used TV advertisements to scare the American people into thinking that if Goldwater was elected, he would start a nuclear war with Russia. Since creating that straw man of Goldwater's ideas, no American politician has dared to say that any American problem needed any radical solution. "Radical" does not mean "bad" or "cool." It simply means "going to the root." A radical position is one which goes to the root of a problem.

Another good example of Straw Man was televangelist Pat Robertson's remark about the Equal Rights Amendment in a speech to the 1992 Republican convention. The ERA had been defeated long before, but he attacked it anyway. He said: "It's about a socialist, anti-family political movement that encourages women to leave their husbands, kill their children, practice witchcraft, destroy capitalism and become lesbians." Robertson knew that the news media will always repeat the nastiest, "hottest", wildest, most negative remarks. It doesn't matter how exaggerated and distorted they are. Sure enough, this remark was quoted in *Newsweek*, 9/7/92, p. 15.

Making nasty, "hot" wild, extremely negative comments "wins" debates, but only in the eyes of *fools* who always agree with the loudest - mouthed, sharpest - tongued speaker. Politicians who deliberately use language like this are called "demagogues" (say DEH-mah-gogs). Another controversial example of straw man is the way some conservatives try to label some progressives "politically correct." What they really mean is "stuck-up cranks." They try to imply that people who don't think it is right to make racial or sexual remarks or jokes are thought-police trying to violate their right to free speech. This sometimes becomes a straw man. Meanwhile, progressive people return the fallacy favor by implying that any conservative position is bigoted. This is equally untrue.

In Straw Man a person or group "A" is claiming that another person or group "B" holds a certain position "p." So one test question for deciding whether this fallacy is present is simply to ask: Is there a person or group A, here, saying 'Person or group B holds the position that p'?" The "acid test" question for this fallacy however, is to ask "Would any sensible, responsible person be likely to hold this position, exactly as it is stated, or assert it in public?" If the answer is "NO, no sensible person would hold or assert this position publicly", then the position is a Straw Man. Robertson was claiming that supporters of the ERA are people who encourage women to kill their children, practice witchcraft, become lesbians, and so on. However no group would hold or assert such exaggerated and wrong views.

ARROW DIAGRAM FOR STRAW MAN

<u><B holds "P"> + <"P" is wrong, stupid, irresponsible, extreme.></u>

 Weak

So B is wrong, stupid, irresponsible, extreme.

False Dilemma is the fallacy committed when an arguer asserts as a basic reason a statement which falsely reduces the number of alternatives in a situation, usually to only two. Another basic reason asserts that one of the two alternatives is wrong, stupid, irresponsible and so on. The arguer then goes on to conclude that the other alternative, is right, intelligent, responsible and so on. The other alternative, of course, is his own or his party's.

Kahane (1992) pointed out that politicians often use this fallacy in connection with Straw Man and Argument Against the Man. First a politician will create a Straw Man to put in place of his opponent's real position. Then he will create a False Dilemma between the Straw Man and his own position. His own position now comes out looking like the wisdom of King Solomon. Then he will conclude that his own position is the only correct one and that the opponent is stupid, irresponsible, or whatever. That is the Argument Against the Man.

Ayn Rand was a narrow, shallow philosopher - novelist. She has become a cult-figure for non philosophers (Shermer, "The Unlikliest Cult",1993) because people find in her writings excuses for their own selfishness. Here is an example. "Do not hide behind such superficialities as whether you should or should not give a dime to a beggar. That is not the issue. The issue is whether you do not have the right to exist without giving him that dime. The issue is whether or not you must keep buying your life, dime by dime, from any beggar who might choose to approach you. The issue is whether the need of others is the first mortgage on your life and the moral purpose of your existence. The issue is whether man is to be regarded as a sacrificial animal" (Rand, 1982, p. 172.) The Straw Man is that no liberal, communist or Christian says: "If you don't give a dime to a beggar, you don't have a right to exist." The false dilemmas are: either buy your life by giving a dime or forfeit your life, either the needs of others are first mortgage and moral purpose of your life or your own needs are these things.

ARROW DIAGRAM FOR FALSE DILEMMA

<u><There are only two choices: P and Q> + <P is stupid, irresponsible, etc.></u>

↓ Weak

So Q is right, intelligent, responsible.

Inconsistency is a fallacy for two reasons. First, rules of ordinary logic make it possible to prove any statement from inconsistent reasons. Second, while any argument from inconsistent reasons is deductively valid, no such argument can ever be sound. The reason is that at least one of the inconsistent reasons must be false.

Often inconsistency is more or less hidden. An example would be that most people want to be modern and to sound scientific. So if you ask them, "Do you believe in ghosts?", they will say "no." But suppose you ask them at a later time if they believe in life after death. They will say "yes." But what is a ghost, if not the disembodied soul or spirit of a person which has left the body after death? If there is life after death, there have to be ghosts. If there are no ghosts, there can't be life after death, at least on earth.

A related inconsistency is this. Many people think that the mind is identical with the brain. They think that the functioning of the mind depends completely on electro-chemical activity in the brain. There seems to be good evidence that we cannot think or remember or do anything without brains and some electrical currents firing the neurons. They also believe that there is survival of the mind or soul after death. But after death, *all* electro-chemical activity eventually ends and the whole brain rots away to nothingness. It can't both be true that there is life, consciousness, mental activity after death *and* that the mind is the brain or depends completely on the brain to be able to function.

An advertisement in a local paper claimed "A *free* healing prayer book will be sent with the Lourdes Crystal Rosary to those offering $12 or more for the ministries of the Missionary Oblates to the poor." It is inconsistent to say one has to send $12 for something "free." Another example is advertising pitches which say "*Buy* now and *save* $50.00 on this $450 item." Of course one is asked to *spend* $400.

Test questions for inconsistency are these. "Are there statements here which can't both be true? Is there opposition between a statement and an action?" "Is the arguer being hypocritical or applying a double standard?"

ARROW DIAGRAM FOR INCONSISTENCY

<u><P> + <NOT-P></u>

↓ Valid but not possibly sound

Q (any conclusion)

Lastly, *Evading the Issue* is avoiding a specific question and thus refusing to put forth any conclusion and argue for it at all. Evading the issue can be done by attacking the questioner or answering a different question from the one asked, like irrelevant reason. Sometimes someone put "on the spot" tries to use humor or to introduce a "red herring." A red herring is a different, highly emotional or interesting issue to distract from the question asked.

There are such things as personal questions. If someone asks a personal question where no one else has a right to know, it is appropriate to answer, "That's personal and *none of your business.*" In countries like ours with freedom of press, we have tabloid journalism. That's the kind of sensation seeking personal stuff written about in grocery store newspapers like the National Inquirer, The Weekly World News, The

Star, and so on. We also have self-promoters who are eager to "let it all hang out" for money - or just to get on TV. Largely conservatives and tabloid reporters and talk show hosts have created the view that public figures, especially politicians, have no rights to privacy at all. Since nobody is perfect, this "character issue", as it is called, is a dangerous idea. Puritans are not likely to make tolerant rulers in a diverse land.

A recent example of both evading the issue and the double standard is this. During the campaign of 1992, Republicans and journalists repeatedly asked Democrat Bill Clinton whether he had ever smoked marijuana. Clinton at first refused to answer. But his campaign eventually figured that this question, like the sex question, would never go away unless answered. They decided that it was not wise to turn the issue around and ask George Bush if he ever drank alcohol. Alcohol may be far more destructive than marijuana. But so long as young people do not turn out to vote and the average voter is a middle aged white male or female, the issue of alcohol versus marijuana would have been a loser for Clinton. These older people have a double standard according to which use of marijuana is evil, while use of alcohol is OK.

Clinton finally answered by saying "I never broke any *state* laws" (italics are this author's.) Clinton was relying on people's trust to believe he only smoked it in college in Oxford, England. Meanwhile, the Bush administration was alleged to have used federal prison system officials to keep locked up and shut up a prisoner who claimed to have sold Vice President Dan Quayle marijuana on many occasions. But many people felt that Clinton had evaded the issue. Clinton went on to say that he didn't inhale. This unbelievable remark earned him the nickname "Slick Willie." In March, 1996 he was at it again. This time he "didn't remember" making illegal fund raising calls "from the Oval Office." So he was not exactly lying if either he made them from another location in the White House or even if he made them from there - he just "didn't remember." In May of 1997 he "didn't remember" having a state trooper summon a woman to a private meeting with him.

The student should now do Exercise 16 on Moderate to Fallacious Arguments.

PART THREE

EVALUATING
UNSUPPORTED BELIEFS

9 JUSTIFICATION, PARADIGMS, AND REASONING

SECTION 9.1: BELIEF, TRUTH AND JUSTIFICATION

This part is concerned with what we should and should not believe. "Epistemology" means the theory of knowledge. "Epistemic agents" are people who try to come to know facts (Double, 1997, p. 10.) *Critical thinking is about becoming good epistemic agents.* Good epistemic agents believe statements when they get epistemic reasons to support the statements. They reject statements when epistemic reasons are against them. When there are neither epistemic reasons for or against a statement, they suspend belief until they get justification for believing one way or another. Non epistemic reasons for beliefs are ones which motivate belief without raising the probability that our beliefs are true. Epistemic ones are "truth tracking," that is, they justify our belief by raising the probability that it is true.

Experience teaches us that actions based on true beliefs are more likely to be successful than ones based on false beliefs. So one of our basic goals as epistemic agents is to use our senses and reasoning to get a large body of true beliefs. When we feel a belief is highly justified or highly unjustified, we say it is "definitely true" (or definitely false.) But truth and falsehood lie in relationships of correspondence and non correspondence between our thoughts and facts in the world. Justification is both an activity and a state which relates our beliefs to truth. Justification as an activity tends to distinguish those of our beliefs which are, in fact, true from those which are false. Being justified as a state helps us hold onto truth.

Justification as a state applies both to persons and to the beliefs themselves. We may say either "Person S is justified in holding belief P," or "Belief P is justified (for S.)" Alston (1985) pointed out that justification is an evaluative, not a factual concept. *Justification is warrant, probability or plausibility, permission to believe for the goal of getting a large number of non-accidentally true beliefs.* Evaluation that a belief is justified is not made from the point of view of what it is "smart" to believe, what feels good, or what it is loyal to believe. Justification is a matter of degree, source and context. Some statements are more justified and others less so. For simplicity and briefness, we will classify most statements as either highly justified, justified, unjustified or highly unjustified. This corresponds to natural ways of evaluating statements as "definitely true," "probably true," "probably false" and "definitely false." A small class of statements, called theological claims, would probably be better classified as non justified. For simplicity this small class will be left out for now.

Critical thinking seeks justification for beliefs. It asks "What is the justification for believing that P?" What exactly makes for justification has been under discussion by philosophers for a long time. In one dialogue Plato has Socrates come to the temporary conclusion that knowledge is true belief which is justified in the sense that the believer can give an account or explanation of the belief. This idea came to be taken as a definition of the necessary and sufficient conditions of knowledge. In other words, S knows that p if, and only if 1) S believes that p; 2) p is true, and 3) S is justified in believing that p. This definition was regarded as satisfactory from about 368 B.C. for about 2,330 years until in 1963. (368 B.C. is when scholars say Plato probably wrote the dialogue in which the definition appeared. Gettier published some counterexamples in a 1963 paper.) These examples showed that a person could sometimes have justified true belief, but not knowledge.

A **counterexample** intends to show a definition, generalization or universal statement to be unjustified, probably false. Gettier counterexamples are generally cases in which some circumstance or fact unknown to the person who believes p "defeats" his or her justification for belief in p. They point to the fact that we want our beliefs to be non-accidentally true. Pollock (1986) gives this example. Suppose S sees a ball which looks red to him. On this basis he correctly judges that it is red. But unknown to him, the ball is lit up by red lights and would look red to him even if it was not red. So he does not have knowledge that it is red even thought he has justified true belief in it. A response to patch up the definition is to add another adjective, "undefeated," in front of "justified." *Knowledge may then be defined as undefeated justified true belief. In other words, S knows that p if, and only if 1) S believes that p; 2) p is true, 3) S is justified in believing that p and 4) S's justification for p is undefeated.*

Does justification for a belief lie entirely in other beliefs or mental states of the believer, or does it depend partly on factors outside of the believer? The view that it depends only on other mental states is called "Internalism." The belief that it rests in part on outside factors is "Externalism." An example on which Internalists and Externalists might differ was given by Bonjour (1985) and discussed by Baergen (1995.)

Bonjour asks us to imagine a man named Norman, who is a completely reliable clairvoyant in some circumstances on some subjects. He has no evidence for or against the existence of clairvoyance or for or against his having this power himself. One day he comes to believe that the President is in New York City. He has no evidence for or against this. But it is true and results from his clairvoyant power under circumstances where it is completely reliable, that is, it has always produced only true beliefs. An internalist would say Norman is unjustified in his belief. He is clueless as to why he should believe that the President is in New York. An Externalist might say Norman is in fact justified in holding his belief even if he doesn't know it is justified.

Internalism comes in two forms, Foundationalism and Coherentism. *Foundationalism* says that some beliefs are basic. They are justified because they are self-evident or undoubtable. Other beliefs are non-basic, justified by being derived from basic beliefs by deduction or induction. *Coherentism* says beliefs are justified by the way they are related to other beliefs. There is no set of basic beliefs from which all others are derived. Externalism comes in two forms. *Probabilism* says that beliefs are justified by the likelihood that they are true. *Reliabilism* says they are justified in terms of the extent to which the process by which the belief was formed generally produces true beliefs. Unreliable processes are interestingly described in Gilovich (1991.)

Critical Thinking is interested in *internal* justification. It seeks to develop ability to justify beliefs and to evaluate claims. Sometimes claims are presented as reasons to support conclusions, sometimes just as claims. We will shortly examine some groups of claims. We will freely adapt from theories of justification whatever seems clearly involved in internal justification or lack of justification of these beliefs. But first, it is necessary to note a couple more points about beliefs.

Our many beliefs are somewhat like the many things a rich man owns. We use the same words, like "having" a thing and a belief, "getting" one, or "holding" one. The rich man can fail to be aware that he owns a specific thing. We can have a belief even if we have never acted on it or thought of it. Yet he, and we, can admit to having a thing or belief if some evidence is pointed out to us that we do, indeed, have it. Beliefs, like things owned, can be organized. The best example of basic and non - basic beliefs is geometry. In geometry hundreds of theorems and constructions are deduced from only five axioms, three or four rules of reasoning and thirty to forty definitions. Beliefs can also be thought of as organized into background and foreground or central and peripheral beliefs.

However, there are significant differences between the collections of our beliefs and the possessions of the rich man. Most of our beliefs are true or false, and justified in some degree or unjustified. Things are neither true nor false, justified or unjustified. Also, beliefs have logical and probability connections with one another which things do not share. **Some claims are not consistent with one another. Some are not inconsistent, yet make others improbable.** *The Principle of Consistency says inconsistent statements can't both be true (in the same senses of all the words.)* This is among the most highly justified statements known to us. To convince yourself of this, recall examples of contradictories and contraries from Chapter Four.

Baergen (1995) gives this example of statements inconsistent in probability. Suppose a set of beliefs includes both the belief that a certain coin is fairly flipped one hundred times and the belief that on this set of flips it comes up heads 100 times. These two statements are not logically inconsistent. However, each makes the other highly improbable.

To complete our comparison, most ownership is voluntary. You get to choose if you want to own things. But most getting of belief is not voluntary. We don't voluntarily choose our beliefs. We can, however, voluntarily *evaluate* our beliefs. In many cases we can revise our estimates of how justified they are in relation to other beliefs. That is one of the things critical thinking is about. Avoidance of inconsistency and probabilistic inconsistency will be major principles in evaluating claims.

Distinctions can be drawn between conditional and non-conditional justification and between prima facie and a fortiori justification. Conditional justification is given to a claim by a valid argument for it. Non-conditional justification is the kind of justification some statements have when they are justified "in themselves" or by evidence which is not in the form of a statement. Examples of statements non-conditionally justified are "a priori" (say Ay PRY-oar-eye) statements and self-made, sincere sensation statements.

The term "prima facie justification" (say pry mah FAY she) is adapted from John Pollock (1986.) Prima facie justified statements are ones which seem justified to us "at first sight." We do not need persuasion or evidence to accept them. *They are ones we are justified in holding unless we have some evidence or reason against holding them.* S's statement above, "I see a round, red ball," when the ball is lit by a red light, is an example of a prima facie justified statement. When S is told that the ball is lit up by a red light, his former justification is defeated. Such statements are more or less easily *defeasible* (defeat-able.) "A fortiori" (say ay for she OAR eye) means "much more." *An a fortiori justified statement is one which may be defeasible, but is held for stronger reasons than a prima facie justified statement.* It is harder to defeat, if it can be defeated at all.

The distinction between prima facie and a fortiori justified statements is a psychological and epistemological one. It is a relative distinction and is not exclusive. A statement originally prima facie justified can become unjustified when its justification is defeated and rejustified, a fortiori justified, when it is confronted with a defeater, but there is a defeater of the defeater.

Lehrer and Paxson (1969) developed this example of defeating defeaters. You see a man walk into a library. He hides a book under his coat and takes it out of the library. You are sure it was Tom Grabit, because you saw him yesterday in class. This is defeated when Tom's mom, Mrs. Grabit, says that Tom was a thousand miles away but his identical twin brother John was in the library. But suppose the police chief to whom you report tells you that Mrs. Grabit is a known pathological liar. There is no John Grabit. She has told the same type of lie to keep Tom out of trouble before. This defeats the defeater. In this case the original claim "Tom Grabit stole the book" was prima facie justified, defeated, and now is both prima facie and a fortiori justified, although we are more inclined to call it just "a fortiori justified."

Three fields produce claims with high level a fortiori justification. In philosophy the process called "dialectic" involves putting forth claims, objections and replies, arguments and counter arguments. In science, hypotheses are put forth, predictions made and the hypotheses are confirmed or defeated. When defeated, new hypotheses are tried. Finally, in law evidence is often put forth to prove a charge, to defeat a claim or defeat a defeater claim. Guilty verdicts require high a fortiori justification, justification "beyond a reasonable doubt."

SECTION 9.2:   PARADIGMS OF HIGHLY JUSTIFIED BELIEFS

A particularly clear example of something is called a "paradigm" (say PAH rah dime.) Since the writings of Ludwig Wittgenstein and Thomas Kuhn philosophers have come to recognize the importance of paradigms to understanding concepts. After stating paradigms we can consider how close or far away other cases are from them. We can put cases into some sort of near - to - far - away order. To learn how to evaluate unsupported claims it will be good to set forth paradigms of highly justified, justified, unjustified and highly unjustified claims. It will help to give examples with their degrees of justification.

One kind of prima facie, non-conditionally highly justified statement comes from logic. The Principle of Consistency is one. (1) "Inconsistent statements can't both be true (in the same senses of all the words.)" Others are rules of inference which come from geometry. An example would be (2) "A thing is identical with itself" or, in symbols, "A=A." Can you imagine a thing not being identical with itself? "I'm not myself today" makes sense when taken to mean "I'm not feeling or reacting as I usually do." But "I'm not me" doesn't seem to make sense or even be imaginable. Other examples would include (3) "Things equal to the same thing are equal to each other." (4) "If equals are added to or subtracted from equals, the results are equal." (5) "Wholes are greater than their proper parts."

Rene Descartes (say day-CART) wrote a book called *Meditations*. In it, he tried to sort through his beliefs, to justify and organize them from most highly justified foundations, or basic beliefs to less highly justified ones. He seems to have had in mind statements which are prima facie and non-conditionally highly justified, like (6) "I am now doubting." He also claimed that "I" means only "a being which thinks." So if (6) is very highly justified, then (7) "I exist" must be also. (Descartes thought he was arguing that (6) was justified in the highest degree so (7) must be conditionally justified.) We will call such highly justified statements "Cartesian statements."

Thinking seems to be intentional. "Intentional" means it is about something. Whenever you talk about experiencing "things," you are using "physical object language." Descartes recognized that all such statements are less highly justified than what might be called "sensation statements." Self-made sensation statements are sincere descriptions of what one is sensing at the moment. Statements like (8) "I am sensing roundly and redly now," made to oneself or others when no deception is present, would be self-made sensation statements. Statements like (9) "I see a round, red ball" are self-made physical object statements. Such statements are less justified than ones like (8) because it is at least logically possible that you are having an hallucination or a dream. This situation would leave (8) true and (9) false. Sensation statements made by others in the same words as (8) are less justified than our own because the others could be lying or pretending for some reason. Sensation statements made about others, like *"She* is sensing roundly and redly now" are also less justified than (8.) Their justification requires an inference based on reasons including that she has the same qualities of experience that you have when you use words like "red."

Other-made physical object statements present a problem for evaluation. In a textbook exercises can only be given missing a context of use. To meet this problem, the student should adopt what will be called the *Socratic skeptical attitude.* This is the attitude that generally speaking, *"I am not going to agree that a statement is justified if I don't know who or what it is about."* The student will get exercises like this. If the statement refers to something that can be looked up in a credible source, then the student has the choice of doing the research work to get more credit for an answer or being less ambitious and simply evaluating the statement as unjustified or highly unjustified.

Suppose the problem is to evaluate (10) "I am over 7' 6" tall." Do not assume that "I" refers to yourself! One cannot look this up anywhere. The Socratic, skeptical attitude requires that it be evaluated as "highly unjustified because it is not known who 'I' refers to and it is very improbable. Most beings known to be capable of making statements are humans and less than 7' 6" tall." Similarly, if the statement was (11) "I am under 2' tall," it would get a little credit to evaluate it as unjustified because one did not know who it referred to. However it would get more credit to be clever and explain that "it is unjustified or highly so because all known beings capable of making statements are over the birth height of human babies (21-24 inches.)"

Rules of inference like 1 - 5 have been called "self-evident," or "indubitable," not able to be doubted. They are "incorrigible," not able to be corrected, or "infallible" (not able to be wrong.) Davis (1993. p. 172) suggests three marks or criteria of self-evident statements. They are believed with the deepest conviction. We can not think up any experiment which might show them to be false. Finally, it seems unimaginable that they are false. For comparison, consider a claim from the Declaration of Independence. It says there "We hold these truths to be self-evident: That (12) all men are created equal." Consider the statement (12) to mean "people are all equal in physical power or social position at birth." In this sense it certainly is not self-evident. It seems highly unjustified. Some people are born healthy, some ill, some handicapped. Some are born to wealth and high status. Others are born to poverty and discrimination by race, sex or class. "Self-evidence" in this statement meant something different. It was used to make the claim, however insincere, that the signers intended to construct a society in which people would have equality of rights.

Philosophers have developed some distinctions to mark off prima facie justified statements from others of lower degrees of justification. Statements 1 - 5 have been called "necessary truths," ones which are true in all possible worlds. Necessary falsehoods would be statements false in all possible worlds. Statements like 6 - 10 are "contingent statements," that is, they are true in some possible worlds and false in others.

Other similar distinctions are between *"a priori"* and *"a posteriori"* ("empirical") statements and between *analytic* and *synthetic* statements. *A priori statements are ones whose truth can be known without inductive sampling* (Double, 1997, p. 6) *Empirical ones are ones whose truth or falsity can only be justified by inductive sampling.* A priori truths are supposed to be universally true, discoverable merely by thought. Empirical truths are supposed to be only generally true, and discoverable only by experience.

Analytic statements are ones whose truth or falsehood depends solely on the meanings of words in them. They are supposed to be merely explicative. The negations of analytic truths are self-contradictory. One of Kant's examples of an analytic statement was: (13) "All bodies are extended." Other examples of analytic truths would be (14) "A mother is a female parent" and (15) "Old computers are computers." *Synthetic statements are ones whose truth or falsity does not depend solely one the meanings of their words.* They put together genuinely separate ideas in the subject and predicates. Examples of synthetic statements would include almost any claim as to a "matter of fact" like (16) "Lake Erie is in North America" or (17) "Lake Erie is not in North America." Such statements are contingently either true or false. They are less and differently justified from analytic ones.

So far we appear to have two exclusive distinctions. How are they related to each other? David Hume and most other philosophers thought that all analytic truths were a priori and vice versa. They also thought that all synthetic statements were empirical and vice versa. Kant believed that there are also a priori synthetic truths, ones which can be known independently of experience, which are universal and necessary and yet whose predicates join a genuinely separate idea to that of the subject. Kant's examples of a priori synthetic statements were: (18) "All bodies have weight," (19) "The shortest distance between two points is a straight line," and (20) "Every event has a cause." Notice the difference between (20) and the statement (21) "Every effect has a cause." (21) is an analytic statement and necessarily true just by the meanings of the words in it.

We will say that some claims are justified or unjustified *by meanings of words in them*. Those that are justified by the meanings of words in them, like 11 - 14, are analytic truths and very highly justified. Definitions and consequences of definitions are like this. Those that are unjustified just by the meanings of words in them are called *self - contradictory*. The contradictories of 13 - 15 are self-contradictory. An Examples would include (22) "A mother is not a female parent" and (23) "Old computers are not computers." By contrast, synthetic statements are justified or unjustified by evidence that they correspondence or do not correspond with reality or facts.

Mathematics provides other types of highly justified statements. Equations of arithmetic are highly justified. Consider (24) "7 + 5 = 12." Kant thought that such statements were synthetic. Why? Modern logicians have developed axiom systems that justify such equations conditionally. Suppose I tell or show a person unacquainted with Arabic numerals that by "+" I mean the operation of adding, putting together. I then show him three groups of sticks: /////, /////// and /////////////. Still, to get him to understand, above the first group I must put a sign with "5" on it, above the second "7" and above the third "12". Otherwise he does not learn that "5" means ///// and so on. Then I push the first group against the second. Finally I take each stick of the "added" groups and put it below a stick of the third group. I have created what mathematicians call "a one - to- one correspondence" between members of the one group and members of the other. I have also "proved" that 7 + 5 = 12.

The need to put the numerals "5", "7" and "12" above the groups is probably why Kant said such statements are a priori but synthetic. Most philosophers think that the connection between signs like "5" and objects or classes is a non-necessary empirical connection. That is why some philosophers regard such statements as a little less justified than analytic ones. But the same thing applies to the words in "analytic" sentences. They are not "natural signs" either. Later, different consistent, useful number systems were created in which perhaps 7 + 5 does not equal 12. But this does not change the fact that such equation statements are justified to a very high degree. They can be proved, easily, and are part of a deductive system with rules and definitions known to many of us.

The same points can be made of theorems in geometry, such as the Pythagorean Theorem. (25) "The square on the hypotenuse of a Euclidian plane right angle triangle is equal to the square on the two other sides." This is usually put in the formula $a^2 + b^2 = c^2$. In Plato's dialogue "Meno," he has Socrates draw a diagram and ask questions of a slave boy about the diagram. He gets the boy to state another theorem of geometry. The point is, the boy had never studied any geometry. Nevertheless he can be led to make and be highly conditionally and a forteriori justified in stating a theorem of geometry.

The philosopher Thomas Hobbes relates that when he first picked up Euclid's Geometry and opened it, he looked at a theorem and thought that it was impossible. So he went back through its proof and further back until, at the beginning, he realized it was necessary. This is a process of thinking which changed the status of the theorem from highly unjustified to highly justified for him. By following the reasoning it became highly justified conditionally. If he accepted the axioms as unconditionally justified, then the theorem deduced from them inherited their prima facie quality but also became a fortiori justified for him.

There are many obstacles to becoming a critical thinker so truth tracking methods are essential to it. Double (1997, p. 10) lists these obstacles: 1) inattention to whether our own beliefs are justified, 2) sticking to our beliefs too much and not looking at contrary evidence, 3) defense of our own egos, 4) wishful thinking, 5) desire to conform to others, 6) reinforcement of our beliefs by others, 7) confusion over "epistemic authority," what really justifies belief, and 8) mistaking firmness of belief for an indicator of truth. Deductively valid and strong forms of reasoning are powerful truth tracking methods. This is illustrated in the next section.

SECTION 9.3: REASONING AS A SOURCE OF CONDITIONAL JUSTIFICATION

By reasoning, we can come to be conditionally justified in the highest degree in believing even visual matters. This is true even of visual matters that cannot be known to a person, because of circumstances, by sight. There is an old logic problem about a jailer who has three prisoners (call them "1," "2" and "3.") The first prisoner has normal vision. The second has only one eye. The third is totally blind. The jailer told them that from 3 white hats and 2 red hats he would pick 3 hats and put them on the prisoner's heads. Each of the prisoners was prevented from seeing what color hat he had on his own head. The jailer brought them together and told each of them in turn that they could go free if they could tell him with the highest justification what color hat they had on their own head. The first prisoner with normal eyes admitted that he couldn't tell to this degree of justification.

Here is a picture of the situation. The blind prisoner reasoned from the fact that the first prisoner couldn't tell, that 2 and 3, himself, could not both have red hats on. (If 1 had seen two red hats on them, 1 could have said with certainty that he had a white one on.)

Reasoning as a Power: The Prisoners and Hats Problem

3 hats are picked from among 3 white and 2 red ones.

The second prisoner with one eye to see the colors of the hats on the others' heads had to admit that he couldn't tell for certain either. Can you now figure out the reasoning of the third, blind prisoner? From the fact that 2 could not tell, the blind prisoner was able to draw the conclusion that 1 and 3 did not both have red hats on. (If 2 had seen two red hats, then he could have told with certainty that he had a white hat on.)

Then the blind prisoner reasoned it out and said "I know for certain that I must have a white hat on." He was right and the jailer had to let him go.

After the one eyed man said "I don't know," the blind prisoner was in a position to reason this way. "If I have a red hat on, then 2 would have been able to tell that he had a white one on, because he knows that 2 and 3 do not both have red hats on. Since 2 can't tell, I must have a white hat on." Let us take (26) "I have a white hat on" as said by the blind prisoner as an example of a statement justified in the highest degree conditionally.

The point of the prisoners problem is that *reasoning has a real power of extending our beliefs,* sometimes even with the highest degree of conditional justification. Sometimes it can do so even without sight. Sometimes it can do so even about visual facts which people with vision are not in a position to know! We are all like blind prisoners in our knowledge of the world. Our senses and ability to travel to "see for ourselves" is very limited. Yet there is very much that we can be highly justified in believing about the world by using a combination of instruments to extend our senses *and* reasoning.

There is one qualification which must be put on high conditional justification. Goldman (1967) gives this example. Suppose S has strong justification for believing Q: "J. owns a Ford." S has a friend, B. Choosing Barcelona, Spain, at random, S validly deduces by addition a statement P: "Either J. owns a Ford or B. is in Barcelona." Suppose further that J. does not own a Ford but by accident B is in Barcelona. Since "Q, therefore P" is deductively valid, S has high conditional justification for P. However, he does not know it.

What makes P true is the fact that B is in Barcelona. This suggests that our definition of knowledge needs a fifth qualification. **S knows that p if, and only if: 1) S believes that p; 2) p is true, 3) S is justified in believing that p , 4) S's justification for p is undefeated and 5) S's belief that p is caused, in an appropriate way, by the fact that p.** By so strict a standard, we know much less than we think we know.

Inductive reasoning also provides conditional justification, although in lower degree. Here is an example. The moon rotates on its axis about as slowly as it goes around the earth. So nobody has ever and perhaps nobody will ever see about 40% of its' surface. But the same conditions of lack of atmosphere, exposure to comets and meteorites, and so forth, which exist on the visible side exist on the non-visible side. So we can conclude that (27) "it is probable that the non-visible side of the moon has craters, mountains, and lava 'seas' like the visible side."

Conversational implicature, or presumptive reasoning of the sort found in moderate arguments dealt with in Chapter Eight provides some lesser conditional justification. When, for example, an authority is accepted by both sides in a discussion, is an authority in the field of a claim "p" and makes claim "p", then "p" is justified so far as the discussion goes, unless and until it is made unjustified.

Note that there are also unreliable reasoning processes. Gilovich (1991) gives an excellent treatment of some. Humans often reason from random data to some sort of pattern. People draw conclusions from too little or unrepresentative data. They interpret ambiguous and inconsistent data in ways that fit their preconceived theories. Our motives, frequently our self-esteem, combine with erroneous reasoning from data to produce incorrect but self-serving beliefs. This will be dealt with in some detail below.

People reason that if something is told to them, it is original or only second hand from that source. So *we too often believe what we are told.* We tend to overlook the fact that information is often second hand or more remote from the original source. That applies to almost everything in this very text. The author has attempted to check many quoted sources. The best policy for any student, even of this text, is to check out claims for herself. We also fail to notice that the person or medium relaying information to us often has a motive to sharpen some elements of a story and flatten others to prove his or her message worthy of our attention. We also over-estimate the number of people who think like us.

SECTION 9.4:   WORLD VIEWS, WISHFUL THINKING AND SELF-DECEPTION

Standard reference works, government publications, news media and textbooks are generally credible sources. However, there are areas where they are biased by self - interest, self - deception, wishful thinking or editing. "Research" by lobbying groups and executive and congressional staff members is to be trusted only as to the interest of the person or group it is written for. Writers of such "research" are employees of corporations, foundations, unions or elected politicians. They leave out or minimize negative things which, if publicized, would offend their employers or funding sources.

There are, on the other hand, critical, reality oriented, and even science-driven governmental bodies whose reports are produced by career civil servants and which are generally reliable. Examples of such bodies would be the U.S. Bureaus of the Census, Labor Statistics, General Accounting Office, Congressional Budget Office, Surgeon General, Centers for Disease Control, Health and Human Services, and Inspector General's offices. Reports of United Nations bodies are likely to involve persons from other countries. This gives them a different perspective on the U. S. and world affairs which should be valued rather than rejected out of knee-jerk nationalism. Reports of non governmental voluntary organizations (N.G.O.'s) like the International Red Cross, the World Watch Institute, The People-Centered Development Forum and Amnesty International can also be trusted.

From parents, siblings, priests, peers, teachers, newspapers, magazines and TV we get a large part of our **world view**. *A world view is a set of general beliefs about ourselves, family, our nation and the rest of the planet.* It includes general beliefs about our place in the universe, human nature and economic systems. Consider news media. News media are businesses which don't want to lose money by criticizing advertisers or contradicting readers' or viewers' prejudices (Kahane, 1992, p. 220.) An example is this. In 1976 20 older, white male veterans died of a new disease called "Legionnaire's Disease." The New York Times published 33 articles about it, 11 on the front page, in the first 30 days of the epidemic. By the end of 1982, 2 years into the AIDS epidemic, with 634 cases reported, the Times had only published 6 articles about it, none on the front page (Public Media Center, 1997.) American society, government and science got started slowly on AIDS, and is still slow in educating people how to avoid it, because of irrational hatred of its original U. S. victims: homosexuals, minorities, sex workers, and victims of drug pushers. Where AIDS started, it is a disease of heterosexual non addicts.

Ownership of news media is highly concentrated. For example, in recent years NBC has been owned by G. E., CBS by Westinghouse, ABC by Disney. Newspapers are owned by large chains: Knight-Ridder, Gannett, and Newhouse Communications. In a recent election year about 640 papers editorially endorsed the Republican presidential candidate, only somewhat over 100 endorsed the Democrat. None of any significant circulation endorsed any alternative candidate. Reporters and editors go through a milling process. Those who want to report truths contrary to the interests of the owners quickly learn that they can not do so or they will be edited out and eventually fired. Thus "freedom of the press" comes to belong to those who own the press.

Newspapers print all sorts of superstitious paranormal claims without challenge. They practically never follow them up. It is almost never possible to reach groups making such claims (MacDougall, 1983, p. ix.) Textbooks too are censored by editors or writers themselves. They want to sell books, not get them rejected by redneck school board members offended at the truth about some events of past history.

The world view we develop has a powerful influence on how warranted, how credible we find unsupported claims. Parenti (1986) gives these examples. During the Cold War owners of American news media did not allow favorable reporting of improvements in the quality of life in countries which had nationalist revolutions with Soviet help, like Cuba or Nicaragua. They also suppressed reporting of torture and death squads by governments favorable to corporate interests, at least until those governments became so intolerable that they were going to be overthrown. However, such suppression left ordinary Americans finding it hard to believe truths about improvements in life conditions or death squad activity on the few occasions that they were reported by fringe sources.

Gilovich (1991) makes another relevant point. Any communicator needs to prove his communication worthy to the recipient. One way to do this is to make it entertaining. The goal of being informative can conflict with that of being entertaining. Entertainment value is increased by sharpening some points and flattening other "detail" of context which may, nevertheless, be very important. Having to sell newspapers or get audience shares and advertising causes news media to turn out a product better called "infotainment" than "news."

Time, Newsweek and NBC news have each been caught doctoring photos or film, ABC for fraud in doing an undercover story. TV news has broadcast video press releases done by public relations firms as news.

Talk shows look for dysfunctional people and don't check their stories too well for truth. At least one, the Jerry Springer show, was fooled. Three Canadian comedians went on and pretended to be a dysfunctional love triangle. People who watch such shows should remember that they are for entertainment, not intellectual development. The participants go on for money and may be pretending, exaggerating, acting, looking to make more money by having a book written, etc. Lately, even staid old networks have taken to showing "Real TV" videos during "sweeps" weeks which make "entertainment" out of disaster or death, almost as bad as "snuff" flicks, if the footage is real.

There are certain desirable qualities to have in any world view. Above all, it should *correspond to the facts.* Further, it should be as *comprehensive* as possible. It should be *consistent.* It should be more than consistent. It should be *coherent* in the sense of having some over-all structure. The deductive structure of geometry is one example of what is meant by structure. Science is another. Rescher (1976) provided another framework for dealing with cognitively dissonant, conflicting information.

There are some powerful parts of human nature which distort our world views, making us poor epistemic agents. The main ones are *ego, self-deception* and *wishful thinking.* "Egotism" means thinking that you are better than others "Egoism" means "looking out for Number One." Both often lead to "rationalization." Rationalization is reasoning from reasons which falsely favor oneself and ones' group. In general, people tend to think too highly of themselves, their own family members, school, church, nation. They also think too lowly of others. Gilovich cites surveys which show that large majorities of people think that they are more intelligent, fair-minded, less prejudiced, and better drivers than the average person. It is mathematically impossible for large majorities to be better than average. We are able to deceive ourselves, because these selves are loose-knit collections of subsystems, not single souls which can "see" all our beliefs at once.

Excess self - esteem causes inconsistent thinking. For example, most people know that the politicians in our federal government aren't doing a good job, but most people surveyed think *their own representative* is doing an at least a fair job. Another example would be that most people (except current students!) think schools are failing badly. However they also think that *their own* school is doing a pretty good job. Of course current students too, are influenced by egotism. Who wants to admit, "I am getting a lousy education?"

Self - deception is another big distorter of our world views. Self - deception means fooling oneself, kidding oneself. There are fairly standard examples of deceptions we sometimes use on others because of our jobs or roles in life and ones we use on ourselves. Here first are some *standard other - deceptions:* excuses, lies, rationalizations often made by people in particular positions. "The check is in the mail." "You'll have your car back by noon, Sir." "Of course I'll still respect you in the morning!" "My athletic scholarship doesn't give me enough money for textbooks." "You can earn a 200% profit and your money is completely safe." "This book will change your life!" "Affirmative Action gives them everything I have to work or pay for." " If you don't buy it now, it won't be available later." "I saw these 3 problems, but I didn't see the 7 problems on the other side of the test." Last let's mention the one which made a lot of people in the Midwest miserable in the Summer of 1993 and Spring of 1997: "The river never gets high enough to flood this property."

Now here are examples of *self* - deceptions. How many of them does the reader kid him or herself with? The smoker says: "I've smoked for 25 years. It can't hurt me any more now." A student doing poorly in college thinks: "I'm not lazy. My courses are dull and irrelevant to my interests." Who signed up for those courses? This author once heard a heavy - set lady in front of a three way mirror turn to her friend and say: "This dress makes me look fat." Styling can have a dramatic effect on appearance. In this case, however, it was her fat that made her look fat. "Aww... Just one drink in the morning to take the edge off can't hurt." "I can eat 'junk food' so long as I get exercise." "Because I'm a white male, these liberal profs. won't give me a break." "I control my cocaine use, it doesn't control me." "So it keeps opening and bleeding.

So what! It's just a little mole!" (If it is on your body, see a real doctor at once. It may be skin cancer.) "Our marriage could have worked, if she'd just been half - way reasonable." The problem was all hers, I wasn't in the least at fault!

Optimism is better than pessimism, because life is action and an optimistic person will act. A pessimistic one will be slow or weak in action or paralyzed by pessimism. But there are two kinds of optimism. *Wishful thinking* is optimistic belief that something is true because you want it to be true. *Rational hope*, on the other hand, is optimistic belief that something is true based on evidence. Let's conclude by illustrating this distinction with somRI)uestions which are beyond the scope of this book. Which of the following are examples of rational hope based on evidence? Which ones are examples of wishful thinking, and s ŸN-deception? "If I study hard and party less, I can improve my grades." "If we *pray* sincerely for world peace, social justice, a cleaner environment and better future for our kids, God will make it happen." "If we *work* for peace, justice, a cleaner environment, maybe we can make a better future." "If I take good care of myself, I can beat the odds and live longer than expected, even though I will eventually die." "I have a second father: eternal, all-powerful, who loves me and will make everything turn out alright in the end." "I will survive death and live again forever in a place even better than the earth."

Wishful thinking and self-deception may be necessary at extreme crises in life, such as when a person has to face dying. Then they serve to reduce anxiety. Can it be though, that a mature, critical thinking person does not need these crutches during most of his or her life? The borderline between rational hope and wishful thinking is not always clear. But it is always clear that beliefs based on wishful thinking and self-deception as opposed to rational hope are unwarranted and not likely to contribute to truth, sound argument or rational action.

SECTION 9.5: WARRANT AND PROBABILITY

"Warrant" means belief-worthiness, credibility, or assertability based on justification or reasonable grounds. A warranted statement is worthy of belief, credible or assertible. It is a statement a person will classify as "definitely true" or "probably true" because she feels she has good reasons for accepting it. She does not need to be able to present those reasons in a sound argument right at the moment she judges the statement to be warranted. But she should be able to give some account of why the statement is warranted. An unwarranted claim is one which is not worthy of belief, because *either* there are no good reasons to believe it or there are good reasons *not* to believe it.

All true statements ought to be warranted. But we do not find them all to be such. Furthermore, *some warranted statements are not true.* Sometimes we can be justified in accepting a claim tentatively if the evidence we have is in favor of it, even if it later turns out to be false. Critical thinkers know that critical thinking itself and scientific method, and not either bias or any system of metaphysics or religion, are our best guides to determining the truth or falsehood, warrant or unwarrantedness of any statement which puts together words about things in our experience.

An unsupported claim is warranted if either it is an analytic statement, or it comes from a credible source, or what it claims is something probable, and it does not conflict with what you have observed, your background beliefs or other warranted claims.

A credible source is a person known to you to make generally warranted statements or an expert. Expertise is demonstrated by education, experience, accomplishments, reputation, or being an eyewitness under good conditions. Often the name of an authority is used to argue for a conclusion or especially to advertise a product or candidate. Such arguments from authority were dealt with in Chapter Eight.

Probability: *usual, normal, or ordinary occurences are explainable by scientifically established laws of nature. Such regular events are probable. Unusual, or extraordinary occurences which would violate laws of nature are improbable.* Statements claiming extraordinary events without extraordinary proof are unwarranted. The more unusual, abnormal or extraordinary the event claimed, the more unwarranted the statement. Consider the old nursery rhyme: "The cow jumped over the moon." Even children do not believe this. They know from experience that this is very improbable. *A critical thinker regularly applies his or her sense of probability to judge claims to be warranted or unwarranted.*

An understanding of basic facts about probability is another truth tracking method. Two events are independent of each other if the occurrence or non-occurrence of one has no effect whatever on the occurrence or non occurrence of the other. There is a simple law governing the probability of independent events. We can illustrate it with the possible outcomes of tossing a coin. Assume for simplicity that we don't have to deal with the possibility that it will land on its edge. For one toss, there are only two possible outcomes: heads or tails. The probability of each is 1 in 2, 1/2 or .5 If we toss it twice, or toss 2 coins once, there are 4 equally possible outcomes: H - H, H - T, T - H, and T - T. The probability of both heads is thus 1/2 x 1/2 or 1/4, .25. The probability of no heads is also 1/2 x 1/2 or .25. However, there are two ways that we can have one head and one tail (H-T and T-H) so this probability is .25 +.25 or .5 Letting "P(a)" stand for "the probability of event a", the rule here is: *The probability of independent events jointly occurring is a multiple of the probabilities of the individual events.* P(a and b) = P(a) x P(b). Since probabilities are fractions or decimals, when multiplied the result always gets smaller, not bigger. This simple fact has many consequences for critical thinking which most people don't realize.

If we make a bar chart for these coin toss probabilities it looks like this.

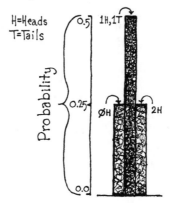

Now suppose we flip a coin 6 times, or make 6 flips of the same coin. The probability of all heads or no heads is only 1/2 times itself 6 times (1/64). Because there are always more ways of getting combinations of heads and tails, the probability of combinations of heads and tails is greater. The highest probability will be for equal numbers of heads and tails. Of all the 64 combinations we could get, 20 have 3 heads and 3 tails, 15 have 2 heads, 15 have 4 heads, 6 have 1 or 5 heads,1 has 6 heads and 1 other has 0 heads. This makes the following graph.

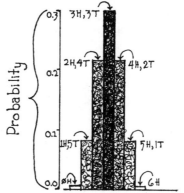

If we flip the coin 16 times, or make 1 flip of 16 coins, or more, the trend continues. The smallest probability is for having no or all heads, the next smallest is for having only one head or all but one head, while the combinations with equal numbers of heads and tails remains the most probable and those with nearly equal distributions of heads and tails are somewhat less probable. This is shown in the following graph.

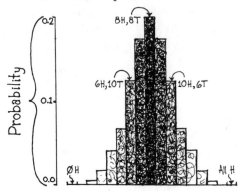

Notice the shape that is starting to emerge at the top of these graphs. If they were line graphs and the points were connected, the more flips we considered, the more the curve would look like what is called a **normal distribution** or **normal curve.**

A normal curve exhibits the distributions of many chance events and human performances on various measurements, tests, contests and characteristics. So it is worth taking a moment to describe some features of the normal distribution. An *arithmetic average* or *mean* is gotten by adding up items of a group and dividing by the number of the items. A *median* is a number such that half the numbers of a group are above it and half below it. A Greek letter "mu" (μ) is used to stand for the mean. A vertical line is drawn from the horizontal base up to the highest point of the curve where this point lies. A *mode* is the most common number in a group. *In a normal distribution the mean, median and mode are all the same and identified with this highest point of the curve.*

Because so many countable events and measured qualities or performances have this normal distribution, it is useful to determine also what are called standard deviations from the mean. For this we use the Greek letter "sigma" (σ). The first standard deviation from the mean, marked by vertical lines on either side of the line to the mean, or the numbers +1 and -1, includes about 68% of all the numbers in the group. The second standard deviation, marked by +2 and -2, includes about 95% of all the numbers and the third, +3, -3 includes almost 100% of the numbers. Thus, knowing the standard deviations is very helpful for getting a sense of the range of variation of a group.

The standard deviation can be called "the spread." When presented with a statistical claim about an "average," a critical thinker wants to know two things: first, *is this a mean, a median or a mode?* Second, *what is the spread?* If the distribution is not normal, and many economic statistics are not normal, the median and mode may be far different and usually lower than the mean. For example, in a company with 1,000 workers earning $27,000 each, 10 managers earning $270,000 each and one owner receiving $2,700,000 the mode is a revealing $27,000; the median is similarly low, while the "average" in the sense of the mean is a little misleadingly high at about $32,335. (Top executive's compensation is even higher than $2,700,000 - see Chapter 15.)

The spread is important because there are actually many normal curves. Here are three, the first with a mean of 70 and standard deviation of 8, the second and third both with means of 50 but one with a narrow spread of only 4, while the second has a spread of 12.

Three Normal Distributions with Differing Spreads

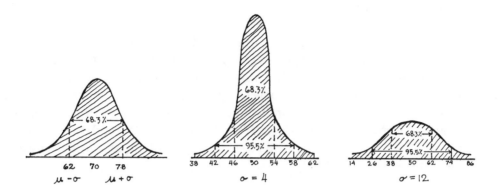

To conclude, when we compare human groups on vague qualities like "intelligence" or "strength," what is found first is that there are differing normal curves for different groups. However, the situation is not at all simple. *There are extremely large areas of overlap,* so large that no generalizations can be made which form premises for strong arguments about how individuals should be treated.

Claims like "Women are not strong enough to be firefighters" or "Blacks are not as intelligent as whites" are "sophomoric generalizations," insufficiently defined, under-quantified, and made for discriminatory purposes. The whole logic of Chapter Six is designed to show that such statements are inaccurate and need to be replaced. Intelligence comes in many forms and neither individuals nor races can be ranked in a straight line on "it," as if "it" were one kind of thing only. I.Q. tests are fair predictors of school performance, because school work 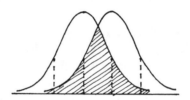 is set up to reward data skills much more than people and thing skills. (Thing skills are essential even for experimental physicists to design equipment to make observations or test theories.) Nor can we separate the effects of heredity from environment. See Fraser (1995, p. 5-10) for arguments on the so-called "bell curve." Our economic system, mechanized as it is, also unequally rewards data skills. No one should confuse what our market system rewards with most money with what is most valuable or needed by human beings.

Performances and qualities which show a normal curve, when repeatedly measured, show what is called "regression to the mean." Once a norm and high or low are established, the tendency for a repeat measurement is to be closer to the mean again than to the high or low. This regression is often misinterpreted. Gilovich (1991) gives the example of thinking that one should not praise good performance by pilots in hitting targets because if one does, the praised pilot gets careless and then misses. Regression to the mean is at work here, not psychological causation. If high I. Q. parents find themselves disappointed with normal children, they ought to find something other than data skills to be proud of in their children. The best argument against selective breeding is that people of low normal I. Q., without heritable defects, by regression, are likely to have children higher in I. Q. than they are.

There is an important point which needs to be added to the earlier claim that "usual, normal, or ordinary occurrences are probable while unusual, abnormal, or extraordinary events are improbable. Because of how probability works, *many amazing coincidences are highly probable.* Paulos (1988) gives numerous examples. A simple example is this. If one shuffles a deck of cards thoroughly, and deals any hand of any specific 13 cards, the probability of exactly that set of cards being drawn is only 1 in 635,013,559,600. Two points follow. First, in a sense, enormously improbable events are usual, normal, ordinary occurrences. We can deal hands of bridge every day. Second, when think we are fantastically lucky or unlucky, it is because of an interpretation or valuation *we* put on events, not because there is some wondrous harmony or evil conspiracy at work in the universe. The chance of getting all 13 spades is no more, no less, than of getting any other specific set of cards.

Paulos makes several related points: "A tendency to drastically underestimate the frequency of coincidences is a prime characteristic of innumerates, who generally accord great significance to correspondences of all sorts while attributing too little significance to less flashy statistical evidence. If they anticipate someone else's thought, or have a dream which seems to come true... this is considered proof of some wondrous but mysterious harmony that somehow holds in their personal universe. Few experiences are more dispiriting to me than meeting someone who seems intelligent and open to the world but who immediately inquires about my Zodiac sign and then begins to note characteristics of my personality consistent with that sign (whatever sign I give them)" (Paulos, p. 35).

As to that "less flashy statistical evidence" the biggest problem comes about from complexity and conflicting numbers. One type of this problem arises out of conflicts between base rates or projections and personal experience. Gilovich (1991) deals with this. During the early 1990's AIDS activists estimated that "1 in 10 babies may be AIDS victims" and "1 in 5 heterosexuals could be dead from AIDS in the next 3 years." Notice the weasel words "may" and "could be." *Weasel words* are qualifications which make a statement ambiguous and allow the maker to escape falsification. When we claimed a person could make "up to" $100 per day we were not claiming he would make even one cent.

Andersen (1997) gives a couple examples. Murders of 23 black children in Atlanta, Georgia and the kidnapping of Adam Walsh made child kidnappings a movie-of-the-week social issue. Estimates were printed of 20,000; 50,000, even 100,000 children kidnapped per year. Andersen did simple arithmetic to see how many kids such estimates would mean for New York City. He then called police departments. He asked how many reports of child kidnappings they actually had. The results were far fewer reports than would support such estimates. It has been claimed that every day 5,000 Americans were trying cocaine for the first time. In 1987 this incredible factoid appeared in official data of the National Institute on Drug Abuse. In fact, Andersen himself had constructed this statistic in 1983. He took what he thought was a credible 1982 estimate of Americans who used cocaine and subtracted from it the comparable 1980 estimate. Then he divided the result by 720 (days in two years.) According to Charen (1994) two feminist authors wrote in books that 150,000 females die of anorexia per year. However, the National Center for Health Statistics says the annual death toll is fewer than 100.

One problem Gilovich mentions with such claims is that it can be very difficult to get accurate, relevant base rate statistics. How can any estimate of such illegal activities, usually done in secret and not admitted, be gotten at all? Personal experience should be distrusted when it conflicts with well established statistical generalizations. However, one should multiply out or divide any statistical projection and compare the result to one's experience. Facts should be trusted, but the reliability of sources of projections needs to be considered. Vivid personal testimony should not be mistaken for evidence about how common a problem may be.

Sometimes there are apparently conflicting statistical claims and conclusions based on them. During the Vietnam war it became an issue as to how much support the so called "Vietcong" were receiving from out - of - country communist sources. Statistical claims ("SC's") and conclusions ("C's") like the following were heard. One side, #1, might say: "(SC) Of the 1500 weapons captured in the enemy stockpile, 247 were Czechoslovakian rifles, 38 were machine guns of Chinese Communist manufacture and 15 were Soviet made 122 mm. rockets. (C) It is obvious from this that the enemy is receiving very substantial aid with its weaponry from Communist sources outside the country." The other side, #2, might argue this way: "(SC) Six times as many of the weapons in the stockpile were of American or allied manufacture as were of Communist manufacture. (C) The enemy is therefore not receiving substantial aid with its weaponry from Communist sources outside the country."

With such a situation, the following possibilities present themselves. A. The statistical claims in the two passages are inconsistent, so that one must be true and the other false. Therefore at least one of the two arguments is unsound. B. The statistical claims in the two passages are not inconsistent and the degree of support that the SC in 1 gives to its conclusion is higher than the degree of support that the SC in 2 gives to its conclusion. C. The SC's in the two positions are not inconsistent and the degree of support that the SC in 2 gives to its' conclusion is higher than the degree of support that the SC in 1 gives to its' conclusion. D. The SC's are not inconsistent and provide about the same amount of support for their conclusions. E. The conclusions are too ambiguous or vague or the statistics are at cross purposes, so the issue is not really resolved by the information given.

The weapons problem, similar to charges and counter charges which occur again and again in civil wars, has some element of vagueness in that it is not defined what constitutes a "substantial" amount of aid. However, a good critical thinker should always reduce *apparently conflicting statistics to the same type of numerical expression if possible.* Here the SC in 1 says that 300/1500ths. or 1/5 of the weapons in the stockpile were of Communist manufacture while the SC in 2 says that "six times as many" were non-communist, in other words, 1/7 were of Communist manufacture. The number of Communist manufactured weapons in the same stockpile presumably cannot be both 1 in 5 and 1 in 7. So A is the best answer for this sort of case. Here is another also with made up numbers: 1. (SC) Surveys reveal that 89% of all Episcopalians support open (integrated) housing while only 81% of Jews do so. (C) Therefore Episcopalians are more favorable to open housing than Jews are. 2. (SC) Just about 1/2 of all demonstrators for open housing are Jews while only 11% of them are Episcopalians. (C) Therefore Jews are more favorable to open hosing than Episcopalians. Here the student should be able to see that the statistical claims in 1 and 2 are not inconsistent and that E is the best alternative. 1 seems to be taking "more favorable" in an extensive sense and 2 seems to be taking it in an intensive sense. We don't know the numbers of Jews and Episcopalians and even if we did, we would have to semantically clarify "more favorable" before that information would be of any use to us.

The Student should now do Exercise 17 on Statistical Problems.

10

SEEING, REASONING AND SCIENTIFIC JUSTIFICATION

SECTION 10.1: SEEING, BELIEVING AND SCIENCE

Carl Sagan (1995, p. 304 ff.) insists that science is open to bizarre and counter intuitive ides that ought to be a source of wonder. Some of the most familiar claims of science seem bizarre and counter intuitive when compared with what is prima facie justified. There is an old saying that "seeing is believing." Statements can become prima facie justified by *looking and seeing for yourself.* Sometimes students get the idea that it is critical thinking to only believe, as justified, what their own eyes "tell them" or things for which they have eyewitness testimony. But this would be a simple-minded and *wrong* position to take! Seeing shouldn't always be believing. A road appearing to get narrower toward the horizon does not cause one to say "Gee, I hope my car wheels will shrink so I can still fit on this road." One knows it is an illusion.

When we describe in physical object language what we think we merely see and sense in other ways, we are in fact *interpreting* our sense experience. This will be illustrated by contrasting some formerly prima facie justified claims with counter intuitive claims scientists now find to be a fortiori justified. What scientists tell us is also based on what *they see* in laboratory experiments and also *reasoning* about what must be so, if we see these things. Most of us automatically hold a prima facie philosophical view called "Naive Realism." "Naive" (say N-eye-eve) means inexperienced. *Naive Realism* says: (28) "We see things as they are." For example, we reason that "Grass is green, because it looks green". We seem to see a world of colored, solid, relatively sharp-edged objects spread out in space around us. So we think that (29) "there is a world of colored, solid, relatively sharp-edged objects spread out in space around us." We have this idea that our eyes are like windows and seeing is simply looking out through them on the "real world," as if no causal process is occurring.

To people before Aristotle it was prima facie justified that (30) "The earth is roughly flat." But additional experience and reasoning had, by Aristotle's time, made a fortiori justified that (31) "The earth is roughly round." If one does not know reasons for this belief, one should wonder why we now believe (31.) Many people who are supposed to be educated in science believe it but cannot give good reasons why. Kuhn (1954, p. 29) gives reasons known by Aristotle. "The hull of a ship sailing from shore disappears before the mast. More of the ship and the sea is visible from a high point than a low point. [Also,] the shadow of the earth on the moon in a lunar eclipse is always circular."

To this day a small number of people believe that the earth is flat. "Flat earthers" are fundamentalists. **Fundamentalism** holds that every sentence of the Bible is *inerrant* (not capable of error, literally true.) The Flat Earth Society makes this argument. Every sentence of the Bible is literally true. So every conclusion drawn by a deductively valid argument from any sentence of it must be true. The Bible says water was created first and it is the nature of water to be flat. Also the Bible repeatedly refers to Heaven as "up." But there would be no "up" if the world were round. So the world cannot be round. So you must choose between the reasoning and evidence of science or the implications of the Bible as literally true in every sentence. If you choose the literal truth of the Bible, you will need to be able to explain something unusual: why photographs of the earth from space seem to show a round planet.

Fewer than 1 in 10 adult Americans can explain a molecule. Only 1 in 5 can explain DNA. Only 2% understand that science is essentially development and testing of theories (National Science Board, 1996, P. 7-8, 10.) One reason is that the phenomena studied by science are often anomalous (unusual) and its' theories inconsistent with prima facie justified claims. The **steps of Scientific Method** are: 1) Observation of an anomalous (unusual) phenomenon. 2) Formation of an hypothesis, also called "inference to the best explanation." 3) Derivation of a prediction from the hypothesis. 4) Testing the prediction by observation and experiment. 5) Drawing a conclusion. If the prediction is true, the hypothesis is confirmed; if false, it is disconfirmed. However, science education is poor. It takes short-cuts and presents theories without the *inferences* by which they were developed. It leaves out "common sense" objections brought against theories and replies to the objections. Scientists like Galileo are easier to understand in many cases than modern textbooks which leave out the reasoning! Justifications for fundamental claims such as "the earth is round" are somewhat complex. They require knowledge of reasons which are not part of everyday experience or life goals. Also, the news media, a profit-making "infotainment" business, do not continuously reeducate us even to such basic facts and the a fortiori justification for them.

A second example is this. It was prima facie justified that (32) "The sun and the moon are almost exactly the same size." But scientists have justified a fortiori that (33) "The sun is roughly 865,000 miles in diameter and the moon about 2,160." The sun is about 400 times bigger than the moon but also about 400 times farther away. This is why the sun and moon look like disks about the size of a coin at arms' length.

Third, it was prima facie justified that (34) "The planets sometimes wander backward through the Zodiac constellations." However, a brilliant Pole, Copernicus, established a fortiori justification for believing that (35) "The earth in its orbit passes or is passed by the planets." Suppose you look at something in a foreground or middle ground position. Next move from one side of it to another. You see it against a different background. Copernicus reasoned that the earth passing or being passed by the planets in circular orbits makes it only *look like* the planets are sometimes moving backward.

Suppose now there are three stars, A, B and C, and that B is much closer to us than A and C. Then if B is close enough, when the three stars are seen from one point of the earth's orbit, they should look a little different than when seen from the other side of the earth's orbit. At one point, B should look closer to A and six months later it should look closer to C. This phenomenon (say "FEH-nah-men-on") called "stellar parallax", was, in fact, finally observed. But there weren't telescopes and star angle measuring tools available to observe this until the 1840's, nearly a couple hundred years after Copernicus and Galileo. So they must have *reasoned* out the conclusion that the earth and planets go around the sun.

Fourth, it was prima facie justified that (36) "The earth stands still and the sun, moon and stars rotate from east to west around it." Copernicus established a fortiori justification for the statement (37) "The earth rotates from west to east as well as revolving around the sun." How fast? Well, would you believe you were going 1,000 miles an hour in rotation? The earth is about 25,000 miles around at the equator. It rotates completely around once every 24 hours from west to east. So if you were at the equator you would be going about 1000 miles an hour just in that one direction! Could you give good reasons to justify believing something as counter intuitive as (37)? Ancient thinkers like Ptolemy (say TAH lem ee) thought that the moon, planets and stars were stuck on big clear crystal balls which went around the earth. Our flat earthers agree with William Jennings Bryan. Bryan was a fundamentalist, who, in the trial of a man named Scopes for teaching evolution, pointed out that Joshua commanded the sun to stand still, not the earth. One should wonder how anyone could reason out that the earth moves, and so fast.

Copernicus's reasons had to do with how much simpler it was to predict the positions of the heavenly bodies assuming (37) than (36). Easier understood reasons were given by Galileo, in his *Dialogues on the Two Great World Systems*. Suppose someone, he argued, climbed up to the dome of a cathedral, and wanted to see the city around him. Would it be more reasonable to turn himself around, or to demand that the whole city turn around under him? Obviously it would be more reasonable for him to turn himself. Similarly, it is more reasonable that the earth turns than the whole universe turns around it.

The planets appear to go around from west to east. It is simpler to say that the earth rotates from west to east than to have the stars rotate from east to west while the planets go the opposite way. Galileo knew about centrifugal force also. This is the force which makes a rotated object tend to fly off in a straight line when you are spinning it around. He figured the planets were far from the earth because it took years for them to go all the way around and that the stars must be even further. So he asked, if the planets and stars are going around on spheres so far out and so fast, why don't they fly off? Finally, he asked, if all these other things are in motion, why shouldn't the earth be in motion also?

Fifth, if you look around a classroom, it is prima facie justified that the bodies in it are at rest. It looks like they need some force to put them in motion. It also looks like moving bodies, like a rolling basketball, always finally come to rest. So Aristotle said that (38) "Rest is the 'natural state' of bodies." Newton developed the theory of gravity and generalized Kepler's laws of the heavenly bodies and the laws of falling bodies developed by Galileo into his First Law of Motion. He thus gave a fortiori justification to the statement (39) "Motion is the natural state of bodies." Newton's First Law says that a body, when in motion, tends to remain in motion and in a straight line at a constant velocity. It doesn't look this way. So one should wonder what *reasoning* could justify such a thought? How about this, just for a start? When you roll a basketball uphill, it slows down. When you roll it downhill, it speeds up. Therefore, when you roll it on a level surface, it should keep rolling at the same speed forever! (It is friction, not having a natural state of rest, which slows it down.)

A sixth point about bodies is this. It was prima facie justified that (40) "Bodies can be definitely located in a certain volume of space." Space seems describable independently of an observer. Space looks to be absolute. But suppose a man is standing beside a railroad. He sees approaching him a train containing a flatbed car on which is a ping pong table and a man bouncing a ball on the table. Suppose he bounces the ball once so that it lands for a second time in what is exactly the same place (for him.) To the man standing beside the tracks the whole train is moving and he will say that the second bounce happened some yards away from the first bounce. So space is relative.

Seventh, it was prima facie justified that (41) "Bodies have no effect on space itself." Space *looks like* just nothing. However, the Theory of Relativity, or rather confirmation of predictions based on it, imply that (42) "Bodies curve space around them." One must wonder at the idea that space can be curved. Eighth, it was prima facie justified that (43) "Speeds may be added infinitely." For example, suppose Julio can throw a baseball 70 miles an hour. However, he needs to throw it 90 miles an hour. So he should be able to get in a car going at least 20 miles an hour and throw it so that 70+20=90 miles per hour. However, scientists named Michelson and Morely provided experimental a fortiori justification that (44) "Speed can't be added beyond the speed of light."

Ninth, it was prima facie justified that (45) "Events can be located in a definite time period without reference to an observer." In other words, time flows uniformly in all places. But physicists have evidence and *reasoning* to the conclusion that (46) "Events can only be located in time with reference to an observer." Time is relative too. The rate of flow of time varies with the velocity of a body. (The closer to the speed of light, the slower time goes.) Is this not a bizarre, astonishing idea?

All this adds up to several conclusions. First, seeing is not a simple matter. We interpret what we see. So the statement "Seeing is believing" is an oversimplification. "Seeing" should not be believing that things are the way we *think* they look! Second, Naive Realism, the view that (28) "We see things as they are," is false. The fact that it takes light time to travel from an object to our eyes implies that we never see things as they are, but at best, as they *were.* You are now highly justified in believing that (47) "We do not see things as they are." Third, the Atomic Theory in particular implies a contrary of (29) "there is a world of colored, solid, relatively sharp-edged objects spread out in space around us." It implies that (48) "Things in the world are not colored, not solid, not relatively sharp-edged." Fourth, all this suggests the thesis of Representative Realism: (49) "What we see is caused by and only in some ways represents things as they are." Fifth, there is plenty that is wondrous and astonishing, even in the most familiar and basic findings of science.

SECTION 10.2:   THEORETICAL TERMS AND SCIENTIFIC EXPLANATION

There are three processes which generally produce highly justified statements. By describing what is generally involved in them we may get clearer on what is required for many statements to be highly justified at least a fortiori. These processes are scientific method, philosophical dialectic and American legal procedure leading up to a verdict. None of them produces or claims to produce eternal truths. Each of them has gone wrong now and then, even spectacularly so. Their specific results have been later shown quite unjustified. This does not prevent them from being generally reliable processes for producing claims whose justification withstands further attempts to defeat them.

In the last section we examined nine pairs of statements. An example was (30) The earth is roughly flat" and (31) "The earth is roughly round." In each case the first was a prima facie justified claim of what is called "folk physics." The other is an inconsistent claim established by scientific method. There the claims were carefully chosen to be about concrete visible objects. But it is notable that scientific method, philosophy and legal procedure all involve technical terms and frequently establish claims about unseen "theoretical entities" such as motives. So we begin with a brief account of theoretical terms.

Thinkers make up words to help talk about things. For example, the Greeks talked about "Zeus's thunderbolts." They meant what we now call "lightning". Suppose an ancient Greek said, "To the west, Zeus's many thunderbolts light the sky." Was she really talking about some real things? In such a case we are inclined to say "yes." In context we could evaluate such a statement as justified. The term "Zeus's thunderbolt's" refers to a sense experience and involves a theoretical entity (being) Zeus, as a proposed cause.

A clearer example of a pure theoretical term would be "epicycle." It was introduced by Ptolemy to explain the apparent backward motion of the planets in the Zodiac. He claimed that the planets went around on "epicycles." Epicycles were little circles on the large circles which they followed in going around the earth. A theoretical term is supposed to stand for some non-sensible thing and to help explain or predict the behavior of sensible things.

Some people seem to behave like two or more different people. Medieval priests tried to explain this strange behavior. Following the Bible, they theorized that such people were "possessed by demons". "Demon" thus became a theoretical term. This led them to practices such as beating such people or making them eat and drink foul substances. The theory was to make the body unpleasant for the demon. This treatment didn't help to explain or predict split personality behavior. Worse yet, it added to the misery of the sick person. So eventually people stopped saying things like (50) "Fat red demons make people violent, while thin green ones make them sad." Were these medieval exorcists really talking about anything when they talked this way? Most of us would be inclined to say "no."

A medieval philosopher named William of Ockham stated a principle of thinking which has come to be called "Ockham's Razor." For him, it was a principle of required sufficient reason to justify claiming that something existed. Its' full expression is something like this. "We are not allowed to affirm a statement to be true or to maintain that a certain thing exists, unless we are forced to do so either by its self-evidence or by revelation or by experience or by logical deduction from either a revealed truth or a statement verified by observation."

A shorter form of Ockham's Razor is *"What can be explained by the assumption of fewer things is vainly (that is uselessly, wrongly) explained by the assumption of more things."* According to an Ockham specialist, Phil. Boehner, Ockham did not actually write the form he is usually quoted as stating: "(Theoretical) entities are not to be multiplied beyond necessity." The Principle is called "Ockham's Razor" because it can be used to "shave off" unnecessary theoretical entities.

Ockham's Razor is a principle of critical thinking which has come to be deeply involved in philosophy and science. "Ontology" means the study of what kinds of beings exist (and maybe of what kinds don't exist.) Let's call the list of things we believe to exist our "ontological commitments." Ockham's Razor says we should be parsimonious (say par sih MOAN e uhs), that is, stingy, in what we believe to exist. We need to have good reason to believe that something exists. It must be necessary to actually explain or predict something. It implies that we should prefer theories which make fewer ontological commitments but explain or predict the same things over theories which require more commitments, provided the simpler theory explains and predicts with the same accuracy.

From examples like "demon" and Ockham's Razor has developed the idea of "the Ontological Fallacy." *The Ontological Fallacy is the fallacy of making a thing out of words.* When people hear a word, particularly a noun, used in a sentence, they automatically think there must be some thing which the noun stands for. But this is not always true, as we see in the case of "possession by demons."

Chemistry developed out of alchemy. Alchemists were using natural processes like burning to try to turn common metals into gold. They found that if you keep all the products of burning or rusting together and weigh them before and after, they actually weigh more after. They had no concept of a gas. So they made up the word "phlogiston" to stand for an alleged substance of fire, "fire-stuff." They said that it was driven out of bodies when they burned or rusted. But no alchemist ever isolated "phlogiston." It didn't help to explain or predict any reactions. Then the concept of a gas was developed. Laviosier isolated oxygen and demonstrated that it was absorbed in burning. Phlogiston could never be isolated. It didn't help really to explain or predict anything. So nobody talked about phlogiston again.

The same use of Ockham's Razor is seen repeatedly in the history of science. In addition to "epicycle," "possession by demons" and "phlogiston," the following words and phrases which were made up, used for a while and then shaved off with Ockham's Razor: "caloric," the so-called substance of heat, "ether," "vital force," "N-rays" and "polywater." Proposed theoretical terms, to function in highly justified claims, must occur in statements which are *testable* and *consistent with other justified claims. The statements must explain and predict events and enable us to act successfully on the world.*

David Hume had presented a philosophical problem called *"The Problem of Induction."* The problem is 'What justifies inductive inference?' For example, why do we think that the sun will rise tomorrow? Because it always has in the past. An example of a "constant conjunction" of properties would be something's being white and a swan. Hume thought that no matter how many white swans you had seen, you were not justified in concluding that all swans are white. According to Hume, it can't be argued with deductive validity that the future will be like the past. Let's call this *the Principle of Induction:* (51) "The future will be like the past." Also, all inductive arguments rely on (51) as an unwritten premise. Therefore no such argument can be used to prove (51) without being circular.

In the late 1950's a philosopher of science named Karl Popper proposed that the problem of induction was insoluble. So he proposed a different method than induction for science, a deductive one. His method claims that a scientific hypothesis is, in essence, a *testable* one. It is one which can never be conclusively verified, proven true. It can, however, be corroborated (say koh ROB oh ray ted.) Corroboration comes in degrees but is not probability. A hypothesis, for Popper, could have a low probability and high corroboration. The scientific way to deal with a hypothesis is to deduce predictions from it and other statements and see if they "come true" or not. If they do, the hypothesis is corroborated. But nature might always change course. So no hypothesis can be conclusively corroborated. However a scientific hypothesis is *conclusively falsifiable.* "Falsifiable" does not mean false! It means there must be some prediction deducible from it and other statements which can be compared to some imaginable experiment or observation which would show it to be false. If there is no such experiment, the hypothesis is unfalsifiable non science.

A good example might be the pair of claims "God is one" and "God is three in one." No prediction arises from them nor any imaginable experiment or observation which could show one of these false or true. They are non science. A good example of cluelessness about this aspect of scientific claims is Stine (1994.) Stine gives directions for construction of dowsing rods, pyramids, and an "energy wheel" which, he claims, works by telekinesis. After the description of how to construct each machine, he has a little section titled "What if it doesn't work?" "Machine" means "something which *reliably* changes direction of force or form of energy." Stine claims that if it doesn't work, it's not because the claim is false, but because you don't have the mental power to make it work! If none of them work under controlled conditions in which one could not influence them physically, what experiment would show that a person lacked the "mental power" rather than that the claim that they work is false in the first place?

Popper's rejection of probability and emphasis on falsification guaranteed that his views could not become widely adopted. Falsification points to a difficulty many people will have in scientific reasoning. Wason's research (1972) on the psychology of reasoning shows that people have difficulty in understanding negative sentences. We mistake valid Denying the Consequent arguments for invalid arguments. So we must also have difficulty with reductions to absurdity and understanding, much less creating, hypothetical reasoning which deduces falsifiable consequences.

Wason invented a problem in inductive reasoning called "The 2-4-6 problem." In simplest form, a psychologist tells a subject that she has in mind a rule obeyed by triplets of numbers. She says she will give the subject one example of a triplet that obeys the rule. She gives the numbers "2, 4, 6." The subject is to try to guess the rule after giving triplets of his own which he thinks obey the rule, but only when he is sure he is correct about the rule. He is given a sheet of paper to write down his examples and the reasons for trying these examples. He can also write down the feedback he gets from the psychologist. This feedback is that the triple does (or does not) obey the rule, and that his rule guess is correct or incorrect. The experiment continues until the correct rule is given or the subject quits.

When the rule is the very general one, "Any ascending sequence," Wason found interesting results. Subjects tend strongly to formulate more specific hypotheses. They tend very strongly to test only positive examples of it. They don't try to falsify their hypotheses. They also often cling to a proposed hypothesis, just rewording it somewhat even after they have announced it and the psychologist has said it was wrong. Here is where texts in critical thinking, logic and philosophy of science can be useful. When you encounter claims or consider hypotheses, always ask **"What, if anything, would falsify this claim?"** If there is nothing that could falsify it, either you have a very highly justified analytic or a priori claim, or you have a physical (or "metaphysical") object statement which is unjustified and can't be justified at all.

Popper's concept of scientific method (deducing predictions from hypotheses and seeing if they fit or are falsified by data) raises two more points. First, *phenomena, to be real for science, must be repeatable.* It must be possible for other scientists to observe very similar events or get very similar results from the same experiments. Eyewitness testimony about unique, non-repeatable events in which something was observed are not uncritically accepted. They are not accepted unless the conditions can be repeated and the same thing is again observed. If it is not, then the original claim may have been based on an illusion, a hallucination, some defect of observation or experiment or even untruthfulness.

Second, explanation is similar to prediction. To predict or explain an event's occurrence is to deduce it from two kinds of statements: a) statements of initial conditions including the occurrence of earlier events and b) well justified general laws. A paradigm was given by Carl Hempel (1942.) Let the event to be explained be the cracking of an automobile's radiator. Initial conditions which help explain this include the following. The car was left out all night. Its' radiator, which is made of iron, was completely filled with water and the cap was screwed on tight. The temperature went down at night from 39 degrees to 25 degrees. The air pressure was normal. The radiator metal would burst at so and so much pressure.

The well-justified laws involved in the explanation must include the following. Below 32 degrees under normal atmospheric pressure, water freezes. Below 39 degrees the pressure of a mass of water increases with decreasing temperature, if the volume remains constant. When the water freezes, the pressure increases more. There would also need to be a quantitative law relating the change of pressure of the water as a function of its volume and temperature.

Notice two things. First, an explanation that allows one to deduce the event to be explained requires both "causes" (events and conditions) and laws. Second, a great deal of information is required to be able to fully explain by deduction. In ordinary life we might acceptably answer "Why did the radiator burst?" with "Because it got below freezing last night." The adequacy of an explanation, like justification, is related to the context in which it is given.

Inference to the best explanation is an important theory - construction process. Some datum D (a given fact) needs to be explained. D, the cracking of the radiator, is "explained" by theories T_1, T_2, T_3. Let's say these are the 3 theories. 1. "It was God's will." 2. "A demon did it." 3. The water expanded as it froze." *An explanation is unjustified when it 1) relies on unprovable or improbable claims as initial conditions or laws and 2) uses unnecessary entities.* Police often run into such circumstances. A 65 year old woman complains to the police that a very expensive ladies Rolex watch is missing and presumed stolen by a young man she let in her house. The man, aged 24, is picked up for a traffic violation and police search his car. They find the watch. He explains: "I'm her boyfriend. She gave me this watch." There are several improbabilities in his story and the police detain him.

Horrendous examples of both circumstances 1) and 2) are given by Robbins (1959, p. 18). In 1608 an Italian Friar named Guazzo explained why a priest cut his own throat while waiting to be burned at the stake. The priest was 90 years old. He had been tortured. He was desperate over his fate. But Guazzo "explained" that a demon appeared to him and tempted him so that ... he cut his own throat with his knife. A papal judge named Paulus Grillandus gave an "explanation" why a witch can not escape from prison. The devil could, after all, change her shape and enable her to crawl through the keyhole. However, "when the devil has once got control over [witches] he is eager that they should be put to death, in order that they should not escape him by recanting and penitence."

Often what needed to be explained had an obvious explanation which could not be accepted. An example was the torture and murder of people based on false accusations. An Inquisitor named Bartolemeo Spina "explained" why oxen which were left unguarded and allegedly killed by witches were later found alive and in their original condition. The Church would have been committing a mortal sin to torture and murder innocent people on false charges. But the Church cannot commit mortal sin. So he "explained" that witches kill the oxen and eat them but then, with the help of the devil, they put the skin back on the bones and bring them back to life. Demonologists had to explain how a woman could be seen in bed at night by her husband and still be far away at a witches' sabbath. A "deus ex machina" (say DAY uhs eks mah keen a) is a "god in the machine," a nonsensible, personal being assumed to exist just to explain some event without careful study of the laws and causes involved in that event. Since it has no known laws governing its' behavior, it is a "wild card". It can be used to give a "pseudo explanation" of any event. Assuming "wild card" supernatural powers and a devil, inquisitors could pseudo explain evidence of witchcraft and even treat non-evidence as evidence.

Among competing explanations those are better which: 1) explain numerical detail of an event or object more precisely, 2) explain similar events in detail, 3) explain other types of events, 4) enable precise prediction of future events, 5) enable or make it easier for humans to have effects on events though the development of tools, instruments, machines or procedures, 6) do not leave the event or data to be explained surprising, 7) do not allow for raising unanswerable questions. Such explanations are also 8) simpler and 9) consistent with other explanations and theories which are better in the same senses. *Nonsensible personal beings which can violate the laws of nature (spirits, souls) are useless to provide any specific explanation to fix, predict or control anything and are worse than scientific explanations on these criteria.*

Spirits can do anything...
    except explain, predict, and control!!

Giere (1991) has given a clear, modern analysis of scientific method which avoids Popper's overemphasis on falsification and exclusion of probability. Scientific method begins with a problem or question, not with a dogma, theory, solution or answer. Scientists construct *models* of some aspect of the real world. The model may actually be a physical scale model, an analogy or a theoretical description of some thing or event.

A theoretical model is like a map. A map does not pretend to be complete. It does not give a perfectly accurate description of all the features it represents. Understanding the map depends on understanding conventions. These conventions allow you to interpret symbols on the map as standing for things in the place mapped. Good examples for our purposes would be map - models of chemical compounds. In her pioneering work *Silent Spring*, Rachel Carson (1962) gave these examples of map - models of compounds.

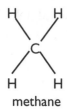

methane

methyl
chloride

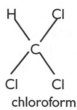

chloroform

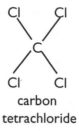

carbon
tetrachloride

Such models have parts in relationships which may or may not correspond to parts and relationships in reality. In order to understand such a map a student needs to know that "C" stands for carbon, "H" for hydrogen and "Cl" for chlorine. She needs to understand that "methyl" is formed from "methane" and that "tetra" atoms combine so easily with others that they form the basis of many compounds. This occurs when chlorine is substituted for hydrogen. She will then understand why methyl chloride, chloroform and carbon tetrachloride are called "chlorinated hydrocarbons."

Jargon is the use of extra-complex words to dress up what is usually a simple, highly prima fascie justified claim. One February day in Syracuse, New York, a fellow graduate student greeted me while walking across campus with the claim (52) "It's sufficiently frigid to sever the glandular appendages of a bimetallically alloyed simian." That was jargon. Jargon requires paraphrase. It meant (53) "It's cold enough to freeze the testicles off a brass monkey." It was well justified that day. *The technical terms and hypotheses of science are not jargon.* There are non-technical names for the first, third and fourth compounds: "marsh gas," "chloroform," and "cleaning fluid." But "cleaning fluid" covers other compounds not including carbon tetrachloride. Complex, unfamiliar scientific terms are needed because reality is complex and much of its specific composition is unfamiliar to the average person. A scientific hypothesis is an attempt to state something about this complex reality, not to communicate some matter of everyday fact. So it should not be faulted for jargon for the use of technical terms.

Scientists frame hypotheses which claim that their models do actually correspond to elements and relationships in reality. The construction of a model must often take account of principles involved in the construction of other earlier, more general models. A scientific theory is a family of models and a set of hypotheses claiming that the parts and relationships of these models correspond to specific things and events of the real world.

Scientists try to determine whether their models fit the real world by collecting data. Data can only be gotten by observation or experiment with the part of the real world the model is supposed to represent. It can't be thought up or invented. Relevant differences in data must be reliably detectable. If they can't be, then one has only information, not useful for evaluating hypotheses and models. To count as a scientific hypothesis, an hypothesis must enable reasoning and calculation from it to determine one or more predictions.

Predictions are claims that, given such a model, certain data should be observed. To be scientific, they must be specific enough to be checked against actual data. Claims too vague or otherwise unable to yield predictions which are testable in this way are not scientific hypotheses. Examples of scientific hypotheses are James Watson's first hypotheses about the structure of DNA: (54) "DNA has a helical structure with three polynucleotide chains" and (55) "DNA has a helical structure with two polynucleotide chains".

When a prediction disagrees with data, this is taken as some evidence that the model and theory are incorrect. Hypothesis (54) predicted that a certain amount of water would be found with DNA. On analysis in the lab the predicted amount of water was only about one-tenth what was actually found. However, this did not lead to immediate rejection of (54). Two other possibilities were also considered. They are that there was some mistake in the collection of data or in reasoning and calculation from the model or even in the design of an experiment to test the model. A prediction from Hypothesis (55) did agree with the data and also with other data. So (55) was adopted as better justified.

When a prediction agrees with data, this is frequently taken as some evidence that the model is correct. However, it is not so taken when there are other models which yield the same prediction. Watson and Crick knew other models, even three-helix models which would have predicted the amount of water actually found. This shows something very important for understanding scientific method. *Agreement between predictions and data alone do not justify a model and hypothesis!* To justify a model and hypothesis scientifically one always has to consider *whether there are other models and hypotheses consistent with previously justified hypotheses, which predict the data as well or even better.* Other data may need to be considered or a crucial observation or experiment performed.

A crucial experiment is one which allows a clear choice between rival models. Such an experiment will require two models to make distinctly different predictions of some datum. It then allows choice between the hypotheses that these models are correct on the basis of which predicts the datum correctly. In plainer terms, a critical thinker always asks: **"Is there another explanation for this consistent with established scientific theory?"**

An example of a crucial observation is this. The Ptolemaic model of the universe had the Earth at the center and then Mercury, Venus, the Sun, Mars, Jupiter and Saturn going around it in that order of distance. This model predicted that Venus, being lighted by the sun from behind, would never show an almost fully lit up disk. Copernicus' theory was that the Sun was at the center and the planets went around it in the order Mercury, Venus, Earth, and so on. Copernicus' theory predicted that Venus would show up an almost fully lit up disk when it was on the other side of the Sun from Earth. The disk of Venus could not be seen until Galileo invented a telescope. When he did, he made the critical observation that Venus did indeed become nearly fully lit up.

This case illustrates a method Giere sets up. The method can be used to decide whether a claim is a scientific hypothesis or not and whether it is justified. The first step is to describe some part of the real world that the claim allegedly deals with. Second, describe the model used to represent that part of reality. Third, pick out the data that have been gotten by observation or experiment involving the things studied. Fourth, identify a prediction which says what the data should be, if the model is a good fit to the part of reality dealt with.

Giere's fifth step is to decide whether the data agree with the prediction or not. Here vagueness becomes a major disqualifier for justification. A predictive claim as a whole is *vague* when it leaves out so many specifics that one cannot clearly tell if it agrees with observed data or not. It is vague if any number of likely situations "agree with it" in a very general way. Finally, the sixth step is to ask whether the prediction was likely to agree with the data even if the model was not a good fit to the real world. Are there other models which are more plausible and which make the same predictions? Are there other explanations for the data which fit better with already justified claims, like laws and well justified scientific theories? Here is one place where critical and scientific thinkers part company from pseudoscientists. Pseudoscientists speculate and create alternative models. Critical and scientific thinkers ask these questions and follow their answers. Pseudoscientists do not exercise such self-discipline.

The development of scientific and critical thinking is slowed not only by pseudosciece but also by anti-science. From the Enlightenment through the 19th. Century many people thought there would be endless progress through science to utopia. (A *utopia* is someone's idea of a better or ideal society.) Two 20th. Century world wars and books like Orwell's *1984* and Huxley's *Brave New World* turned the tide. Since then many technology-based dystopias (bad societies) have been presented in fiction and film. Some academics, religious leaders and medical ethicists have actually become hostile toward science (Gross and Levitt,1994.) Their movement is called *"Anti-science."* Some of it takes the form of legitimate interest in the consequences of certain sorts of technology or the interest of animals in humane treatment. However, the effect of anti-science is to slow or stop scientific research. An example would be research by Dr. Robert White (1996) on transplanting whole heads to different bodies. This could save lives of people whose brains are fine but whose bodies dying. Anti-science is generally contrary to our human interest. That interest is in gaining knowledge, using it for our betterment and afterward dealing with the problems it creates.

SECTION 10.3: HOW WE KNOW AND PHYSICAL IMPOSSIBILITY

Many findings of science are wondrous and astonishing. However, there remain limits on the wondrous and astonishing nature of reality. Milton Rothman (1988) discusses these well. He begins by asking "How do we trace the boundary between fantasy and reality?" (p. 9 ff.) In slight paraphrase, the answer is "By means of science." A science deals with real things in space and time. A science has an outlook according to which the real world consists of lawfully changing concrete things instead of lawless, ghostly things. It involves a realistic theory of knowledge which holds that there are things in an external world which do not depend for their existence and nature on our minds. The contents of science change over time as a result of new knowledge. Members of a scientific community are specially trained, communicate information among themselves and practice free inquiry. Theories in science are frequently mathematical and have specific predictive content, rather than being empty. The goal of a science is to systematize data and hypotheses into laws and theories and to use such laws and theories to make specific predictions and develop devices of practical use to human beings.

Rothman notes that the laws of nature discovered by physicists are of two kinds: laws of permission and laws of denial. Laws of permission, like Newton's Second Law of Motion, permit us to predict what things are likely to happen. Laws of denial tell us what can not happen. Among these are the laws of conservation of energy and momentum. It is common for people who like to read science fiction or fantasy and pseudo scientists to claim "Anything's possible." This claim is false. First, there are things which are logically impossible because they are self-contradictory. For example, a round square cannot exist, nor will anyone ever be able to make one, because round squares are logically impossible. Second, there are describable "things" and "events" which are physically impossible because they violate these enormously well-confirmed physical laws of denial.

Rothman also notes that people attracted to science fiction, fantasy and pseudoscience often ask "How do you know that..." so and so, where "so and so" is some controversial or fantastic idea. "How do you know that..." is in many cases a legitimate critical question. He therefore explains clearly how we know some of the ideas of science fiction are fantasy and always will be fantasy. Krauss (1995) does the same for the impulse engines, transporter and other machines in Star Trek.

Rothman makes the following predictions (p. 148 ff.) to show the reasons for regarding some ideas as not ever more than fantasy. This is no fun, but reality. No one will never be able to jump over the moon without mechanical aid, because human muscles can not supply enough energy. No one will never spontaneously burst into flames, because molecules of burnable body components and oxygen cannot just suddenly get the motion energy to start combustion, getting it from nowhere. No one will ever suddenly levitate (rise up) off the floor, because an object at rest has to interact with another object to start movement. No one will ever build a flying machine able to hover high in the air on magnetic fields, because nothing happens without interactions between pairs of objects and the earth's magnetic field is simply too weak for the repulsive force required for this. No one will ever build an "anti-gravity drive" either, because there is no such thing as "gravity repulsion." Electromagnetism is both attractive and repulsive. Gravity is always attractive. No one will ever travel to the stars faster than the speed of light, because this would generate situations which are as self contradictory as round squares (Rothman, Appendix.)

Other impossibilities deal with time. No one will ever build a workable time machine. Such a machine would violate fundamental laws about how the universe behaves and generate paradoxes which are logically impossible (such as living before one was born, or after one died.) No one will ever send a message through space that does not diminish in intensity as it travels away from the sender, because conservation of energy requires that as energy spreads out in space it must decrease in intensity. No one will ever send a message faster than light or instantaneously because it takes energy to transmit any information and energy can travel no faster than the speed of light. The whole concept of something happening instantaneously depends on an under-analyzed concept of simultaneous events (Rothman, Appendix.) No one will ever make a killing in the stock market by foreseeing the future, because no effect comes before its cause. No event can be seen or known before it occurs. No one will ever influence the position or motion of any kind of physical object from a distance (telekinesis or psychokinesis) just by thinking about it, because the brain is incapable of transmitting enough electromagnetic energy to affect distant bodies.

The student should now do Exercise 18, "The Devil Made me Do it."

11

JUSTIFICATION IN LAW

SECTION 11.1: LEGAL PROCEDURE AND HIGH JUSTIFICATION

Law is a system of justification. It is limited and it is flawed. It is limited in seeking to justify statements about particular, past, non repeatable events. It seeks to justify two types of statements. One type is factual claims about what happened. The other is interpretive or evaluative. It is interpretation, for example, when one side claims that a killing was murder. The other side offers the interpretation that it was only manslaughter or accidental. These interpretations require use of non scientific folk psychological "mental object" terms such as *mens rea,* a "guilty mind."

Many Americans look only at a few controversial verdicts in cases covered in the news media. The case of O. J. Simpson, accused of murdering his wife and Ronald Goldman, is a good example. People conclude that the system of justice which produces verdicts like the one in that case is hopelessly flawed or unjust. They forget that the news media only feature the *unusual,* sensational cases. They do not tell of the thousands of cases where the dialectical process in courts produces results most people would regard as justified. They are not aware of the processes of justification gone through. They do not know or remember the historical reasons for the procedures and rules in effect.

There *are* very serious problems and distortions which deform our system of justice as a whole. Trials are not really searches for the truth. They are adversarial. That is, they are contests between sides bound by rules designed to be more or less fair. The contest is to persuade a judge, jury or both that acts occurred (or did not occur) which are described and "explained" in folk psychological language, acts that have been defined and prohibited in statutes and cases. *Exclusionary rules* sometimes prevent the introduction of real evidence which would be decisive if it was allowed. Worse yet, from a truth-seeking point of view, evidence of past wrongdoing is often ruled irrelevant and may not be admitted. This is contrary to scientific, inductive reasoning which establishes a probability of similar behavior if it has been observed before. But the legal system is not science. It is supposed to protect individual liberty by requiring a high level of evidence strictly relevant to some violation of law with which a person is charged.

In unusual cases, the rules do not ensure fairness. White collar crime by white, well-educated, well-paid men goes under-investigated. The system fails to try many white collar criminals. Many cases become administrative hearings. They end in slaps on the wrist. The system fails even to require fines which take the profit out of crime. White collar crime *does* pay. Those with money can get better lawyers. Therefore poor people of minority groups are much more frequently jailed than middle class or wealthy people. In civil and criminal court trials what is called "junk science" by fringe "expert witnesses" is sometimes introduced (see Huber, 1991.) This may be done for wealthy defendants or by lawyers who themselves are simply looking to win large settlements. However, all this does not prevent criminal trial procedure from *generally* producing very highly justified findings of fact and somewhat less often highly justified verdicts as conclusions.

There has always been a close relation between philosophy and law. They grew up together in Western Civilization in Ancient Greece. Political leaders had to persuade assembly members to make certain laws or carry out government activities using argument in situations where back and forth dialectic of argument happened. Also there were lawsuits where people had to argue with adversaries. There remains today a healthy field of philosophy called "philosophy of law." Bishin and Stone (1972, vii) state that "...every legal problem ... has its roots and perhaps its analog in traditionally 'philosophical' realms [such as] the nature of reality, of knowledge, of language ... the requisites of morality ... the 'good life' ... the nature of man."

Kenny, (1978) an analytic philosopher of law, correctly states that "When we explain actions in terms of desires and beliefs we are not putting forward any explanatory *theory* to account for the action. It is true that desires and beliefs explain action; but the explanation is not of any causal hypothetical form. It is not as if the actions of human beings constitute a set of raw data - actions identifiable on their faces as the kinds of actions they are - for which we seek an explanatory hypothesis. On the contrary, many human actions are not identifiable as actions of a particular kind unless they are already seen and interpreted as proceeding from a particular set of desires and beliefs" (p. 12.) This can be true even of such basic, apparently physical actions as killing and letting die. Kenny illustrates his point with some fascinating cases involving laws against witchcraft in Africa in modern times. (Alleged witch doctors can cause real harm while trying to find out who is a "witch" by making suspects drink some liquid possibly fatal through anxiety to people who believe they are witches.)

Kenny's work has been followed by others considering similar problems. One such is Katz (1987) whose book carries the subtitle "Conundrums of the Criminal Law." "Conundrums" means, precisely, philosophical problems. Katz organizes his treatment of these problems by starting out with the deficiencies of the 10 Commandments to be criminal law. Since the purpose of this chapter is to describe law as a system of justification and give the student historical insight as to why its' provisions are there, they will be stated.

First, The Commandments don't allow for any exceptions. But we think there are many exceptions. Suppose we never killed anything. We would not kill anyone in self defense, defense of another or even to eat. We would all die. Second, they don't define the acts prohibited. Third, they don't mention state of mind. However, a firm (folk psychological) principle of criminal law is that a person must have a *mens rea,* a criminal intent or guilty mind in addition to doing a wrong act to be guilty of a crime. He or she must know what they are doing. Fourth, they do not discuss causation. However, exactly who or what event caused another can be a very difficult problem. Fifth, they have nothing to say about degrees of responsibility for others involved in helping someone to violate a Commandment. Sixth, they do not bother with attempted crimes, even so serious as attempted murder.

To go through the history of how the modern system of justification arose would require a whole book. Instead, we shall look at its major provisions with special application to criminal law and an occasional backward glance to see why it has developed as it has. Whether criminal or civil, a legal proceeding first begins with someone formally stating to the legal system some complaint that the system accepts as one it can take action on. Second, the opponent in a legal action must be notified of the complaint and given the opportunity to prepare a defense. Third, the adversaries have to be given all reasonable chances to learn the factual and legal arguments of the other side. Fourth, if the matter does go to trial it is carried out in a dialectical, adversarial manner in which each side has every chance to challenge the arguments of the other side. Fifth, decisions at trial are supposed to be based on the evidence and arguments presented. Sixth, procedural error overrides the goal of getting a verdict. Any failure to follow procedure may be taken as a basis for appealing that the process was incorrect.

The Constitution of the United States establishes a three part government with separation of powers: executive, legislative and judicial. This separation allows for "checks and balances" to protect individuals accused of crimes. Articles One and Three of the Constitution provide for writs of Habeus Corpus and trial by jury. They ban the making of bills of attainder and *ex post facto* laws. A writ of habeus corpus allows an imprisoned person to challenge the lawfulness of the government in imprisoning him. In past times there was little possibility that an accused person could challenge a priestly accuser, a baron or the kings' magistrate. These same officers were often judge, jury and executioner. *Ex post facto* laws were laws which made certain conduct criminal after it was committed. Making such laws was a way for government to "get" people for doing acts which, at the time of doing, were not illegal. Bills of Attainer were bills which singled out one person or a very narrow group and were also used for vengeance.

The first ten amendments to the United States Constitution are called the "Bill of Rights." They include freedom of religion and freedom from other peoples' religions. They also include freedom of the press, the right to assemble peaceably to ask the government to correct wrongs it had done to people, and the right to refuse to put up the government's soldiers in your house. In a more recognizably legal area it included the rights to be secure against unreasonable search, and various due process rights which were first won from King John of England by barons, who, in 1215, forced him to sign the Magna Carta. These include rights to be accused only by indictment before a grand jury, and to have warrants issued only on probable cause supported by an oath and describing in particular the places to be searched and persons or things to be taken. Additional rights specified include the rights to be informed of charges against you, to non-excessive bail, to counsel, to trial by an *impartial* jury, to compel witnesses to appear for your defense, to a speedy and public trial, to refuse to testify against yourself and to not be tried twice on the same charge.

Unless a person knows something about the history of legal proceedings, he or she will not appreciate these freedoms and rights much. Each of these rights was included specifically because there were past times when they were not recognized and gross miscarriages of justice resulted. Sagan (1995, p. 275) relates the tale of Miles Phillips, an English sailor who was stranded in Spanish Mexico. Phillips and others with him were brought before the Inquisition in the year 1574. They were asked whether they believed that the Host (communion wafer) and wine were the very body and blood of our Savior Christ, Yes or No? Phillips related that if they did not answer "yes," they would have been murdered. This sort of scene was repeated time and again among so-called "Christians" of slightly different beliefs and Christians and Non-Christians for hundreds of years. So it is little wonder that the framers of the Constitution provided for freedom *from* others' religion!

Before modern legal concepts of evidence there were some very strange ideas of how to justify claims and resolve disputes. Among the earliest was trial by ordeal. The accused party was threatened or actually subjected to fire, or partial drowning. The theory was that God would make the innocent strong to withstand the ordeal. Another form of justification was trial by battle. This was tough going for an innocent, scrawny runt at the hands of a guilty bruiser accuser.

People often criticize the right to refuse to testify against yourself and the Miranda warning about the right to remain silent. They will be better appreciated when one recalls that terrible torture used to be used in witchcraft trials to get confessions. Then the confessions were taken as evidence justifying a guilty verdict. The process of inquisition became so obviously unjust that even a Jesuit priest, Friedrich von Spee, exposed it. In 1631 he published a work called *Precautions for Prosecutors*. Sagan (1995, p. 407) relates some of von Spee's points. One of them is that judges who delayed trials were sent a special investigator. The Investigator was paid a certain amount of money for each "witch" burned!

Is it any different today, when one side is the Government or has much more money?

Another was that if the accused confessed without torture, she would be burned. However, once torture was begun, the accused would always be burned as well, because it would disgrace the investigators if she was acquitted. A right to remain silent, to not testify against ones' self, is needed to avoid strong temptations to torture accused people to gain confessions. Strict rules on admissibility of confessions are then also needed.

Following trial by ordeal and by combat, parties to disputes were often required to swear oaths before some god. Sometimes others were required to swear to opinions about the parties even though they might not have anything to do with the facts under dispute. The theory again was that a god would at least later punish a liar, so the sworn oath would be true. When this did not work, confession came to be thought of as the best sort of evidence. It became accepted practice to question witnesses in secret and torture was regarded as an acceptable means of getting a confession. A split then developed between systems in which the judge held investigative powers and the adversarial system in which the judge was supposed to be neutral and it was up to the parties to find their own evidence.

The Catholic Church thought itself infallible on matters of faith and morals and eventually a Pope declared it such. But long before that, in the Inquisition, Von Spee noted it acting as if it were infallible. Accusation that someone was a witch led, in many cases without any opportunity to make a defense, to torture, "confession," conviction, and murder. In other words, the burden of proof was on the accused and was impossible to meet. **The "burden of proof" is the requirement that assertions be justified by evidence.** After political power decisively shifted away from "infallible" religions to governments, people rebelling against kings shifted the burden of proof to government. As civil law became distinct from criminal, the burden was shifted further to the party which made the accusation or complaint. This is a very important point for critical thinking in general. **The burden of proof is on the maker of a claim. He or she must present evidence to justify it. The hearer or reader is not required to prove it wrong.**

An important conclusion follows from the principle that **the burden of proof is on the maker of a claim. This is why a person is innocent until proven guilty.** Evidence submitted must be *relevant* to the charge in question. An area of controversy is that some legal processes allow evidence of past similar crimes while others do not. Here it seems the practice in American criminal law of excluding such evidence runs contrary to the principle of induction. However, there is no good evidence that many or a majority of criminal trials which should end in conviction fail to do so because of the exclusion of evidence about prior similar acts.

Evidence must also be *admissible*. Some possible witnesses testimony, for example, that of very young children may be excluded for incompetence, others as hearsay, or because of an established privilege such as that against self-incrimination, or against disclosing government secrets or confidential material that comes to a person in certain professions. There are good reasons for such exclusions. The original speaker who is quoted in hearsay cannot be cross examined. Young children are not as trained observers of detail as some adults. They can be more influenced than many adults. Doctors, lawyers, clergymen, journalists and employers need some protection of confidentiality or people will not tell them things they need to know to perform successfully.

The standard *means of proof* are witnesses, the parties (accuser and accused) experts, documents and what is called "real evidence" (things involved in the crime, the bloody knife, and so on.) Oaths are still required to try to establish credibility of witnesses. But cross examination does much more to establish or wreck credibility. Leading, misleading and argumentative questions are generally not allowed. Cross examination is generally limited to subjects brought up on direct examination. Admissions made in or out of court are admissible, but involuntary confessions are not.

Documents, to be admitted, may need to be proven genuine by testimony of their authors, signers, witnesses or experts. This process is called *"authentication."* There is a rule called the *"Best Available Evidence" rule*. Original documents must be presented, if they are available, copies only second or not at all. Spoken evidence is inadmissible to vary, contradict or add to the terms of a written agreement. Real evidence must also be shown to be relevant and authentic to be admitted. Highly scientific techniques are used to justify conclusions about real evidence such as cause of death, blood and semen types, fingerprints, or whether a particular gun fired a particular bullet.

Criminal procedure includes the rights described above. After a crime has been discovered and reported, police investigate. They identify a suspect. They also have the power to arrest and accuse someone without a warrant when they have probable cause to believe that a crime has committed and that the person they arrest was the perpetrator or one of the perpetrators. But by the Miranda decision, they must warn the suspect of his right to remain silent and to have a lawyer present at questioning. Also, if they exceed their authority they may be sued for civil rights violations or for false arrest in general. Not only minorities have a remedy against false arrest. Arrest is the apprehension of a person to make him or her answer to a charge of committing a crime. Arrest corresponds to acceptance of a prima facie belief that this person committed such and such a crime.

Through long experience, police have developed very effective non-violent, non-illegal techniques of interrogation. An excellent summary of them is found in Inbau, Reed and Buckley (1986.) They report that a good police interrogator will play upon guilt feelings of a subject may have. He will show confidence about the guilt of the subject. He will point out some of the evidence against the person. If they show signs of nervousness, he will point that out and ask them why they are so nervous. He will pretend to understand and sympathize with the suspect. He may even invent his own stories of similar acts he claims to have performed. He will try to get the suspect to place him or herself at the scene of the crime or in association with others involved in it. He may make up evidence to see what the subject will say to explain it away.

If more than one person was involved in a crime and two or more suspects are being questioned, interrogator(s) will compare notes for inconsistencies and try to play one off against another. Given the long experience police have had at interrogation, it would be very surprising if they had not developed highly effective non-violent, non-illegal methods of getting confessions out of guilty people. The getting of a confession may be sufficient for the interrogator himself to think that he is a fortiori justified in believing that the subject committed a crime. But it is far from sufficient for the procedure as a whole.

Assume that no confession is gotten. After a suspect is arrested, he or she must be brought before a magistrate without delay, usually within no more than twenty-four hours. This is called a "preliminary" or "first appearance," "hearing" or "arraignment." The accused will be informed of the charges and his or her legal rights. The judge will determine whether there is probable cause to believe that a crime was committed and that the defendant committed it. If the judge does not think either is the case, she can dismiss the charges. If charges are not dismissed, the accused will have to plead not guilty, guilty or no contest. Bail will be set and if the accused feels it is excessive, he or she can request a hearing on it. The court, under federal law, must set the least restrictive conditions of release which will make sure the person appears in court.

Legal justification deals with claims about unique, non repeatable events. Nevertheless, the occurrence of arraignments or preliminary hearings shows something similar to the process gone through by scientists. Scientists' hypotheses get tested first by comparing predictions from them with data. After that, when the scientist goes to publish her results, she will do so by sending a report of findings or a paper to journals in her field. These scholarly journals have referees, people who are experts in the area. Referees read papers and try to determine whether the claims they present are well justified or not. Only papers approved by the referees will be accepted into the journal. The best scholarly journals accept only five or ten percent of the papers submitted to them. Similarly, in the criminal process, the prosecution side must convince *independent* persons from a magistrate through a grand jury to the trial jury that they are justified in believing that a crime was committed and that the defendant committed it.

Charges of the most serious felonies are brought by indictment (say in DIE t ment) by a grand jury or by an "information" by a prosecutor. Both indictment and information are written accusations. Grand jury hearings are not adversarial. They are secret, witnesses can be compelled to testify or imprisoned and the prosecutor generally has control of them. However, even if the grand jury finds probable cause and indicts, he must meet the burden of proof at trial. Even before trial, the defense can move to suppress evidence improperly obtained. It also gets to know by a process called "discovery" what evidence there is against the defendant. Finally, *the burden of proof is higher for crimes than for civil cases and increases as the process goes on toward its final stage.*

"Arraignment" is the technical term for the court session in which a defendant gets to make a plea. This plea may generally be only one of four: not guilty, not guilty by reason of insanity, guilty, or *nolo contendere.* "Nolo contendere" means the defendant will not contest the charges. It will be treated as the same as a guilty plea but can not be used as an admission of guilt in other criminal or civil trials. If a defendant stands mute, a plea of "Not guilty" is entered.

"Insanity" is thought to make it impossible that a defendant had the *mens rea,* the criminal intent to commit the punishable act. The old test of insanity still in use in many places is basically the *M'Naughton Rule.* "Did the accused suffer from a defect of mind such that he did not understand the nature of his act or did not know that it was wrong?" This test is a can of worms precisely because it involves folk psychological terms like "mind," and "understand." Some jurisdictions, fed up with what people see in some courts are seeking to add "guilty, but insane" as another plea to allow punishment in some such cases. This area will continue to be a can of worms until it is recognized that "mental illness" is neurobiological. That is, it results from tumors, chemical imbalances and other brain disorders. When it can be controlled by treatment, it will be easier to say who is responsible for what acts or omissions of the "mentally ill."

At trial, there are *three standards of proof in American law:* preponderance of evidence, clear and convincing evidence and proof beyond a reasonable doubt. In civil law the common burden of proof is preponderance of evidence. *Preponderance of evidence* is evidence which is of greater weight than what is opposed to it. It is evidence that is more credible or convincing than opposing evidence. This is too low a standard to justify depriving a person of fundamental rights such as life or liberty. *Clear and convincing evidence* goes beyond a preponderance. It is evidence which renders its conclusion highly probable or justified. *Proof beyond a reasonable doubt* is proof which precludes every other reasonable hypothesis except the one it supports. It is proof which is logically consistent with a defendant's guilt and establishes so high a probability of guilt that no reasonable person would accept a different hypothesis.

Only about 5% of civil and criminal cases ever get to trial. Many criminal defendants are poor. They are intimidated by multiple charges into plea bargaining. They often go to prison without trial or for less than the worst crime they may have committed. All parties feel unjustly treated. Yet "Law and Order" conservatives who complain about this and shortened sentences also want to cut government spending for programs which lessen some of the conditions associated with crime, such as poverty and drug abuse. They fail to note that a system which prohibited plea bargaining and required full sentences would cost enormously more for courts and prisons.

For those who do go to trial, the process is somewhat self-correcting by appeal. An example is "Satanic" child abuse cases which got started in the early 1980's. Although 200 people were convicted in these cases, by 1996 140 of them had charges dismissed, appeals granted or convictions reversed. Some people were unjustly imprisoned even before trial on the basis of a kind of junk science. This is the testimony of so-called "experts" in child abuse. Some appear to have brow-beaten children into claiming that they were abused or induced False Memory Syndrome in suggestible adults. Those imprisoned may sue their persecutors, but cannot be made whole. Also, survivors of law enforcement massacres, such as the people in MOVE or Waco are punished with unusually long sentences. Instead of officials resigning, they hold "show trials" to prove their victims were serious criminals. Being a government official means never admitting error.

Huber (1991) deals with a flaw many people today find in tort law. A *tort* is a private wrong not arising out of a contract. Product liability is a tort. According to Huber, *Frye vs. the United States,* (1923) established the precedent that expert testimony is admissible only if it is founded on theories, methods and procedures "generally accepted" as valid among other experts in the same field. In the 1960's and 70's however, a law professor Guido Calabresi, wrote a book called the *Cost of Accidents.* He persuaded many lawyers and judges that the cost of accidents could be most efficiently controlled by charging the person who might have prevented it most cheaply. Often this is the manufacturer of a product.

There are a couple of other principles with which Calabresi's argument combined to make for bad decisions. One is that in tort law the defendant "takes the plaintiff as he finds him." In other words, he does not blame the victim. Another is *"in dubio pro laeso."* This is a principle for judges which means "When in doubt, favor the injured." On this basis judges have abandoned the principle established in the Frye case and let all sorts of junk science cranks testify in product liability cases. Tort lawyers have created a pseudoscience Huber calls "Liability Science." This pseudoscience seeks for distant causes which "may," "might," or "could possibly" be involved in the causation of accidents, illness, injury or premature death. It fixes liability there while ignoring much more plausible immediate causes known to cause these things.

Huber gives some examples which partially make his point. Judges used to award damages for cancer believed to be caused by one - time injuries. Apparently the Audi 5000 was not subject to sudden acceleration. People were accidentally putting their feet on the accelerator instead of the gas pedal. After CBS *"60 minutes"* did a story on it, there was an enormous jump in reports of such "rare" sudden accelerations. It appears that Bendectin, a morning sickness medication, did not cause birth defects. Suits cost its manufacturer so much that it offered $120 million to settle and stopped making this non defective medication. Some alleged expert witnesses were less than truthful in their own work and representations about their credentials (see Huber, 1991 p. 92 on Bertram Carnow and p. 126 on William McBride.)

Huber, however, minimizes the need for tort lawyers and firms to have enough wealth to take on corporate giants in cases where liability is real. He is best in describing the necessities for claims to become established scientific fact. It is not true that everything in science remains tentative. There are stopping points when claims are testable and have been falsified. There is genuine progress when experiments are replicated, predictions are verified, peers review work, it is published and consensus develops. There is a "causation pack" of many factors which *may* be involved in some accidents, illnesses and premature death. But only some of them are immediate and important.

The unfortunate truth is that *the main causes of illness and premature death involve tough lifestyle problems.* As a risk, tobacco smoke dwarfs all sorts of other headline - grabbing pollutants. Key risks of reproductive diseases come from sexual habits, not contraceptives. Alcohol is the number one cause of auto accidents. Bad diets and lack of exercise contribute greatly to heart disease. Want to live as long and healthy a life as your genes allow? The Surgeon General, chief medical officer of the United States, has put forth the true *scientific* prescription to increase your probability of doing so. 1) Stop smoking or don't start. Get second hand smoke out of your environment. 2) Cut alcohol consumption. 3) Don't have casual sex with many partners. 4) Eat less and eat right. 5) Exercise. 6) Have periodic checkups. 7) Use seat belts and obey the speed laws.

To summarize. Legal procedure requires an attempt to equalize a contest between parties, to authenticate evidence, and to test credibility of witnesses. It requires getting agreement of increasing numbers of other, supposedly neutral persons. It defines and upholds higher and higher standards of evidence. It allows for appeals for self - correction. It is a method of producing findings of fact and verdicts which should be well justified. In some cases, the process is deformed, even badly so. One must remember that justification is not identical with truth. It simply tends in the long run to truth more than lack of justification. The point was to review the detail of the process as a paradigm of how to produce high justification. As the student does exercises, he or she should think of the extent to which similar processes have been gone through to establish the claims in the examples.

SECTION 11.2: EVALUATING EYEWITNESS TESTIMONY

Law differs from science in dealing with unique, non repeatable events. So cases often involve eyewitness testimony. *Eyewitness testimony is much less credible than most people believe.* Sociologists study how juries form beliefs. They have found that if you give a jury an eyewitness identification and then thoroughly discredit that identification, *many jury members still believe the identification.* Let the jury hear a witness say "I saw that defendant there stab the victim in the alley. I saw it from across the street." Now have a cross examiner prove that it was a moonless, misty night. Let her prove that the nearby street lights left it too dark for almost anyone to see into the alley. Let her prove that the witness was too near-sighted to recognize anyone across a street. Let her prove that he did not have his glasses with him at the time. Let her establish an alibi for the defendant. Many jury members still will give great weight to the eyewitness testimony.

Magic also illustrates the When you see a good magician, man or woman who is admitting tricks. An honest magician does objects with his mind or telling has drawn by reading their mind, or sawing somebody in half and back together again. But as an would have to testify you saw. unreliability of one's eyes. you are witnessing an honest that he or she is performing not really claim to be bending which playing card someone or making a person float in air then somehow putting them "eye witness" that's what you

Should seeing be believing?

Many factors can affect eyewitness testimony: surrounding conditions like distance from scene, light, and weather may affect it and produce illusion. Too much light or too little can leave us unable to see details. Rain, fog, smog, smoke or heat can cut visibility.

Observer conditions like alcohol, other drugs, stress, hunger, and disease may produce hallucination. Some skeptics (doubters) believe that visions of heaven as a place where people drink from silver chalices and feast off of golden plates are exactly the kinds of visions one would expect to find in the dreams and hallucinations of very poor people who live in desert areas and sometimes eat spoiled, unhealthy food. A person who has been robbed at gun or knife - point may not be a good eyewitness even if she was no further away from the robber than three feet. When someone is pointing a gun or knife at you it is very stressful! You are likely to be uncool. You may be looking only or largely at the weapon. You are not calmly memorizing the attackers' features while handing over your money!

There is also something called the "context of expectancy" or inference set by prior beliefs. A way of explaining this is to say that a person who expects a miracle or crime may "see" one, even if it doesn't happen. Some years ago a professor and three of her students tested this. Two girls took a filled duffel bag to a bus station. They would sit near somebody and talk about having their professor's tape recorder in the bag. Then they would get up to go make a 'phone call, leaving the bag a couple of seats away from the person waiting for the bus. While they were gone a male student, unshaven and sloppy, walked up and bent over the duffel bag briefly in such a way as to block the waiting persons' view. Then he went away. The girls came back, opened the duffel bag, appeared upset and talked about how their professor's tape recorder was missing. They asked the waiting person if he or she would be a witness that they didn't take it. Some refused to become involved. Eventually enough said they would for a good experiment. The girls got their names. A week later the professor, posing as an insurance agent, called these "eyewitnesses" up. Among questions she asked was "Did you actually see the man take the tape recorder?" About 50% of the "eyewitnesses" said "Yes", *even though there never even was a tape recorder.*

The subjects in this experiment had done what most people do. We mix up what we actually see with our eyes with *interpretation and inference,* which may well be wrong! These cases are very similar to the fallacy called *"subjective validation."* Given that we already accept a certain theory, or trust certain individuals, we tend to "see" things which confirm what we already think. We also are largely unconscious of doing this and think we are "just seeing what's there."

What about other eyewitnesses to the same event? The testimony of other eyewitnesses can help. But they could be suffering a shared context of expectancy or interpretation or delusion. What about photographs? Couldn't we have photographs or videotapes of events which would corroborate (say kohr-ROB-or-ate, support) eyewitness testimony? Unfortunately photographs are increasingly easy to fake. You yourself could cut photographs out of newspapers or magazines, use a photocopy machine to blow up or shrink images to appropriate sizes and then cut heads out of one picture, stick them on bodies in another picture, touch up the cut lines and then photocopy the result to make a new picture. Students have done this with yearbook pictures of hated teachers.

Older cameras can make double exposures. With a little knowledge, double images can be created in photographic development and printing. Computer hardware and software can take photographs as input and change them upon command. Finally, movie making special effects can create very realistic images of things which do not exist. One can find an explanation of how the aliens' bodies in "Alien Autopsy" are made in (Stokes, pp. 21-23.)

What about TV? Video recordings are notoriously subject to interpretation based on that context of belief. Many Americans thought they saw Rodney King helpless on the ground being beaten by police. But the first jury didn't see it that way. They had a shared interpretation which was very different from many Americans and from the later civil trial. One juror even claimed that "Mr. King was directing the action." That first verdict may have seemed an outrageous and racist injustice to many Americans. It does illustrate though, that what people "see" can be very heavily influenced by what they believe.

Two points should be noted. First, unique eyewitnessed events are not repeatable. That is why eyewitness testimony about them is highly regarded. *However, eyewitness testimony about them is, given the non-repeatability, untestable.* Its credibility can be attacked and it can be contradicted. It can not be falsified like a scientific hypothesis. Without corroborating testimony of others or supporting physical evidence like photographs, it can only be judged in terms of its probability. A good illustration of both the unreliability of eyewitness testimony and the partially self correcting nature of the legal process is to be found in DNA fingerprinting. An Associated Press story "DNA Testing Gets its' Day in Court" (1/26/97) reported that "More than 30 men have had rape convictions overturned by DNA evidence in recent year(s)." DNA fingerprinting has shown that eyewitness identifications are unreliable in rape cases.

If one has to decide whether to believe uncorroborated eyewitness testimony, therefore, one has to consider two things. First, is the kind of event it claims a usual, ordinary or normal event? In that case, the statement of it may be justified. If it is testimony of an unusual, extraordinary or abnormal event, then it is unjustified in the degree to which it is unusual, extraordinary or unjustified and requires evidence beyond testimony. Second, one has to consider how specific the testimony is. The more specific, as in "I'm absolutely sure he (or she) did it," the more evidence one must have to justify everything claimed.

SECTION 11.3: A CLOSING REALITY CHECK

A generally favorable account has been given of law as a system of justification. Several serious problems with its' administration were noted at the beginning. Here are some more. While white collar crime goes under-reported and not sufficiently punished, minorities suffer significantly harsher penalties for nonviolent crime than white youth. While white suburban youth accused of theft are often released to their parents, minority youth are imprisoned. Young people in the juvenile system can be "detained" without trial under brutal conditions for long periods of time. Outrageous police and prosecutorial misconduct do occur now and then. Sensation-seeking "news" media pile on, helping deprive innocent people of liberty and reputation in ways that are never and perhaps can never be totally remedied. Public defenders are underpaid and overworked. Because salary commands talent in a labor market, public defenders are not the most experienced lawyers and some are not competent.

There is widespread agreement that the system places too much emphasis on punishing nonviolent property crime, drug use, petty theft, and so on by imprisonment. It does little to get at the causes of crime or even to prevent it. Imprisoned petty criminals are not rehabilitated but taught more crime commission methods. Brutalized, they become hardened criminals in prison. More persons are imprisoned in "the land of the free" per 100 in the population than in some of the world's worst dictatorships. It has been claimed that at least one in every four males in America has an arrest record ("America Busted," The New Yorker, 2/24 - 3/3/97 p. 49.) This author suggests some spreading of multiple arrests over non arrested persons in this statistic. It is still somewhat impressive. In the meantime, both white collar criminals who violate positions of trust and violent criminals are either not imprisoned at all or released or released too soon. Building further prisons to house small-time drug users and dealers seems simply not to work to solve the crime problem.

The student should now do Exercise 19, Jury Research and Legal Justification.

12

PHILOSOPHICAL DIALECTIC AND HIGH JUSTIFICATION

SECTION 12.1: SOME FUNDAMENTALS OF PHILOSOPHY

The word **"Philosophy"** comes from two Greek words "philos" meaning "love of" and "sophia" meaning "wisdom." **Wisdom** is knowledge of profound matters having to do with the nature of reality, knowledge and values. Philosophy differs from other fields in being **"problematic."** It deals with apparently inconsistent beliefs all of which seem true. Like scientists, individual philosophers construct theories. Like law, its' method is **dialectical** critical thinking. One after another, philosophers use arguments, objections and replies to analyze, support or attack or sometimes harmonize inconsistent beliefs and theories. Inconsistencies are more or less hidden contradictions, that is, sets of statements which can't possibly all be true.

Philosophical writing also differs from other kinds of writing. Because philosophy is dialectical, it moves back and forth between questions which formulate problems and theories which offer answers to the questions or between arguments and counter arguments. The following are important items to look for in reading philosophy: *1. Concepts, 2. Distinctions, 3. Definitions, 4. Theories, 5. Questions, 6. Arguments, 7. Analogies, and 8. Objections and Replies.*

A *concept* is the technical meaning of a word. Often it is elaborated, explained in a number of sentences. For example, the word "argument" has the ordinary meaning "fight," "disagreement," or "dispute." In Philosophy, however, it means a groups of statements called "premises," made to persuade someone of a conclusion. We distinguish deductive and inductive, sound and unsound arguments. The first statement is a *definition*. The second draws two *distinctions*. Both express part of the concept of an argument. A correct definition gives other words which have the same meaning as the word defined. A distinction divides up a general concept or says there is a difference between two or more concepts. A *theory* is a claim or group of claims, important to a philosopher, and about whose subject there is disagreement. It is usually a conclusion of inference to the best explanation of some datum (given fact.) Examples of theories are proposed solutions to the problems below. An *analogy* is a statement which says one thing is like another. Distinctions, definitions and analogies often become premises of arguments.

To spot definitions, look for quote marks around words (" ") and verbs like "means", or "signifies." To spot distinctions, look for words like "differs", "2 (or 3) types", and so on. To spot arguments, look for conclusion indicating words like "so", "thus" or "therefore", or reason indicating words like "since" or "because". To spot analogies, look for words such as "like", "is similar to", or "resembles." To spot objections, look for words like "but," or "on the contrary."

The *major fields* of philosophy include: 1. *Logic,* 2. *Ethics,* 3. *Metaphysics,* 4. *Epistemology,* 5. *Philosophy of Art,* 6, *Philosophy of Science,* 7. *Philosophy of Religion,* 8. *Philosophy of History,* 9. *Philosophy of Law,* 10. *Philosophy of Education,* 11. *Social Philosophy,* 12. *Axiology* and area studies such as *13. African Philosophy,* and *14. Eastern Philosophy. 15. The History of Philosophy* is divided into Ancient, Medieval, Modern, 19th Century, Contemporary and Postmodern periods.

Probably many philosophers would agree that **logic, ethics, metaphysics,** and **epistemology** are at the core of philosophy. **Logic** is the study of the methods and principles for distinguishing correct from incorrect reasoning. It can be applied to arguments in any field: science, courts, political debate and everyday life. **Ethics** is the study of right and wrong, good and evil in human action and character. It helps us examine moral problems rationally and decide, choose, and act rightly.

Metaphysics is an attempt to distinguish reality from appearance. It has a part called **"Ontology"** which asks "What exists?" and "What is real?" It tries to reconcile the scientific view of the world with our sensory experience and deals with the conflict between religion and science. Our senses tell us that the world contains many colored, solid, relatively sharp edged and smooth things spread out in space outside ourselves. The Atomic Theory of Matter implies that color, smoothness and solidity are not in the objects outside ourselves. They are in us. Both the scientific and sensory world views give evidence that nothing is permanent. So they conflict with religious hopes people have for survival after death and eternal life. We will deal with the conflict between science and religion in Chapter 13.

"Epistemology" means "the theory of knowledge." This field deals with defining knowledge. It distinguishes between knowledge and opinion. This is extremely important for critical thinking, scientific investigation, law, political debate, and everyday life, as well as metaphysics.

"Axiology" is the name of the general theory of **value.** As a noun, the most general meaning of **"value"** is "the worth of a thing." As a verb, "to value" means "to prize," "cherish," "esteem" or like something. Values may be material or spiritual; economic, moral, aesthetic, religious; intrinsic or extrinsic, and so on. Examples of values would be right, good, justice, beauty, truth, utility, pleasure, holiness, wisdom, self-realization.

A philosophical problem is an inconsistency among beliefs about some profound matter having to do with the nature of reality, knowledge or values. Each problem can be formulated as either an inconsistency between beliefs or as a question. Philosophical theories are inferences to the best explanation of the inconsistencies in problems. They are attempts to offer the most-likely-to-be-true answers to philosophical questions. *Four philosophical problems, by name, are:* "Knowledge versus Skepticism," "Free Will versus Determinism," The "Mind/Body Problem," and the "Problem of the Coexistence of God and Suffering."

The Problem of Knowledge versus Skepticism is the inconsistency that 1. "We know some things for certain," yet on the other hand, 2. "On examination, everything seems open to doubt." This problem could be put by the simple question: "Can we have any real knowledge at all, or is everything we think just a belief?" A *skeptic* thinks we do not have knowledge but only at best well confirmed beliefs, opinions or thoughts. He or she holds the theory or position expressed by 2. If the atomic theory is correct, we cannot be sure even that we know of the existence of the objects we think we are seeing right now. Descartes pointed out that instead of seeing a real page, blackboard or professor in front of you, you might be dreaming it, or it might by an illusion, hallucination, or an effect of a cause very different from what you ordinarily believe. And if you can't even know, for sure, what you see, can you know anything for sure?

The *Problem of Free Will versus Determinism* is this: The Libertarian position says: 1) "I am free in some of my actions and choices. It is up to me what I choose or do. Sometimes I could have done otherwise." This is why we hold people responsible for their actions and praise or blame them and even reward or punish them sometimes. On the other hand, the Determinist theory includes: 2) "Every event has a cause." From this belief and other statements of Determinism, we can make a chain of arguments to the opposite conclusion, that we are *not* free and responsible. It is customary to write down premises first, then draw a line and write the conclusion below the line as follows:

The chain of arguments for Determinism goes like this.

> Every event has a cause. Premise (Basic Reason)
> Every human action is an event. Premise (Basic Reason)
> Therefore, every human action has a cause. (Intermediate Conclusion)
> A cause is something which makes its effect happen. (Basic Reason)
> Therefore, every human action has something which makes it happen. (I.C.)
> Therefore, we are not free in our actions or choices (I.C.)
> Therefore, we are not responsible for our actions. (I.C.)
> Therefore, we should not be praised or blamed or rewarded or
> punished for our actions. (Final Conclusion.)

So the question posed by the Problem of Free Will is "Do we really have free will or are all of our choices and actions made to happen by causes ultimately beyond our control?" To make this plausible, think about the idea of Spinoza who said "we only believe that we are free because we are ignorant of the causes of our actions." If you believe, for example, that there is an electrochemical state of your brain which occurs before you raise your arm and causes your nerves and muscles to contract so that your arm goes up, or that some psychological science could predict your behavior, then you are a determinist, you believe your actions have causes which <u>make them</u> happen. This is true even if you also happen to believe the apparent contradiction that you are free.

The Mind/Body Problem is related to the Free Will versus Determinism problem insofar as both involve the idea of a cause. The kinds of words and descriptive expressions we use with nouns give us a fairly clear indication that the words "mind" and "body" stand for very different types of things. About the body or any part of it like the brain, we correctly use physical object words describing their weight, size, color, location, etc. However, it sounds funny to use such words about the *mind* or "mental objects" like ideas or thoughts. For example, it makes good sense to say my brain weighs about 48 ounces, has a volume of 1,500 ml., is pinkish and grayish in color and is located in my head, which, with the rest of my body is 20 feet from the door. But it wouldn't make sense to say "I have a 48 oz. mind." Do you think your *mind* has some color or shape? If not, you realize that the words "brain" and "mind" appear to refer to very different kinds of objects, although they are closely related.

Similarly, about an idea or thought we might say that it is clear or confused. This does not seem to make sense to say about a brain or brain process. My mind is clear or muddled, my brain is not. If words make sense with and are true of one subject but not another, the two subjects cannot be identical although, like brain and mind, they may be closely related. When we look at the different words which apply to mind and body, we can see, as Descartes pointed out, that mind seems to be a thinking, unextended (that is non spatial) object while body is an unthinking extended substance. In fact, Descartes noted that we think that: 1) "The mind is a nonphysical soul or spirit." This is part of the theory called "Dualism."

The Mind/Body Problem is that we also believe that 2) "Mind acts on body and body acts on mind." This position is called "Interactionism." For example, when we have an idea and then do something, we think that this is mind causing body to move. When we are stuck with a pin and feel pain, we think that this is a bodily event causing a mental event (the pain.) But the problem is, "How can a nonphysical mind act on a physical body or a physical body act on a nonphysical mind?" In the ordinary case of causality, it is like one billiard ball hitting another straight on, stopping dead and making the other move by making contact with it and transmitting force to it. But if mind has no extension or physical location, there can be no contact and transmission of force between body and mind.

The Problem of the Coexistence of God and Suffering can be explained as follows. Some people tend to believe both 1.) "There is an all-knowing, all-powerful, perfectly good God who created us and loves us as a father loves his children" and 2.) "Innocent children and apparently good people suffer." But how can God's being all-powerful, etc., be reconciled with the existence of such suffering as the painful death of babies in natural disasters? Why, if there is such a God, do bad things happen to good people or innocent children? It would seem that either God is not all-knowing. He doesn't know about such evil. Perhaps instead He is not all-powerful. He can't do anything about the suffering. A third possibility is that He is not perfectly loving, just or merciful. He doesn't care to eliminate all the suffering.

There is a customary way to try to explain this suffering away. It is to say that God gave man free will. Man sinned and thus brought all suffering into the world. This does not work on cases of the suffering of newborns in earthquakes, floods, tornadoes, and so forth. Most people seem to think that it would be wrong to punish all the students in a class and even future classes for the actions of one or two people. This is called "collective guilt" or "collective punishment." If it is wrong when a teacher does it with students, why is it alright when God does it to everybody for what just Adam and Eve did? Even as "a test," what strength of character or faith is there in a newborn to test? Or, how can it be just for a God to inflict suffering and death on an innocent newborn to test *somebody else,* such as the child's parents?

There are many different **schools** of philosophy in different senses. In metaphysics there is **Monism versus Dualism.** A monist philosopher holds the theory that there is fundamentally only one kind of substance in the universe. A dualist takes the position that there are two kinds of substances. "Dualism" is also used to refer to the theory that a human being is a nonphysical mind together with a physical body. A further example of schools is **Idealism versus Realism** and Materialism. Both idealist and materialist are monists. Idealists believe that everything exists is either a mind or depends for its existence on a mind, like ideas. Realists believe some things at least exist and have qualities independent of minds. Materialists think that everything real is physical, that is, it takes up space and behaves only in ways described by laws of physics and other sciences. Mental phenomena are really physical.

Associated with the Idealism - Materialism distinction is that between **Supernaturalism** and **Naturalism.** **Supernaturalism** says that natural events can be satisfactorily explained, predicted and controlled by assuming that they are caused by nonphysical personal beings. These beings are not bound by laws of nature. A single God or gods or demons, devils, gremlins, spirits, poltergeists, ancestor ghosts, nymphs of the woods and so forth would be examples of such personal nonphysical beings.) **Naturalism** says that natural events can only be satisfactorily explained, predicted and controlled by assuming that they are caused by physical particles and interactions which occur by laws of nature. A related distinction is that between **Vitalism** and **Mechanism. Vitalism** says that life is caused and sustained by a supernatural being (such as a soul.) Mechanism says that life is caused and sustained by the same natural physical particles and interactions as non-living processes.

Another major set of schools is **Rationalism versus Empiricism.** This pair of schools divides up philosophers in epistemology. Empiricists such as John Locke, George Berkeley, and David Hume believed that all knowledge comes from experience. Rationalists like Descartes and Leibniz believed there is some knowledge which we can have independently of experience. Emmanuel Kant worked out a solution to the conflict between these two schools of philosophy.

The early to middle Twentieth century was dominated by five schools. **Marxism** holds that societies are conditioned by the struggle between social classes; that is, workers vs. owners. Marxists are also concerned with the issues of economic inequality and worker alienation (being "turned off.") **Pragmatism** is America's contribution to philosophy. It holds that truth is what works and meaning is determined by practical differences in one's life. **Linguistic Analysis** holds that philosophical problems are best handled by examination of the uses of words. It stress clarity as the goal of philosophy. **Existentialism** asserts that man's existence precedes his essence. Existentialists believe that the best approach to philosophy lies in pure, detached observation and descriptions of phenomena of consciousness, called "Phenomenology." **Humanism** rejects belief in the supernatural, finds the individual to be precious, and seeks the fulfillment and enhancement of human life through reason, science and democracy (Humanist Manifestos 1 & 2, 1933, 1973.)

Post-1960 English language philosophy has been concerned with the nature of language and political life. Philosophers such as Noam Chomsky seem to agree with European philosophers that there are universal structures of mind and language. In Europe the new school was called "Structuralism." By the 1970's some philosophers became more interested in a kind of philosophy called **"Deconstructionism."** Deconstructionism seems to hold that almost all traditional texts in philosophy, science, literature and other areas can be shown to undermine and refute their own main points. Deconstructionism has now developed into **Postmodernism.** Postmodernism seems to contradict Modern Philosophy by holding that there is no independent reality or absolute truth. Every thing and phenomenon is a "text" and any group's interpretation of that text is as good as any other group's interpretation.

Below is a list of the most famous Western philosophers of all time. It is not a judgment of their importance or value to philosophy. The period just before the beginnings of Western Philosophy, **800-500 B.C.,** saw the appearance of many of the **world's largest and oldest religions:** the Hindu Upanishads; Gautama (the Buddha) 560-480; Confucius, 551-479 B.C.; Lao Tze, 604-517?, the founder of Taoism; and the pre-exile prophets of Israel 750-586 B.C. (Gautama was born a Hindu in India but Buddhism spread to and developed in China, Korea, and Japan.) This development of religion contributed to philosophy the idea of general rules or laws (at least of human behavior.) Examples would include the *5 purely ethical commands of the 10 Commandments. Thou shalt not: 1. murder, 2. steal, 3. bear false witness or 4. covet your neighbor's things and 5. Honor you parents. It also includes the "Golden Rule": Do unto others what you would have them do unto you.*

Here is the list of most famous Western Philosophers. Numbers 1 - 5 are the famous names of Ancient Philosophers.

1. Socrates 469-399 BC	16. George Hegel 1770-1831
2. Plato 428-348 BC	17. John Stuart Mill 1806-1873
3. Aristotle 384-322 BC	18. Karl Marx 1818-1883
4. Epicurus 341-270 BC	19. Soren Kierkegaard 1813-1855
5. Epictetus 50-130 AD	20. Fredrick Nietzsche 1844-1900
6. Augustine 354-430 AD	21. William James 1842-1910
7. Thomas Aquinas 1224-1274	22. John Dewey 1859-1952
8. Thomas Hobbes 1588-1679	23. Bertrand Russell 1872-1970
9. Rene Descartes 1596-1650	24. L. Wittgenstein 1889-1951
10. Baruch Spinoza 1632-1677	25. Martin Heidegger 1889-1976
11. John Locke 1632-1704	26. Jean-Paul Sartre 1905-1980
12. George Berkeley 1686-1753	27. Jacques Derrida 1930-
13. David Hume 1711-1776	28. Michel Foucault 1900-1995
14. Gottfried Leibniz 1646-1716	29. Noam Chomsky 1928-
15. Emmanuel Kant 1724-1804	

Six and seven are the greatest names of Medieval philosophy, eight through fifteen are Modern philosophers (1600-1800); sixteen through twenty were Nineteenth Century philosophers; twenty-one through twenty-six could be called Contemporary philosophers. Twenty-one and twenty-two were American Pragmatists; twenty three and twenty-four were Linguistic Analysts. Nineteen, twenty-five and twenty-six were Existentialists. Numbers Twenty-seven and Twenty-eight are Deconstructionist - Postmodern philosophers. Twenty-nine is perhaps the best known current philosopher of language.

This list contains only the names of dead, white, European, largely Christian males. Important Islamic philosophers include Al Farabi 875-950, Avicenna 980-1036, Al Ghazali 1058-1111, and Averroes 1126-1198. Jewish philosophers include Philo Judeaus 20 B.C. - 40 A.D., Maimonides 1135-1209, Baruch Spinoza 1632-1677, and Martin Buber 1878-1965.

Sexist social structure is largely responsible for the lack of diversity in this list. Women have not had chances to study and publish philosophy and have it widely read enough to become among the best known philosophers. Higher education changed its focus and at the earlier time this author went to college, Eastern, African and Native American contributions to philosophy and religion were not subjects of study. Deconstructionism, Postmodernism, Feminism, and Afrocentrism did not yet exist. In any case, they are beyond the scope of this book. **Feminism** says that women as a group have been oppressed by men. A more just society will result with the liberation of women from oppression. Women philosophers include Hypatia 370-415 A.D., Mary Wollstonecraft 1759-1796, Simone DeBeauvoir and Ayn Rand. Native thinkers include Black Elk (*Black Elk Speaks,* translated by John Neihard.)

Afrocentrism says that: 1. Many of the ideas of the Greek philosophers came from ancient Egypt and 2. that ancient Egypt was a multiracial society in which black people were among the most important contributors to Greek thought. Some scholars believe these points to be true. Other scholars believe either that such theses are untrue, or that there is not sufficient evidence to prove them. Present day Black African philosophers include Kwame Appiah, *In My Father's House,* Kwame Gyekye, *African Philosophical Thought,* John Mbiti, *African Religions and Philosophy,* Kwasi Wiredu, *Philosophy and the African Culture.*

Many philosophers, like some religious leaders, have been persecuted for their freethinking in the long process of putting wisdom and justice into government and other human institutions. Socrates was executed. Anaxagoras was banished and Aristotle had to flee from Athens. Zeno of Elea was tortured. Hypatia was murdered. Seneca was forced to commit suicide. Boethius was imprisoned and executed. Bruno was burned at the stake. Spinoza was excommunicated by the synagogue and the victim of attempted murder. Hobbes, Locke and Marx had to flee their countries. Gramsci was imprisoned for a long time. Through a long struggle of development, the values in moral rules finally came to be protected as specific rights, such as those set forth in the first ten amendments to the United States Constitution, called "The Bill of Rights." These include *freedom of religion and* **from** *others' religions, freedom of the press and of assembly to ask the government for a redress of grievances. The liberty right became the specific rights to refuse to host soldiers, to be secure against unreasonable searches, to be accused only by indictment by a grand jury, to be informed of charges against one, to bail, to counsel, to compel witnesses on your behalf, to a speedy trial, to refuse to testify against ones' self, and to not be tried twice on the same accusation.*

We should not leave the grim impression that all philosophers end up as martyrs in the struggle for morality and good government. Analytic philosophy is closer to law in development than to science or religion. Its instruction in logic helps students to score better than average on graduate school entrance tests. Philosophy majors frequently find employment in computer science, counseling, law, politics and entertainment. Successful philosophy majors include William Bennett, former U.S. Secretary of Education; Game show host Alex Trebeck (Jeopardy), comedian Steve Martin; and musicians Taylor Dayne and Sting.

SECTION 12.2: BASIC PHILOSOPHICAL IDEAS BEHIND CRITICAL THINKING

We will now look at a specific dialectic in philosophy, that about the Mind / Body Problem. We shall see that philosophical dialectic is often negative. It shows us what theories do not work. This can be of great value, especially in dealing with problems where "solutions" are tied up with deep hopes and wishful thinking. This is exactly the case in the Mind / Body Problem, where some proposed "solutions" are tied up with a hope for a life after death. Our presentation will be oversimplified for illustration.

Critical thinkers believe in a view called **Realism** (or "Truth Absolutism" or "the Objective View of Truth.") **Realism says there is a way that the world is independent of what anyone thinks.** It says that there are facts which are independent of what anyone wishes or hopes the facts might be. It is the view that the truth really is "out there." It holds that much important truth is objective, not subjective or relative to individuals, societies, or sets of concepts. It disagrees with the view that we humans make our reality. That view could be called "Idealism" or "Truth Relativism" or "Truth Subjectivism."

There are several problems with trying to believe that truth is subjective or relative. Schick and Vaughn (1995) sum up these arguments nicely. According to relativism, if you or your society in general believe that a claim is true, then it is true. However, *if you or your society could make a statement true just by believing it, then you would be infallible!* You could never be wrong. You could never make a mistake. If you or your society believed that the earth was flat and the sun, moon and stars went around it, that would be true. What then, would you do if you were given evidence that the earth was round and that the sun and moon did not go around it?

Belief that truth is subjective makes disagreement and all attempts at rational solution of it useless. Suppose you were a judge. Two men came before you each claiming to be the sole owner of some property. Suddenly a feeling that truth is relative and subjective came over you. You could not decide the issue. *Truth Relativism paralyzes the ability to decide between inconsistent claims.* Furthermore, people who claim to be truth relativists can not be consistent in everyday life. Suppose you were a relativist and one of the parties to an ownership dispute over a valuable piece of property. Would you give up insisting the property is yours because the other guy believed it was his also?

Finally, truth relativism is not consistent with itself. If we make our own reality, if everyone is always right, then even those who reject truth relativism would be right. The belief that truth is independent of what we believe would be as true as that it is dependent on what we believe. If truth was relative to what a society believed, then it would be true that black people are inferior to white, fit only to be slaves. That, after all, is what white southern society believed. It would be true that Jews ought to be exterminated, as the Nazi's believed. But these things would also be false, because they were disbelieved by other societies.

The theory that truth is statements and the facts is a illustrated that idea with the Let's imagine you have a cat or after one. The cat has made a Relativism, from the Truth here.

correspondence between our natural ally of Realism. Earlier we sentence "The cat is on the mat." are responsible for cleaning up mess on the mat. New Age Truth Realist's point of view, is shown

Other ideas presupposed by critical thinking are materialism, mechanism, naturalism and humanism. Dualism is the view that there are two radically different kinds of substances in the universe, minds, or spiritual objects and physical objects. *Minds* are supposed to be nonphysical objects which do not take up space. They have no mass, are non sensible, and private. Because they do not take up space and are utterly simple, they cannot decompose, rot, die. *Physical objects* are spatial, have mass, or at least location, and shape. They can make contact with each other, can decompose, and are publicly observable objects. A general argument for dualism is that it seems impossible to reduce the mental to the material or vice versa. We have not been able to translate statements about pain or belief into ones about something physical and/ or chemical where the statements are true or false under exactly the same conditions. This does not entail, however, that there are no roughly equivalent ways of describing the same process.

Dualism is usually found with Supernaturalism and Vitalism. Supernaturalism says that natural events can be satisfactorily explained, predicted and controlled by assuming that they are caused by non-physical personal beings. These beings are not bound by laws of nature. Vitalism says that life is caused and sustained by a supernatural substance (such as a soul.)

The trouble with supernaturalism and vitalism is that they are unproductive of any useful predictions, prevention, treatments, inventions, etc. They are not an inference to the best explanation of anything! Naturalism, embodied in science, does provide specifics which help explain why natural events happen and how to control them or at least get the most good out of them or tend to avoid the worst they can do. Consider the cracking of a car radiator exposed to extreme cold and wind. Any talk about it being "God's will" or "God ha[ving] a plan" into which the event fits, or it being the work of spirits, demons, and so on is just a pseudo-explanation. It tells us nothing useful! An explanation in terms of repeatable, observed natural events like the expansion of water below certain temperatures tells us all we can know to explain, predict, promote the occurrence of or try to prevent such events.

Vitalism in biology or psychology does not provide any real explanation of anything either. If some substance was life itself, then reintroduction of that substance into a brain-dead corpse would bring it back to life. Introduction of some material substances like blood, drugs, or electrical energy has, indeed, revived non brain-dead individuals. Medical science can also explain acceptably, if not exactly, how this happens. It has also made great advances in saving dying people. *Where are the demonstrated, repeated advances in religious or vitalistic raising of the dead?* No spiritual substance has ever been isolated. In no documented case has reintroduction of any substance into a brain-dead corpse ever brought it back to life. So there is no evidence of this sort that life is some supernatural spiritual soul substance.

Supernaturalism, vitalism and most versions of dualism have a further problem. In excusing their theoretical entities, God and the soul or mind from obeying natural law, they make them what might be called "explanatory wild cards." A "wild card" can be used as any card. Wild cards are fine in games. But coming to know reality is not a game. Money, effort, even health or life itself may be involved in coming to know reality. TWA flight 800 exploded off Long Island in 1996. The Federal Aviation Administration and Coast Guard spent millions of dollars and thousands of hours trying to find out what caused the crash. The goal was to prevent such accidents from happening again. This process has been repeated many times. It has made flying much safer. Ministers, on the other hand, tried to comfort grieving relatives. They "explained" that the crash was "part of God's plan." If that is satisfactory, why painstakingly reassemble its parts? Why not just "explain" the crash as God's will?

If one excuses God and the mind or soul from obeying natural law, one can't really satisfactorily explain anything with them. They make easy pseudo-explanations. However, they become of no use to predict or control anything.

A strong general argument against Dualism is that if it is true, then *Solipsism* is a reasonable position. Solipsism says that your own mind may be the only mind in existence. If the mind is a non sensible, private object which only the possessor has access to, then you cannot be certain that there is a mind animating any other body. Other bodies might just be complicated physical and chemical mechanisms. But it seems very clear that Solipsism is not a reasonable position. Nothing seems more obvious than that there are other minds than my own. If my mind was the only one, then somehow I wrote the works of Shakespeare, the music of Bach and the theories of Newton and Einstein. However, I can't even understand these things, much less write them.

The opposite of Dualism is **Monism:** the view that there is only one type of substance in the universe. An argument for Monism comes from Ockham's Razor. William of Ockham lived 1290 - 1349. He put forth the principle of theorizing that "It is vain to do with more what can be done with less." This is often not accurately stated as "(Theoretical) entities are not to be multiplied beyond necessity." In other words, one should assume the existence of as few theoretical entities as possible which are necessary to explain and predict any things or events. Materialism is a main form of monism.

Materialism is the view that there is only one type of substance in the universe, matter. Materialism is usually found coupled with **Reductionism,** the view that higher-order objects are really nothing but a sum of lower-order parts. For example, the view that the mind is nothing but the brain is reductionistic. So is the view that thinking is nothing but brain processes. The opposite of reductionism is **Holism,** the view that higher-order wholes are greater than the sum of their parts and have non-reducible properties. A strong argument for Materialism is that it explains why we have no doubt that other people have minds (since it holds the mind to be either visible behavior or potentially visible brain states.) An obstacle to the acceptance of Materialism is that if it is true, then there are no souls in the sense of Dualism, and no afterlife, and people do want to believe this.

Descartes developed a specific form of dualism known as Dualistic Interactionism. This theory says a person consists of a mind which is an unextended (non-material) thinking thing and a body which is an extended unthinking thing. It fits with our ordinary ways of describing and explaining human behavior. For example, we say, "She raised her hand because she wanted to answer a question." This looks like explaining a bodily behavior by a mental cause. We also say, "He felt pain because he was stuck with a pin." This looks like explaining a mental effect by a bodily cause. As Gilbert Ryle (1949) put it, according to such theories a person lives through two parallel histories, a stream of mental events and a stream of bodily events.

Parallel lines with a broken line between them and arrows from one event to another will represent the idea that one event causes another. A wavy "ghostly" line around the mental "things" or events represents Descartes' idea that they have no mass, volume, or location in space. Imagine a situation in which at one time T_1, a sharp pin pricks your hand. At time T_2 you feel pain. At T_3 you experience a desire to move your hand and at T_4 your hand moves. Descartes' theory is represented by the following diagram.

Diagram of Dualistic Interactionism

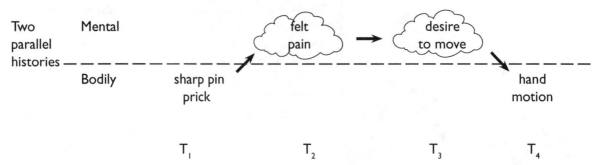

There is, of course, a correlation in time between bodily and mental events. If you are struck with a pin 100 different times, you are likely to feel pain, then a desire to move, and then your hand will move. However correlation is not identical with *causality!* Every time there is a day, then there is a night after it and vice versa. But this is correlation, not causality. Day does not cause night any more than night causes day. Descartes' claim is that, despite the extreme difference between mind and body, mental events do cause bodily events and vice versa.

As soon as Descartes imported Dualism from religion into philosophy it came under attack. Another natural philosopher, Pierre Gassendi, raised serious questions about Descartes' theory. If you are not in your body like a sailor in a ship, then you must be united or intermingled with it. How can there be a union and in-termingling of mind and body if one takes up space and the other is not greater than a point? How will that which is bodily seize on that which is non-bodily to keep it conjoined with itself, or how will the non bodily seize on the body to bind it to itself? Essentially he was asking how the body and soul could keep "together" with each other. Surely we see enough endurance of terrible pain. Why does not an immortal soul simply wander away from an unattractive, old, ill injured, severely pained body? How and why would a God "hold" such different things together for so long?

Another problematic question is, "How could this nonphysical extensionless mind possibly interact with a physical body?" If it has no extension and location, where would it interact with a body? Gassendi may be seen as suggesting that Descartes' mind and body are so different that there is a Wall of Causal Impossibility between them, preventing interaction.

GASSENDI'S VIEW

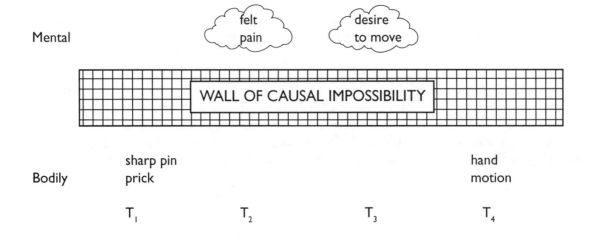

Another serious objection comes from the core of science, physics. Physicists after Descartes' time firmly established three principles called "Conservation Principles." *Conservation of Energy* means that the total energy of an isolated physical system always remains the same in quantity. This principle has been repeatedly confirmed. Whenever it looked like it was violated, physicists have discovered some new form of physical energy into which the apparently lost energy was transformed. For example, when a falling body hits the earth, its kinetic energy is transformed into sound and heat.

If a nonphysical mind could actually effect a physical body, then there would be a gain of total energy in the physical system without any compensating loss or transformation. If an event happening to a physical body could cause some effect upon a nonphysical mind, then there should be a loss of energy from the physical system. This is never observed!

Where does the energy come from when I raise my hand? My muscles released chemical energy. The chemical energy comes from my muscles oxidizing food. The food got energy which came to plants from the sun. The plants converted the energy of sunlight into chemical energy by photosynthesis. The radiant energy of sunlight came from nuclear fusion in the sun. The sun's hydrogen nuclei were created in the Big Bang at the beginning of the universe.

But *why* did you raise your hand? The "Why?" question invites a confusion of contexts. You can give a folk-psychological "explanation" in terms of reasons and desires, purposes of a ghostly mind. It might provide some practical insight useful for judging my action and rewarding or punishing me for it. But it will not be of great use to accurately predict and control my hand-raising behavior in the future. A physicist or neurophysiologist can not give a specific scientific explanation for several reasons. 1) This is an under - described fictional example. 2) Humans are so complex and one hand - raising so trivial that probably no scientists have ever wired up anyone to try to find this out. 3) The monitoring would affect the subject's behavior so the action would not be in the normal context in which we think of people doing things out of reasons or desires. 4) An average person would not understand the technical language the neurophysiologist would need to use to give a causal "why" explanation. Does this mean that simple-minded folk psychological explanations are correct and scientific ones are not? Certainly not. They are not even competitors except when we come to philosophical questions of what exists.

Descartes' followers could not answer questions about interaction. They then proposed another dualistic theory called Parallelism. **Parallelism** is the view that a person consists of a nonphysical mind and a physical body but owing to the vast differences between them, they do not causally interact. There is a severe problem for Parallelism. If mind and body don't interact, how come there is so much regularity or correlation in time between mental and bodily events? For example, how come if you are struck with a pin 100 times, you will feel pain an instant later every time? Normally this correlation between A happening 100 times and event B 100 times after is explained by saying "A causes B."

Descartes' followers' solution was to drag another theoretical entity into the answer, God. Their theory was called Occasionalism. It said that on the occasion that God causes an event to happen to your body, like a pinprick, at the next moment He causes an event to occur in your mind like felt pain. Next God causes you to feel a desire to move and finally He again acts to cause your hand to go up. This is incredibly over-complex. If your own mind can't move your hand, then how can God, being a spirit also, Himself break through the Wall of Causal Impossibility and make pins stick a person or a hand move? Furthermore, with God so closely involved with individuals' mental life, it seems to leave no room at all for free will and responsibility.

No significant new dualistic theory came forth until one called **Epiphenomenalism** developed in the 1800's (say EH pih feh nah men al izm). This is the view that people have both physical bodies and nonphysical minds but that only the body acts on the mind. Mind and mental events are an off-shoot or by-product of bodily, particularly, brain events. The mind is to the body as the babbling of the brook is to the water rushing over the rocks. To illustrate this we take down the Wall of Causal Impossibility and put up a thin line with gates -/ which open only one way, from the bodily to the mental. We put in intermediate bodily events which had been learned about by Nineteenth Century scientists, nerve firings. We use heavy arrows among them to indicate real causal relations. Finally, the cut off cones represent beams of "light" by which the physical events somehow bring to consciousness the mental events.

Epiphenomenalism

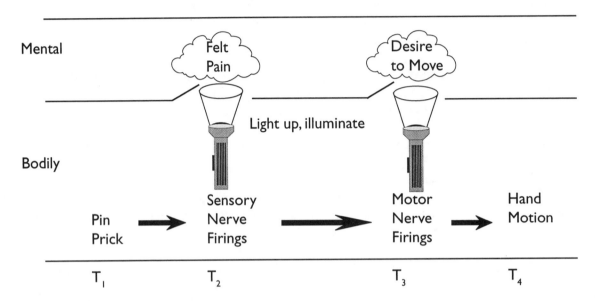

Aside from the interaction problem, the conservation problem and making Solipsism seem reasonable, dualism has a fourth severe problem. The dualist's mind must be simple, have no parts, to survive death and disintegration. But it needs parts to explain complex activities that humans can perform. So the mind begins to be talked about as if it were a little person inside the person. Such a being is called by the Latin word "homunculus," meaning "little man." What do we see dream images with at night when we sleep with our bodily eyes closed? It seems natural to say "the eyes of the mind." Conscience is described as a "still small voice" inside ourselves. From ancient times people believed that they were sometimes possessed by demons, personal beings. Socrates speaks of his demon in *The Republic*. We are claimed to "grasp" concepts with our minds.

Minsky (1988), a physicalist, has written that "Mind is a meat machine." He describes the problem by saying that it is useless to try to explain how some complex thing accomplishes complex activities by claiming that there is another thing like it inside of it. If the mind is simple, then it has no parts with which to explain the complexities of the activities. If the mind is another complex thing inside the person and like it in causal powers, then we mind homunculus does *its* work. body to move" and so on? The theory will then have to refer to that one, and so on. This is called regress. Going on forever, it explanation, not a real one. All philosophers and scientists to held by religion and by people problems.

will have to ask how this How does it "see" or "will the person who puts forward this another homunculus inside an infinite explanatory produces only a pseudo - these difficulties led abandon dualism. It is now unaware of its unsolvable

The next theory to develop in the dialectic about the Mind/Body problem was **Behaviorism.** Behaviorism is the theory that the mind is not a non material object but behavior or dispositions to behave in certain ways. The meaning of mental terms is behavioral and every sentence containing mental terms can be translated into sentences referring only to behavior or dispositions to behave. For example, to be "intelligent" is to be capable of complex behavior varied appropriately to the circumstances. An argument for Behaviorism is that it explains why we can often be certain exactly what mental state another person is in. An argument against Behaviorism brought about its' abandonment. It is that one cannot translate all sentences containing mental terms into ones not containing them. It seems that there really are images and pain feelings, not just pain behavior.

The next theory to develop was "The Identity Theory" or **"Physicalism."** This theory says that *the mind is identical with the brain.* So-called "mental objects" like pain are really identical with brain processes like firing C-Fibers. An advantage this theory had over Behaviorism is that it distinguished between the sense of words and their references. The *sense* of a word is the other words used to define it. Its' *reference* is the thing or things for which it stands. Words like "mind" and "brain" and behavioral terms may not have the same dictionary meaning but can refer to the same object. This distinction enables physicalists to hold that the mind is identical with the brain even if one can not translate mental conduct statements into equivalent neurophysiological words or vice versa.

We find evidence apparently supporting Physicalism in the progress of medicine. Doctors treating brain damaged people and brain researchers have established that *every so-called "mental" function is damaged or destroyed when parts of the brain are damaged or destroyed. Therefore the mind, soul or spirit is either identical with or totally dependent on the brain.* So what is there left for a nonphysical mind to do (except hopefully survive death?) But how would a disembodied mind without a brain and senses work? Drugs can alter almost all moods, forms of thought or behavior. Scientists conclude that all so-called "mental illness" is neurobiological, due to damage or chemical imbalances in the brain. This is evidence for the dependence of mind on brain. Further evidence is that extreme age brings brain shrinkage and deterioration of memory and personality. What is left to survive death?

Heart stoppage is not death. If reviving one whose heart and respiration have stopped is a miracle, Dr. Robert Spetzler, who has done over 50 cardiac stand-still operations, has performed over 50 miracles. Death occurs when electrochemical activity ceases irreversibly in the brain. There are no documented cases of anyone ever returning to life after irreversible brain death. The "white light" and images of dead relatives have been reported by people who obviously were not brain dead. They have been reported also by nonbelievers and explained as hallucinations produced by anoxia, lack of oxygen.

There is an objection against Physicalism as well. Two things can't be identical if they have different properties. A mental image may be orange. No brain event is orange. Therefore an orange mental image cannot be a brain event. Mental objects like images and pains seem to have "qualia." The sharpness or dullness of pain is another example. It does not seem that these are equivalent to any brain processes.

In the 1970's **Functionalism** was developed. This is roughly the view that *the brain is a computer and the mind is its programming.* Mental states are computational states of the brain caused by sensory inputs and its current state and producing later states and behavioral outputs according to formulatable rules about transition from one state to another. Pain, for example, is the state caused by injury and causing fear and avoidance or repair action. Functionalism avoids most objections against earlier theories except perhaps those against physicalism. It allows that aliens might have intelligence, and other mental states.

Functionalism makes use of Alan Turing's idea of a State Table. (Turing developed the mathematical theory of the computer.) In Thomas (1976) it is shown how such a table could be used to give a full systematic description of a particular human mind. However, Functionalism allows anything which has the same functional states as a mind to have a mind of its own. This allows inorganic and non-alive computers and robots to have minds. But such things don't seem to have the inner qualia of mental states like the throbbing or sharpness of pain which we think only living beings can experience.

What is this brain physicalists give so much credit to? Weighing about 44 - 48 ounces, about 1,000 milliliters in volume, it is really a very redundant ("massively parallel") electrochemical organ. It is so active it requires 20% of the heart's supply of blood. Life emerged between 3.85 and 3.46 billion years ago. So this brain is the highest product of about 3.5 billion years of evolution. Its processing units are 50-100 billion neurons organized into many sorts of patterns such as receptor and motor networks. These neurons are supported by even more nutrient glial cells.

Most neurons have a cell body ("soma") dendrite trees (receptors), and an axon (sender) with tree branches at its' ends. The axon fiber transmits the processed signal to the synapses (gaps between it and the next dendrite branches.) At the end of the axon branches chemicals are released which flow across the synapse to neighboring dendrite trees. There the chemicals excite or slow down the receiving neurons' firing rates. Neurons fire at rates up to about 1,000 pulses per second.

Is there any place for a spirit to somehow influence such an incredible machine? It seems impossible to understand, physically, how it could do so. There is nothing even so "light" or delicate in it. Is there anything in its operation which could not be modeled by an inorganic computer, any place for free will or spontaneous creativity? A few modern scientific thinkers have speculated that there might be. A man named Kurt Goedel proved that there are statements which humans can know to be true but which nether we nor any computers will ever be able to prove. Roger Penrose, a mathematical physicist, has argued, based partly on Goedel's work, that artificial intelligence will never be able to do everything the human brain can do.

Penrose (1989, P. 400 f.) speculates that there may be quantum level effects in the brain. One portion of Quantum Theory is indeterministic. To speculate thus, he must assume two levels of amplification from a cell as sensitive as a retinal one which can be activated by a single neuron. However, he must admit that the threshold for awareness of the activation is above this and that "our consciousness is not needed" for collapse of the indeterministic wave function. His critics, such as Stenger (1995) agree. Stenger says, "I personally find it incomprehensible that quantum gravity, which only comes into play at the Planck scale, can have a profound role on the scale of biological processes." (p. 275.) So it seems that it is not possible for even an almost indetectably light or small spirit to start or affect a neuron signal, a much larger region of positive charge traveling in a normally negative axon channel.

We can't "explain spontaneous creativity." This implies nothing about its' being undetermined. The brain will perhaps always be too complex to learn exactly how creativity works. If we feel that we are free, this may be because we have no means for deep monitoring of our own brain processes. Our brains evolved to cope with external problems, not for meditation. Feelings can be deceptive. There is a strong argument that the "Free Will Problem," is a pseudo problem anyway (see Double, 1991.) We can distinguish between social, economic and governmental conditions under which there is more *freedom of action,* and those under which there is less. This is what really counts for human life, not freedom of will.

There are still many physicalists and some functionalists. However, all critical thinking philosophers have abandoned dualism in favor of some form of materialism about the mind and the Mind/Body problem. This simplified dialectic should be taken as an example of how difficult it is to get justified theories about some subjects. Philosophers have worked 350 years from Descartes on to find, develop and evaluate a half dozen theories. Dualistic Interactionism, Parallelism, Epiphenomenalism and Behaviorism have been found unjustified. Physicalism and Functionalism are still being worked on. None of the theories are as yet fully justified.

13

RELIGION AND SCIENCE

SECTION 13.1: FUNDAMENTALISM

There are two areas in which philosophy touches on both religion and science. One is in the field of ethics, upon a theory called "Theological Ethics." The other is in the field of metaphysics, which must be concerned with the conflict of religion and science. **Fundamentalism** will be defined as the belief that the scriptures of one's religion are inerrant. "Inerrant" means "without error." Fundamentalists believe that every claim in the scripture of their religion is literally true and other religions are "false religion." Ecumenicalism (say EH q men ih kal izm) says many religions' scriptures express some important truths symbolically. It admits that some claims are not literally true. This chapter deals with a fundamentalist view of theological and especially ethical claims from scripture.

Tertullian (150 - 230 A. D.) said that the incarnation of Christ "is certain because it is impossible." He also said, "Credo quia absurdum est," I believe *because* it is absurd. He seemed to recognize that theological statements are absurd, highly unjustified, by a standard of evidence applied to factual claims. Their distinctive absurdity is a reason for their being held at all. Distinctive absurdity seems to be a necessary quality in statements settled on to be "articles of faith." Theological claims are picked to be confessed, not professed or asserted. They are membership-confessing statements (see Cowley, 1991 p. 7.) In marketing terms, they differentiate brands, like Joe Camel and the Marlboro Man.

A look at early Catholic creeds tends to confirm this. Many such confessions of faith exist. One is the Creed of Nicaea which was set forth (in 325 A. D.) explicitly to define the membership boundaries between Catholics and Arians. The parts meant to mark off what Catholics believe from what Arians believe have been put in italics.

We believe in one God the Father All-sovereign, maker of all things visible and invisible; And in one Lord Jesus Christ, the Son of God, begotten of the Father, only-begotten, that is, of the substance of the Father, God of God, Light of Light, true God of true God, begotten not made, of one substance with the Father, through whom all things were made, things in heaven and things on the earth; who for us men and for our salvation came down and was made flesh, and became man, suffered, and rose on the third day, ascended into the heavens, is coming to judge living and dead.

And in the Holy Spirit. *And those who say 'There was a time when he was not,' and 'Before he was begotten he was not' and that, 'He came into being from what-is-not,' or those who allege, that the Son of God is 'Of another substance or essence,' or 'created,' or 'changeable,' or 'alterable,' these the Catholic and Apostolic Church anathematizes.* (Bettinson, 1947, p. 36)

Such non - reality - based disputes are settled only by political struggle, war or schism (splitting.) Early bishops preached against one another, sought alliances, deposed each other and won or lost at Church Councils (see, e.g., Harnack, 1957, p. 285f.) Conquerors of one religion said to conquered people of others: "Accept our theological beliefs, political authority and ethical rules or we will kill you." "Minister" means "agent of some foreign power," not "one who helps." Confessions of faith in theological creeds need to be differently absurd from what the conquered believe. They are dominance-acceptance rituals. *Fundamentalism makes religion into pseudoscience.* By its belief in inerrancy, it turns such dominance-acceptance rituals into claims of deep and important factual knowledge about the world, including predictions (revelations) which are very important to how life should be lived. Critical thinkers can get along, uneasily, with Ecumenicalists. With Fundamentalists, it's total war. If abortion stops a beating heart, Fundamentalism stops a thinking mind.

SECTION 13.2: BIBLICAL MORALITY

Theological ethics says simply "Whatever God wills is what ought to be done." There are significant difficulties to applying this theory. First, it assumes that there is a God. Most people in America accept that assumption. But suppose one were arguing with an atheist. To claim that "God wills such and such" is not going to be persuasive. One would have to first persuade him that there is a God. This would prove difficult because of the Problem of Suffering. Second, one's claim might not be persuasive to people who practice a different religion. Religions differ over what is right and wrong. They differ even over matters like whether it is alright to kill other human beings.

Within the Judeo - Christian tradition parties can agree on the Bible as the basic moral authority. Some Judeo-Christian religious moral commands have influenced or caused much good behavior. Christianity also has inspired much very great music and art. However, the morality in the Bible itself is simply not consistent even on taking human life. We will quote from the King James version of the Bible. There are other translations. However, most say the same thing on the points we will quote. The quotes reveal what might be called "the Good, The Bad and The Ugly" of the Bible. Some of them students may have never seen before. *Look them up;* they can be found in the Bible. Other translations may clean up or soften some of the "bad" or "ugly," mean-sounding statements. But it is doubtful that they are accurate if they differ very greatly from the King James version.

After Adam and Eve ate the apple, God, according to Genesis, Chapter 3: V.16, punished Eve. He said, "I will greatly multiply thy sorrow... in sorrow thou shalt bring forth children; and thy desire shall be to thy husband, and he shall rule over thee." He also punished Adam with having to work to get bread (V.19). These passages raise the question of whether it is moral to punish a whole group of people, many as yet unborn, for the deeds of a very few. It seems that God practices collective punishment. But is it right to punish non responsible members of a group, as well as responsible ones? The passage has also been used to justify denying women anesthetics or being indifferent to their pain in childbirth. The "rule over thee" part represents God as squarely behind sexism. Should husbands rule over wives, or should marriage be an equal partnership?

Shortly thereafter God seems to take slavery for granted. In Ch. 17: V 13, He tells Abraham: "He that is born in thy house and he that is bought with thy money, must needs be circumcised." No disapproval of slavery is offered. In the New Testament 1 Peter 2:18 slaves are urged to be subject to their masters, even harsh ones. No serious opposition to slavery occurred among even the fathers of the Catholic Church hundreds of years later. Augustine, writing in *The City of God*, around 400 A. D., says that slavery is not natural. However, "... it is with justice, we believe, that the condition of slavery is the result of sin" (Bk. XIX, 15.) He tries to justify 1 Peter by arguing that the particular slave may have done nothing wrong but, oh well, somebody somewhere along the line must have sinned.

On the other hand, in Genesis Ch. 18, when God wants to destroy Sodom, Abraham is able to bargain with Him. God says He will not destroy Sodom first if 50 righteous people are found in it. Abraham is able to get it down to 20. So it looks like God does not practice collective punishment. But He does destroy Sodom and Gomorrah. These were two cities. Were there not any babies in these two cities who did not deserve to be killed? Lot and his daughters did some things which would not seem to make them very deserving of saving either. When Sodomites came to "know" (have homosexual relations with) two visitors to Lot's house (angels) Lot offered to let the Sodomites rape his daughters instead! Nevertheless, the girls later get Lot drunk and have sex with him while he "perceived not when [they] lay down nor when they arose." This certainly suggests that they raped their father against his will. Couldn't these women have gone back to Zoar to get men?

One statement of the 10 Commandments is found in Exodus, Ch. 20. Four are specifically religious. Thou shalt have no other Gods before Me. Thou shalt not make idols. Thou shalt not take God's name in vain. Thou shalt keep the sabbath holy. A related fifth seems like the first labor law. Six days shalt thou labor, but not do any work on the seventh. The remainder seem more purely ethical and progressive. Honor thy father and mother. Thou shalt not kill, commit adultery, steal, bear false witness against thy neighbor, or covet his wife or possessions. Much other "progressive morality," more in keeping with modern ideas, is expressed elsewhere in the Bible. Many such passages are collected in Bachman (1989.) There are, however, more very serious passages we need to expose and others which are not consistent with these progressive ideas. Sex, violence and plainly strange passages in the Bible are catalogued in Smith (1995.)

In Ch. 21 God makes regulations without disapproving of indentured servitude (being sold into temporary slavery). Among them is the rule that if a master gives a wife to a servant and she has children, when he goes free, she and their children remain the master's property. If he insists on staying with his wife and child, he becomes a slave forever. (Ch. 21, V. 4-5.) This seems cruel for a God. God also says "He that curseth his father, or his mother, shall surely be put to death." (Ch. 21, V. 17.) If the death penalty were applied to everyone who has ever cursed his father or mother, how many people would be left alive? This too seems cruel and thoughtless.

In Ch. 21 V. 21 God rules that if men are fighting and a pregnant woman is injured so that her fetus is stillborn, the injurer is not guilty of murder of a person. He shall pay a fine. But in V. 23-25 the principle of "an eye for an eye" is stated. "If any mischief follow, then thou shalt give life for life, eye for eye, tooth for tooth, hand for hand, foot for foot, burning for burning, wound for wound."

Many situations involving killing human beings are right and even prescribed, allegedly by God, in the Old Testament. Leviticus Ch. 20: V. 9 repeats the death penalty for anyone who curses his parents. Chapters 9 - 12 and 14 - 16 prescribe the death penalty for adultery, various sexual relations among kin by marriage, and for having sex with animals. Verses 21 and 22 have God saying that if people have sex with animals, the animals have to be put to death too! One wonders how many people would be left if we inflicted the death penalty on adulterers. Verse 13 says "If a man also lie with mankind, as he lieth with a woman, both of them have committed an abomination: they shall surely be put to death." Either the Bible Commandment "Thou shalt not kill" is not to be taken literally or the Bible is inconsistent by also containing all these death penalties. If the Commandment meant "Thou shalt not murder" the Bible is inhumane, since it must be understood as saying that killing homosexuals, adulterers, sheep lovers and parent-cursers is not murder but obedience to God's Will.

Exodus Ch. 22: V. 18 says something which became the justification of one of the greatest evils humans have ever inflicted on other humans. "Thou shalt not suffer a witch to live." Under this justification, "During the 14th - 17th centuries, somewhere between 200,000 and half a million people were executed (burned, beheaded, drowned, hanged or strangled) on accusations of witchcraft" (Ben-Yehuda, N. 1981, p. 328.) Accounts of the Inquisition in particular reveal that investigators were paid for gathering evidence from the estates of the very people they persecuted. They also reveal that priests used fantasies about witches having sexual relations with demons and Satan himself in order to strip the women being tried for witchcraft to examine their bodies, especially the genitals, for marks of sexual acts with demons (see Sagan, 1995, p. 120 f.) Inconsistency, we see, is useful. Hide it from oneself and one can commit the greatest obscenities, torture and murder for profit and for religious, political and sexual domination.

SECTION 13.3: BIBLICAL GENOCIDE

Many wars are described in the Old Testament. In Exodus Ch. 15: V. 3 Moses and the children of Israel sing: "The Lord is a man of war." In Numbers Ch. 31: V. 7-18 it describes the fate of the Midianites. After the Israelites defeat them, they kill the kings and all the men. When they bring the women and children to Moses, he gets angry and says: "kill every male among the little ones, and kill every woman that hath known man by lying with him. But all the women children that have not known a man by lying with him, keep alive for yourselves." In Deuteronomy Ch. 2: V. 31 - 34, Moses relates that God gave Sihon and his land to the Israelites. Moses says (V. 34) "And we took all his cities at that time, and utterly destroyed the men, and the women, and the little ones, of every city, we left none to remain." These religions prohibited birth control so they could outbreed others to build bigger armies. Retrograde fundamentalists still try to prohibit it while there is an environmental crisis and they have lost control of governments and the ability to field armies at all.

To kill a large number, or all men, women and children; civilians, is called **"genocide."** It is widely condemned among nations today as barbaric wrongdoing. Yet God threatens or orders it repeatedly. In Deuteronomy Ch. 3, genocide is committed against all of the three score (60!) cities of Bashan (V. 4.) In Ch. 7, V. 2 it is commanded against 7 nations. In Joshua, Ch. 10, God "delivers" 6 cities, "and he [Joshua] smote [them] with the edge of the sword, and all the souls that were therein; he let none remain." Check out 1 Samuel 15:2-3 and Hosea 13:16 on ripping open pregnant women and dashing infants. With such images of God, it is no wonder that a fundamentalist American-Israeli M.D., Baruch Goldstein, could forsake his medical oath, take up a submachine gun and slaughter worshipers in one the holiest Islamic mosques in Israel. Lately they have wished to kill each other over a red cow and an offensive drawing of Mohammed.

SECTION 13.4: RIGHT NOW, WRONG LATER?

It is sometimes claimed that the morality of the Old Testament is something called "the Mosaic Dispensation." This means the moral law as given to Moses. It is claimed that this was changed by the advent of Jesus. There is certainly a sharp contrast, even explicit inconsistency, between these representations of God's moral rules and those set forth in the Sermon on the Mount in the Gospel of Matthew. Jesus several times says things like (Matt. Ch. 5: V. 21) "Ye have heard that it was said by them of old time, thou shalt not kill; and whoever shall kill shall be in danger of the judgment: But I say unto you, That whoever is angry with his brother without a cause shall be in danger of the judgment." Again, he says, "Ye have heard that it hath been said, An eye for an eye, and a tooth for a tooth: But I say unto you, that ye resist not evil: but whosoever shall smite thee on the right cheek, turn to him the other also. And if a man will sue thee at the law, and take away thy coat, let him have thy cloak also, and whosoever shall compel thee to go a mile, go with him twain... Love your enemies, bless them that curse you, do good to them that hate you... etc." This passage also contains the Golden Rule (Matt. Ch. 7, V. 12) "Therefore all things whatsoever ye would that men should do unto you, do ye even so to them."

But could killing adulterers, homosexuals, really have been *right* up to Jesus's time and then wrong thereafter? Are Jesus's rules really the right way to react to evil or wrongdoing? Should evil not be resisted? If a group or nation is keeping people in slavery or actually practicing genocide on them and we have the capacity to stop it, have we an obligation to "resist not" such evil? Did not Jesus set up moral standards opposite to those of the Old Testament? Are they not wrong for human beings? Are they not as impossibly too high as the Old Testament Mosaic dispensation was too low for us? As soon as Christianity gained political power it accepted and justified slavery and capital punishment, persecution of people for holding other religions, inquisitions into heresy, burning hundreds of thousands of women at the stake and wars such as those of the Crusades and the Reformation. Has it not also laid a heavy load of guilt on people because of our inability to live up to Jesus's moral rules?

SECTION 13.5: MARRIAGE, THE FAMILY AND HOMOSEXUALITY

There are also some areas in which the morality of Christianity has not seemed too much of an advance. One area is that of marriage and family life. Another is the treatment of homosexuality. Jesus made no provision for divorce except for adultery (Matt. Ch. 5: V. 32.) He also said (Ch. 10: V. 34-5) "Think not that I am come to send peace on earth: I came not to send peace, but a sword. For I am come to set a man at variance against his father, and the daughter against her mother, and the daughter in law against her mother in law." This may refer to the strife which occurs when part of a family changes religion. But just before that he said that whoever would deny him before men he would deny before his Father in heaven (V. 33) This seems at least not merciful, even if truthful.

The explicit passages of the New Testament about the inequality of the sexes in marriage and homosexuality are these. In Paul's letter to the Ephesians Ch. 5, V. 22-24 he says, "Wives, submit yourselves unto your own husbands, as unto the Lord. For the husband is the head of the wife, even as Christ is the head of the church: and he is savior of the body. Therefore as the church is subject unto Christ, so let the wives be to their own husbands in every thing." It matters little that he goes on immediately to say that husbands should love their wives as themselves, nourish and cherish them as their own bodies. A clearly unequal structure has been set forth.

In his letter to the Romans (Ch. 1: V. 26-7) Paul describes unrighteous and ungodly people this way: "And for this cause God gave them up unto vile affections: for even their women did change the natural use into that which is against nature; And likewise also the men, leaving the natural use of the woman, burned in their lust one toward another; men with men working that which is unseemly, and receiving in themselves that recompense of their error which was meet." After calling them many sorts of names, he says this about them: "Who knowing the judgment of God, that they which commit such things are worthy of death..." (V. 32.) If God gave homosexuals up to "vile affections" are they responsible? And are Christians supposed to love their homosexual neighbors or kill them?

SECTION 13.6: HELL IN CHRISTIANITY AND ISLAM

Other arguments concerning moral defects in Christianity and Islam can be found in Russell (1961) and Warraq (1995.) About the doctrine of Hell as a place of eternal torment for sinners, Russell said, "I really do not think that a person with a proper degree of kindness in his nature would have put fears and terrors of that sort into the world." *Infinite torture is unjust punishment for finite wrongs!* When Salman Rushdie published a soft critique of Islam in a work of fiction, *The Satanic Verses,* Islamic clerics said he should be killed. Warraq claims that Muhammad had several opponents assassinated. He claims that almost all Muslims believe the Koran is the exact word of God, dictated in perfect, pure Arabic by an angel to Muhammad. However, there are verses by Muhammad to God, non-Arabic words, variant readings, grammatical and historical errors and self-contradictions in it. Self-contradiction is taken care of by a doctrine that later sayings abbrogate (cancel) earlier ones.

Warraq claims that Islam is sexist, racist and imperialistic like Christianity. Its doctrine of Jihad, or Holy War, is simple: Kill all unbelievers (those who join other gods with God) wherever you find them (sura 9.5-6.) The Koran is mostly in favor of predestination, yet claims that many people will suffer terrible torments in Hell for things they (were predestined to) do. Islamic civilization has reached great heights, Warraq claims, in spite of Muhammad's teachings and Islamic law. All passages of the Koran preaching tolerance are found in early suras (chapters) while all featuring killings, decapitation, and maiming are found in later ones. Thus intolerance in Islam abrogates tolerance.

Fundamentalist Christians in America have recently called occasionally for killing homosexuals and people who work in clinics where abortions are done. A couple of such killings have happened. An AP dispatch from Israel in December 1996 claimed that Rabbi Ovadia Yosef told a rally of 10,000 Orthodox Jews that people who work on the Sabbath ought to be put to death. Death - dealing intolerance is characteristic of fundamentalism. We have concentrated a bit unfairly on Judeo-Christian religions. For an excellent account of "Holy Hatred" and slaughter among Hindus, Buddhists, and Sikhs as well as Christians and Jews in the 1990's see Haught (1995.)

Extreme inconsistencies like these have led philosophers in general to reject Theological Ethics. They pose the following dilemma. Either something is good *by definition* because God wills it, or God wills it because it is good. If it was good by definition if God willed it, then if God willed undeserved suffering, torture or death, then that would be good. But believers in a God do not accept this idea. However, if God wills things because they are good, then even God has some evidence on the basis of which He decides what is good. So if we humans have moral disagreements, claims as to the commands of a God, without evidence, will not result in a rational resolution of such moral disputes. When we disagree, we have to trust our sense of what is right and wrong to decide what God wills. We can not trust our sense of what God wills to decide what it right and wrong. This view is called *The Autonomy of Ethics* (from religion.) "Autonomy" means "being a lawmaker for itself." "The autonomy of ethics from religion" means that we humans have a sense of right and wrong independent of what it says in scriptures, perhaps what is called "conscience."

SECTION 13.7: TESTABLE STATEMENTS IN THE BIBLE

We consider Fundamentalism to necessarily involve belief that every statement in the Bible is literally true. A couple of passages of the New Testament make claims which ought to be testable, if the Bible is literally true. One is Matthew Ch. 17 in which Jesus says to his disciples "If ye have faith as a grain of mustard seed, ye shall say unto this mountain, 'Remove hence to yonder place'; and it shall remove and nothing shall be impossible unto you." Unless this was meant to apply only to the disciples, anyone with even a little faith, for a grain of mustard seed is small, ought to be able to move a mountain. This has suggested to some non fundamentalists a test. Ask a believer in the literal truth of the Bible if he or she has faith. If the answer is "yes," ask to see his or her Bible. Check that the quote just given is the same. If it is, ask him to read it aloud. Then challenge him to move some massive object visibly, some distance.

If the person claims that the passage applied only to the disciples, there is a more unqualified testable statement at Luke Ch. 10: V.19 which Jesus apparently said to seventy disciples: "I give you power to tread on scorpions and over all the power of the enemy; nothing shall by any means hurt you." If this too, is claimed to apply only to the disciples, there is one more similar passage, concerning which this author has heard the following test. **Warning: the author of this text is simply expounding what he has read elsewhere. Do not do this. It is probably illegal.** "Carry a bottle of some harsh chemical liquid with you, such as an ammonia based cleaner. Ask your fundamentalist opponent whether he has faith. If he answers 'yes,' ask him if 'To drink something' means to swallow, to take down into one's stomach. If the answer is 'Yes,' ask to see his Bible. Check the Gospel according to Mark, Ch. 16: V. 17-18 to see whether it says this. "And these signs shall follow them that believe; ... they shall take up serpents; and if they drink any deadly thing; it shall not hurt them." If it says that, ask him to read it aloud. After he does so, offer him the bottle of poisonous chemical and ask him to drink."

This test, although no one should urge another to perform it, would prove either the literal truth of the Bible or that the person claiming literal belief does not have faith in the literal truth of the Bible. There are, indeed, small groups of snake handling ministers. Some are bitten and survive. But bites of most American poisonous snakes are not fatal to adults, whether they believe or do not believe. On the other hand, this author has never seen any good evidence of any fundamentalists drinking any deadly thing and coming away unhurt.

SECTION 13.8: RELIGION TRIES TO SUPPRESS SCIENCE

Metaphysics has had to deal with a long term conflict between religious fundamentalism and science over the nature of reality. Bertrand Russell (1961) described the conflict from a very pro-scientific viewpoint. The basic point of science, according to Russell, is by observation and reasoning to discover truths about the world. These truths are learned by induction and are regarded as tentative and only probable. A religion, on the other hand, consists of a church, a creed and a code of morals. The creed is a set of abstract statements, vast generalizations which are taken on faith to be certain. From these statements others are deduced which come into conflict with claims established by science.

Russell argues that Catholicism resisted developments in science because some of them contradicted claims in the Bible. If the Catholic or other Christian churches admitted that there was even one factual error in the Bible, then it would not be the perfect word of God. It might even be in error on more important matters, such as moral judgments. There can be no doubt, historically, that Christian religions resisted various developments in science. The first major battle was over the theory of Copernicus that the sun, not the earth, was the center of the solar system. Prior to Copernicus' time the church had accepted the earth - centered theory of a second Century A. D. astronomer named Ptolemy. His theory fit well with the idea that the earth was a special creation to God and that man was special as well, having been created in the Garden of Eden.

Copernicus, fearing trouble with the church, delayed publication of his theory until just before his death in 1543. Protestants were almost more bitter in their condemnation of his theory than Catholics. Russell quotes Martin Luther as saying "People give ear to an upstart astrologer who strove to show that the earth revolves, not the heavens or the firmament, the sun and the moon. ... This fool wishes to reverse the entire science of astronomy; but sacred Scripture tells us that Joshua commanded the sun to stand still, and not the earth." John Calvin quoted Psalm 93: V. 1 which says "the world also is established, that it cannot be moved." He then added: "Who will venture to place the authority of Copernicus above that of the Holy Spirit?" John Wesley claimed that the new doctrines in astronomy "tended toward infidelity."

Kepler worked out the laws of motion which would describe the motions of the planets in a sun - centered system. They were much simpler than those required by the earth - centered Ptolemaic system. He managed to avoid serious trouble with the Church. Galileo discovered the laws of motion of falling bodies and the telescope. His invention of the telescope led to discovery of moons orbiting around Jupiter, the phases of Venus and sunspots. The first two discoveries showed that not everything went around the earth. The third showed that not everything in the heavens was a perfect creation. His discoveries about falling bodies contradicted claims of Aristotle which had been adopted by the Church.

Galileo's ideas were condemned by the Inquisition. Russell quotes the following condemnation. "The first proposition, that the sun is the center and does not revolve around the earth, is foolish, absurd, false in Theology, and heretical, because expressly contrary to Holy Scripture... The second proposition, that the earth is not the center, but revolves about the sun, is absurd, false in Philosophy, and, from a theological point of view at least, opposed to the true faith" (Russell, p. 36.) He was ordered to come before the Pope and give up his "errors." He did so on February 26, 1616. He was forced to say he would not teach Copernicus' view anymore. All books teaching that the earth was not the center were put on an Index of books Catholics were forbidden to read.

Galileo then wrote a book on the Ptolemaic and Copernican systems. He pretended to simply compare them. In 1632 he was ordered to come to Rome again. He was put into prison and threatened with torture if he did not take back what he had said. He was forced to say publicly and on his knees that things he knew to be true were false. Despite doing so, he was sentenced by the Inquisition to house arrest for the rest of his life. Says Russell: "Satisfied that the interests of religion and morals had been served by causing the greatest man of his age to commit perjury, the Inquisition allowed him to spend the rest of his days in retirement and silence, not in prison, it is true, but controlled in all his movements, and forbidden to see his family or his friends. He became blind in 1637 and died in 1642 - the year in which Newton was born."

Russell's book, in part, skims a massive two - volume work by Andrew D. White (1896.) White should have called his book "The Warfare of Theology *Against* Science." Here is a little more of what White relates about Galileo. Galileo begged to be buried in his family's crypt. This was denied. He was buried apart from his family, without ceremony, without monument, without even an epitaph. Only forty years after his death did anyone dare to write an epitaph. Attempts were made to damage his reputation.

In the 1850's a Monsignor Marini attempted to sanitize the Church's proceedings against Galileo. It was claimed that the theories and findings of Copernicus and Galileo had never really been condemned. Galileo had been personally condemned for contempt. The condemnation was by cardinals of the Inquisition, not the Pope. Blah, blah, blah! Only in 1867 were the records of his trial fully released for publication by independent biographers. The infallible Church did not admit that Copernicus and Galileo might have been right and it might have been wrong for 330 years.

White's *History* reveals that Christian religions had developed a detailed view of the world from statements or implications of statements in the Bible taken literally. This world view contradicted most developments in modern science. So the Christian religions all found themselves opposing new scientific ideas. They had believed that the earth was created in six days. They also believed that it was only a few thousand years old. So they opposed the view of geologists that it took millions of years to evolve. The word "evolution" refers to gradual development over a long period of time. In science it is thought to apply to the universe as a whole, to the earth, and to life in particular. Christian thinkers came to oppose evolution in all its scientific forms.

These thinkers believed that each species was created separately by God. Extinct ones perished in the flood from which God saved Noah. So they opposed the theory of biological evolution, and some still do today. The problems with the Genesis story were becoming obvious even before there was solid scientific argument against it. There were millions of species. How could Adam have named them all? Biologists found themselves having to create thousands of new names. How could Noah have possibly gotten two of each of them, with food for forty days on a boat? Why did Chaldean tablets much older than the Bible tell a legend of a flood extremely similar to the Bible but about a time long before Noah was calculated to have lived?

If it rained enough in forty days to cover the entire earth up to the top of the highest mountain, then it would have had to rain about 30 feet per hour. This is gotten by dividing the height of the highest mountains, 29,000 feet, by 40 days (960 hours.) A storm which produced that rate of rainfall would capsize a modern aircraft carrier or any smaller ship. How could a wooden ark withstand it?

SECTION 13.9: EVOLUTION AND THE TREATMENT OF HUMANS

Physicists have carefully measured the rate of decay of radioactive parent minerals into daughter isotopes. If the earth is only about 6,000 years old, why does radiation dating show it to be about 4.5 billion years old? There are about 250,000 species of plants and 750,000 of insects alone. If each species of plants and animals were created separately, why is there such similarity of anatomical structure among them, as if they descended from a common ancestor? Why is there such chemical and genetic similarities between them? Why are their embryos so similar they can hardly be told apart? Why do they behave so similarly? Why can they be grouped into larger natural kinds so easily, like genera, orders and phyla?

Further questions arise. Why is there a fossil record showing animals and plants existing long before humans? Why does it show obvious series of animals similar to one another? If death came into the world with "Adam's Fall," why are there fossils of so many carnivores in strata before human bones are found? Why do some contain the bones of other animals apparently eaten? Why do humans have parasitic viruses and bacteria which can not live outside us, but are similar to external ones? Were humans created with such parasites? All such questions are plausibly answered by evolution and not by sudden, separate creation.

An example of religious opposition to the development of science in this area is what happened to Buffon. Buffon, a naturalist, published a book called *Natural History* in 1749. He claimed that the mountains and valleys now on the earth were produced by secondary causes after the creation. His work was condemned by the faculty of the Sorbonne. He was, to quote, "dragged forth by the theological faculty, forced to recant publicly, and to print his recantation. In this he announced, "I abandon everything in my book respecting the formation of the earth, and generally all which may be contrary to the narrative of Moses'" (White, *History of the Warfare*, Vol. 1, pg. 62.) In geography, early Church fathers had also decided that there were no humans living on the other side of the (flat) earth. This opposite side was called the "antipodes." Centuries later their followers even argued against Ferdinand and Isabella funding Columbus's voyage to the New World.

The early church fathers thought that astronomy was useless. However, they accepted the Ptolemaic theory that the earth was the center of the universe and opposed Copernicus and Galileo. They thought that comets were in the atmosphere. So they opposed the view that comets were heavenly bodies. They believed that storms were caused by Satan, "The Prince of the Power of the Air" or by witches. So when there were storms, they prayed or persecuted Jews or "witches." So they opposed the development of meteorology. There were religious scruples against the use of Franklin's lightning rod in America, England, Austria and Italy.

Roger Bacon was an experimental scientist who had the misfortune to be born in the 1200's. For advocating an experimental attitude, he was sentenced to 14 years in prison. Christian religions were very suspicious that changes in matter brought about in alchemist's laboratories were made to happen by magic. So they opposed the development of what became chemistry. They opposed the development of scientific associations in Italy and England, and scientific education in France, England and Prussia.

The religious theory of sickness and disease was that they are either God's punishment for sin or caused by demons. So they opposed medical research and treatment. In fact, there was little progress in medicine during the era that Christianity dominated European civilization. Dissection for the study of anatomy was forbidden because the Church supposedly abhorred shedding of blood. A lingering effect of this even today is the shortage of organs for transplant. About 40,000 people are awaiting transplants in the United States and 9 or 10 die every day. You could die early because most churches are not leading any drive to get their congregations to donate organs, no matter how charitable it is.

Surgery was also opposed. Charges of magic and Mohammadanism were made against physicians. Later there was theological opposition to inoculation, vaccination and the use of anesthetics. Epidemics were thought to be caused by unseen powers. So there was no reason to practice sanitation.

As to the treatment of "mental" illness, a whole pseudoscience of "Demonology" replaced medicine. Demonology held that exorcisms, rituals and relics were useful to cast out devils. Part of the theory was that since pride was the Devil's chief characteristic, he could be driven out by being humiliated. Under this theory people with mental illnesses in particular were mistreated with whipping and torture, and forced consumption of foul substances. The idea was to make the body uncomfortable and humiliating to the prideful devil. Needless to say, this "diagnosis" and "treatment" simply damaged the ill person more!

In early 1997, a universal chorus of religious nay-saying greeted the development of cloning. Because scientists first did the easier step of cloning whole sheep and monkeys, the silly argument is offered that it would be "immoral" to clone whole humans to replace oneself or use as an organ bank. Not even a billionaire thinks his clone would be him, that somehow he could escape death by cloning. Nor would anyone think it legal or practical to clone and grow a whole adult person to take its organs. However, cloning techniques may be used to turn off cancer cells, regenerate spinal nerves, grow new skin for burn victims, culture bone marrow for cancer patients and sickle cell anemia victims and even create drugs which mimic maternal factors and may prevent birth defects.

Anti-science is now a respectable movement (Gross and Levitt, 1994.) In the 1970's, Dr. Robert White transplanted a monkey's head to another body (White, 1996.) Such research could save lives. Animal "rights" activism discouraged such research. Would an anti-scientist say to Stephen Hawking, "Sorry, you have to die slowly, because I feel bad about the sacrifice of small monkeys?" Anti-science tends to be parasitic and hypocritical. A parasite lives off its host. Anti-scientists lead longer, healthier, happier lives because of science. They see by science-made artificial light and are warmed with its heat. The fabric of their clothes is made by science, the safety of drinking water and food is ensured by it. They can travel rapidly, work less than ancestors, word process on computers because of science. Yet they do nothing to support it and even oppose it. That is parasitism. Still, when it becomes possible to turn off cancer cells, or regenerate spinal nerves, most will avail themselves of the "miracles" which let them live or walk again. That is hypocrisy.

SECTION 13.10: PRAYER - NEVER KNOWN TO FAIL?

In Chapter Four we saw that to determine if X causes Y, one must look also at cases of X without Y and Y without X. If prayer, relics and rituals had been effective, why did half of Europe die from the Black Plague of 1348? Christians killed thousands of cats. The Plague came to Europe from Constantinople in fleas carried by rats. The killing of the cats allowed rats to multiply. Cats which escaped this idiocy probably helped end the Plague. Did these faith-full people not pray for their lives? Untreated Bubonic Plague kills more than 60% of the people it infects. Prevention with prayer stops nothing. Tetracycline prevents almost all of it. Streptomycin kills the causing bacterium, Yersinia Pestis, and reduces the disease to killing less than 5% of infected people.

Millions of prayers have been said for every dying Pope. Every one died anyway. Yet Christian "Science" holds that prayer is the way to treat disease. Religious medals can be bought and shrines like Lourdes still do good business. Anecdotes are only vivid illustrations, but here is a tale of two families dealing with deadly illness in a child.

According to O'Reilly, (1997) Luke John was born to Bridget and Joseph Hooker, Catholic activists. Joseph had made two pilgrimages to Medjugorgie, during the first singing the complete rosary on three days running and the second time meeting Bridget, his wife to be. Despite the double gospel name "Luke John," in July 1995 the boy developed a deadly form of liver cancer at age 2. The family bought all sorts of glazed statues, icons, medals, tapestries and so on. They started prayer circles and Catholic magazines, Christian radio stations and a Catholic cable channel picked up the story. Mother Teresa sent a miraculous medal and handwritten note. A Cardinal blessed him and said mass for him. The family took him to anti-abortion activities. They took him to Rome where the Pope blessed him. They took him to Lourdes. They got him first communion three years earlier than normal. They also sought the best medical treatment they could find. When that did not work, they turned to homeopathy and naturopathy. For all this, the poor child died in February 1997 anyway.

So what should non-medical persons do when a beloved child is very ill, if not pray? The film *Lorenzo's Oil* is an inspiring story about the Odone family whose child, Lorenzo, was stricken with another terrible disease which attacks the fatty Myelin insulation that helps nerves conduct electrical impulses. (One suspects from the film that the Odone's are also Catholic.) The struggle they put up for the life of their child is certainly a great tribute to placing a very high value on human life. The Odone's cared for Lorenzo as well as they could. When they found medical science unable to stop the progress of their son's disease, *they made themselves experts on the disease.* They actually found a substance now called "Lorenzo's Oil" which was able to arrest the cause of the disease and has helped other people since that time. Their son, Lorenzo, is alive. He is severely disabled but they saved his life. Furthermore, they are working on remyelination to cure or lessen the effects of the disease. To learn more, contact The Myelin Project, Suite 950, 1747 Pennsylvania Ave. N. W., Washington, D. C., 20006 or http://www.myelin.org/. It is unfortunate that Americans spend billions a year on ineffective religious "warding off" and healing rituals instead of learning how to live a healthy life and contributing to medical research long before our inevitable death.

A person can remedy deficiencies in their own education and make a fight for life, possibly helping others also. Recall that if reviving someone whose heart and breathing have stopped, whose body has cooled to about 60^0 is a miracle, one brain surgeon alone has performed over 50 such "miracles." There will eventually come a fatal illness: deal with it! For accurate, non mystical information on one's ultimate fate, read Wilson (1992) on traumatic death (rare) or Nuland's more general *How We Die* (1995.) This book gives descriptions of the course of typical causes of natural death. From it one can learn what diseases one may need to fight. Modern anesthesia, including large doses of morphine can eliminate almost all severe pain in dying.

SECTION 13.11: CONTRIBUTIONS OF DENOMINATIONS VERSUS SCIENTISTS

A newspaper column gave this summary of the history of theology. Judaism was founded about 4,000 B.C. Hinduism developed around 1,500 B.C. Gautama began the split of Buddhism from Hinduism about 500 B.C. Catholicism began with the death of Jesus in 33 A. D. Islam began with the teachings of Mohammed around 600 A. D. The Eastern Orthodox Church separated from Catholicism around 1,000 A. D. The Reformation saw Lutheranism begin with Martin Luther's 95 theses in 1517. The Anglican Church split from Catholicism in 1534. Presbyterianism began with the teachings of John Calvin and John Knox in the 1560s. Unitarianism has origins going back to the 1500s. Congregationalism developed out of Puritanism in the early 1600s. The Baptist religion began with John Smyth in Amsterdam in 1607. Methodism was founded by John and Charles Wesley in England in 1744. Episcopalianism formed into a separate religion founded by Samuel Seabury in 1789. Mormonism was founded by John Smith in Palmyra, New York in 1830. The Salvation Army began with William Booth in London in 1865. The Jehovah's Witnesses religion was founded by Charles Taze in the 1870's. Christian Science was founded in 1879 by Mary Baker Eddy. Pentecostalism was founded in the United States in 1901.

Which of these 19 religions were founded on the discovery of some new, repeatable phenomenon of nature? Which have led to theories confirmed by others' observations? Tools and inventions are machines. The essence of a machine is *reliable* performance. Which have contributed any tools or inventions for the production of food, clothing, shelter, or medicines for prevention or cure of diseases? Which have not been in conflict with others for followers? Only critical thinkers ask such questions. Major religions have hundreds or thousands of denominations. There are no Orthodox, Pentecostal, Adventist or Jehovahs' physicists. This suggests that if there is one Reality, science is getting at it, theology is not.

Many scientists and inventors have, of course, been deeply religious people. A few persons whose official work was primarily religious have been scientists. However, consider lists of tools, inventions, machines in general. A *machine* is anything which reliably changes force, motion or energy. There are 5 simple machines. Three, the lever, inclined plane, and wedge, were developed in the Stone Age. Simple machines have mechanical advantage. They enable humans to exert lesser amounts of force over longer distances and times to move things they could not move directly.

A ramp is an inclined plane. Work is effort times distance. If the sloping side of a ramp is twice as long as its height, it will take only about half as much effort to drag something up the ramp as to lift it directly up the height. With a first class lever, the fulcrum between the effort and the load, a person can use his or her own weight and gravity to move a heavy object. Does anyone think that 100,000 years before Judeo-Christian religions some Stone Age person got these inventions by prayer as a revelation from the one true God?

Simple Machines

The Inclined Plane

Half
Effort
Required

Full Effort
Required

The Lever

Effort
aided by
weight,
gravity

Archimedes, it is claimed, said: "give me a lever long enough and I will move the earth." Other simple machines like the pulley, screw and wheel and axle were developed by Archimedes. The pump was developed by Ctesibius and Hero, the treadmill, water wheels and mills by the Roman engineer Vitruvius. In the Middle Ages the horseshoe, padded collar and stirrup harnessed the energy of the horse. The windmill and spinning wheel were developed, along with gunpowder. The first printing press went to work in 1448.

Galileo and Newton began the development of modern physics. Galileo invented the telescope and developed the compound microscope. Ocean-going sailboats came about when someone got the idea to equip a boat with both the large, rectangular sails of Europe and the small triangular ones of Arab dhows. Navigation became possible by development of the sextant and an accurate chronometer. Later steam engines and boats were developed. Jethro Tull developed a mechanical crop sower to increase food production. Robert Boyle began the development of chemistry. The theory of electricity was developed by Farady, Votla and Ben Franklin. Faraday invented the electric motor. Edison invented the light bulb, phonograph and synchronization of sound and pictures which made movies possible. He held over 1,300 patents for inventions. Cooke and Wheatsone developed the telegraph and Samuel Morse its' code. Marconi developed radio. Colonel Edwin Drake first successfully drilled for oil in the United States in 1859. The internal combustion engine was developed by Lenoir and Otto and the motor car by Daimler and Benz in 1885.

Orville and Wilber Wright developed the first airplane in 1903. Television was developed in 1926 by Baird, Farnsworth and Zworkin. The liquid fueled rocket was developed by R. H Goddard in 1926 and the jet engine in 1930 by Frank Whittle. The helicopter was designed by Igor Sikorsky in 1939. The first mechanical computer was designed by Charles Babbage in 1830. The first programmer was his assistant, Lady Ada Lovelace. The first electronic computer was built by Eckert and Mauchly. Nuclear power was a result of the theories of Einstein and the engineering design of the physicist Enrico Fermi.

We could go on like this about the transistor, magnetic tape, stereo, microchips, CD's and so on. The point is this. Some important scientific minds have had theological educations or even vocations such as Gregor Mendel and Charles Darwin. But how many of these theories, discoveries and inventions were given to the human race by people whose *primary* work in life was ministry? How many were given to humanity by priests, nuns, reverends, gurus, prophets, etc., as *revelations given to them by God?* Very few, if any. *How many were given by all the psychics, mystics, and gurus the world has ever had?* How many of them, on the other hand, were the result of hard work by scientists and inventors? Who is really, concretely, effectively ministering to people's needs and who is only producing temporary "feel-good" words?

A second list one should consider is developments in medicine. Zacharias Janssen, a spectacle maker, actually invented the compound microscope. Vaccination was practiced in the East and was popularized in Europe by a gentlewoman named Mary Wortley Montagu and then first practiced by a physician, Dr. Edward Jenner. Physicians like Dr. William Witherington developed foxglove for the digitalis it contains as a heart medication. Louis Pasteur developed the Germ Theory of Disease and Joseph Lister the idea of antiseptics. A doctor named Morton first demonstrated anesthetics at Massachusetts General Hospital in 1846.

James Young Simpson experimented on himself by inhaling various substances to find that chloroform was an effective anesthetic. Nor has he been the only scientist who has risked his or her own body to benefit humanity or the environment. One should remember Jonas Salk tested his polio vaccine on himself and Jane Goodall and Dian Fossey's self deprivation and risk-taking until one of them was killed by poachers during her study of gorillas. These two women are only among the latest examples of people who have sacrificed quite as much of life's comforts for scientific knowledge as monks and nuns have sacrificed for personal salvation. Who is really ministering to people's needs and serving humanity in such cases?

Bacteriologists, not mystics, developed arsenamine, effective against what was the AIDS of past centuries: syphilis. They also developed sulfanilamide against streptococcus, penicillin against staphylococcus, streptomycin against tuberculosis and vaccinations against typhoid, tetanus, diphtheria and yellow fever, all dreaded diseases of mankind. Microbiologists discovered insulin which enabled diabetics to live longer, much healthier lives and cortisone which diminished the crippling effect of arthritis. Vitamins were recognized as necessary for nutrition by a biologist. Sulfones were identified as effective against leprosy, a disease mentioned in the New Testament. Biologists developed DDT which was very useful in controlling the population of mosquitoes which bore malaria, and quinine to treat it. (DDT later became a problem on its own.)

Operations of all sorts were developed by surgeons, not clergymen. These include operations for removal of cancerous parts of the bowel or lungs, brain surgery for abscesses and tumors, and appendectomy. A physicist, William Roentgen, developed the X-ray, of great value in diagnosis.

Physicians developed blood transfusion, clotting prevention so blood could be stored and intravenous saline solution to prevent dehydration. They are also responsible for life-saving heart, liver, lung, kidney and pancreas transplants. Now microbiologists are working out the human genetic code with some concrete results already in curing or lessening the effects of inherited diseases. Meanwhile "There is an epidemic of clergy malpractice claims" (McMenamin, 1986, Cornell, 1992.) Owing to ignorance and repression clergy are being charged with outrageous conduct, child sexual abuse, and counselling leading to divorce or suicide.

SECTION 13.12: MORE WARS, COSTS VERSUS BENEFITS IN RELIGION

They don't sing "Onward Christian Soldiers" for nothing. Martin Marty, a well known theologian, recently wrote: "Religion motivates most of the killing in the world today" (1996, p. 14.) Sometimes it is difficult to count distinct wars. There are almost always other sources of conflict as well. So we will count only roughly by area or dates wars which have had religious conflict as a major element. Between 711 AD and 1492 there was war between Muslims and Christians as the Muslims first moved into Spain and later were driven out. Christendom replied with 9 to 12 Crusades from 1096 to 1291 in which Catholics and Moslems butchered each other over control of "The Holy Land." Between 200,000 a half million people were murdered in the Inquisition, but we will not even count this war by the Church largely on its own people. Between 1562 and 1598 there were 7 civil wars between Catholics and Protestants called the "Wars of Religion." The English Civil War 1642 - 1649 involved an element of religious conflict. Anglicans and Catholics were loyal to the King, Puritans to the Parliament. There were 10 wars between Christian Russians and Turks between 1676 and 1878.

Wars occurred between Moslems, Hindus and Buddhists in India between about 700 and 1700 A. D. (see Warraq, p. 219 -225.) Because of a belief in reincarnation, pacifism is a core belief of Buddhism. One might be killing a reincarnation of an ancestor. However, even Buddhists in Japan had standing armies in the Middle Ages to pressure emperors to do the bidding of temples. According to the *Millennial Prophecy Report* (7/96) Aum Shinri Kyo, the group accused of putting poison gas in the subways in Japan, retains a belief in a final great war (Apocalypse, Armageddon) between Buddhism and Christianity. It is preparing for this with bomb shelters, weapons, and so on. Many colonial wars have had religious elements or at least justifications. European slavers justified kidnapping of people on the theory that it was alright to do so to Christianize them to save their immortal souls. The Indochina War and Vietnam wars involved elements of Christian Frenchmen and later Americans fighting Communists and Buddhists. At one point the government of the southern part of Vietnam, which was supported by the United States, forbade the Buddhists from holding an annual religious procession. To protest this religious persecution, a Buddhist monk burned himself to death in the street.

Add to the list 5 wars between Moslems and Jews over Palestine since 1948, the Lebanese Civil War of 1975 between Moslems and Christians and the same two religions pitted against each other in the war and "ethnic cleansing" in Bosnia in the 1990's. In the Sudan in 1997 there is conflict between Christian rebels and an Islamic government. Terrorism inspired by religious fanaticism troubles the world today. The Founders who wrote the Constitution were aware that religious differences were the cause of persecutions and wars. They deliberately left God and Christianity out of the Constitution and put in two separate prohibitions against religions using government to subject people to others' religions. In Article VI they stated: "No religious test shall ever be required as a qualification to any office or public trust under the United States." In the First Amendment they added: "Congress shall make no law respecting the establishment of religion, or prohibiting the free exercise thereof." Fundamental rights like life and freedom from others' religions are not subject to vote. Those who push prayer in public school should be reminded of the bloody religious riots over it in Philadelphia in 1844.

Victor Stenger (1995, p. 31) has said: "Selling eternal life is an unbeatable business, with no customers ever asking for their money back after the goods aren't delivered." Estimates vary as to how much money is spent supporting religions each year. For the United States, contributions, according to the American Association of Fund - Raising Councils (Religion beating sports at the gate p. 9A) amounted to $56.7 billion. Another estimate (Niebuhr, 1993) is that "Americans drop about $40 billion in the collection plates of churches, synagogues and mosques. About $6 billion of that goes directly to social service work, playing a critical role in helping hard-pressed U.S. cities."

Take the lower figure. Perform a thought experiment. First subtract all of the inventions, discoveries, machines, medicine and conveniences of modern life due to science. After subtraction, what will one's life be like and how long will it be? A person is probably reduced to a shivering medieval peasant. Now put it all back. Now imagine that everyone takes a one year sabbatical from organized religion and contributes the $34 billion ($40 - 6) for church operations to science, particularly medical research. Give it 20 years at a rate of growth higher than the current one because of the $34 billion. Cancer is stopped. So is heart disease. So is AIDS. Most brain tumors are successfully removed. Many genetic disorders and possibly Alzheimers' is cured. People can live healthily to maybe 100 and die quickly and painlessly.

SECTION 13.13: TWO OBJECTIONS AND ANSWERS

"But if the Bible is inconsistent, who's to say what's right or wrong?" When asked this question, the student's answer should be "You are." "You, with your billion-year-evolved-brain, have as much equipment and right to make moral judgments as anyone else, even on the practices of whole societies." How? Here one can adopt a strategy from John Rawls. Rawls (1971) ask you to imagine that you have to select the institutions and moral rules of the society you are going to live in after your choice. However, you have to do so without knowing what characteristics or position you will have in that society. You do not know whether you will be male or female, healthy, ill or handicapped, how intelligent you will be, or your race or religion. Any type of act, institution, practice or rule you would disapprove of under these circumstances (because you might be treated unjustly under it) is wrong.

"But I don't want to die at all. Religion gives me hope of immortality." Neither do I want to die. But if you and I don't die, either we must have no children or grandchildren or they must die, or we all will become impoverished. We live on a finite planet. In John Ch. 10: V. 10 Jesus says "I am come that they might have life and have it more abundantly." But the world's population went from perhaps 300 million at the birth of Jesus through all the ages of faith to about only 550 million by 1650, the beginning of modern science. In the nearly 350 years since then it has increased ten-fold to about 5.9 billion. All the time under religious belief humans' life span was about 20 - 30 years and most children died young. Under the development of science, the life span has risen to 40, 50, 60, 70 and is now approaching 80. So what, indeed, has come that we might "have life more abundantly?"

Natural laws and facts make it unreasonable to believe that we will be able to colonize other planets. A little carbon dioxide on Mars or ice on the moon or Europa do not mean they could shortly be made livable for millions of people. Stars are light years away. There is no known way to quickly accelerate to nearly the light speed for practical space travel. Each shuttle launch costs about $450,000 per astronaut. You can not have infinite expansion of population on a planet of finite resources. If we can lead long, healthy, happy lives made meaningful by our own goodness to other people and die quick, painless deaths thanks to science, for what more should we ask?

SECTION 13.14: A LOOK AT REINCARNATION

One might ask whether Eastern religions theories of reincarnation fare better in terms of consistency with science, solving the Problem of Suffering or having reasonable moral implications. Paul Edwards (1996) deals with these topics in a funny book. First he gives some definitions. *Reincarnation* is the belief that humans live many, perhaps an infinite number of lives. They get a new body for each incarnation. It holds that souls are eternal, not created at some time (p. 11.) The doctrine is found in the Hindu *Bhagavid Gita.* It is held by the God Krishna. Eventually those who have lived good enough lives will become enlightened and reach Nirvana. Nirvana is a kind of cosmic consciousness. Then they will not be reborn anymore. Some believers hold we can be reborn only as humans. Others think our souls can be incarnated as animals or even in inanimate objects.

The Law of Karma maintains that there is justice in the world. Everything good that happens to us is a reward for some previous good deed of ours, and everything bad that happens is punishment for an evil deed. A Christian may rationalize birth defects and accidents to children as punishments for the sins of their parents or original sin. This is incredible. A believer in Karma may rationalize such conditions as deserved punishments for bad deeds done in earlier lives. This must apply to the people born black (who became slaves), born Jewish (who were exterminated in the Holocaust), to people killed in the Lisbon earthquake, to those born Armenian (who were slaughtered by the Turks.) It must also apply to people born female (to be burned as witches or otherwise oppressed.) The Kennedy brothers, Martin Luther King, and the 7 Challenger astronauts, according to the theory of Karma, got what they deserved. This is as unbelievable as the Christian treatment of nature-caused suffering.

The "Law of Karma" has no predictive value whatever. You can't use it to predict, e.g., whether a given airplane will crash or not. It is compatible with anything happening, e.g., with a good man coming to a bad end and his next incarnation being a long horrible nightmare of torture and persecution. This doesn't disconfirm the "Law." "He did evil in a previous life." Also, because it implies that illness, birth defects, accidents are just punishment, it does not prescribe we help people who suffer them.

The biggest problems with reincarnation are: (1) that all the evidence for it can be explained in other natural ways, (2) the *modus operandi* problem. This, Edwards explains, is the question: "Exactly how does a law of Karma or even spiritual 'lords of Karma' register good and bad deeds, decide what kind of body and where a soul's next incarnation will be, decide what characteristics the body will have, invade a woman's womb and fuse this soul to an embryo?" Reincarnation is clearly based on extreme, Cartesian-like dualism. I am a non-physical mind. If a continuing body is necessary for personal identity, then the theory is false. Nor can it provide a real answer to the "how" or *modus operandi* question.

Edwards catalogs common sense objections which have been made against reincarnation. 1) How does a soul exist between bodies? 2) Tertullian's objection: If there is reincarnation, why are not babies born with the mental abilities of adults? 3) Reincarnation claims an infinite series of prior incarnations. Evolution teaches that there was a time when humans did not yet exist. So reincarnation is inconsistent with modern science. 4) If there is reincarnation, then what is happening when the population increases? 5) If there is reincarnation, then why do so few, if any people, remember past lives?

To answer these objections believers in reincarnation must accept additional assumptions. They assume that when a human dies, before he is reincarnated, he exists as an *astral body* invisible, completely undetectable by scientific instruments, yet somehow able to travel at very high speed and penetrate material objects like walls, roofs and human bodies. He can travel and see things even though deprived of a brain and eyes and means of locomotion. After a period of time, one's astral body picks out or is thrown into a woman's body at the moment of conception. Even though the person may have been very old and knowledgeable at death, when reborn he has a new, different baby's body and none of his memories. Yet he is somehow the same person.

To account for the great increase in population, it must be assumed that many souls incarnated on this earth did not live on it previously. They must somehow have migrated from some other planets or dimensions or god knows what. Finally, most people must have done bad in past lives because they will enter the wombs of mothers in poor, over-populated countries where their lives are likely to be miserable. Acceptance of these silly assumptions, Edwards says, amounts to a crucifixion of one's intellect (p. 253.)

14 PSEUDOSCIENCE AS UNJUSTIFIED STATEMENTS

SECTION 14.1: THE NATURE OF PSEUDOSCIENCE AND THE PARANORMAL

The term "pseudoscience" means "pretend" or "fake" science. The pseudosciences present a lot of claims as true, as known, as providing important factual knowledge of reality, as useful for prediction of events and gaining some wisdom and control over one's life. Yet on examination such statements turn out not even to be justified. Subjects in which pseudoscientific claims are made include abduction (kidnapping) by aliens, ancient astronauts, astrology, the Bermuda Triangle, crystal and pyramid power, cults, demonic possession and exorcism, Freudian psychology, ghosts and channeling, health and nutrition quackery, monsters (like Big Foot and the Loch Ness monster), New Age Millenarianism, psi phenomena, (including telepathy, and telekinesis), satanism and witchcraft, and UFO's as "flying saucers."

Hines excellent treatment of pseudoscience lists the most common qualities of the pseudosciences as follows. 1) They look for or actually manufacture "mysteries." 2) They claim that these "mysteries" can not be explained by science. 3) They make unfalsifiable hypotheses. 4) They uncritically accept myths or Bible stories as literally true. 5) They uncritically accept eyewitness testimony of unique, non-repeatable events for the existence of phenomena which careful scientific observers can not reproduce. 6) They accept as real phenomena events which probably did not happen at all or which can be explained in natural terms, or in terms of hoax, fraud or magicians' tricks. 7) They refuse to revise or change their findings substantially in light of new evidence (Hines 1988.)

We can add to Hines' list several more from Radner and Radner (1982.) 8) The pseudosciences also engage in anachronism, that is, they present as new, ideas which are sometimes old and long discredited. 9) They make false analogies or ones at least very weak. 10) They make pseudo explanations of events by scenarios rather than scientific explanations by causal laws. 11) They are "armchair fields." They substitute interpretation of texts (like the Bible or people's reports) for real-world laboratory or field research.

The *"paranormal"* is that area of pseudoscience which relies on dualistic pseudo explanations. The paranormal includes extrasensory perception (ESP), telekinesis, ghosts, poltergeists, near-death experiences as "proof" of life after death, reincarnation, and faith healing. As we saw in Chapter 12, dualism has such severe problems that it is unjustified to hold it. Therefore, it can not explain and certainly can not justify the existence of these alleged phenomena.

If there is one principle that students who wish to become critical thinkers should absorb from the following exposure to pseudoscientific claims it is probably one stated by Sagan (1995.) The principle is this. **Extraordinary claims require extraordinary proof!** If someone claims she saw an apple fall off a tree, this is an ordinary claim. If she says she saw an apple leap off the ground and attach itself to a tree, this is an extraordinary claim and requires extraordinary proof. The claims below are, to critical thinkers and scientists, roughly in the same ball park of improbability with the apple leaping up. In some cases generalized claims of a sort made by a pseudoscientist have been put in quotation marks without reference just to set it off. Many of the claims are simply *exposed* or only lightly criticized. They are so far from the paradigms of justified statements given earlier the author has followed the path of Martin Gardner. Gardner pointed out that true believers will not be persuaded out of their silly beliefs. But, as H. L. Mencken said "One good horse laugh is worth a thousand syllogisms." Prepare to laugh yourself silly.

SECTION 14.2: SEEING STARS

Astrology makes the claim that "The positions of the sun and planets on the day a person was born influence and allow prediction of a person's personality and future." This claim is highly unjustified. We do tend to agree with vague, flattering descriptions of ourselves. We can find agreements between vague predictions and what happens to us by chance, if we are biased toward looking for them in the first place. But the stars in the Zodiac constellations have no physical connection to each other. The constellations are products of a culture. Other cultures do not even group the stars into the same constellations. There is no mechanism for constellations to influence us. So why should Aries or Pisces, say, influence human personality?

Astrology assigns dates to constellations such as "Aries, March 21 to April 19." These assignments were made 2,000 years ago. The sun is supposed to be 'in' a Zodiac sign like Aries during those dates. This means the sun, as seen from the earth, is in the same place in the sky as that constellation. But the position of the sun changes with respect to the Zodiac signs. Now, 2,000 years later, the sun is not in Aries but Pisces for almost the entire time of March 21 to April 19. Astrologers, being pseudoscientists, don't care about the facts. Tell them you were born between March 21 and April 19 and they will read you as an Aries, even though the sun was actually in Pisces for most of the period you were really born in! *Pseudoscience does not revise or correct itself.* Only real science does that (Hines, p. 144.)

Astrology is based on only 5 planets in addition to the sun, moon and earth (Mercury, Venus, Mars, Jupiter, and Saturn.) Astronomy has precisely predicted many eclipses and predicted three more planets and found them (Uranus, Neptune and Pluto). Astrology predicted a planet Vulcan, to account for deviations in Mercury's orbit. However, that was explained by Relativity theory and nobody has ever discovered Vulcan. Astrologers even contradict each other on which signs are compatible with which others (Hines, Fig. 7.) Repeated studies have been done of astrological predictions of personality on groups of people. They show no correlations between Zodiac signs and personality types. People's personalities are simply not uniformly influenced or caused by what Zodiac sign they were born in. People of all different sorts of personality traits are born in all the various signs (Hines, p. 148 ff.) Finally, a typical newspaper horoscope often contains just good advice for anyone or multiple "predictions" so vague that anyone looking to have them confirmed will find something to confirm them. Multiple, vague predictions are the trick by which Nostradamus remains popular as a seer.

Ruchlis (1991) gives the following example of astrological claims. Nancy Reagan was worried about President Reagan's appearance at a ceremony honoring German war dead in World War Two. The appearance was controversial. Many Americans thought no American President should honor soldiers who had exterminated Jews and killed Americans in the war. She consulted astrologer Joan Quigley who advised scheduling the event for 11:45 A.M. In her book, *What Does Joan Say?*, Quigley is quoted as saying, "At the time I chose, the Sun, which ruled the event itself, was in a very elevated position in the 10th. house of great prominence and prestige. The sun and the proud, honorable and dignified Leo Ascendant described the nature of the event. Jupiter, the planet of benevolence and good will, represented the public. Two planets in the 9th. house indicated global attention; Mars in the 10th showed a kind of victory."

Ruchlis asks the following questions. Why should the sun high in the sky and in a certain part of it give the president's ceremony "great prominence and prestige?" Does the sun have a brain that can understand what is happening in Bitberg, Germany and does it do the same for all other events happening at the same time? How can it "give the ceremony prominence and prestige?" Why should a chance collection of stars called "Leo," billions of miles away, be "proud, honorable and dignified?" How could they "describe the nature of the event?" How does the planet Jupiter bestow "benevolence and good will" or "represent the public" at a ceremony millions of miles away? How does Mars give the President's ceremony "victory," whatever that means.

False analogy, stretched far beyond the breaking point, is seen here. Kings are powerful. Some are proud, honorable and dignified. A lion is powerful, so it is the "king of the beasts." So, it was concluded, lions were "proud", "honorable" and "dignified." "Honorable" is a stretch where old man-eaters are concerned, and the other adjectives seem not very meaningful. Then ancient Greeks formed constellations in the sky, one of which was Leo, the Lion. It is just a chance collection of stars, the brightest of which look to most people today like a question mark followed by a triangle, not a lion. However, astrologers stretched the analogy more and said the constellation was "proud, honorable and dignified."

Quigley claims the fact that the constellation was Ascendant (coming up) at a certain time "describes the nature" of events on earth. Why? Ruchlis says: "Astrologers do not understand what a fact is." Worse yet, making claims like this seems to show lack of understanding of the boundaries distinguishing factual, informative claim - making from grammatical, but scrambled word - salad writing which does not make sensible, factual claims at all. What she wrote makes no clear sense at all. Other examples of such claims in pseudoscience will be exposed later.

By contrast to the verbal garbage of Quigley and empty, useless "predictions" of astrology, note in passing that there are scientific methods which can predict a number of specific, very useful facts. Such facts include where oil or other valuable resources are likely to be found, when dangerous events such as tornadoes and earthquakes are likely to occur and even whether a person will develop certain diseases (Huntington's and Hemochromatosis.)

SECTION 14.3: TALL TALES OF EARLIER VISITS

The visiting of earth by aliens was greatly popularized in the 1970's by Charles Berlitz and Erich Von Daniken. According to Berlitz (1974) "The Bermuda Triangle is an area in which a large number of mysterious disappearances of ships and airplanes have occurred." But each of Berlitz's cases has been carefully examined by Kusche (1975.) Kusche is a reference librarian and pilot. In the case of the disappearance of a large freighter, the Marine Sulfur Queen, for example, Kusche notes that Berlitz is simply wrong on some facts and leaves out detail which would tend toward natural explanations.

Berlitz claimed that the Sulfur Queen "vanished without message, clues, or debris," (p. 39) "disappear[ing] in good weather on February 2, 1963" (Berlitz, caption to photograph of ship). However, Kusche quotes from a Coast Guard Board of Inquiry that another ship estimated to be 40 miles from the Sulfur Queen at noon on February 3 reported high winds, very rough seas and decks awash. A personal message from a member of the crew of the Sulfur Queen was transmitted from it after this, showing that the ship was still afloat on February 4. Also, 8 life jackets, 5 life rings, 2 ship name boards and other debris were found. Many rips in the life jackets indicated possible attacks by sharks rather than alien abduction. The ship probably sank in a storm. But the Board of Inquiry listed other possible causes. It could have suffered an explosion of gases from its molten sulfur cargo, or of fumes from a space surrounding its cargo holds. The ship had a history of fires in the insulation on one of its holds. It could have broken in two, or capsized or had a steam explosion.

Many cheaply made movies for television exploit the idea of the Bermuda Triangle as a place of mystery, possibly alien contact. But the student should not confuse entertainment with reality. The Bermuda Triangle is a high-volume shipping area. There are more disappearances there than in some other sea areas because there are more ships there. It is also subject to storms and high seas, amateur sailors, reefs near islands and occasional pirates and drug runners. This is quite enough to explain most disappearances there without anything mysterious about them. Critical thinking admits that there are unexplained events. It simply insists that we have justification beyond stories and "eyewitness reports" of unique, non-repeatable events. It insists that we seek alternative explanations in terms of highly justified natural laws and causes before we jump to paranormal or pseudoscientific hypotheses.

Erich Von Daniken (1970) claimed that "Aliens landing on earth in ancient times explain the building of the pyramids and the destruction of Sodom and Gomorrah." But if it is improbable that aliens are visiting the earth at all, this is certainly even more improbable. Destruction of cities "by fire and brimstone" sounds very like volcanic eruption, if, of course, it happened at all. Von Daniken repeatedly voices indirect racist contempt for "primitive" peoples of past times. They could not do what they did, so aliens must have helped them. But ancient Egyptian illustrations from inside pyramids reveal quite clearly that the Egyptians had the necessary technology of wheel and ropes necessary to build the pyramids. It is also easy to explain how the large drawings with near perfect circles in the Nazca desert in Peru were made by primitive peoples. Dig a hole. Put a pole in it. Tie a rope to it. Walk around the rope. Nickell (1982-3) showed how six people using only sticks and cord could create a full sized, 440 foot Nazca drawing in only a day and a half. As to the more recent phenomenon of crop circles, two Englishmen confessed that it was a hoax. They made the circles themselves and demonstrated how they did it.

SECTION 14.4: UFO'S, ET'S AND ABDUCTIONS

NASA scientists have announced the first possible evidence that primitive life may have existed on Mars about 4 billion years ago and possible water on Europa. But it would be an enormous jump to "conclusions" some people have been stating. They have made claims like "I was abducted by aliens who took me into a space ship and did experiments on me." A few have claimed that "Many (thousands or more) Americans have been abducted by aliens." These claims are a logical offshoot of the claim "UFO's are space ships controlled by aliens who are visiting earth."

"UFO" means "unidentified flying objects." Critical thinkers certainly admit the existence of unidentified flying objects. However, despite hundreds of "reports" not one case has been presented in which there is evidence highly justifying the claim that they are space ships piloted by aliens. These are "eyewitness reports" of unique, non-reproducible events. No scars which could not have been produced by earthlings have been demonstrated. Only a very few pieces of "crashed saucers" or "implants" have been offered as evidence. Every one has been tested in laboratories. None has been found to have unearthly properties.

Earlier it was noted how unreliable eyewitness reports can be. They can be affected or caused by everything from a desire for publicity to hysteria. Sagan (1995, p. 109) points to sleep paralysis as part of a probable cause for abduction experiences. Many alleged saucer "abductees" describe waking up feeling paralyzed.

Sleep paralysis is a well known phenomenon. In it, a person wakes up partially and feels no control over his or her body. If the person is also easily influenced (suggestible), he or she may dream about flying saucers and abduction and mistake the dream and sleep paralysis for a real experience.

Goya said: "The sleep of reason brings forth monsters." This author had a similar experience. He awoke one morning very early, feeling paralyzed and seeing, out of "the corner of his eye," a long-fingered claw-like black hand apparently about to grab him by the face. It was a terrifying experience, until the author recovered from the paralysis, jumped up in a fright and then realized that it had been his own hand! While asleep, he must have raised his right arm so that his forearm rested on his head and his hand hung over the left edge of his face. Coming partially to consciousness in early morning gloom, the hand had looked black against the white ceiling, and the claw-like appearance was produced by the hand's relaxed state and the angle he saw it from.

Many reports of UFO's are explainable in terms of misidentification of common objects like weather balloons, clouds or aircraft or the deliberate creation of a hoax. Some were probably the result of deliberate leaving out of some of the facts. Hines (p. 189) gives this example of manufacturing a mystery. Jim Fawcett wrote that astronauts Lovell and Aldrin reported seeing 4 UFO's linked in a row and that they were not stars. A skeptic named Oberg found the original debriefing document. One of the astronauts said they had discarded a used-up life support system and 3 bags. Two to four orbits later they looked out again and saw 4 objects lined up in a row and they weren't stars known to them. The astronaut also said: *"They must have been these same things we tossed overboard."*

The Air Force created a commission of independent scientists which studied sightings of UFO's. It issued a report in 1969. The report is called "the Condon Report" after the chairman of the committee, Edward Condon. The report concluded that there was no evidence that UFO's were of extraterrestrial origin. When it comes to UFO's as space ships piloted by aliens and abduction claims, two principles of critical thinking should be noted. First, *it is not the quantity of reports that count to demonstrating the reality of something, it is the quality of the evidence.*

In a video, "UFO's are Real," physicist Stanton Friedman cites "thousands" of UFO reports as evidence they are real. However, in the Middle Ages thousands of people reported that others had used witchcraft against them. Heinrich Institor and Jakob Sprenger, in their book, *The Hammer of Witches*, wrote: "Who is so dense as to maintain ... that all their witchcraft and injuries are phantastic and imaginary, when the contrary is evident to the senses of everybody?" (Huber, p. 9.) Martin Gardner pointed out that there will always be a residue of unexplained and unexplainable cases. Cases may be unexplainable because they are lies, or hallucinations or just because we do not have enough information to explain them. So, second, *the existence of unexplainable claims does not justify the extremely improbable hypothesis of alien landings when alternative, more probable explanations are available.*

There are several reasons why claims of alien space craft landings are unjustified. They are not probabilistically consistent with highly justified laws and characteristics of the universe. Few planets are known to us and they show no evidence of life on them. They are also very far away. According to Relativity Theory, it would take a very long time for aliens just to reach the Earth. In science fiction, it is assumed that space travelers have gotten "faster than light speed" drives. But this is *fiction,* not reality! It would violate Ockham's Razor to pile "faster than light speed drives" onto "intelligent aliens" on top of "alien visitors to earth" in order to believe claims about abductions. Why would advanced aliens come all the way to earth rather than just study it by telescope?

We have no good grounds for believing that civilizations which develop science and technology will exist for very long times after doing so. Humans have been civilized for only some thousands of years. We may yet easily destroy ourselves with nuclear weapons or pollution. It is fairly well justified to believe that the universe is billions of years old. Life might have emerged and become intelligent at any time and then died out. But belief in alien *visitors* requires belief in a seven-fold improbability: that *(1) life, which evolved to (2) intelligence (3) emerged on another planet,* at the *(4) right time* as well as the *(5) right place* to visit us, *(6) that it has a motive* to do so, and *(7) can and has violated laws of nature* known to us to do so. While the first, second and third of these items may be probable, the fourth through sixth are improbable and the seventh extremely so. Many scientists accept that there might be (or have been) 10,000 to 100,000 intelligent species among the 200 billion stars of our galaxy

We humans already understand almost all there is to know about the biology of sex. Why would such an advanced civilization be so retarded in biological knowledge to need to experiment on live humans? If there is anything to these reports, why don't agencies of the government which have an interest in getting more money, like NASA, support them? NASA, is a civilian agency. No one can effectively order all its members to keep from secret whistle blowing. Why, for all the reports and claims since 1947, is there not one bit of hard, physical evidence of alien space craft, bodies, monstrous hybrid births, or humans with body modifications which cannot be explained by natural, scientific means? Why are aliens, so rude and invasive as to kidnap people, careful to leave them back in their own beds or at least near the locations from which they kidnapped them?

SECTION 14.5: MEDIA PROMOTION OF UFO'S

Strieber (1987) a horror fiction writer, claimed he was really abducted by aliens. Perhaps he took a clue from David Rorvik. Rorvik claimed that *In His Image: The Cloning of a Man* (1978) was nonfiction. Rorvik's publisher was sued by a researcher who claimed Rorvik had misused his work. A judge ruled the book was a hoax. However, it made $700, 000 (Sifakis, 1996.) Strieber's work has been examined by Klass (1988) and Swords (1987.) Both point out that Strieber relates a number of highly improbable incidents. Strieber claims to have had a threatening encounter with Mr. Peanut. He claims to have been assaulted by a skeleton on a motorcycle at age 12. He awoke one night and saw a tiny humanoid run by him holding a red light. He was awakened at a cabin in the Catskill Mountains one night by a strange blue light in the fog. Swords counted 33 improbable experiences related in *Communion*. Thirty are not confirmed by anyone else. The remaining three are confirmed only in ordinary details. Strieber has told several tales which he has later taken back as untrue. In *Communion* he himself writes: "For years I have told of being present at the University of Texas when Charles Whitman went on his shooting spree from the tower in 1966. But I wasn't there." (p. 103.)

On August 28, 1995, TV stations owned by Rupert Murdoch showed parts of a film called "Alien Autopsy." Murdoch also owns tabloid "newspapers" which gossip about celebrities, and tell a lot of "stories" of pseudoscience, and have advertisements for good luck charms, psychics, and fortune tellers. Celebrities frequently sue these newspapers for printing falsehoods and often win. It was claimed that the film must be genuine because the first few feet, the leader, contained information showing it to be from 1947. But Kodak, which was able to verify that, was never given

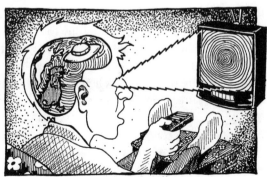

" I Believe !! "

the whole film. It is possible that the film itself was shot much later as a hoax. Stage setting and special effects can produce whatever was seen on the film. For an explanation of how, see Stokes (1996, pp. 21-23.)

Probably the main cause of continued belief in UFO's as space ships is TV "dramatizations" and "documentaries." Here we see TV at its worst in blurring the line between fantasy and reality. An early "sighting" was one in which a Captain Charles Mantell, in 1947, flew toward 20,000 feet to try to identify a UFO and then crashed. TV drama: "it was a probable shoot-down by a space ship from another world." Circumstances make it look very unmysterious. It appears that Mantell was chasing a Skyhook weather balloon released by a different branch of the government. He was flying a propeller plane not equipped with oxygen, blacked out, lost control and crashed. James Randi (1980) described a TV dramatization of this case as containing no less than ten falsifications! For example, it showed an actor in a jet and having oxygen. Apparently the producers felt you can't lie if you don't say something, just show pictures which are false to the facts.

Klass (1996) has written about how skeptics have been treated for appearances on an NBC's *Unsolved Mysteries* and other recent UFO shows. He brought with him former top-secret Air Force documents relating to the "Roswell Incident." It is claimed that a flying saucer crashed and alien bodies were found there. The documents, according to Klass, show that if an extraterrestrial craft crashed in New Mexico in July, 1947, no one informed top Pentagon intelligence officers who should have been the first to know.

The documents Klass had gotten showed top Air Force officials thinking that UFO's might be Soviet spy vehicles. Klass was given only 20 seconds of air time and none of the documents were shown. A Larry King 1-hour special on UFO's aired 10/1/94. Klass and Carl Sagan were given a total of less than 3 minutes to state skeptical views. They were taped weeks before pro-flying saucer people so they could not respond to wild claims made by them. Again, the documents were refused air time.

The Learning Channel's *Science Frontiers* did a show called "UFO." Not one "expert" interviewed was a skeptic. CBS contacted Klass for an interview with *48 Hours.* He met them at Roswell. Klass pulled one of the documents out of a pocket and held it up to the camera. CBS did not include any of the interview with him at Roswell in the program. There *is* a cover-up about UFO's. It is a media cover-up of the uninteresting but highly probable truth that UFO sightings are misidentifications of common objects or illusions or hallucinations or self-promoting lies. This is covered up because UFO's have entertainment value. UFO shows sell advertising space. Uninteresting truth does not.

In March 1997, media promotion of UFO's contributed to a tragedy, when beliefs in dualism, life after death and UFO's resulted in the tragic multiple suicides of 39 members of the Heaven's Gate UFO cult - religion in southern California. *People do what they are told and believe what they see on TV!* In 1988 a Dallas disk jockey, Ron Chapman, started saying on air, "Send $20.00 to [his station.]" He gave no reason at all. People sent in $243,000, enough to buy assassination attempts on world leaders. Chapman gave the money to charity ("Briefly," 1988.) Two groups of boys lay in the middle of roadways, imitating a stupid stunt in Disney's movie *"The Program."* After *Gilligan's Island* started showing, some called the Coast Guard to go pick up those people stranded on that island (Martindale, 1996.) Networks should be required to put on "Heaven's Gate Warnings" such as "This show is fiction. Belief in souls which survive death and alien - piloted space craft have facilitated mass suicide." If you agree, write the Network Presidents (all addresses are in New York, NY.) ABC-TV, 77 W. 66th. St. Zip 10023; CBS-TV, 51 W. 52 St., Zip 10019; FOX-TV, 1211 6th. Ave., Zip 10039; NBC-TV, 30 Rockefeller Plaza, Zip 10112.

SECTION 14.6: A TESTABLE THEORY OF UFO'S

Persinger (1990) proposes a Tectonic Stress Theory. It is that "most UFO phenomena (not due to frank misobservation) are due to natural events, generated by stresses and strains within the earth's crust." He and colleagues have done extensive statistical studies which show that the strongest correlations between sightings of anomalous luminous phenomena, (ALP's) including "earthquake lights" and UFO's, are with the occurrence of earthquakes. According to the theory, both ALPs and earthquakes are generated by release of the earth's stress.

Tectonic Stress Theory fits UFO sightings under a larger class of phenomena observed and recorded long before the first "saucer" sightings of 1947. It makes many testable predictions about the occurrence of these phenomena which have, in fact, been verified through statistical analysis of the data about earthquakes and UFO sightings. It offers plausible, terrestrial, physical mechanisms to explain production of these phenomena without resorting to improbable intelligent aliens. The general idea is that some of the mechanical energy of the stresses are transformed into thermoelectric, piezoelectric, chemical luminescence or still other forms of energy. Because of variations in the earth's crust, these transformations will vary from place to place and produce the wide variety of UFO phenomena observed. The theory predicts that strong electromagnetic fields would be generated which might give off all colors of the spectrum and whose magnetic effects might interfere with lighting and ignition systems. Finally, it explains the general characteristics of experiences reported by people who claim they were abducted by aliens in terms of the effects of such electromagnetic fields on the temporal lobes of the brain (Persinger, p. 129 ff.)

SECTION 14.7: PREDICTING THE FUTURE

Astrology, psychic powers like clairvoyance (the alleged seeing of the future) and fortune telling are based on the desire to reduce anxiety about the uncertainty of the future. Fortune telling for money is illegal in many areas. Why? It is illegal because it has so often been found together with con artistry. People go to fortune tellers frequently because they are troubled about love, money or health. Just by looking at the person the fortune teller can tell their approximate age, income and sometimes amount of education. This gives them good clues as to which problem it is. Fortune tellers often tell their clients that their troubles are caused by a curse. The fortune teller will lift the curse for a price. The price keeps going up.

The technique of the fortune teller is called "cold reading." She predicts what the type of problem is by noting the characteristics of the person. She will engage in apparently idle conversation before the reading, from which she gains more information. She uses self-excusing remarks like "My readings are symbolic and have to be fitted to your life." Perhaps she will say that "listening to the spirits is like listening to 5 'phone conversations at once." She will probably give a stock spiel about the patron's personality. This stock spiel contains statements which describe the patron one way in one phrase and nearly the opposite in the next phrase. Hines (p. 39) gives this example: "At times you are extroverted, affable, sociable, while at other times you are introverted, wary and reserved." The stock spiel is generally flattering but not to the extent that the sucker will feel it was insincere. The fortune teller will then ask vague questions like "I see a troubling change in your life?" The patron, already a believer, will almost certainly respond somehow, thus offering more information. The fortune teller may then say vague things like "I'm getting part of a name," or "some letters." Does the name 'Robert' mean anything to you?" The patron, eager to help, may well find someone in her life who has that name, give more information and come away thinking the fortune teller told her things the fortune teller "could not have known."

Psychic hotlines may work similarly. Callers may *volunteer* information, but a good 'phone worker could get age, education and type of problem just by listening and getting the subject's birth date. They don't have to hit up the mark for money to lift a curse. $3.99 per minute equals $240 per hour! If a person suffers from anxiety or depression about the future, she can see a psychiatrist for less than half that price. The psychiatrist can prescribe medications that will really work. "Psychic Friends Network" currently brings in about $100 million per year, "Psychic Readers Network" $50 million, and "Your Psychic Experience," $35-40 million. They also use the muscle of big 'phone companies A.T. & T and M.C.I. to collect. One only gets "free" minutes by making paid calls.

Review a simple argument from Chapter 4, Section 4. Causes always come before effects. So something must happen before it can be seen or known in any way. Astrology, clairvoyance and fortune telling are expressions of self-deceptions that we are not responsible for our futures, they are unchangeable "destiny" and can be known in advance. Critical thinking rejects such claims as highly unjustified.

Each year the tabloid newspapers National Enquirer, National Examiner and Weekly World News have so-called psychics make predictions. Here are some of the things they predicted for 1996 (Emery, 1997.) The psychics for the Enquirer predicted that Jay Leno would lose his *Tonight Show* hosting job to Johnny Carson. O.J. Simpson would confess to murdering Nicole Simpson and Ron Goldman and become a minister. *Good Morning America* Hostess Joan Lunden would become engaged to Shaquille O'Neal. Johnnie Cochran would play a defense attorney in a new "smash hit" TV comedy. Barbara Walters would be kidnapped by middle eastern terrorists. The Globe predicted that Marcia Clark and Chris Darden would be married and O. J. Simpson would enter a monastery. It also predicted that Susan Lucci would finally win an Emmy. The Globe also predicted (1/2/96) that Jerry Lewis and Dean Martin would have an emotional TV reunion. Unfortunately for the Globe, Martin died in December 1995!

The psychics for the Examiner predicted the following. Michael Jackson would undergo a complete sex change and insist everyone call him "Michelle." Rush Limbaugh would quit his job as a conservative talk radio commentator and star in a remake of the TV series *Jake and the Fat man.* Nuclear missiles would be used to break up a giant asteroid found to be coming toward the earth. The Sun predicted that Rush Limbaugh would be the Republican nominee against Bill Clinton. The tiny island nation of Tonga would somehow land and strand people on the moon and the U.S. would rescue them. Finally, it predicted that the American and National baseball leagues would disband and that NFL owners would sell their teams to the players! All of these predictions proved false.

Could God have included predictions of specific events in a Bible code (Drosnin, 1997?) Computers running very many codes rapidly will likely find "astounding matches" by coincidence (Begley, 1997.) The Hebrew has to be interpreted. Drosnin read what he wanted to. He has also "predicted" the past and made vague, multiple predictions of "for everyone, the terror," but of disasters or just delays, and in 2,000, 2006 or 2,014 AD (Drosnin, p. 138?)

SECTION 14.8: NEW AGE MILLENNARIANISM

A millennium is a period of 1,000 years. The Book of Revelations in the Bible says that there will be a period of 1,000 years during which Jesus will rule with the souls of those who were killed for him and never worshipped the devil. This has been called "The Millennium". In Bible - influenced thinking "The Millennium" has come to mean a golden age, a good time in which war and poverty are abolished, everyone lives in peace and harmony, health and happiness. There could hardly be a clearer example of wishful thinking than cults of people who believe such a millennium, including an end of the world as we know it, is coming soon. At least 49 such predictions have been made and failed (Randi, 1995, Appendix II.)

Millenarian cults often following charismatic (say KAH riz mah tik) leaders. In the Nineteenth Century there were millennarian cults of people who, believing the world was coming to an end, gave away all of their property. The 900 people who were killed following "the Reverend" Jim Jones in Jonestown, Guyana, were millennarian cultists. So were the eighty or so followers of the self-called "David Koresh" at Waco. There was a rise of millennarian cults around the year 1000. With Waco, the Aum Shinri Kyo cult in Japan, mass murders in the Solar Temple cult and mass suicide at Heaven's Gate, we seem to be seeing a new rise of millennial cults as we near the year 2000.

According to Melton (1988) The New Age traces its origins to the study of Eastern religions among counter - culture groups like the Hippies and Age of Aquarius in the 1960's. By the 1970's the study of eastern religion and transpersonal psychology had achieved great popularity. A big difference between the Age of Aquarius and the New Age is the attitude towards drugs. The New Agers are generally against their use. Another difference is that Aquarians were very politically active. New Agers tend to be apolitical because all suffering serves good karmic purpose.

The actress Shirley MacLaine has published five (5) autobiographies! This suggests more than a little egotism and self-obsession. Her third (1983) dealt with her growing interest in reincarnation and the paranormal. It became a best seller. The book uses terms like "energy vibrations," "Karma," "other dimensions," "auras," "out of body experiences," "synchronicity," "ESP," "precognition," "holism," "Atlantis," "Lemuria," "UFO's," "the Shroud of Turin," and "discarnates." It was made into a TV movie telecast January 18 and 19, 1987.

An astronomical event called "the Harmonic Convergence" occurred in August of 1987. It would, according to Arguelles (1987) begin a final 25 year earth-age. He claimed that at the end of that cycle the human race will unify and be projected into an evolutionary domain that is presently inconceivable. Here is a quote from Arguelles about the end of the cycle.

> ... the moment of total planetary synchronization, 13.0.0.0.0 on the beam will arrive - the closing out of the evolutionary interim called homo sapiens. Amidst festive preparations and awesome galactic - solar songs psychically received, the human race, in harmony with the animal and other kingdoms ... will unify as a single circuit.
> Then, as if a switch were being thrown, a great voltage will race through this finally synchronized and integrated circuit called humanity. ... A current charging both poles will race across the skies, connecting the polar auroras in a single brilliant flash. Like an iridescent rainbow, this circumpolar energy uniting the planetary antipodes will be instantaneously understood as the external projecting of the unification of the collective mind of humanity. In that moment we shall be collectively projected into an evolutionary domain that is presently inconceivable.

The compiler of this quote, Robert Basil, thinks Arguelles' intention with this language was not to instruct but to delight. What, however, is it to be taken to mean? Arguelles also predicted UFO's to fill the skies at the Harmonic Convergence and that we would all become telepathic. Of course, neither happened. Telepathy, whereby everyone could instantly know what anyone else was thinking, would seem to this author to be one of the worst things that could happen to human relations. We survive and relate satisfactorily because we can behave differently from the way we think about others.

SECTION 14.9: DOES THE SPIRIT MOVE YOU?

Belief in demons, ghosts and poltergeists, near death experiences as "proving" life after death, reincarnation and faith healing have in common that they are based on dualism. Also, they generally involve wishful thinking that people somehow survive death. Belief that "There are demons" was one of the mainstays of the Inquisition. Belief in demons has revived lately in fundamentalist thinking. It was a killer in the Middle Ages. It still is a killer today. In 1994 a 19-year-old French woman was killed in an exorcism ("Muslim Cleric Gets 7 Years") and in July 1996 a South Korean woman was killed in Los Angeles. She allegedly consented to the ritual at the beginning but suffered serious internal injuries during it ("Woman Dies" 1996.)

The claim is advanced that "Near death experiences prove that there is an afterlife." In "near death experiences" people sometimes report feeling that they are floating, seeing their bodies below them, or a white light. Feeling that one is floating and seeing a whitish light were experiences known to medicine before anyone "hyped" (stressed) them as providing evidence for life after death. They can be produced in laboratories and have been shown to involve loss of oxygen to the brain. It has recently been recognized that death does not occur when the heart stops beating.

Irreversible death occurs when the brain ceases electrochemical activity because of lack of oxygen. Between heart stoppage and brain death, the brain, deprived of oxygen, gets more and more damaged. Is it any wonder then, if it produces hallucinatory experiences of floating, seeing ones' body, tunnels, white light, or ones' dead relatives? We don't take the descriptions of people on hallucinogenic drugs as accurate descriptions of reality. This is because we know their brains have been altered at least temporarily by the drug. So we certainly should not take descriptions of experiences had by people at times when their brains are under the most abnormal condition of all, near death, as experiences of reality.

Belief in poltergeists and spiritualism began in the 19th. century. It was actually started by two young girls, Kate and Margaret Fox, 11 and 13 years old. Strange knocks and rapping sounds were heard in their house which were interpreted to be communication from spirits. People set themselves up as "mediums," claiming that "it is possible to communicate with the dead." Mediums held seances in which this was alleged to occur. Mysterious happenings occurred in seances. Tables and Ouija (say we gee) boards seemed to move by themselves. The scientist Michael Faraday investigated table movement and was able to show by experiment that tables were actually moved, consciously or not, by tiny muscle motions of the medium themselves. Other illusions of magic could explain objects apparently floating in air and so on. Mediums' knowledge of their subjects could be explained in the same terms as the apparent knowledge of psychics. Houdini, Brandon and Dunninger have explained mediums' tricks (see Hines, p. 319 ff.) Finally, Margaret Fox herself confessed in 1888 that their case was a fraud. She and her sister produced all the noises by tying an apple to a string and bouncing it up and down to frighten their mother.

The most famous cases of alleged "reincarnation" have been thoroughly explained by natural causes. These are the cases of Virginia Tighe who claimed to recall a past life as "Bridey Murphy" and Jane Evans. Evans apparently gave accurate details of six past lives. This included one as a maid in the house of a well known merchant of Fifteenth-century France. It turned out that his house was one of the most photographed in all of France. Also, her account was missing a detail that would not have been missed by any maid. She claimed the man was not married and had no children. But he was and had five children. This is also missing from a novel about his life written by a well-known author. It seems much more probable that she learned about his life from this novel than that she and the author both left that important information out.

SECTION 14.10: ETHICAL BLATHER ON THE RAMTHA CHANNEL

Mediums don't call themselves "mediums" any more. Like corporations and criminals which have gotten bad names, they have changed names. They now call themselves "channelers." What sort of philosophy and theology is being taught by some of the New Age spirits? Here are some quotes from "Ramtha," an alleged 35,000 year old spirit "channeled" by J. Z. Knight. According to Martin Gardner, people have packed seminars at $400 to $1,000 for a whole weekend to hear this sort of stuff. The following quotes are taken from Weinberg (1994.) "The God that I know ... is a God of complete and unjudgmental love" (p. 29.) " "God, of itself, is wholly without goodness or evil" (p. 30.) "What need is there for punishment, lady? You have been doing it to yourself all your life" (p. 38.) "But God, the principal cause of all life, has never been *outside* of you - it is you" (Ch. 5 p. 41.) "There is not a plan for life... There is only *isness*.... [anything goes?] Indeed!" (p. 122.) Ramtha addresses others as "Master." "Master: So you don't even think that killing someone is evil? Ramtha: That is correct. Because I have not limited myself by believing in the ending of any one thing, for nothing is ever destroyed... Master: So you're saying that even murder is not wrong or evil. Ramtha: That is correct."

For a being 35,000 years old, Ramtha does not seem to have learned much about right and wrong. Perhaps Charles Manson was an incarnation of him. Ramtha bloviates (speaks too long) anti-ethical garbage. It is made up to make people who feel guilty feel better about themselves. That's what the suckers are paying $400 to $1,000 for. In "est" therapy, they paid a lot to be kept in rooms where they could not go to the bathroom and were insulted by being called the worst swear words.

SECTION 14.11: FAITH HEALING

Faith healing is on the border between the paranormal and quackery. It claims that "People with even fatal illnesses can be cured through faith and laying on of hands." In some cases of illnesses with psychological origins, faith healing may be followed by temporary (or sometimes even permanent) relief. Medicine has long known that for any disease there are cases of "spontaneous remission." In other words, the course of illness is not a straight downward one. A disease may simply stop without faith healing. A person may get better, then worse, then better and so on. Faith healers have been caught in various kinds of fraud such as "healing" accomplices who only pretended to be ill.

Faith healing is probably the most dangerous pseudoscience. Belief in faith healing causes people to refuse science-based medical treatment and die sooner and more painfully than they would by taking medical treatment. In Altoona, Pennsylvania, in 1996, the family of Shannon Nixon came under investigation. Shannon died at age 16 of a heart attack, the result of untreated, chronic diabetes. Shannon's parents are Christian Scientists. She died three days short of her 17th. birthday, when she could have sought medical care on her own.

Nixon's parents were previously prosecuted and convicted of involuntary manslaughter and endangering the welfare of another child. A son of theirs died from complications of an ear infection in 1991. The Nixon's are members of a church called the Faith Tabernacle Congregation. Five children of church families died of measles in recent years. After that, a court ordered vaccinations of the remaining children. The church still appealed to the state Supreme Court. Why don't such people learn? The case illustrates self-excusal or failure of pseudoscientific hypotheses and refusal to revise opinions. Failure to be healed can be excused by claiming that the ill people or their faith healers simply did not have enough faith, or that it was not God's will that they be healed. The opinion that faith healing works keeps its grip on some people even when their children die because of it. Nixon's parents have been convicted in her death also. As they have nine remaining children to endanger, the court ruled that social service agencies can intervene to take temporary custody when their children are seriously ill to save them from their parents' "faith."

According to Sagan (1995, p. 10) from pre-agricultural times to Late Roman and Medieval times human life expectancy was about only 20 to 30 years. It did not rise to 40 years until about 1870. By 1915 it reached 50. By 1930 it reached 60; by 1955 it was 70 and it is now approaching 80 *in those countries with advanced science, medicine, and public health measures.* When one looks at history, it becomes clear that no religion, no faith healing, no savior brings us life more abundantly in a plain, literal sense. When ill, one should see a physician, not a faith healer!

As to miraculous cures still heard of today, consider the case of Lourdes. Sagan relates (p. 232 f.) that since 1858 when a vision of Mary was allegedly seen there, about 100 million visits have been paid to the site. The Roman Catholic Church itself rejects many claims of miraculous cures there but accepts 65 such cases in about 150 years. The rate of spontaneous remission of all types of cancers is 1 in 10,000 to 1 in 100,000. So if only 5% of the visitors were there for cures for cancer, it would be expected that there would be 50 to 500 cures of cancer alone just from spontaneous remission. But only 3 of the 65 cures accepted by the Church are of cancer. Thus, Sagan observes, "the rate of spontaneous remission at Lourdes seems to be lower than if the victims had just stayed at home."

Sightings, we might note, have always been good for local business. Nor does it seem, in our times, to matter much what is sighted. The Loch Ness monster myth is worth $42 million dollars in tourist money to the area of Loch Ness ("Loch Ness..." AP, 5/29/90.) For a piece of $42 million a lot of people, including officials of the local government and the tourist board will be powerfully tempted to report such sightings. Photographs and videotapes always seem to be a little fuzzy, so that what is photographed could be a log or something else. The "best" videotape of Bigfoot is fuzzy and looks to this author like a man in a gorilla suit walking at a distance from the camera. Footprints are easier to fake than even than alien crop circles. A section of highway in the United States has been renamed "The Extra Terrestrial Highway" in an overt attempt to draw tourists.

SECTION 14.12: ALTERNATIVE, BUT IS IT MEDICINE?

Human societies have probably had people who falsely pretend to medical skill and knowledge from their beginnings. Stalker and Glymour (1985) state that the holistic movement includes many treatments based on unjustified claims. These include acupuncture, therapeutic touch, cancer therapy through visualization, Rolfing, reflexology, homeopathy, diet therapies, chiropractic, aroma therapy, chelation, colonics, and iridology, to name just a few. This is one area of pseudoscience in which some quite despicable acts are done. Ill people are preyed upon, taken for money, and their lives are sometimes shortened by using pseudoscientific therapies based on unjustified claims.

Stalker and Glymor claim that holistic medicine gets a degree of acceptability by mixing with its unjustified claims some claims which are justified. For example, it claims that we should focus on prevention rather than cure. Second, it says people are to some extent responsible for their own health. It admits that there are behavioral, environmental, and social causes of illness. Its' practitioners rightly point out that traditional doctors have for too long treated the disease while ignoring the whole patient. Nevertheless, they say (p. 10.) "The essays in this book make it apparent that the science of holistic medicine is bogus; that the philosophical views championed by the movement are incoherent, uninformed, and unintelligent; and that most holistic therapies are crank in the usual sense of that word: they lack any sound scientific basis."

This is an area in which there are a lot of errors of accepting anecdotes and testimonials. Additionally people assume that because a person got better after a "treatment" that the treatment must have been the cause of getting better. The human body has an immune system which often makes one get better despite useless or even somewhat harmful treatments. The student should remember that *anecdotes and testimonials are never good evidence of the effectiveness of medical treatment*. Patients are the best source of information on their symptoms. However, if they pay for some sort of therapy, they are likely to feel better after it just because they had it. This is called "the placebo" effect.

A *placebo* is a demonstrably non effective medication or treatment given to a control group in a study to determine the effectiveness of a medication on an experimental group. This is done by comparing the number of people who get better with the placebo versus those who get better just by having been given some treatment which they think might be effective. To be scientific, such experiments need to be conducted in a careful manner. The researcher whose medication is being tried should not either pick the experimental group or examine it to determine the results.

Effective testing of medical treatments requires "double blind" experiments or studies. *"Double blind"* means that some patients get the real therapy and others get a placebo, but the selection of subjects is not made by the proposer of the treatment, and still a third party evaluates the results. If the proposer of a treatment can select the subjects, her bias can affect the outcome just as if she picks who gets the placebo or evaluates the results.

Here are definitions of some "therapies" which critical thinkers have claimed to be quackery based on unjustified claims. Acupuncture is a technique of traditional Chinese medicine that involves inserting needles in the body to produce pain relief and claimed to treat ulcers, high blood pressure, and depression. It is based on the claim that "The human body contains 'Qi,' vital energy, flowing in meridians." Acupuncture points are located on these meridians and are supposed to allow excess Qi to be released or deficiencies to be corrected. "Qi" is undetectable by science.

Quantum Holistic medical writers think that Quantum theory shows their approaches are correct while traditional medicine is incorrect. Capra (1975) claimed to find in Quantum theory confirmation of or parallels to mystical teachings of Eastern religions. This author does not have a grasp of the mathematics of Quantum Theory to offer opinions on the subject. However, Rothman (1988) and Stenger (1990, 1995) make what look to him like very strong arguments against these ideas.

Quantum Theory is alleged to require consideration of wholes and consciousness as shaping reality. Dossey and Canton (in Stalker and Glymour, p. 118) say that Quantum medicine claims that "Patients actually influence the cause of their own illness... through the impact of their consciousness on the physical world - which contains their own bodies." What there is can be determined by what you want there to be or how you feel about things. Dossey and Canton say that Quantum Theory has not led real physicists to place any emphasis on "consciousness" as a causal factor in physics. "Quantum medicine" is the old psycho-physical causation of dualistic interactionism. We saw in Chapter 12 that it does not work, no matter what you call it.

Reflexology or Zone Therapy is massaging the soles of the feet or underside of the hands. It is supposed to have therapeutic effects on all parts of the body. This is based on the theory that "Each part or organ of the body is connected to some part of the foot or hand." A similar claim is made for diagnosis by iridology. The claim is that diseases of the body or whole person can be diagnosed by examination of the iris of the eye. This is based in part on the ancient idea that the eyes are the windows of the soul.

Homeopathy is based on the claim that "Like cures like." The claim is that substances which produce symptoms in well people similar to those of certain diseases can, in extremely small quantities, cure the disease in people who really have it. Chronic disease results from suppression of the itch or psora. This looks like the theory behind inoculation, which does work. But homeopathic practitioners try to use it for cure, not prevention. Also, they use substances in such extremely small quantities as to be impossible to have any therapeutic effect.

Chelation (say KEE la shun) has been claimed to be useful therapy for many conditions including arteriosclerosis. It is the practice of administering EDTA, a molecule which removes calcium in the blood. Chelation is the binding of a metal ion. EDTA was approved by the FDA in 1953 for use in heavy metal poisoning and one illness named Wilson's Disease. This author requested information from a local clinic which recently began chelation therapy. Included was a release form which contains the following words. "I understand that although Disodium Ethylenediamine Tetra-acetic Acid has been used for thirty years in clinical practices, it is still considered experimental by the American Medical Association and its affiliated groups. It is my desire to undertake this treatment and release XYZ from legal responsibility for any harmful effects or lack of improvement in connection with the use of chelation therapy in my particular case." Also included was a pamphlet offering an inconsistent explanation indirectly stating that medical insurance was not likely to cover costs of this therapy unless one sued the insurer.

SECTION 14.13: A BODY TO DIE(T) FOR

Nutrition Therapy is a group of beliefs to the effect that "Proper diet can greatly extend life and health, including prevention or lessening of heart attacks and cancer." It includes macrobiotic diet and megavitamin therapy. The claim that megavitamins, herbs or a macrobiotic diet can prevent cancer or retard advanced cancer is unjustified.

Health and nutrition quackery includes fad diets, excess vitamins and minerals and questionable therapies. Each year billions of dollars are spent on new books on how to lose weight, vitamins, minerals, herbs, and pseudo-medical and "fitness" gadgets. People buy diet books because they did not lose weight or keep it off on last years' fad diet. Some of these diets have very bad effects on the body. One such diet book claimed: "You can lose weight and keep it off on a diet of liquid protein." More than 50 deaths were caused by the liquid diet since 1970. It can damage the heart, liver and kidneys. According to Hines (pg. 253 ff.) the claim of Harvey and Marilyn Diamond (1985) is "You should only eat certain kinds of food at certain times of day because the body processes of digestion, absorption, and elimination go on only at certain times of the day." This, Hines says, is utter nonsense. Harvey claims to have a Ph.D. in nutrition. In fact, his "degree" comes from an unaccredited school which was never authorized to grant degrees.

Fad weight loss and anti-aging diets and megadoses of vitamins result partly from wishful thinking that there is an easy way to keep good health and a slim body forever. The claim is offered that "One can eat oneself thin." But weight is probably significantly controlled by genes. No superficial treatment is likely to be effective against excess weight. Fad weight loss dieting is frequently semi-starvation. The body may respond to this, when one goes off a fad diet, by storing more fat. Megadoses of vitamins have not been shown to be clinically effective against colds or cancer and sometimes harm people.

The best advice is to eat a balanced diet from the "Food Pyramid." The base of one's diet should be 6 - 11 servings of grains per day. On top of this one should eat 2 - 3 servings of vegetables, 2 - 4 servings of fruit, 2 - 3 of milk products, 2 - 3 at most of meat, fish, dry beans, eggs and nuts, and only sparing amounts of fats, oils and sweets. If one does that and eats moderate quantities, one will get all the vitamins and minerals needed by the body. Megadoses are excreted and can be harmful.

There is a tee-shirt, no doubt worn by critical thinking joggers, which says: "Eat right! Exercise! - Die Anyway." This is the truth. But there is good evidence that moderate exercise helps keep some weight off, helps retain or regain some muscle strength, reduces stress and enables people to feel better through the release of natural chemicals called endorphins. It takes self-discipline to eat a reasonable diet and get exercise. We will continue to age and die anyway. Therefore it is certain that fad diets, especially anti-aging ones, will be an on-going big business pseudoscience.

SECTION 14.14: THE EXAMPLE OF CHIROPRACTIC

Chiropractic is a model for the holistic movement, according to Stalker and Glymour. Chiropractors are licensed everywhere in the United States. Chiropractic is covered in Medicare. The American Medical Association has allowed association with chiropractors and others who use therapies regarded as unscientific. Chiropractors achieved this against evidence that their theories of healing and disease are unjustified, and in the absence of any good evidence that chiropractic has specific good effects. They have won the day through lawsuits (generally antitrust suits) and lobbying. (Stalker and Glymour, pp. 10-11.) Chiropractic makes the claim that "Misalignments of vertebrae cause subluxations, pinched nerves which cause numerous diseases, curable by manipulating the spine." Chiropractors are forbidden by law from prescribing drugs, because their education and experience does not enable them to do so safely. So they try to persuade clients that medicines only mask symptoms of disease where they alone can cure its causes.

Edmund S. Crelin, a Doctor of Science, not an M.D., but a professor of Anatomy in the Department of Surgery at Yale University, quotes T. A. Vondarhaar, President of the Northern California College of Chiropractic, as stating Chiropractic's claim this way:

> Because of the various stresses to which the spine is subject, individual vertebrae can become misaligned. Such misalignments can create pressure on nerve tissue, and thus interfere with the conduction of nerve impulses to other parts of the body. Chiropractors call the condition a *subluxation.*
>
> Nerves travel to various tissues and organs from each vertebra of the spine. A subluxation reduces the nerve signals to the affected tissue or organ, resulting in dysfunction and eventually disease. The subluxation of the spine, because it reduces the nerve supply, is considered by doctors of chiropractic to be a main *cause* of disease. The point in the body at which disease becomes apparent is the *symptom.* Physical trauma is one major cause of subluxations.... Mental stress is another cause of subluxation. Tightened muscles resulting from tension can pull the vertebrae out of alignment. Finally, chemical ingestion associated with faulty nutrition or consumption of drugs can cause misalignment of the vertebrae.

Crelin designed an experiment he said shows the basic claim of chiropractic to be completely false, that is, that there are vertebral subluxations. He dissected out the intact spines or vertebral columns, with their attached ligaments, from three infants and three adults a few hours after they died. He exposed the spinal nerves as they passed through the opening inside the spines. He put the spines in an ordinary drill press. He wrapped a thin wire around the nerve in the spinal cavity. A different wire was put against the wall of the space in the spine. He then applied force to the front and back of each vertebra. He also twisted and bent the spines. If the space inside the spine became reduced in size to the point that its walls touched the spinal nerve going through it, the wires would touch and cause a meter to register it.

The forces applied to the spine reached the level where the spine was about to break. Not once did the walls of the space push upon the spinal nerves passing through them. In order to have that happen he had to break the spine! This, Crelin claims, is definite scientific proof that the chiropractic subluxation causing pinching or pressure upon a spinal nerve is a myth. This experiment was published in 1973. The President of the American Chiropractic Association claimed that Crelin's findings were irrelevant because they were done on dead bodies.

Crelin replied that if a vertebra could be subluxed to squeeze a spinal nerve, it would have occurred more easily in a dead body. In a living person there is a reflex response by the powerful spinal muscles to fight any forces that would sublux a vertebra to the degree that it and/or spinal nerves could be damaged. In the spines Crelin tested the only resistance to displacement of vertebrae were the attached passive ligaments. Thus, if the pinching on the nerves could not happen in a dead body, it definitely could not happen in a living one. (Stalker & Glymour, p. 205).

Keating (1997) asserts after 13 years of teaching and research at several chiropractic colleges, that chiropractic is both science and antiscience. Chiropractors' belief systems lie all the way from the scientific to unscientific, uncritical dogma and circus. There is more than one theory about spinal lesions and they have not been adequately tested. By an operational definition chiropractic is a science, because some of its practitioners engage in real scientific activities. However, its practitioners' theories of knowledge as to why it works are largely uncritical rationalism and personal experience.

Chiropractic may produce relief from low back pain. However, when chiropractors try to persuade people that spine manipulations are the real cures for many serious diseases like diabetes, and not to take medicines, their claims should be rejected. They also claim clients need indefinite numbers of return visits ("preventive maintenance.") In other words, if we fail to cure your illness, it's your fault for not paying us enough.

SECTION 14.15: FREUDIAN PSYCHOLOGY

Psychology has been infected with dualism as much as philosophy. It is home to a number of pseudoscientific hypotheses. Freudian psychology claimed that "All young boys around age 5 desire to have sex with their mothers and kill their fathers." This was called "the Oedipus Complex" (say E duh puhs) after a mythological Greek king. Oedipus was supposed to have killed his father and slept with his mother. Freud believed that "Young boys get to see the genitals of a young girl and, thinking that their fathers mutilated the girl, develop 'castration anxiety'." He claimed that "Little girls see boys' sexual organs and develop 'penis envy'." Oedipal feelings would be desires to kill one's father and sleep with one's mother. Freud claimed that "Oedipal feelings are repressed." He thought of repression as a means of keeping anxiety-provoking, dangerous thoughts out of consciousness.

These beliefs led Freud to analyze dreams as containing symbols of early desires and fears. But the concept of repression made Freud's claims about interpretation unfalsifiable. If a patient denied an interpretation Freud made of a dream object, Freud could simply excuse this by saying that the patient had repressed the desire or fear too well to recognize it.

Freud also claimed that "Early toilet training is profoundly influential on later personality in life." But he associated strict toilet training either with a child's becoming neat, orderly, careful with money, and over-controlled or rebellious, messy, disorderly, wasteful and under-controlled. He made similar opposite predictions about gentle toilet training. It should be obvious that this makes the original claim non-predictive and so not falsifiable. Actual behavior and personality traits can't be predicted even if we know how a person was toilet trained, because either kind of training is consistent with opposite behaviors.

It is worth noting that all symbolic interpretation of dreams has a questionable element to it. Dreams are vague, like the descriptions and predictions of psychics. People convinced that psychics or psychologists are right or that some dreams are predictive can always find something in their dreams or daily lives which they can interpret to count as evidence for their beliefs. It is wrong, however, to think that a single person who already holds a hypothesis, can accurately evaluate it in the face of vague evidence. Hines (1988, P. 112) calls this the *"fallacy of personal validation."* Accurate validation requires precise prediction and data clear enough for many observers to determine whether the hypothesis fits them. "It works for me" won't cut it. Each of us has a confirmatory bias.

SECTION 14.16: RELIGIONS, CULTS AND MILITIAS

Cults, religions and militias are groups of people organized around beliefs which are non scientific and sometimes contradicted by science. Their beliefs are controversial, widely disagreed with and thought by others to not correspond with reality. Some such beliefs do, in fact, correspond to reality. Others are literally false, some are exaggerated, some are distortions of reality, over - generalizations, and prejudice. Other beliefs of such groups, such as conspiracy theories, are untestable. It is hard to give precise definitions of such groups but easier to draw distinctions among them. Religions and cults compete for members and money. Both have run up against governments over whether their businesses should be taxed. Individuals have sued cults claiming they have been suckered into giving the cults great sums of money. Sometimes this was for worthless treatments. Other times the suits were simply over misuse of money. From this competitor a lot of critical information has developed.

Large, established religions will be called "churches" for short. According to information from the Cult Awareness Network, churches allow members freedom of association. Cults tend to require isolation from others except to gain money or new converts. Cults encourage leaving jobs, family, friends and relocating unless a person has a well paying or influential position. Churches teach family love and unity, although under parental authority. Cults teach that parents and other relatives are demonic, bad influences. Churches teach honesty and respect for law, government and society. Cults teach that they have superior knowledge of "The Truth" and so are being persecuted. Therefore it is alright "work the system" for their purposes, to break laws for a higher cause, to be deceitful. Churches teach that the human body is a sacred vessel of the soul. Many cults in practice show little or no concern for the body. This is shown in their techniques of gaining control over the minds of their converts. Most churches do not emphasize what may be called self - hypnosis or thought - stoppage by endless repetition of chants. Some cults do emphasize this. Churches put somewhat less pressure on their converts for money than do cults and less pressure against leaving the group. Churches are "up front" about their beliefs, often requiring some form of public "confession" of faith. Cults often try to keep some of their beliefs secret and use the need for secrecy as a basis to pressure members to stay in the group.

Cult members are not all simple - minded dopes. They are frequently well educated. They may come from troubled families where they have been held to high achievement standards which they have come to resent. They may also be troubled with "mental" problems and lonely. The techniques used by cults to take control of converts' minds include the following. They "love bomb" the person - express total, unconditional love and support for the convert. They provide instant friends and peers. They make lots of physical contact - putting their arms around the convert, looking her in the eyes. They take the convert to unfamiliar surroundings to make the person feel like a dependent guest. They put the convert in an environment in which he or she may lose track of time.

Time spent in a cult often includes long hours of work and endless meetings. This deprives the person of adequate sleep. Cults feed converts diets low in vitamins and protein. They have converts engage in a lot of activities which appeal to emotions rather than intellect. This includes repeated attendance at meetings where there is "personal testimony" by others about how bad their lives were before they joined, stirring sermons and singing. They teach "secret" doctrines which they claim are "The Truth" which makes them superior to others. They foster elements of paranoia that terrible things will happen if someone leaves the group.

Some individuals and groups were identified by the Cult Awareness Network in 1988 as ones about which they had received complaints. These included the following: The Unification Church (Moonies), Hare Krishnas, Scientology (Dianetics, Narconon), Ramtha (J. Z. Knight), The Bible Speaks, Rajneesh Ananda

Marga, Transcendental Meditation (TM), Muktananda, Nicherin Shoshu of America (Soka Gakkai), National Democratic Policy Committee (Lyndon LaRouche), Divine Light Mission, Posse Comitatus, the Christian Identity Movement (The Order and The Covenant, Sword and Arm of the Lord), the Worldwide Church of God, The Forum (est, Hunger Project), The Farm, Move, and The Peoples Temple at Jonestown, Guyana. It should be clear from the names that these groups sometimes use political names and worthy causes such as fighting drug abuse or hunger to collect money.

The Cult Awareness Network was bankrupted by a lawsuit. A convert to a cult alleged imprisonment by deprogrammers recommended by the Network. The court awarded $1.8 million which put the Network out of business. A different sort of watch on cults is kept today by the Millennium Watch Institute. The author of most materials on the MWI's World Wide Web Site (http://www.channel1.com/mpr) is a folklorist, Dr. Ted Daniels. Dr. Daniels has a less oppositional attitude than CAN and the critical thinkers who write for Prometheus Books' *The Skeptical Inquirer* or *Skeptic Magazine*. He regards cult figures, particularly millennarians with some sympathy and academic detachment as "mythographers." To him, they are primarily expressing humans "utopian longings," longings for a better society than that which we have now. On his web site can be found materials on The Montana Freemen, The Branch Davidians, The Order of the Solar Temple and Heaven's Gate.

The People's Temple, MOVE, The Branch Davidians, Solar Temple and Heaven's Gate all ended in tragic loss of life. This shows how beliefs out of touch with reality can be heavily involved in getting people killed. Nor is it only beliefs of "far out cults" which sometimes bring death. On June 19 and 23, 1994, papers around the U.S. carried A.P. stories titled thus: "Girl, 6, stood in front of train 'to become an angel'" and "Woman who feared cancer kills children, then herself." In the first case it was reported that the child committed suicide so she could be in heaven with her terminally ill mother. In the second, the woman believed that no one could take care of her children like she could, and that they would go to heaven with her. An autopsy revealed that she did not even have cancer, only "strep throat" and influenza.

Despite the danger of such beliefs, Daniels takes a generally non judgmental, "let it all in" approach and reports beliefs of many tiny groups or even individuals. As a result on his web site one can read wonderfully imaginative, outrageous pseudoscientific nonsense. Recent subjects have included the Ascended Masters, The Rose and the Cross, Ashtar Command, The Photon Belt, End-Time Handmaidens, Cyber - prophecy and Third Density Terran Existence. For perspective, one should compare such beliefs in amount of evidence and reasonableness to one's own religious beliefs, if any, and those found in *The Book of the SubGenius* (1983.)

Militias are an outgrowth of the "Patriot Movement." There may be up to 12 million Americans in this Patriot Movement, united in their strong opposition to the United States government. Militias seem to have some aspects of cults. Members are usually poor, rural whites squeezed out of the economy. They grew up without contact with diverse people. They received poor educations and so are not able to get decent jobs in the technical economy. They have military training. They are frequently of fundamentalist Christian religions. They believe **the United States government is indifferent to their problems or actively hostile toward them. In this belief, they are exactly right** (see Chapter 15.) However, they also believe that Blacks and Latinos are inferior races and that the U.S. favors "minorities" and foreigners. Some think there is a secret "Zionist Occupation Government" (ZOG) running the United States. Thompson (1994) claims the U.S. "exploit[s] the people through the Federal Reserve System." County government is the highest legal authority. IRS and BATF "men in black" oppress the people. The United Nations is ruler-to-be of a conspiracy to create a "New World Order," one world government. Armaggedon (final war) will be Rahowa (a racial holy war.) The true Children of God (Identity: White Christians) will exterminate the Jews and "Mud People." None of these beliefs is well justified (see Chapter 15.)

Daniels thinks militias have aspects of cargo cults. Militias make use of symbols and trappings of government of their own. A Cargo Cult is a group of colonized people who start behaving like colonists in the hope of attracting some of the wealth which they see the colonists receiving. Melanesian natives were excluded from the system that brought white colonizers cargo on airfields. They organized cults in which they made rifle - like sticks, organized drills, and had "officials" who shuffled meaningless papers. They cleared "airstrips," built a "control Tower" in which sat a man with wooden imitation earphones on. They kept torches burning all night. Daniels points out that the Montana Freemen and Republic of Texas militias in their extensive use of legal forms and their own "common law" courts are like Cargo Cults.

What the Freemen and Republic of Texas have done is treated by law enforcement as conventional "working the system," civil wrongs and crimes. In any case, there is little doubt that as long as our economy continues to lower wages, export jobs and deprive small farmers of their family farms, the unjustified views of the Patriots will lead to more misplaced, violent actions like the bombing of the Federal Building in Oklahoma City. Patriots have, in fact, the same sort of sexist, racist, anti-semitic views which led to fascism in Germany and Italy before World War Two. If their members are not educated to economic reality, their growing militancy in future years will make life in America very difficult for Jews, Blacks, Latinos, immigrants, foreigners, women, gays, probably Catholics and democracy as well as themselves.

SECTION 14.17: SCIENTOLOGY AS A THERAPY CULT

Pseudoscientific cult ideology may be more negative than Ted Daniels thinks. Often it exploits troubled people for a great deal of time, labor, money and other resources. Scientology has been repeatedly alleged to be such a cult. Scientology calls itself "scientific" but also a religion, perhaps for tax-avoidance purposes. Considering the radical differences we have seen between science and religion, this seems doubtful in itself.

In 1988, a controversy erupted over Scientology's purchase of $15 to $18 million dollars of real estate in the Clearwater, Florida area. Since 1975 Scientology had acquired several hotels, motels, apartments, a former bank and office building and a teen night club. Elsewhere it owns a 500-passenger cruise ship, the Freewinds. (Koff, 1988b.) The *St. Petersburg Times* claimed that Scientology's Clearwater operations alone brought in $1.5 to $2 million a week. Scientology, it said, charged converts $8,000 for 12 1/2 hours of basic counseling (Koff, 1988a.)

The basic Theory of Scientology is similar to psychoanalysis. Its founder (Hubbard, 1950) wrote: "The mind records continuously during the entire life of a person. 'Unconsciousness' is possible only in death. All mental and physical derangements of a psychic nature come about from moments of 'unconsciousness'. Such moments can be reached and drained of charge with the result of returning the mind to optimum operating condition." "The sentient portions of the mind, which computes the answers to problems is *utterly incapable of errors*" (italics are Hubbard's.) Dianetics proposes "a single source of all insanities" and "a therapeutic technique with which all ... mental and psychosomatic ills ('aberrations') can be treated with assurance of complete cure in unselected cases." This technique is called "auditing." Auditing is supposed to clear "engrams," memories of pain and fear, out of the "reactive mind," memories which one got when one was 'unconscious.'

The critical thinking reader may see here first the unjustified theory of dualism behind all of this. Second, it appears to involve great over - simplification, generalization and exaggeration. One cause and one therapy for all sorts of aberrations, and always totally effective? Clearing is sometimes carried out just by auditing, a form of "talking cure." Sometimes it involves a device called an E-meter. Like a simplified lie detector, the E-meter is supposed to measure reactions from the palms of the audited person's hands. A person who has been cleared is called "a clear." Hubbard claims the following about clears (1950): "All individuals who have organically complete nervous systems respond in this fashion to Dianetic clearing [that is, they pass tests to show they are unaberrated]." "Tests of a [Clear's] intelligence indicate it to be high above the current norm" (Hubbard, p. 12). This author takes these two sentences to imply that clearing will raise many people's level of intelligence.

Hubbard also claims that clearing improves all of people's senses, memory and general health: "When the stage of glasses is entered, [eyesight] is deteriorating on the psychosomatic principle ... One of the incidental things which happen to a clear is that his eyesight, if it had been bad as an aberee, generally improves markedly." In Book Three, Chapter Two he claims, "[A clear's] physical vitality and health are markedly improved ... He has greater resistance to actual disease. . [His] longevity is most certainly raised" (p. 187.) "A clear, for instance, has complete recall of everything which has ever happened to him or anything he has ever studied."

It is difficult for this author to see how anyone could believe such claims, or pay thousands of dollars to someone making them. Hubbard, after all, was mainly a science *fiction* writer. The reader, however, should get ready for worse. In a slick, expensively produced 8 1/2 x 11" Scientology booklet, "L. Ron Hubbard, the Rediscovery of the Human Soul" it is explained that "The individual man is divisible into three parts. The first of these is the spirit, called in Scientology the *Thetan.* The second ... is the mind [and] the third ... is the body" (p. 45). The Thetan (spirit) is described in Scientology as having no mass, no wavelength, no energy and no time or location in space. It is the creator of things. The usual residence of the Thetan is in the skull or near the body" (p. 46.) Wait a moment. How can it have no location and its usual "residence" be in the skull or near the body? This is self-contradictory.

It gets worse yet. The Thetan story so far told is only for people not yet "into" Scientology. The booklet above is one of at least 16 "Ron Series" of booklets put out by the "L. Ron Hubbard Personal Public Relations Office." This office also runs an "L. Ron Hubbard Life Exhibition." Has anyone heard of an Isaac Newton or Albert Einstein personal public relations office putting out an "Isaac" series or an "Al" series? Is this the sort of thing done by scientists or cult worshipers? Scientists are endlessly trying to find anomalies (abnormalities) to show earlier scientists' theories wrong in some area.

Korff (1988c) revealed teachings about the Thetan allegedly kept secret until a convert had already gone through some expensive elementary therapy. There are 6 or 7 grades to clearing, and above that 15 levels of "Operating Thetan." Scientology processing to this level requires twelve courses (L. Ron Hubbard, A Profile, p. 91) At Operating Thetan III the converts were allegedly charged $6,500 to learn the following "truths" and have "implants" removed. The story is that 75 million years ago a Titan named "Xenu" or "Xemu" ruled a galactic federation of 70 to 90 planets. There were 200 to 500 billion beings per planet. Zemu rounded up artists, revolutionaries, criminals and those "too smart" (Forbes 400, 10/27/86.) He had their lungs filled with alcohol or glycol, transported them by spaceships to earth (then called "Teegeeach") and deposited them near volcanoes. He then dropped nuclear bombs on the volcanoes. The beings were destroyed in a wall of fire.

After the explosions, the Thetan spirits, deprived of bodies, were packaged by Xemu and electronically implanted so they would reproduce in later generations of human beings. Each human today is a cluster of Thetans with one dominant. This is the cause of aberration, internal conflict, and unhappiness. Only through paying for the costly further Scientology training could humans break through the wall of fire, revisit the Xemu incident, have their less dominant Thetans removed and at last become unabberrated, mentally healthy.

Whew! How does anybody know what Earth was called 75 million years ago? Where is the geological, radioactive or archeological evidence of any of this? How does anyone know "Xemu's" name? Gerald Armstrong, a Scientology defector, claimed Scientology leaders know it because Hubbard made it up! The story, Kroff claimed, is identical to the plot of a screenplay for "Revolt in the Stars," a film script written by Hubbard, but which never got commercial financing and was not released (Korff, 1988c.)

This would not be the first time claims that something was fact derived from fiction. In an excellent book for children, Nickell (1989) relates three stories about boys or young men named Oliver who vanished from the earth. They all seem to have been "converted" to claims of fact from a fiction story by Ambrose Bierce. However, in this author's opinion the Xemu claims may be the biggest crock of unjustified claims ever sold to people for $6,000.

Scientology has received a lot of exposure since a *Time Magazine* 5/6/91 cover story. In 1997 *The Auditor,* (#262) a Scientology Monthly newspaper which advertises books and courses for sale, carried an advertisement for a course on "Suppressive Persons" and "Potential Trouble Sources." A "Suppressive Person" is defined as one who seeks to suppress any betterment activity or group. A "Potential Trouble Source" is a person or preclear who "roller coasters," i.e., gets better, then worse. He is in some way connected to and being adversely affected by a suppressive person. He is called a potential trouble source because he can be a lot of trouble to himself and others. A "Suppressive Person" sounds to this author like a critical thinker or a friend or relative, while a "Potential Trouble Source" sounds like a person who has paid a lot of money to Scientology, been dissatisfied and may sue or expose it.

Further critical information on Scientology can be found in the *Time* cover story and on the Internet at Alt.Religion.Scientology and at http://www.cybercom.net/~rnewman/scientology/home.html. Warning: according to *60 Minutes* (12/28/97) Scientology, after bankrupting the Cult Awareness Network, bought its name and logo at bankruptcy sale and now has Scientology members operating CAN.

SECTION 14.18: PARAPSYCHOLOGY AND EXTRASENSORY PERCEPTION

Parapsychology claims that "Some people's minds have extra- sensory perception, (ESP), specifically telepathy, precognition ('clairvoyance') or psychokinesis." Telepathy is the alleged ability to "read other people's minds," to know specifically what they are thinking. Precognition is the alleged ability to 'see' the future. Psychokinesis (PK) is the alleged power to move objects with the mind alone. According to Hines (p. 77) starting with the work of Rhine (1962) *there have been over 3,000 experiments in parapsychology. Yet the vast majority of scientists remain unconvinced that ESP even exists.* Phenomena have to be repeatable for science to acknowledge that they exist. When an experiment can't be repeated and get the same result, this tends to show that the result was due to some error in experimental procedure, rather than some real causal process. ESP experiments simply have not turned up any repeatable paranormal phenomena (Hines p. 80.)

Rhine's experiments were in having people try to "psych out" which of five symbols was on a card seen by another person or to predict the sequence of upcoming cards. By chance any person would get 1/5 right, about 20%. Most subjects did about chance. Some subjects did somewhat better and were tested further. But the original "Zener cards" with the five symbols were defective. The designs were stamped on. The stamping was done so hard that in some cases the design could be seen through the back of the card. In other cases, some cards were transparent enough to see the design through the back.

The methods used to prevent subjects from getting evidence were not adequate. In some cases a shield was used between a "sender" who saw the cards and the "receiver" who's ESP was being tested. But where this was a low partition, it was possible for some receivers to see the symbol reflected in the sender's glasses or even in their eyes. It was possible for them to get some clues from other sources. Senders wrote down clues and the sounds their pencils made could be heard by receivers. Receivers could get some evidence from tones of voice and gestures of senders. Record keeping was sloppy. Sometimes subjects tested got the order of cards before the sender. Other times subjects tested were allowed to help in checking their own results.

More sophisticated experiments have been done by Targ and Puthoff (1977) and later by Schmidt, all physicists (Hines, p. 99.) Remote viewing is the belief that "Some people's minds can receive information about remote locations of a sender by telepathy." Targ and Puthoff had receiver subjects stay in a lab while teams of an experimenter and sender went to different locations and attempted to send descriptions of their location. Receiver subjects wrote descriptions which were then turned over to independent judges who were to try to match subjects' descriptions to locations. If independent judges did better than chance in matching, results were regarded as significant. But Targ and Puthoff gave judges unedited transcripts which contained comments by experimenters which gave some clues to the subjects. When this error was corrected by other experimenters, their experiments did not show matching greater than chance.

Schmidt tried to test precognition by using a random number generator to turn on one of several lights. Subjects were to predict which light would come on. They would press the button and then the random number generator would determine which light would go on. It is essential that there be long test runs of the random number generator before the short runs with experimental subjects. But random number generators can give apparently non-random results over short experiments. It is possible for subjects to pick up this non-randomness and predict in accord with it. Such predictions will be interpreted as evidence of predictive ability when it is not.

It has been claimed that "Uri Geller could bend spoons with his mind." But a magician and skeptic named James Randi showed how this could be done by standard magicians' sleight of hand. Geller has refused to perform his feat in the presence of magicians who could ensure that it was not being done by means of magic tricks. It is worth noting that computer literate people and scientists may be no better than non-scientists in detecting magic, con artistry or fraud. Indeed, scientists may be less so, because they are used to honest inquiry into nature, which does not deceive. Targ and Puthoff were taken in by Geller. According to *Internet Underground* ("Sucker," 1996) up to 40,000 computer users were defrauded of more than $6 million in a pyramid scheme on the Internet. Pyramid schemes are old, widely known scams and easy to figure out. All one has to do is multiply to figure out that one is unlikely to get one's money back or make more money.

Gambling represents a sort of ultimate test of ESP, especially precognition and psychokinesis (PK). Billions of lottery tickets have been sold and millions of bets made on roulette and dice. Gamblers with bets down certainly want and try to influence lottery balls, dice and the roulette ball mentally. Some people are banned from casinos because they can actually count cards in blackjack. But the House always wins in the long run, not because its owners have ESP, but because of the physical setup and rules of their "games of chance." This author has heard on only one person who has ever won a large lottery prize twice. If ESP is real, where are the multiple winners of lotteries and roulette? Where are the people with PK banned from lotteries and casinos because of their PK? Why has the United States defense establishment concluded after twenty years study that ESP has no intelligence value? (Hyman, Mumford, 1996.)

ESP makes a good example of how a pseudoscientific hypothesis is made unfalsifiable. Advocates have taken results better than chance as evidence of ESP. But when critics demand presence at experiments and strict controls and results are no better than chance, advocates sometimes say that "ESP powers are 'shy powers' or 'jealous phenomena.' They go away in the presence of skeptics or else the skeptics are using their ESP consciously or even unconsciously to block the subjects." Finally, when results are below chance, they sometimes say that this is an example of the "psi-missing" phenomenon. The receiving subject has ESP, only it works to *avoid* what the sender is sending. It should be clear to the student that if the hypothesis that a certain subject has ESP is compatible with all possible states of affairs, doing better than chance, doing chance-level work or doing worse than chance, then no evidence could ever falsify it. But then one may well ask, what is the difference between having ESP, having only imaginary ESP, and not having ESP at all?

So-called "Psychic Detectives" claim to use ESP to help police solve crimes. Often, if one checks with the police, the police deny that the person making the claim was of any help at all. It is difficult to believe they deny this because they don't want to look bad. There is a great deal of pressure on police to solve cases of violent crimes. If psychic detectives really could do the job, police departments would hire them, wouldn't they? The way some of these "psychic detectives" work is called "retrofitting." First they learn as much as they can about the case, then call up the media or go to the police and give some vague, brief wording. Nickell (1996, p. 18-19) gives this example. The psychic may throw out single words or phrases like "water" and "the number 7." This is no concrete help to the police at all. However, "water" could mean a pond, the sea, a lake, a stream, a river, a water tower or any place name involving any of these words. "The number 7" could be a part of any street, avenue, boulevard, house number, license plate of any vehicle involved, part of a number of miles of any location of importance, a period of time, a number of people involved, and so on. After the crime has been solved, the alleged "psychic detective" can find some facts involving "water" and the number 7 which he can retrofit his clues to. He can count on people who already believe in this stuff to ignore the vagueness, unhelpfulness, and retrofitting of his "clues" and take the coincidence as "proof" of his psychic powers.

15

THE UNITED STATES AND THE GLOBAL CORPORATE ECONOMY

SECTION 15.1: WEALTH RULES!

Critical thinkers are people who can draw distinctions. A very important distinction is that between the American people, our government and our economic system. The American people have made great achievements in the nearly 210 years since the country was founded. However, the thesis of this chapter is: *The economic and governmental systems under which American's accomplishments have been made are terribly flawed.* Furthermore, *inequalities, injustices, social and environmental damage they have created are getting worse, not better. High stock prices, low inflation and increased employment can not make up for the basic inequality of wealth, the decline in Americans' real wages, job insecurity and other negative factors.* The following statistics are taken from Folbre (1996.) Large-scale government surveys, e.g., the Census, are only done every 5 to 10 years. The facts contained in these statistics are more indicative of real, persistent problems than current high stock prices and relatively high employment.

Wealth in the United States is very unevenly distributed. In 1991, the top 20% of households with incomes of more than $53,448, owned 45% of all household wealth. The bottom 20%, with incomes of less than $12,852, owned about 7% (Folbre, et. al. Sec. 1.1.) The rich continue to get richer at the expense of the poor and middle classes. The top 1% increased their share of net worth, or wealth, from 31% to 37% between 1983 and 1989. Their share now exceeds that owned by the bottom 90% of all families. Much of this wealth will be passed on, untouched, to the next generation. The top tax rate on income fell from 90% during the Kennedy years to 31% during the Reagan years (Sec. 1.2.) The richest 10% of families held: 80% of all nonresidential real estate; 91% of all business assets; 85% of all stocks; 94% of all bonds. More than half of the richest 400 people in this country largely inherited their wealth (Sec. 1.4.)

Who are the richest of the rich? The Sultan of Brunei, worth $37 billion, Bill Gates, $36 billion, the Walton family, $27.6 billion, Warren Buffett, $23.2 billion, Paul Allen, $14 billion and the heirs of the Swiss Roche drug company, $14 billion ("Gates Tops Forbes' List," 1997.)

As to income, in 1992, 74% of all people 15 or older worked for some pay; only 7% were self-employed. About 58% of adults earned some interest in 1992 owing to money in savings accounts. However, the average amount was only slightly over $1,000. Only 14% received income from dividends and only 7% got income from rents, royalties, estates, or trusts (Folbre, Sec. 1.3.)

The spring of each year sees corporate reports come out announcing annual meetings and containing interesting information on compensation of chief executive officers (CEO's.) Michael Eisner, the CEO of Walt Disney Company, was paid $750,000 in 1993, in salary, but also received $202 million in long-term compensation. In 1996, the "executive compensation" of W. W. Allen, CEO of Phillips 66, included stock appreciation rights which, if the stock appreciated 5% per year for 10 years, would be worth $5, 496,294. However, if he pushed the stock to a growth rate of 10%, they would be worth $13, 929,941 (Phillips Petroleum Company, 1997.) In 1993, CEO's of large transnational corporations were paid 149 times more than an average factory worker. Back in 1960, they were paid approximately 40 times as much. In Japan, in 1992, CEOs earned only 32 times as much as workers (Folbre, Sec. 1.6.) Folbre does not state what sort of average this is. One suspects it is a mean.

What are American CEO's paid so much for? One theory, to put it in plain language, is that they are paid so much to be bastards, to lay off thousands of American workers, force others to do their work, ship jobs overseas to get lower labor costs, rape the environment, and generally do anything to get higher profits and stock prices. If you were in W. W. Allen's place, and could do such things knowing you would not go to jail for them, would you not do them for the $8.4 million more he will get if he pushes Phillips 66 stock to 10% per year rather than 5%? Sloan (1996) lists layoffs made by some CEO's: Louis V. Gerstner Jr., of IBM, cut 60,000 jobs. Robert Stempel, GM, cut 74,000 jobs. Edward Brennan, Sears, cut 50,000 jobs. Robert E. Allen, AT&T, cut 40,000 jobs. Gerstner's pay for 1996, according to IBM (1997) included the following: salary, $1,500,000; plus bonus, $3,270,000; plus $300,000 in options, plus payouts of a long term incentive program of $2,072,567; plus $128,250 from other sources.

Despite such high pay and "perks," most of these executives are under "employment at will," that is, they can be fired in an instant (subject to their "golden parachutes" contracts being paid off.) Corporate Boards of Directors are very arbitrary. They have been known to sometimes handsomely reward executives after rotten years and fire them after good years. With firing at any age after about 40 the executive loses his bevy of secretaries, his following of "yes" men, his entire status and power. So he's really more a high-paid slave than a unionized worker in a strong union.

One reason for such arbitrariness is lack of communication or false, even fraudulent communication. Caplow (1976) has written, in plain, elegant English, an excellent work on organization theory. There are few general aspects of organizations one needs to understand to run them. One is communication, which must always be able to operate two or three ways freely (down, up and sideways.) A manager must have access to all parts of the organization and build consensus to deal with problems and change. However, the larger an organization and the more secure-feeling its' top managers, the more resistant it is to *critical thinking, to negative facts and bad news*. This has caused any number of large organizations to decline and fall, from the Roman Empire and the Catholic Church to NASA after the Challenger disaster. History records any number of whistle blowers who have been penalized for telling an organization the truth. So critical thinkers have to be careful how and when they disclose negative facts to have a reasonable impact.

A financial statement is a form of communication to stockholders. In the case of corporations, the sums of money involved are big temptations for managers to commit financial statement fraud. The cozy relationship between managements which give out large auditing contracts and the auditing firms themselves promotes the creation in some "legitimate" corporations of something like 'skimming' in the underworld. The Association of Certified Fraud Examiners (1994, p. 1.201) reports that in 1992 the 'Big Six' accounting firms alone faced 4,000 lawsuits for failure to detect false and misleading financial statements. Two thousand six hundred eight Certified Fraud Examiners reported to a survey by the association cases of fraud over the last 10 years totaling $15 billion (Wells, 1996.)

SECTION 15.2: JUKEBOX GOVERNMENT

Put a quarter in a juke box and it plays your tune. Put a quarter million dollars in the political party machinery and government writes laws and makes decisions that you want. Gup (1996) wrote an article imitating the "Forbes 400." It names 400 very wealthy Americans, tells which politicians they gave money to, what they wanted and got for their money. Here are two examples. Fred Lennon, who developed small family-owned pipe fitting business into a billion-dollar corporation, gave $524,450 since 1993 to Republicans. The money helped stack the Ohio Supreme Court with Republican justices willing to reduce corporate liability and damage awards in law suits. It made changes in tax laws to exclude the value of family-owned businesses from estate taxes. William S. Lerach gave $480,043 to the Democrats since 1993. Lerach is the head of a law firm which makes hundreds of millions of dollars out of class action law suits by shareholders against companies. Lerach dined at the White House December 15, 1996. Four days later President Clinton surprisingly vetoed widely supported tort reform legislation.

However, all the money given by wealthy individuals alone is small be comparison to what corporations themselves give. **In terms of money power, giant transnational corporations have become the dominant form of governmental institution in the world today.** Without being elected to any office, they get law written the way they want it by paying off politicians with campaign contributions. In other words, government by corruption is the standard operating procedure of our federal government. It takes so much money to get elected to national office the money can not possibly come from the people in small contributions. Also, no organizations other than corporations have enough money to really influence government, not even unions. In Congressional campaigns in 1991 - 92, business outspent other groups by a wide margin. It invested more than $295 million in its favorite candidates. Organized labor could only raise 15% of that (about $43 million.) Environmental organizations and other "special interests" only raised $18.6 million (Folbre, Sec. 1.7.)

Congressmen are effectively on the payrolls of political action committees (PACs.) Common Cause is an organization trying to get some limitation on special interest PAC money given to parties and candidates. It notes ("Special interests," 1996) that in the 1996 elections PACs gave a record $214 million to House and Senate candidates. 28 Senate candidates raised over $500,000 each from PACs, 7 already in the Senate (incumbents) raised over $1,000,000. More than 95% of incumbents were reelected. Over 90% of incumbents have typically been reelected for many years now. The power of money to keep them in office is too great for the people to overcome.

Here are some of Common Cause's examples of congressmen effectively on the payroll of PACS. Between 1/81 and 6/96 the following congressmen received the following amounts of PAC money. Rep. Richard Gebhart, (Democrat, MO.) $5,374,661; Senator Phil Gramm (Republican, TX.) $4,933,125; Rep. Vic. Fazio, (D-CA.) $4,615,601; Rep. John Dingel (D-MI) $4, 025,802; Sen. Al D'Amato, (R-NY) $3,977,268. The top 5 PAC givers over the same period were largely corporations and in these industries: Banking and finance, $77,622,183; Energy (Oil, Gas, Coal &Utilities) $74,282,291; Agribusiness and Food Processors, $69,571,591; Transportation Unions, $64,812,905; Real Estate & Construction, $59, 511,211 ("Special Interests," 1996.)

Many areas of American industry are effectively monopolized. When 3 or fewer large corporations make most of the sales in an industry, they can effectively control the industry. Industries in which large percentages of sales are made by 3 or fewer corporations include photographic film, 75%; aircraft, 80%; cereals, 90%; long distance telephone service, 65% (Folbre, Sec. 1.9.) The top 100 industrial corporation in the US have substantially increased in relative size. In 1993, they had assets amounting to 30% of total assets of nonfinancial corporations, compared with 22% in 1961 (Sec. 1.10.) Notice your banking fees going up? Aside from giving $77 million, the number of US bank holding companies shrank from 13,000 to 10,000 between 1981 and 1991. The largest 50 banks accounted for 52% of all domestic banking assets in 1989, compared with 41% in 1970. Competition is decreasing among banks. This is good for bank stockholders but not so good for borrowers and depositors (Sec. 1.11.)

How big are the transnational corporations? It is common to compare corporations' annual sales with countries' Gross National or Domestic Product (GNP or GDP.) The first union-sponsored study of this found that of the world's largest economic units, 51 were corporations and only 49 were countries. The first dozen or so were countries, but by the time one got down to 15th. place giant corporations producing more than whole countries started to appear on the list. The worldwide sales of Ford, Exxon and General Motors in 1992 were far greater than the value of all goods made and sold (GDP) in countries like Honduras, Zimbabwe, or the Philippines (Folbre, Sec. 1.12.) The GDP of the entire Philippines was $43.9 billion, while Ford had sales of $98.3 billion, and GMC had sales of $126 billion.

In 1991, the total assets of corporate, state, and local employee benefit funds amounted to over $3 trillion. About 40% of all corporate stocks and 50% of bonds were held by private and public pension funds. Currently, funds are strictly prohibited from using any but profit making criteria in investing. Most pension funds (70%) are run by employers who don't invest them to make jobs, justice or a clean environment (Sec. 1.14.)

SECTION 15.3: STATISTICS ON WORKING PEOPLE'S INCOMES

All we *had* was production. By 1950, more than 50% of workers were employed in service jobs. Since then, the percentage has increased to more than 75% (Folbre, Sec. 2.2.) Nearly 24 million jobs were created between 1979 and 1993. However, the production sector (manufacturing, mining, and construction) lost 3.2 million jobs over that period while the service sector gained almost 24 million. Wages in service are lower, so this shift depressed average wages. The average hourly total compensation in all service jobs in 1993 was $15.51, compared with $20.22 in goods production (Sec. 2.3.) Temporary jobs expanded by 211% between 1970 and 1990, compared with 54% for all employment (Sec. 2.4.) In fact, Manpower, Inc., a temporary agency, is now the single largest employer of Americans. This is pathetic performance for a government which committed itself legally to providing full employment as long ago as a Truman-era post World War Two piece of congressional legislation.

From 1950 to the early 1970's, real average hourly earnings went up. *Real wages have been going mostly down since 1973.* In 1994, the average hourly wage was lower than it had been in 1968 (Sec. 2.5.) Non supervisory workers' average wages in 1996 rose 3.7%, slightly greater than the 3.3% inflation rate. That was the biggest increase since 1990. Median income from wages in 1996 was $490 a week or $25,480 a year (Brenner, 1997, p.4.) Median U.S. household income from all sources rose to $34,076 - the first rise since 1989. The real value of the minimum wage in 1994 was lower than it was in 1950. At $4.75 an hour, it would have to rise to $8.01 to lift workers to the poverty level (Brenner, 1997.)

The distribution of income worsened considerably in the 1980s. The top 5% of income receivers increased their share of income from about 17% to 19% of all income while the bottom 40% declined from 14% to 13%. In other words, the top 5% got a larger amount all household income than the bottom 40%. The middle class is shrinking while the rich are getting richer and the poor poorer. Over the 1980s, the percentage of Americans earning more than 2 times median family income increased, as did the percentage earning half the median or less (Sec. 6.2.)

Workers are doing less well in health care coverage. In 1980, employers paid all health insurance premiums for 71% of all full-time employees in medium and large firms. By 1993, only 37% of employees were fully covered (Sec. 2.8.) At the same time, inequality in earnings increased. In 1973, 24% of all workers could not earn enough to get above the poverty line. By 1993, 27% of all workers earned an hourly wage too low to adequately support a family of 4. Minorities in America suffered more. In 1993, 36% of African Americans and 43% of Latinos earned hourly wages that were below the poverty level for a family of 4 (Sec. 2.9.)

Entry-level wages in most jobs have declined also since 1973. Back then, high school graduates could expect to go to work for the equivalent of $8.56 an hour. By 1993, they could expect only $6.42, a decline of 25%. Opportunities for college graduates have been cut back by corporate downsizing. In 1993, the College Employment Research Institute reported that the job market for recent graduates was the poorest it had been since World War II, with at least 35% of graduates taking jobs not requiring a college education (Sec. 2.10.)

In 1994, the average unemployment rate for whites was about 5%. It was more than twice as high, at 12% for African-Americans and 10% for Latinos. In 1994, the official overall unemployment rate was 6%. However, this leaves out "discouraged workers." When these workers are added, the jobless rate amounts to about 9% (Sec. 2.11.) Unemployment rates in Japan are under 3% (Sec. 2.14.) In 1990 and 1991, about 1.4 million workers lost their jobs to the job killers as a result of plant closings or layoffs. A General Accounting Office analysis shows that about 47% of layoffs affecting 250 or more workers were cases where employers were not even required to give advance warning to workers (Sec. 2.13.) By 1997 media cheerleaders were hailing the lowest unemployment rate in 25 years (while failing to mention wage levels.)

SECTION 15.4: WOMEN IN THE WORK FORCE

Because of the decline in real wages, since 1979, more than half of women over age 16 have been working or looking for work in the paid labor force. By 1993, 60% of married women with children under 6 were in the labor force (Sec. 3.1.) This puts real stress on women. Employed women do about 38 hours of housework a week, on average, compared with 22 hours for employed men. Two or more children added to a household just about doubles a woman's hours of household work, (28 to 51 hours per week.) In 1987, employed husbands did only 32% as much household work as their employed wives (Sec. 3.2.) More women are climbing the professional - managerial job ladder. By 1993, women accounted for 9% of all engineers, 22% of all lawyers and judges, 43% of all managers, and 21% of all doctors (Sec. 3.3.) A reason for this may be that the greater the number of women relative to men in an occupation, the lower the average pay (Sec. 3.4.)

Women are gaining on men. But *in 1992, women still earned only about 71 cents for every dollar a man earned* (Sec. 3.5.) Studies of comparable worth show that women are still paid much less than men for comparable jobs (Sec 3.7.)

Why is there so much childhood poverty in the United States? A growing percentage of families are maintained by women alone. In 1993, more than 1 out of 4 children lived with only 1 parent. 88% of these lived with their mothers (Sec. 3.10.) In 1992, child support enforcement agencies only collected one-quarter of what deadbeat dads owed. In 1989, almost 10 million women were living with children under age 21 whose fathers were absent from the home. Only 50% of these women were awarded child support payments. Only 51% of those due payments received the full amount (Sec. 3.11.) To top it all off, good and inexpensive child care is hard to find.

SECTION 15.5: MINORITIES

About 43 million Americans have physical or mental disabilities, and 66% are unemployed ("Job creation," 1993.) Despite the Americans with Disabilities Act, challenged people, this largest minority of all, face serious risk of poverty. Blacks and Latinos make up about 12% and 10% of the population, Asians and Pacific Islanders, 3%, and Native Americans nearly 1% (Sec. 4.1.) Only 12% of Blacks' households and 15% of Latino's had incomes over $50,000 in 1992, compared with 27% of white households. *In 1991, Latino and Black families had a median net worth of only about one tenth that of white families* (Sec. 4.5.) More than 40% of Black and Latino children lived in poverty (Sec. 4.6.) Job discrimination accounts for much of this poverty. In 1994, 11.8% of black workers and 10.2% of Latinos could not find jobs, while only 5.4% of whites

were unemployed. Unemployment among black youths was 36%; for whites, 16% (Sec. 4.7.)

Even with a college degree, African-Americans and Latinos had far higher unemployment rates than whites in 1993 (Sec. 4.8.) Between 1979 and 1993, minorities' wages declined relative to whites of the same sex (Sec. 4.11.) One reason for this is a decline in unionization. *The number of union members has declined as a percentage of all employees, from over 30% in 1954 to about 16% in 1993.* Between 1980 and 1984 unions lost 2.7 million members, partly because recessions in those years led to job losses. Also, employers' resistance to unionization has grown (Sec. 2.15.) Between 1979 and 1989, the percentage of African -

Americans belonging to unions declined sharply because union jobs were eliminated. The result was a significant loss of earnings for black female college graduates, as well as black high school graduates (Sec. 4.12.)

Once in a while the Equal Employment Opportunities Commission or other agencies send "testers" to apply for entry-level jobs, mortgages or other things. The results of a recent study on jobs: Blacks were 3 times more like than whites to be

rejected. Latinos were significantly less likely to be offered a job interview or a job than whites (Sec. 4.13.) The Federal Reserve Bank of Boston performed a detailed statistical analysis of mortgage applications. It found that even if black and Latino borrowers had the same characteristics as whites (except for race), they were 56% more likely to be denied a mortgage (Sec. 4.18.)

SECTION 15.6: POVERTY

Who are the poor? People with no wealth and little income: largely old people, children, members of minority groups, women stuck with kids. Many of the elderly are poor, but as a group they are better off than children, whose overall poverty rate increased from 17% in 1975 to 22% in 1992 (Sec. 6.6.) Many poor people are either ineligible or unwilling to receive public assistance. In 1992, only 43% of poor people collected cash assistance and only slightly more than half benefited from food stamps or Medicaid (Sec. 6.8.) Aid to Families with Dependent Children, in 1970, averaged benefits of about $622 per family per month (measured in constant 1992 dollars), or about 71% of the poverty line for a family of 3. By 1992, they had fallen to $374, or about 40% of the poverty line (Sec. 6.9.) As of this writing even such payments are under bipartisan attack by Democratic President Clinton and Republicans in Congress. After all, they are not on the payroll of the poor but the rich.

In 1992, *Business Week* estimated that poverty-related crime in the US cost the country $50 billion and that productive employment for the poor could generate $60 billion. In that year, government payments to poor people of $45.8 billion could have brought the incomes of all families over the poverty line. $45.8 billion is less than 1% of the Gross Domestic Product, about 15% of military spending. Poverty among children could have been eliminated by transfers of about half that amount ($28 billion.) According to the Congressional Budget Office, the US could easily have raised that amount of money simply by taxing the richest 1% of Americans at the same rates they were taxed at back in 1977 before Ronald Reagan and the "Republican Revolution" (Sec. 6.10.)

Between 1979 and 1991, housing costs went up a lot, and family income did not go up as much. By 1991, the average homeowner with a mortgage spent 25% of family income making payments, compared with 21% in 1979 (Sec. 6.11.) People lost their homes or housing. Estimates range from 500,00 to several million Americans are now homeless. During the 1980s, the federal government reduced appropriations for low-income housing by 81% (Sec. 6.12.)

On the other hand, average expenditures per pupil in US schools have increased steadily since 1970 (Sec. 6.13.) Most public schools in the US are financed largely by local property taxes. This makes for great inequality in funding. In some states, well-off school districts spend 9 times as much per student as poorer districts. As of June 1993, lawsuits were challenging school funding systems in more than a third of the states, and courts in at least 13 states had found school funding systems to be unconstitutional (Sec. 6.14.) Don't count on Congress or state legislatures to change it though. Legislators are more interested in passing bills that are un- or anti constitutional, forcing religion-specific prayer on kids, funding religious schools, violating kids' privacy with searches or restricting free speech on the Internet or banning uses of the flag to express strong disagreement with the way they run America.

Private universities, on the other hand, now cost more than 50% of median family income, putting them beyond the reach of most families. Faculty salaries have increased hardly at all in recent years. The number of highly paid administrators, however, has grown quite rapidly (Sec. 6.15.) Public aid for higher education has changed dramatically in form and declined as a percentage of per capita income. When this author started teaching college in the 1960's, most aid was grants, gifts! Today's state university students struggling with big loans are amazed to hear this. In 1979, a student from the richest quarter of income receivers was 4 times more likely to earn a B.A. by age 24 than a student in the poorest quarter. By 1994, that individual was 19 times more likely. So much for equal opportunity (Sec. 6.16.)

SECTION 15.7: HEALTH CARE, OR CARE FOR PROFIT?

The United States spends a much larger share of GDP on health care than other advanced industrialized nations, even though 40 million of our citizens - 1 person in 6 - lacks health insurance (Sec. 7.1.) But in an economy where health care exists to make a profit rather than to serve human needs, costs are enormous and benefits very unevenly distributed. While consumer prices increased by more than 3 1/2 times between 1970 and 1993, medical costs grew by a factor of more than 6 (Sec. 7.3.) Competition keeps prices down, right? Not in this case. Hospitals attract doctors and their patients not by advertising the cheapest rates in town, but by offering the highest quality care (Sec. 7.4.)

Since 1970, prescription drug prices have risen much faster than the overall rate of inflation. This author recently had to pay about $4.00 per pill for an antibiotic prescribed by a doctor for a case of bronchitis. In Canada, a country with a single-payer health system, the government negotiates prices directly with drug making companies. As a result, many of the same drugs cost only half as much (Sec. 7.5.) Health insurance is also more expensive because of unnecessary duplication of insurance programs. Private insurance companies' overhead amounts to about 14 cents of every dollar actually spent. In the Canadian public single-payer system, overhead accounted for only about 1% of total program expenditures in 1987 (Sec. 7.7.)

There's an old folk song a line of which goes something like: "If life were a thing the rich could buy, you know the rich would live and the poor would die." This is exactly true of the United States. Twenty-three other countries have infant mortality rates lower than ours. Why? Other countries provide health services on the basis of need, but the US allocates services by patients' ability to pay (Sec. 7.8.) Over 50% of wealthy individuals in the top income group consider themselves in excellent health, but only 26% of those in the bottom group say the same (Sec. 7.9.) The richest fifth spend only about 15% of their income on health insurance premiums, out - of - pocket payments, and taxes devoted to health care. The poorest fifth have to spend 23% of their family income on health care (Sec. 7.10.)

There is a worse effect of this on minorities, of course. In 1991, the black infant mortality rate was 16.5 for every 1000 live births, compared with 7.5 for whites (Sec. 7.11.) More than a fifth of all African Americans and 38% of all Mexican - Americans lacked health insurance in 1992, compared with 18% of Puerto Ricans and 16% of whites (Sec. 7.12.) In 1992, about 36% of all people under 65 with incomes under $14,000 lacked health insurance (Sec. 7.13.) Still, when President Clinton tried to introduce a universal health care program during his first term in office, conservative congressional creeps blocked it. (To be fair, we must add that Clinton's proposed program itself was far from perfect, and would have excessively profited certain segments of the health care industry.) However, it was defeated largely by sexist hot air (as "President Hillary's program") not on the demerits of how it would provide basic health care for all Americans.

SECTION 15.8: THE GROTESQUE NATIONAL PRODUCT

Economists employed by corporations, media and government pretend they are measuring our collective well-being by adding the value of everything that is bought and sold and dividing it by the size of the population. This is the Gross National Product per capita. It is a grotesque figure which includes actual costs of bad things as well as goods and things produced overseas by American-based transnational corporations. It is a figure so large it dwarfs all others. It therefore minimizes all negative figures. A little more realistic figure is the Gross Domestic Product which excludes the value of goods and services produced overseas. However, both such figures include things like the cost of negative things like crime and pollution. They also don't include the value of things used up, damaged or destroyed that don't carry an explicit price tag, such as breathable air, swimmable rivers, and livable neighborhoods. An alternative index of "sustainable economic welfare" (SEW) gives a better picture of the quality of life. It includes the value of purchased items but adds estimates of the value of non market services (such as time devoted to housework and child care) and subtracts the costs of pollution, resource depletion, and long-term environmental damage (Sec. 8.1.)

SECTION 15.9: ENVIRONMENTAL DAMAGE

Large areas of land have been degraded through overgrazing, deforestation, agricultural mismanagement, and pollution. Land degraded as a percentage of total vegetated land 1945-91: in Asia, 20%; Africa, 22%; South America, 14%; Europe, 23%; North and Central America, 8%; Oceania, 13%; the World as a whole, 17% (Sec. 8.3.) Three hundred seven types of Mammals, 226 Birds; 80 Reptiles; 14 Amphibians; 65 Fish and 386 Plants are the number of endangered species, worldwide, as of 1992. Species extinction is to some extent natural. However, humans may be losing species which could be very valuable to ourselves by destroying their habitats (Sec. 8.4.)

Congress created a "Superfund" in 1980 to clean up major pollution problem sources. But in 1991 the Washington Post reported that nearly one third of the $200 million paid to 45 contractors since 1988 was spent on paperwork and coordination. As of 1991, the Superfund had cleaned up only 63 of the 1,200 sites listed by the Environmental Protection Agency as most threatening (Sec. 8.5.) Because of excess packaging, consumers generate more garbage than they used to, more than 4 pounds per person per day (Sec. 8.6.) A quarter of the country's rivers and streams are unsafe. The main problem for water is polluted runoff, particularly from farm chemicals (Sec. 8.7.) This author lives in a small town in a rural state. Yet there is a Superfund site within 4 miles of his home. One of the highest points in the county is called "Mt. Trashmore." It is a landfill. The local lake, a year around asset, is threatened by plant life growing excessively because of runoff from cow manure.

Citizens of the US consume, on average, an amount of energy equivalent to 22,758 pounds of coal a year, compared with 4,311 for the world as a whole. Fossil fuel combustion also increases emissions of carbon dioxide, which many scientists believe is causing a long-run trend toward global warming (Sec. 8.9.) The price of fossil fuels doesn't reflect the hidden costs that their use inflicts on the environment. Electricity from existing coal-fired plants (the source of acid rain problems) would cost 100% more if those hidden costs were added to the price. Higher prices would encourage people to economize, but industry opposition to such increases is intense. Energy price increases when environmental costs are added in: Gasoline, +40%; existing coal-fired electric plants, +100%; new coal fired electric plants, +80%; new oil-fired electric plants, +50%; oil for home heating, +30% (Sec. 8.10.)

In 1980, the Environmental Protection Agency's (EPA) total expenditures amounted to only 0.9% of the federal budget. Since then, they have declined to about 0.4%. Over the same time period, real spending fell from $9.5 billion to $6.3 billion (Sec. 8.13.) In 1990, 437 cities and counties failed to meet at least one of the EPA's ambient air quality standards. 57% of whites, 65% of African Americans, and 80% of Latinos lived in these areas. 3 out of every 5 African Americans and Latinos lived in communities with uncontrolled toxic waste sites. Here is our return gift to Native Americans: all nuclear bomb test sites on the US mainland are on Native American land (Sec. 8.15.) Every industrialized country except the US now favors an outright ban on hazardous waste exports (Sec. 8.16.)

SECTION 15.10: SOME STATISTICS ON GROWTH

Economists employed by corporations, government and media claim that economic growth is the solution to problems of the economy. If only we can get the GNP to grow faster than the population, per capita income will automatically increase and unemployment will cease to be a problem. This has so often been disproved by so much evidence it would be appropriate to call it, coming from a professional economist, a lie. In any case, over the last 20 years, even economic growth in the U.S. has slowed (Sec. 9.) *The American economy is subject to a business cycle of booms and busts.* The sooner the student learns this, and learns to make hay while the sun shines, the better off he or she is likely to be financially in life. The US has had panics or recessions in 1873, '84, '90, '94, 1912, '29-39, '54, '58, '70, '73, 80-82, and '91. The average annual rate of growth in GDP was over 3 1/2% in the 1950's and 60's (Sec. 9.3.) It has recently declined to 1.8% 1990-94 and taken an upturn since then.

Growth depends in part on increases in productivity among workers. Productivity itself has declined from over 2% per hour to under 2% per hour (Sec. 9.4.) Productivity growth in a mechanized society like ours does not depend on how hard workers work. It depends on investment in new tools and machinery and education of workers. Non-residential investment also shows a recent downward trend (Sec. 9.5.) Since the 1980's corporations have chosen to buy productive capacity or create it overseas rather than at home. Personal savings in the US are low as a percentage of GDP. But most savings (about 70%) comes from businesses, which have maintained a high rate. Personal savings have declined because wages have declined and people are struggling to maintain their former standard of living (Sec. 9.6.)

SECTION 15.11: TAXES, POLITICS AND REALITY

American politicians of both parties have gotten into the rotten habit of promising to cut taxes and government spending. What this really amounts to is a bribe to cut a few dollars off the taxes of each well-to-do voter at terrible expense to the poor, their children, minorities, veterans, the elderly, the handicapped, the homeless and others. Here's the reality about taxes, like it or not. *American workers pay lower income and payroll taxes, on average, than workers in other industrial countries (25% as compared with 33%,* Sec. 5.4). Most business also pay higher taxes in other industrial countries. Japan and Germany have steeper corporate tax rates. And their economies are growing faster than ours. Initiative is not damaged by taxation. Although European workers pay more income and sales taxes, they get a large variety of subsidized government services, including universal health care, and much better unemployment compensation than we do. Moreover, they don't have to be ashamed, as we ought to be, about the number of fellow citizens in poverty, homelessness, in ill health or who go to bed hungry at night.

From another perspective, the average American working person's taxes are too high. That perspective is in relation to taxation on the wealthy and corporations. Zepenzauer and Naimen (1996) outline how this works. They assemble data indicating that "wealthfare" amounts to $448 billion per year! *Wealthfare* is the money not collected from the wealthy and corporations in taxes which used to be collected, or ought to be collected, or which is transferred to them from working people's taxes, (Zepenzauer and Neiman, p. 6) We could wipe out the $117 billion deficit by cutting wealthfare just 26%. Wealthfare for the rich costs about 3.5 times as much as welfare for the poor, which is now being cut. Three years of wealthfare costs more than it costs to run the entire federal government for a year. The national debt is now about $5.1 trillion. Less than 12 years of wealthfare at the current rate equals all the deficit spending the U. S. government has engaged in over more than 200 years!

Examples of wealthfare dealt with by Zepenzauer and Neiman, together with the approximate amount paid or left in the hands of the wealthy, in per year amounts, are: military waste and fraud, $172 billion; Social Security tax inequities (lower incomes pay proportionally more) $53 billion; depreciation of purchased machinery before it is worn out, $37 billion; lower taxes on capital gains, $37 billion; the bailout of Savings and Loans, $32 billion; tax breaks for homeowners, $26 billion; farm subsidies, $18 billion; tax avoidance by transnational corporations, $12 billion; tax free municipal bonds, $9.1 billion; and handouts to the media (like free frequencies for new TV stations) $8 billion. Much of these handouts come in forms hidden from the public, such as exemptions from taxation. Nor do such handouts necessarily create jobs with most efficiency. $1 billion spent on capital-intensive military hardware produces 25,000 jobs, while the same amount spent on mass transit would create 30,000 jobs; on housing, 36,000 jobs; on education, 41,000 jobs and on health care 47,000 jobs (Zepenzauer and Naiman, p. 25.)

In 1994, the U.S. spent proportionately less on education, training, employment and social services, natural resources, the environment, and energy than in 1980! Income security, a category that includes housing, food and nutrition assistance, unemployment compensation, and contributions to Aid to Families with Dependent Children increased 0.6%. The only thing which went up was the share of spending on health, which nearly doubled to not great effect (Folbre, Sec. 5.7.)

"Infrastructure" is the word for public works needed for all citizens. Things like sewer, water and storm water systems are taken for granted, but they are very costly, wear out, and tremendously inconvenient to have break down. The New York City sewer system alone is estimated to require $40 billion in repairs (Choate and Walter, 1981.) Imagine the municipal constipation required to weather a major breakdown to it! Federal expenditures on infrastructure such as roads, airports, communications networks, civilian research and development, and education and training are investments that benefit everybody. Yet, from 1978 to 1994, expenditures in those areas declined from 14% to 9% of total federal spending (Folbre, Sec. 5.8.) Every year, about 25% of federal spending goes to the armed forces. In 1992, the US spent almost twice as much on its military as France, Germany, Japan, and the United Kingdom combined (Sec. 5.9.) The Soviet Union has disintegrated, but the military-industrial complex lives on, employing about 6% of the labor force. More than 40,000 private firms make and continue to want the government to buy their war goods (Sec. 5.10.)

Income taxes make up the same share today of all federal taxes as they did in 1960. However, *taxes on corporate income have declined sharply, from 23% to 10% of the total.* Sales taxes are also less important now. Social Security payroll taxes have increased enormously in importance. They now account for 36% of the taxes, relative to 16% in 1960 (Sec. 5.11.) Back in the 1950s, federal taxes averaged about 45% of corporate profits. Today, they average only about 24% (Sec. 5.12.)

Between 1977 and 1992, tax rates on the top 1% of income earners decreased greatly, and almost everyone in the top 20% paid less. But the average tax rate did not change for the bottom 80% of the population. As a group, the top 1% saved $83 billion in 1992, compared with what they would have had to pay had 1977 tax rates remained in effect (Sec. 5.13.) State and local governments rely heavily on regressive taxes (such as sales and property taxes) that take a bigger percentage out of low than out of high family incomes (Sec. 5.14.) We will see in greater detail later, how the rich actually benefit from tax subsidies from tax money collected from working people. One example, price supports, is mentioned by Folbre. Price supports were instituted by the government in the Depression to keep family farms from disappearing when farm labor had become so productive prices fell below costs. However, they have continued endlessly since the 1930's. Price supports amounted to about $29 billion in 1992. More money was paid to largely corporate farms that year than was spent on Aid to Families with Dependent Children (Sec. 5.15.)

SECTION 15.12: DEBT AND DETERIORATION

The wave of mergers and acquisitions of the 1980's was financed by borrowed money. In the 1950's interest payments averaged only about 9% of profits. By the 1980's they were up to 83% of profits. As a result, business failures rose sharply. Among those failures were over 1,500 failures of Savings and Loan associations (S&L's.) Deregulation has been a centerpiece of conservative economists for many decades. In this case, it led to unmitigated disaster. Hundreds of S&L's were simply defrauded by their owners and managers. Other hundreds made terrible investments and lost their depositors' money. However, since deposits were insured by the Federal Savings and Loan Insurance Corporation, taxpayers were stuck with paying the depositors back. The bailout is expected to cost $200 billion (Folbre, Sec. 9.12.) As of 1991 1,500 banks were also in trouble (Sec. 9.13.) Household debt as a percentage of after-tax income has also increased since 1960. It is up from 60% of after-tax income to around 95% (Sec. 9.14.)

Total US. debt in 1994 was about $47 trillion. But the national debt was actually bigger, as a percentage of GDP, following World War II (Sec. 5.1.) No economist then was crying "wolf!" at the national debt. On taking office in 1981 Ronald Reagan said: "This administration is committed to a balanced budget and we will fight to the last blow to achieve it by 1984." He proceeded to cut taxes and build up the military, thus becoming the "biggest spender" of any American president. His protege, George Bush, said: "Read my lips: No new taxes." He then presided over one of the largest tax increases in history. The lies never end (see Clinton on NAFTA below.) Ten years after Reagan's remark, the deficit had grown from 2.6% to 4.8% of the GDP (Sec. 5.2.)

The stock market has been on the rise since the collapse of the Soviet Union. Indeed, the U.S. has seen nearly seven years of steady expansion in stock prices and job growth (at jobs considerably less well paid in constant, uninflated dollars relative to earlier times.) As we have seen, this means little to reduction of poverty or increase in living standards. In fact, the U.S. no longer even has the world's largest GDP. It has been matched by Germany and beaten in that area by Japan (Sec. 10.1.) Japan has been spending about twice as much of its GDP on investment than the U.S. since 1962 and most Japanese investors hold stock for long term gain while the American system involves maniacal concentration on short term profits (Sec. 10.3.)

SECTION 15.13: KORTEN ON DEVELOPMENT

David Korten was born in 1937, in a small town, to a conservative, white, upper middle class family. He attended Stanford University and decided to devote his life to bringing knowledge of modern business management and entrepreneurship to those who had not yet benefited from it. He got an MBA in international business and Ph.D. from Stanford Business School. He served as a captain in the air force in Vietnam, 5 1/2 years on the faculty of Harvard Graduate School of Business, as a Harvard advisor to the Nicaragua-based Central American Management Institute. Then he joined the Ford Foundation staff in the Philippines for 14 years. After that he moved on to work as a senior advisor on development management for the US Agency for International Development. He is no radical or anti-capitalist.

Nevertheless, out of his own experience and research, Korten has written a very revealing book (Korten, 1995.) He states that he gradually awakened to the conclusion that the conventional development practice advocated by conservatives and liberals is the leading cause of *a rapidly accelerating human crisis of global proportions* (Korten, p. 3). "... Externally imposed 'development' [is] seriously disrupting human relationships and community life and causing significant hardship for the very people it claimed to benefit. By contrast, he says, when people found the freedom and self-confidence to develop themselves, they demonstrated enormous potential to create a better world (p. 4-5.) Real development can not be bought with foreign aid monies. Development depends upon people's abilities to gain control and use effectively the real resources of their localities - land, water, labor, technology and human ingenuity and motivation - to meet their own needs. Yet most development interventions transfer control of local resources to ever larger and more centralized institutions that are unaccountable to local people and unresponsive to their needs. The greater the amount of money that flows through these central institutions, the more dependent people become, the less control they have over their own lives and resources and the more rapidly the gap grows between those who hold central power and those who seek to make a living for themselves within local communities" (Korten, p. 5.)

SECTION 15.14: GROWTH AND THE ENVIRONMENT

Korten introduces his subject with words better than this author could find. "We are experiencing accelerating social and environmental disintegration in nearly every country in the world - as revealed by a rise in poverty, unemployment, inequality, violent crime, failing families and environmental degradation. These problems stem in part from a five fold increase in economic output since 1950 that has pushed human demands on the ecosystem beyond what the planet is capable of sustaining. The continued quest for economic growth ... is accelerating the breakdown of the ecosystem's regenerative capacities and the social fabric that sustains the human community; at the same time, it is intensifying the competition for resources between rich and poor - a competition that the poor invariably lose."

Wow ... and largely correct, so far as this author, from his travels abroad and learning from other sources, can tell. Korten mentions that the last half of the twentieth century has been perhaps the most remarkable period in human history in scientific advance, economic growth and trade expansion. Global economic output went up from $3.8 trillion in 1950 to $18.9 trillion (in 1987 dollars) in 1992. World trade exports increased from $308 billion to $3,554 billion (an 11.5 fold increase.) But no Golden Age of peace and plenty has arrived. The things most people want - a secure means of livelihood, a decent place to live, healthy and uncontaminated food and water, good education and health care for children, and an unpolluted environment seem further away then before. Fewer people even in the United States feel secure even in their means of livelihood, their jobs.

He argues that the current environmental demands of our economic system fill the whole available environmental space of our planet. We have reached the limit of the environment's "sink functions," ability to absorb our wastes (Korten, p. 28.) Each year deserts encroach on another 6 billion hectares of once productive land. Tropical rainforests are reduced by 11 million hectares. There is a net loss of 26 billion tons of soil from oxidation and erosion. 1.5 billion hectares of prime agricultural land are abandoned due to salinization from irrigation projects. Per capita grain production has been falling since 1984. Five percent of the Ozone Layer over North America was lost between 1980 and 1990. There has been a 25% increase in atmospheric carbon dioxide in the past 10 years. (Korten, p. 28.)

Plants can convert solar energy. Animals can not. Thus animals depend on plants for food. The amount of energy available for the support of animal species after taking out that which plants need for their own respiratory processes is called 'Net Primary Production" (NPP). A 1986 study concluded that humans were already using nearly 40% of the potential NPP of the earth's land surfaces. This leaves only 60% for all other species, for improving the lives of the 80% of humanity which has only 20% of the wealth and for meeting population growth needs. Given the projected population growth in the next 35 years, humans would require 80% of NPP and leave only 20% for all non plant life (p. 32-33.)

Growth in the Grotesque National Product is, Korten thinks, a dangerous illusion. Growth in labor productivity is neither socially useful nor environmentally sound. Britain's per capita income doubled between 1954 and 1989, but economist Richard Douthwaite found that conditions had worsened on almost every economic indicator - chronic disease, crime, divorce, unemployment. Britain, Korten quotes Douthwaite as saying, squandered its wealth on pallets, corrugated cardboard, non returnable bottles and ring pull drink cans, just like the USA.

Growth is only good under certain conditions (p. 40.) It must produce inherently valuable goods and services. They must be widely distributed throughout the society. The benefits must outweigh bad effects on any parts of society. The GNP makes no such distinctions. Much of what shows up as growth in the GNP results from shifting productive activities from the non money social economy to the money economy. It causes depletion of natural resources at rates far above recovery rates. It requires counting as income the cost of disposing of wastes, cleaning up toxic waste dumps, providing health care for pollution caused illnesses and rebuilding after floods resulting from deforestation, etc.

What poor people want, says Korten, is not growth but land for their own production or jobs at decent wages, health care and education. Growth requires depletion of natural resources. It means shifting control of agricultural lands from people to capital-owning classes and pushing incomes of the poor down. Millions of people have been forced off their land for the sake of growth that actually impoverishes them, rather than making them better off. People separated from their land for the sake of growth include: in Brazil 1960-80, 28.4 million; in India, 20 million over a 40 year period; in Thailand, 10 million; in Mexico, 1 million (pg. 49.)

SECTION 15.15: CORPORATE ECONOMIC MYTHOLOGY

It is Korten's thesis that **corporations have emerged as the dominant governance institutions on the planet.** The largest among them reach into almost every country in the world and exceed most governments in size and power. The corporate interest more than the human interest now defines the policy of nations and international bodies. In 1888 the U.S. Supreme Court ruled that a private corporation is a natural person under the U.S. Constitution and entitled to protection under the Bill of Rights, including freedom of speech. This has enabled corporations, with their vast money power, to effectively dominate public thought and discourse through advertising, ownership of the media, and political campaign contributions.

There is a phony theory called "Consumer Sovereignty." It is the idea that the market is a system in which the consumer is king. The consumer rules, because she votes with her dollars. However, one dollar is one vote and you get as many votes as dollars you have. No dollars, no votes. Thus millions of people are effectively shut out from this anti-democratic system. The philosophers of market liberalism equate the rights of money with the rights of people, market freedom and property rights with human freedom. But when rights are a function of property rather than personhood, only those with property have rights. *358 billionaires in the world have a combined net worth of $760 billion - equal to the net worth of all the poorest 2.5 billion of the world's people* (cited by Korten from Richard Barnet, The Nation, 12/18/94, 654 "Stateless Corporations.") The sources of market liberalist propaganda justifying a system with such consequences are primarily *Fortune Magazine, Business Week, Forbes, The Wall Street Journal, The Economist,* and *The New York Times.*

Corporate economists hold these mythic beliefs. 1. Sustained GNP growth is the path to progress. 2. Freer markets generally result in the most efficient and socially best use of resources. 3. Economic globalization by removing barriers to free flow of goods and money spurs competition, increases economic efficiency, creates jobs, and economic growth which is generally beneficial. 4. Privatization which moves functions and assets from governments to the private sector improves efficiency. The primary responsibility of government is to enforce the law of property rights and contracts. These myths are based on starker falsehoods about human nature: 5. Humans are motivated primarily by greed for individual gain. 6. The action which yields the greatest financial return to the individual or firm is best for the society as a whole. 7. Competitive behavior is more rational than cooperative behavior. 8. Human progress is best measured by increases in the value of what members of society consume. These myths are called "neoclassical," or "libertarian economics," or "market liberalism."

The truth is that certain basic conditions are needed for a market to set prices efficiently. These conditions, set forth by Adam Smith, are: 1. the market must be competitive (today's market is nearly monopolized.) 2. Full costs of production must be borne by producers and included in the price of the product. (Today costs of destroying the environment are externalized - environmental clean-up costs are left to the taxpayers.) 3. Capital must be locally or nationally rooted and its owners directly involved in its management (Korten, p. 75.) Today capital is transnational and managed by non owners. David Ricardo showed that free trade works when 1) capital can not cross from a high wage to a low wage country, 2) trade is balanced and 3) each country has full employment. (None of these are the case now.)

SECTION 15.16: THE CREATION OF A GLOBAL ECONOMY

It is interesting to note that people as far apart in basic theories of how the world works can still agree on many facts. This is the case with Korten and Pat Robertson (1991.) Robertson agrees that the foreign policy of the United States is made by tiny unelected elites, consisting of members of the Council on Foreign Relations, The Trilateral Commission, and members of groups like the Bilderberg. Both mention that two weeks before the outbreak of W.W. II a member of the Council on Foreign Relations met with George Messersmith, Assistant Secretary of State, to plan for a global economy after eventual victory. The Council on Foreign Relations is a group of corporate executives and foreign policy officers of the U.S. government who have dinner meetings and study groups and who publish the journal *Foreign Affairs*. The Bilderberg is a group of powerful North American and European leaders, heads of state, key industrialists and financiers, intellectuals, a few trade unionists, diplomats and members of the financial press. They met first at the Hotel de Bilderberg in Oosterbeek, Holland in May, 1954. Trilateralism is the alliance of 3 regional partners: Japan, The US/Canada, and Western Europe. The Trilateral Commission includes heads of the largest industrial corporations.

According to Korten, the hopes of these influential groups are that the world's money, technology and markets should be controlled by gigantic global corporations. A common consumer culture ought to unify all people in a shared quest for material gratification. There should be, above all, **free trade**, and perfect global competition among workers and localities to offer their services to investors. Corporations should be free to act solely on profitability without loyalty or regard to national or local consequences.

Modern transnational corporations have bought out democracy. Korten reveals the means. 1. They employed large law firms and created legal foundations, programs and seminars in law schools which reflected their interests. Supreme Court Justice Lewis Powell, for example, was employed by the US Chamber of Commerce. 2. They created "front" organizations which look like citizens organizations but are actually funded by corporations. At least 36 such fronts as the National Wetlands Coalition, Consumer Alert, and Keep America Beautiful are funded by Dow Chemical, Exxon, Chevron, Mobil, DuPont, Ford, Phillip Morris, AT & T, etc. 3. They developed their own Washington-based public relations offices. By 1980, 80% of the Fortune 500 had such offices. In 1974 unions accounted for half of all PAC money given to politicians. By 1980 they accounted for only one quarter. 4. They employed larger public relations firms to clean up their image after events like the Exxon Valdez oil spill and the Bhopal chemical disaster. 170,000 people are employed in public relations; this is 40,000 more than actual news reporters! A 1990 study showed that almost 40% of "news" content of typical US newspapers originates from public relations materials.

In the late 1980's the Japanese government and corporations spent an estimated $100 million on political lobbying in the US and $300 million building a nationwide grass roots political network to influence public opinion. They employed 92 Washington law, public relations and lobbying firms, far more than Canada's 55, and Britain's 42. Corporations also created business lobbies like the Business Roundtable. It has 200 members including heads of the largest industrial, banking, insurance, transportation and retailer corporations. At the Roundtable heads of competitive corporations like GM, Ford and Chrysler sit down together to figure out common approaches to making government more favorable to their interests. They are extremely non-diverse. Almost all are white males over 50 earning more than 170 times the per capita GNP. They enrolled 2,300 corporations in a pro-NAFTA lobby. Nine of the state captains of the USA* NAFTA were among U.S. corporations that had already exported 180,000 U.S. jobs to Mexico.

On December 1, 1994 a long step in the direction of their hopes for a global economy was taken. The U.S. Senate approved the General Agreement on Tariffs and Trade (GATT) by a vote of 76 to 24. *"Economic Globalization"* means the creation of a unified global economy through agreements such as GATT, the WTO (World Trade Organization) NAFTA, the EEC (European Economic Community) and APEC (Asia-Pacific Economic Community). However, the same reasons that caused Marxism to fail operate in market economies. These are concentration of economic power in centralized institutions so powerful they are unaccountable to any government, economic motives which destroy the environment, and power - weakening dependence on mega institutions. In short, Big is Ugly, Small is Beautiful. Under GATT, "We're losing our sovereignty" (Nader, 1996.)

NAFTA is a good example of what these "free trade" schemes mean to ordinary Americans. It was passed by a bipartisan coalition in both houses of Congress. It went into effect January 1, 1994. Thousands of American jobs went South of the border (*Vanishing Jobs*, 1996) to Maquiladoras. These are plants where Mexicans work for 1/10th. of what Americans earn (about $1.64 per hour versus $16.17 total.) American made goods flooded the Mexican consumer market, destroying local industry. By August, the newly elected President of Mexico had to lower the value of the Mexican peso. By January of 1995, Clinton had to ask Congress for $40 billion of Americans' tax money in loan guarantees to prevent Mexico from defaulting on bond payments. By February, he was so desperate he unilaterally got Mexico $60 billion. This was probably a violation of the separation of powers which gives only Congress money appropriating power, but both parties praised it. In 1997, after helping corporations export billions of dollars to southeast Asia, he had to put together multi-billion dollar bailouts for Japan and South Korea.

SECTION 15.17: SIZE OF UNITS AND MARKET OPERATION

Korten points out that a market depends for efficient operation on conditions it can not produce for itself: 1. Fair competition, (competition produces winners and losers and oligopoly.) 2. Moral capital - day to day transactions presume trust, but the market can't produce trust itself. 3. Public goods like investment in basic scientific research, public security, and justice, education, and roads. 4. Full cost pricing - sellers and buyers must not externalize costs but bear full costs. 5. Just distribution of income (with economic power more unequally distributed, resources will be allocated in a socially inefficient way to the few with wealth rather than the many with human needs.) 6. Ecological sustainability (the free market is blind to this.)

The size and power of transnational corporations enable them to corrupt governments to do their will and allow continued and increased maldistribution of goods, services and wealth. Twenty percent of the world's population which lives in the wealthiest countries receives 82.7% of all the income. The poorest 20% receive only 1.4% of total world income. In 1950 the income average of the wealthiest was 30 times that of the poorest. By 1989 it had increased to 60 times (Korten, p. 107.) In 1989 the top 1% of American families had more income than the bottom 40% all put together (p. 108.) In 1992 the CEO of Hospital Corporation of America received $127 million, nearly 780,000 times the average per capita income of $163 of the poorest 20% of the world's people. In 1960 the average CEO received 40 times compensation of the average worker. By 1992 Korten's estimate is it was 157 times as much. *Forbes 400 richest Americans got a $92 billion increase in wealth 1982-93 to a total of $328 billion. This was more than the combined 1991 GNP shared by a billion people living in India, Bangladesh, Sri Lanka, and Nepal (p. 108.)*

The rich and powerful atop these corporations live in a different world from you and I and the poor. When Nelson Rockefeller was campaigning for the presidency in the 1970's he and his associates once found themselves at 2 am, hungry and with no restaurant open. So he had his associates break into a delicatessen. They left money to cover food costs and repairs, but did not think it wrong to break and enter. Korten points out that newsmen chuckled when George Bush stared in amazement at a grocery price scanner. He had not shopped for groceries in so long, he had never seen a grocery scanner! Powerful swells like these live in guarded mansions, travel by private limousine or car, have private airplanes, servants, and bodyguards to keep the people away. How can they be expected to know what life is like for average and poor people displaced from their land?

SECTION 15.18: NO CONSPIRACY, BUT...

There is no good evidence that there is a conspiracy afoot to replace the United States government and others with one official, anti-Christian socialist World Government under the United Nations (*Militia Information Packet II*, 1995, passim.) Why would the wealthiest and most powerful people in the world, who can get the most powerful governments to do almost exactly what they want almost all of the time, want to turn their wealth over to a world socialist state? Why would oil company executives or big stockholders want a world government? They can get the U. S. government to send American youth to fight for their oil "rights" in Iraq. One world government might gain significant power in relation to their own corporations. They can now deal from corporate strength and manipulate a chaotic world situation including the most powerful national governments and a large number of very poor, weak, easily bribed ones as well.

The United Nations is a particularly unlikely suspect as a world take-over player. It has no power base, no territory, no population from which it can draft men to fight, and no economy it can command to produce weapons. It is funded by its member countries. It is near broke, because the U.S. has for many years not paid its dues. The U.S. now owes it $870 million. Of course militiamen spot small numbers of foreign troops and police on American soil! For decades the U.S. CIA and military have trained them to fight *their own people* for pro-corporate governments.

Corporations can now produce goods at very low costs in terrible labor conditions in Third World Countries, conditions which they could not produce in under uniform world laws. Why would they want to eliminate Christianity? It has been helpful in getting oppressed workers and poor people to turn the other cheek, to give their cloaks also and to render unto Caesar. To claim that some supernatural power (Satan?) is behind all this is to make large, unnecessary metaphysical assumptions. It is to make assumptions useful for a Christian religious leader to raise funds with. *There is a much simpler, natural explanation for what is going on. The rich are simply doing what they have been doing all along, trying to get richer.* If you, yourself were at the top of this economic heap, would you not do what is necessary to keep the money and power and get more?

Robertson *is* right in arguing that *there now is a New World Order.* "De facto" means "in reality," "as a matter of fact." "De jure," means "legally" or "officially." The global economic system changes and takes on new forms. It has many centers of influence and power. These include large corporations, elite private bodies like the C.F.R., trade policy advisory groups and international banks and pension fund money managers. None is an all-powerful, string-pulling governor of the whole system. All consist of humans who must react to changing conditions or eventually lose their wealth and positions. A couple of these system parts are worth looking at. For now, note that *recently a de facto world economic government has emerged.* It consists of the World Bank, the International Monetary Fund, and GATT, the General Agreement on Tariffs and Trades. ATT, the General Agreement on Tariffs and Trades.

SECTION 15.19: ONE PIECE OF THE SYSTEM - THE MONEY MANAGERS

Korten gives an illuminating account of the international financial system. About 500,000 to 1 million people worldwide are involved in money changing and management. An unrestrained market system develops in addition to production, speculative extraction and concentration of wealth. Extractive investment gets control of sustainable productive resources like land, timberland; even a whole corporation, breaks it up, and sells it off. It can actually *decrease* overall wealth. Coins, paper money, checks, credit and debit cards are useful, but they delink money from things of real value. Note four trends: 1. The U.S. financed its global expansion with dollars which are now held in foreign banks (Eurodollars). 2. Computerization and globalization created a single global market in money. 3. Investment decision making came to be concentrated in many fewer hands. The pool of investment in mutual funds doubled 1991-1994 from $1 trillion to $2 trillion. More than 500 banks merged between September 1992 and September 1993.

Pension funds now have about $4 trillion in assets. They are managed by trust departments of large banks. The fourth trend is that *investment horizons have shortened enormously.* The managers of investment pools are not co-conspirators, but compete with each other based on the returns they can make. Mutual fund results are published daily in the newspapers. Holders can switch funds with a phone call. For the mutual fund manager, then, the short term is a day or less. The long term is perhaps a month! *The time frames involved are far too short for productive investment opportunities.* Also, the returns the market has come to expect exceed what productive investments are able to yield (Korten, pg. 188.) Joel Kurtzman's (former business editor of the N.Y. Times) estimates that for every $1 circulating in the productive world economy, there is $20 to $50 circulating in the economy of pure finance. International currency exchanges alone involve $1 trillion per day.

Money changing and management, Korten points out, create money without creating value. They do so by creating debt or bidding up asset values. Banking gives a simple example of creating a debt. Suppose a farmer, A, sells wheat for $1000 and deposits the money in Bank M. Now M has a $1000 cash asset. M must keep say, a 10% reserve. So it keeps $100 and loans $900 to person B. B puts the money in bank N. She now has a $900 asset and Bank N can loan $810 to person C and so on. The original $1,000 earned by producing a real product and by real consumption allows the banking system to generate $9,000 more in new deposits and new debt. At 6% interest on all of these loans the banks expect to get a return of $540 on money the system created representing no new economic value.

A second form of extractive wealth concentration is arbitrage. This is buying an asset in one market and reselling it for a slightly higher price in another almost immediately. A third way paper money is made is by speculative bidding up of asset values. Demand for stocks and bonds is increased by ever more money available to buy them, so their prices go up. Korten quotes an authority as saying: "If the assets were gold or oil this phenomenon would be called inflation. In stocks it is called wealth creation." Such wealth is very shaky. On October 19, 1987, the New York Stock Exchange fell 22.6% in one day. Investors lost over $1 trillion. There is only about $20 trillion of total productive property around. By 1992 there was $12 trillion in one unstable kind of investment vehicle (called "a derivative") alone. Korten says: "The global financial system has become a parasitic predator that lives off the flesh of its host - the productive economy."

SECTION 15.20: THE NEW WORLD ORDER GLOBAL ECONOMIC GOVERNMENT

Korten says that the framework of the post-W. W. II economy called for by the U.S. and Great Britain required 3 organizations - the World Bank (WB) the International Monetary Fund (IMF) and a trade organization. The U.S. Congress refused to cooperate with creation of the trade organization, because Congressmen were concerned that it would cut into national sovereignty (the right of our nation to pursue its own interests.) Finally, on 1/1/95 the World Trade Organization (WTO) was created during a round of the GATT in Uruguay. Article 16 Paragraph 4 of the GATT agreement creating the WTO says, (Korten, p. 174) "Each member shall ensure the conformity of its laws, regulations, and administrative procedures with its obligations as provided in the annexed agreements." The annexed agreements are all the agreements relating to trade in goods and services. Any member country can challenge any law of any other member that it thinks deprives it of benefits it expects to get from the new trade rules. *This implies that any law that requires imported goods to meet national health, safety, labor or environmental standards that are higher that the exporting country's can be challenged. Any American laws requiring recycled or recyclable materials, banning use of cancer causing food additives, auto safety requirements, bans on toxic substances, labeling and meat inspection could all be challenged.* Conservation measures may be ruled unfair trade practices as could local processing regulations.

The WTO is also a Kangaroo Court. As a court, WTO handles disputes in secret hearings. No provision is made to allow alternative perspectives unless a party wants to allow it. Documents and identities of panelist Judges - trade experts are secret. The burden of proof is on the defending country to prove that its law is not restrictive of free trade. Recommendations of the panel are automatically adopted by the WTO countries unless there is a unanimous vote to reject them (including the original complaining country.) What are the chances of that?

The WTO is also an unelected legislative body, according to Korten. It can change trade rules by a 2/3 vote of WTO member representatives and new rules are binding on all members. A Public Citizen Congress Watch study released in 1991 found that of 111 members of 3 main trade advisory committees, only 2 represented labor unions. An approved vacancy for 1 environmental organization was unfilled. 92 members represented individual companies and 16 represented trade industry associations. These panels rarely announce their meetings and the public is never allowed to attend. 27 of 92 companies represented had been fined by the U.S. EPA between 1980-90 for failure to comply with environmental regulations. News stories published about April 1, 1997 told that one half of President Clinton's 99 appointees to trade advisory committees had been big contributors to his campaign.

SECTION 15.21: ADJUSTING THE POOR TO THE NEW WORLD ORDER

To force millions of people off their land so it could be used for cash export crops, to make them into impoverished, money-dependent wage slaves, has not been easy. It has required first, the usual steps of *colonialism.* Set up a puppet government. Get it to declare all land uncultivated at the moment and forests scarcely populated to be state property. Force money taxes on people who are self-sufficiently farming outside the money economy, so some of them have to go to work for money. When they resist, send in home-country trained counter-insurgency forces. Make war on them, torture them, call in the death squads. When they organize to compete politically, send in political agents and money.

Keeping countries of the world open to "free trade" has required the United States to engage in many military and political interventions in foreign countries. It also requires support of cruel military tyrannies with sometimes civilian figureheads. These governments have made war on their own people, employing torturers and death squads to assassinate students, professors, trade union leaders, leaders of peasant farm cooperatives, priests and nuns, lawyers and other professionals who stick up for the people and criticize the government. Richard Falk (1979, p. 407) wrote that: "the human rights records of both socialism and capitalism are so poor in the Third World that it is quite unconvincing to insist that one approach is generically preferable to the other." Since World War Two the United States has fought 3 major wars in Korea, Vietnam and Iraq. It has sent troops to Lebanon (1958, 1983), the Dominican Republic (1965), Grenada (1983), Libya (1986), the Persian Gulf (1987), Panama (1989), Somalia (1993), and Bosnia (1995.) It conducted war though financing a local army in El Salvador in the 1980's. It mounted at least 14 "covert" actions to overthrow governments unfavorable to corporate exploitation in Iran, Guatemala, Chile, Brazil, Greece, Afghanistan, Angola, Indonesia, Cuba, Libya, Nicaragua, Cambodia, Laos and Iraq (Doyle, 1994, p. 193.)

The struggle of people in these countries to get control of their own land, for human rights and democracy has produced real heroes. Among them are Rigoberta Menchú, Hanan Ashrawi, Vera Chirwa, Megawati Sukarnoputri and Aung San Suu Kyi. Rigoberta Menchú is typical of the harrowing lives these heroes have had to live. In 1954 C. I. A. "Operation Success" overthrew the democratically elected President of Guatemala, Jacobo Guzman. Guzman was a reformer. He had never sought Soviet support. He did take away some of the land holdings of the United Fruit Company. His overthrow was followed by nearly 40 years of U.S.-supported military dictatorship and civil war. About 140,000 people were killed.

Vera Chirwa
MALAWI

Hanan Ashrawi
PALESTINE

Megawati
Sukarnoputri
INDONESIA

Rigoberta Menchu
GUATAMALA

Aung San
Suu Kyi
MYANMAR

Menchú, an Indian, worked in slave conditions in fields and then as a maid in Guatemala City. Her family became involved in the human rights struggle. In 1980 her father, mother and brother were all killed. She escaped to Mexico. She continued the liberation struggle, published a book on the oppression of her people (Menchú, 1983) received the Nobel Peace Prize in 1992 and opposed the imposing of another tyranny on Guatemala in 1993. The extraordinary lives of these heroes were recently retold in "Women Who Fight for Human Rights" by William F. Shultz, Director of Amnesty International. Anyone wishing to know what human rights conditions are really like in countries around the world should become a member of Amnesty International, 322 Eighth Avenue, New York, N. Y. 10001 and read its annual reports on prisoners of conscience.

Korten relates how the World Bank and International Monetary Fund deepen the dependence of low income countries on the global economy and open them to corporate colonization. There are 3 sorts of development policies. 1. The Import Substitution Strategy is to take loans to build domestic industry to produce substitutes for what used to be imported. 2. Export-led Strategies build industries to export products to foreign countries. 3. People-centered Development uses national capital and local people to develop their own human, institutional and technical capacities to make goods and services needed to achieve sustainable improvements in people's quality of life, using resources they already have.

In the 1970's oil price increases put low income countries in a critical foreign exchange situation. Long term external debt of such countries went from $21 billion 1970 to $110 billion in 1980. That of middle income countries went from $40 billion to $317 billion. A great debt crisis loomed as low income countries were unable to pay back their loans. The WB and IMF forced policies of "structural adjustment" on poor and middle income countries. They required restrictions on tariffs on imports and exports, incentives to attract foreign investors. (This often displaced people from their homes and land and polluted their environment.) They required cuts in government spending on social services for the poor, so more money would be available for debt repayment. From 1980 - 1992 total low-income country international indebtedness still went from $134 billion to $473 billion. "The World Bank must be regarded as a governance institution, exercising power through its financial leverage to legislate entire legal regimes and even alter the constitutional structure of borrowing nations" (quoted in Korten, p. 165.) The WB and IMF rewrite countries trade policies, labor laws, fiscal policies, health care laws, energy and environmental regulations.

The results of these policies are resistance, war, turning people into refugees, and child labor under terrible conditions. Hundreds of millions of Southern hemisphere workers are discarded when their work is replaced by machines. There is a competitive race to the bottom. *Wages and working conditions tend to fall to the level of the most desperate workers and countries that corporations can find.* In India, an estimated 55 million children work in servitude under terrible conditions (p. 231.) The automation and computerization revolution are discarding human brains now as well as muscle. In the North hemisphere, the US Dept. of Labor reports that 20% of US college graduates 1984-90 took jobs in which they were underutilized. It is estimated that 30% of graduates from 1994 - 2005 will join the ranks of the unemployed or underemployed (*Time* 11/22/93, "Bellboys with B. A.'s.") All told, Korten estimates 2-3 billion people live less secure and less prosperous lives than did their ancestors.

SECTION 15.22: ALTERNATIVES AND WHAT CAN BE DONE

Are there alternatives to the current problems of the United States and the world as a whole? Of course, but they depend on one's analysis of the problems. Some think our problems are caused by sinful human nature itself. That would make them hopeless. This author thinks human life can be enhanced (*Humanist Manifesto 1*, 13th. point, 1933.) Leftists find a root cause in capitalism, feminists in sexist oppression. Native "primitivists" find it in the industrial system itself (F.C., 1993.) It is beyond the scope of this book to give any but the most superficial suggestions. **Mixed economies** consisting of some large, some medium sized and some small private profit-making businesses, together with some consumer co-operatives, producer co-operatives and some government owned enterprises, according to the kind of productive function involved, might be a better sort of national system than we have now. Alternatives have been sketched by various authors from Shumacher (1960) down though Korten, who has detailed principles for healthy, environmentally sustainable societies (p. 259 ff.)

There are many things each of us as critical thinkers can do. We can read more, particularly non main-stream media on both the left and right. Some of it will be screwball stuff, but when you find large areas of factual agreement between authors of as different perspectives as Pat Robertson and David Korten, you know you are likely on to something. We can travel and talk to people in other walks of life or maybe other countries to learn more of their perspectives on things.

We should try to help others think more critically rather than despise them for not doing so. *Arrogance about what one knows, impatience with other's ignorance, or false belief are killer obstacles to helping other people to be critical thinkers.* Patient attempts to bring enlightenment slowly give the only chance of success.

There are scores of little things we can do to live more environmentally sound life styles ourselves. Many of them involve voluntary simplification of our lives and consuming less, becoming what are called "sustainers" rather than "overconsumers" (Korten, p. 281.) Many specific suggestions are contained in a number of articles and books such as Hawken (1997) or the Earthworks Group (1989.)

We can join all sorts of non governmental voluntary organizations (NGO's) working for change, such as farm to market cooperatives. (Just be careful not to be taken in and join a corporate front or pseudoscientific or religious cult.) *We can look at product labels carefully and buy union-made and "Made in the USA" label products.* Unionized workers are generally less oppressed and paid better wages than non union workers (unless the "union" is a fraudulent company or government organization.) "Made in the USA" should mean "all or virtually all parts made and assembled in the USA." Beware of products only "assembled" in the USA. Information on what products are Union and American made can be gotten from Grant and Burrell (1992) or from the Buy American Foundation, P.O. Box 82, Abington, Pa. whose web site is http://www.libertynet.org/~buyam. The American Federation of Labor - Congress of Industrial Organizations (AFL-CIO) also maintains a Union Label and Service Trades Department at 815 16th. St. N.W. , Washington, D.C., 20006. It conducts research and provides information on union label and American made goods.

Another thing we can do is to become politically active. If the major parties are hopelessly corrupt, there are new political parties like the Green Party USA, 100 Blodgett Mills, New York., 13738 or the New Party, 227 West 40th. St. Suite 1303, New York, N.Y. 10018. There is fertile ground for recruiting among people who are being shoved downward by big corporations and government. So far, members of the Patriot movement have been much more successful in recruiting these people toward their dangerously intolerant views than critical thinkers have been in getting people to understand the system which is limiting their life prospects. Critical thinkers *must* reach out to these people. Their current Patriot leaders would surely silence critical thinkers as well as suppressing other minorities.

If the extensive critical discussion which went before makes the situation seem hopeless, it was not intended to do so. Humanity makes progress very slowly. By critical intelligence over perhaps 7,000 years we have developed science and mastered most of the secrets of the universe. Critical intelligence has made it possible for humans to live long, healthy lives, to develop their talents and abilities, and to contribute to the welfare of others.

There are still tremendous problems. One is the thousands of undisarmed nuclear weapons, desperate people, fanatics and nations which may get and use them. Another is corporate domination, the worsening economic condition of many Americans and the growth of the intolerant Patriot Movement in response to it. However, critical thinkers are not doomed to unhappy irrelevance. Disraeli said, "Justice is truth in action." In his acceptance speech for the Green Party Presidential nomination Ralph Nader (1996) quoted Daniel Webster: "Justice is the great work of human beings on earth." Nader added, "It's truly remarkable what the fulfillment of civic potential does to human beings. They're happier.... So the very pursuit of justice becomes the pursuit of happiness." Now we need to apply our precious critical intelligence to root out unproductive mythologies, to become public citizens, to create the truth-based, just and sustainable societies which will enable us and future generations of the whole world to live happy, full lives in peace and justice.

The student should now do Exercise 23 on Checking Facts and Interpretations. Next, read Appendix II and do Exercise 24 on Evaluating Unsupported Claims.

SUMMARY OF LOGICAL EVALUATION CONCEPTS

Adjectives of logical evaluation: Statements (claims, propositions, reasons, conclusions, assertions) are true or false. The Correspondence Theory of Truth: *What makes a statement true is that it corresponds to the facts in an external world.* False statements do not correspond to the facts. Statements are never valid or invalid, sound or unsound. Reasonings (arguments, explanations, proofs, deductions, inductions) are *valid or invalid, sound or unsound,* never true or false.

"Valid" reasoning in general is reasoning in which if all its' reasons were true, then its' conclusion either would have to be true or would very probably be true. "It's" refers to the reasoning. *"Deductively valid" reasoning is reasoning in which if all its' reasons were true, then its' conclusion would have to be true. "Inductively valid" reasoning is reasoning in which if all its' reasons were true, then its' conclusion would very probably be true.* There are three essential elements in these definitions: 1) the "If... then..." form which implies that validity is independent of truth. Truth of statements does NOT make an argument valid. One can have valid arguments with all false statements. 2) "Were" means *supposing* that the reasons are true, then the conclusion would have to be or is very probably true. 3) It is reasons and conclusions only which are claimed to be true or very probably true, not reasoning.

A "Magic Question" can be used to determine whether any argument is deductively valid or not. It is "Can all these reasons be true and this conclusion false at the same time?" If the answer is "yes," then the argument is deductively invalid. The reasons can still offer a *Degree of Support below deductive validity: strong, moderate, weak or nil.* If it is "no," then the argument is deductively valid. This question works because, in a deductively valid argument, if all the reasons were true, then the conclusion would have to be true. So, if the reasons can all be true and the conclusion false at the same time, then the argument is not deductively valid. The validity or invalidity of a deductive argument depends on its *form. If an argument form is deductively valid, every argument of that form is valid, if it is invalid, every argument of that form is invalid.* If the answer is "Yes," then you have to consider how probable are the circumstances under which all the reasons could be true and the conclusion false. The less probable they are, the stronger is the argument. *A logically sound argument is one in which 1) all the reasons are true and 2) the reasoning is valid in general.* This implies a) all reasons of sound reasoning are true, b) all sound reasoning is valid. Because validity so defined allows a possibility reasons could be true and conclusion false, it is possible but improbable that sound reasoning has a false conclusion.

DIAGNOSTIC TEST ON TRUTH, VALIDITY AND SOUNDNESS

Answer in complete, correct sentences.

1. Explain what makes true statements true and false ones false.

2. Define "valid reasoning" in general.

3. Define "deductively valid reasoning."

4. Define "inductively valid reasoning."

5. Explain the difference between a deductively valid argument and an inductively valid argument in terms of the information presented (claimed to be true) in the reasons and the information claimed to be true in the conclusion.

6. Define a sound argument.

7. State the Magic Question of argument evaluation and explain why it works.

8. After answering the Magic Question, if the answer is "Yes," what do you have to consider to determine the *degree of support* (strong, moderate, weak or nil) the reasons give to the conclusion? Explain!

9. Names of persons, places, things and actions can be expressed by single words. Write 3 nouns which stand for things which can only be expressed in whole statements (Example: claims.)

10. Write 3 nouns for things which can be expressed only by whole reasoning discourses (Example: arguments.)

11. The most common words used to evaluate *statements* are these. A statement is either:

    _____ or _____.

12. The different logical terms used to evaluate *reasoning* are these. A piece of reasoning is either:

    logically _____ or _____.
    Considering also the truth or falsity of its reasons allows us to judge futher that it is either

    _____ or _____ (2 different distinctions are needed here.)

13. Fill in the blanks. To avoid confusion one should not say or write: "It's true," or " It's false," "It's valid," or "invalid," "It's sound," or "unsound." Instead one should write "The _____ is true or false." "The _____ is valid or invalid, sound or unsound."

14. Cross out those of the following statements which do not make sense.

1. That's a true argument.   2. That's a deductive argument.

3. That's a false assumption.   4. That's a valid statement.

5. That's a valid argument.   6. That's a sound conclusion.

7. That's a valid reason.   8. That's a false argument.

9. That's a sound argument.   10. That's an unsound statement.

Write out the whole word "true" or "false."

15. You can have valid reasoning with false reasons.

16. You can have valid reasoning in our general sense with all true reasons and a false conclusion.

17. You can have deductively valid reasoning with true reasons and a false conclusion.

18. You can have deductively valid reasoning with false reasons and a true conclusion.

19. You can have sound reasoning with false reasons.

20. You can have valid reasoning with all false reasons and a false conclusion.

21. The validity or invalidity of an argument depends on its' content.

22. You can have sound reasoning with a false conclusion.

23. You can have valid reasoning with a false conclusion.

24. You can have sound reasoning which is invalid.

25. Soundness = truth of conclusions + validity of reasoning.

CHECKLIST FOR STATEMENT EVALUATION

Evaluating all sorts of unsupported statements requires a background in philosophical concepts, distinctions, definitions, theories and a broad acquaintance with negative, critical facts. To evaluate statements as warranted (definitely or probably true) or (unwarranted unknown, probably or definitely false,) one should be skeptical (doubtful) critical, but not stupidly so. Try to use common sense. The summaries below usually end with the judgment "unwarranted." The student, however, may use "definitely false" where appropriate.

1. Is the statement *analytic* or known to you to be true by your own present or past *observation?* If so, in answering exercise problems, write "Definitely true, because it is analytic" or "because I have observed this myself." Be careful that the statement is about a particular person or event, not a generalization which might have been based on insufficient cases. Also, it must have been observed under good conditions. Be careful not to just believe what you are told by someone else.

2. Consider whether the statement might be *self-contradictory* or in direct contradiction to what you have observed for yourself. Check definitions with a dictionary if necessary! When necessary write "Definitely false, because it is self - contradictory" and write out the definitions which make it so. Otherwise write "False, because I have observed the opposite." Most statements will be *synthetic*. No synthetic statements are true just because they are synthetic. One has to judge them against one's *background beliefs*.

3. *Unknown referent:* If a statement names a made-up person, place or thing, or uses a pronoun for such a thing, then the statement should be classified as "Unwarranted because of an unknown subject." It is not acceptable to use this as a lazy man's way out of doing a little research or even thinking about the meaning of a statement. However, to say: "This claim is unwarranted because I don't know who or what it is about" is often to make an admirably true admission.

4. *Probability:* If a statement talks about real people and events somewhat known to you, you should always ask, "Is what the statement says *probable?* (a usual, normal, or ordinary event)? If so, it is warranted. If not, it is unwarranted. If one cannot decide if the claim is more probable than not, and one is in a position to do the research to find if the claim is true or false, then one should *do the research*.

5. *Statistics:* If an "average" is given, is it possible to determine whether it is a *mean,* (sum divided by number of items), *median* (1/2 above, 1/2 below) or *mode* (most frequent value)? If not, the claim is unwarranted because it is ambiguous. Remember that human qualities like I.Q. and strength fall into normal distributions with much overlap between races and sexes, but wealth and income statistics are likely to have much higher means than medians or modes because of non normal distribution. Note that if the *spread* (standard deviation) is not given, little can be concluded.

6. *Counterexamples and Disconfirming Instances:* If the statement is a correlational or causal claim "X is correlated with (or causes, results from, is attributable to) Y," consider whether there is even a real correlation. To do this one must consider not only the confirming cases of X and Y, but also whether there are disconfirming cases of X without Y and Y without X and how many such cases there might be. If there are many disconfirming cases, the statement should be found unwarranted because of such cases.

7. *Analogies and Differences:* If the statement is an analogy, "X is like Y," consider whether there are significant differences between X and Y. If so, the statement should be classified as unwarranted and the significant differences should be stated.

8. *Explanations:* An explanation of an action by reasons and desires is unwarranted if it ignores circumstances or runs contrary to one's general knowledge of human nature, including our egotism and self- deception. Explanations of natural events by spiritual personal beings which can violate the laws of nature are unwarranted, because such beings are useless "wild cards" which fail to help us predict or control anything. In both cases, *always consider whether there are other, better explanations.*

9. *Moral judgments, circumstances and theories:* If the claim is a *moral judgment* of an act, person, or policy, to judge it one may need to consider circumstances, moral rules, theories and values like "the greatest good for the greatest number" discussed in Chapter Four. Recall that detail is likely to be left out and that it is difficult to make judgments that a claim about a specific act or person is warranted without knowledge of the details.

10. *Testability:* If a statement makes a *pseudoscientific* or *paranormal* claim, consider whether the claim is consistent with the results of science and whether it is *testable* at all. If a statement makes an untestable claim, one should note that this makes it unwarranted. The same applies to *religious existence* claims about gods, devils, angels, demons, etc.

11. *Self- and Other- Deceptions:* If a claim is a *self-deception* or standard *other-deception*, then note that the statement is "Unwarranted, because this is a self - deception," or "standard other - deception." Recall that egotism makes many of us have too high an opinion of our intelligence, fairness, driving ability and that of others we are related to or associated with.

12. *Qualified subjectivity*: If the statement is *qualified* by words like "To me," or "I feel that," as an expression of *subjective* personal opinion and one has no reason to doubt it, write "Warranted, because this is only a personal opinion."

13. *Weasel words and fake precision:* If a statement contains "weasel words" like "may be," "could be," or "up to," note that these words make it vague and hence unwarranted. One cannot know how much is meant by claims containing "up to," and so on. On the other hand, sometimes an estimate is offered which is much more precise than anyone might reasonably be expected to know, or more precise than errors involved in measuring it allow: "unwarranted because of fake over-precision."

14. If a *source* is given, consider the *reliability or unreliability, credibility or bias* of the source in your answer. If conflicting information is available from differing sources, see if it is possible to give the statement a plausibility index. A statement can become unwarranted because its' source is biased or not credible on this subject. Why bias or lack of credibility is present needs to be explained.

15. *Unknowable claims:* With some estimates, such as of base rates of underground activities, ill defined items, or others' mental states, one can find a statement unwarranted by asking, *"How could anyone know that?"* A good example would be opposing guesses about whether "most" women feel guilty or sad after having an abortion. Unless there is good behavioral evidence, neither side can *know* any such claim to be true, because no one can get into "most" women's heads.

16. Consider whether any word, phrase or the whole statement is *ambiguous or vague.* If ambiguous, state the different meanings and explain how one makes the statement warranted while another makes it unwarranted. If the statement is vague, write "Unwarranted because vague," and explain the area in which it is vague (subject, time, place, and so on.)

17. *Jargon or malapropism.* Jargon uses *unnecessarily* complex words to dress up a simple truth. Label such a statement "jargon," or "malapropism" and paraphrase it or explain the misuse. Words are not jargon just because they are polite or technical. Science involves necessary technical terms which are not jargon. *Malapropism* is misuse of big words. An example of malapropism is this: "Evolution strongly motivated the ideologies that preempted WW I and WW II." "Preempted" means either "seized before anyone else could," or more generally "prevented." It makes no sense here.

18. *Abstraction or sophomoric generalization.* Philosophers talk about "Justice," "The Absolute," or "Dasein" and sometimes make claims like "Man is.." this or "Man is..." that. Unless context makes clear what is meant, such statements are unwarranted because they are vague. They leave open questions like "What is really being talked about, just acts or people or principles?" "How many men - all, almost all, most, many or only some? Women too? At all times, in all cultures?"

19. *Euphemism:* euphemism is the use of nice - sounding or neutral words for something bad. For example, there is never any fornication, adultery or rape on a university campus. There is only "radically infrequent, inappropriate penile insertive behavior." State that the sentence contains euphemism and paraphrase it.

20. Be on the look out for *exaggeration and flattery.* Recall that communicators want to make their communications worthy, so they may sharpen some points while flattening others. Too much exaggeration or flattery makes a statement unwarranted, so write "Unwarranted, because of exaggeration (or flattery)" and explain the exaggeration, etc.

21. If the statement is some sort of *game rule,* such as "The bishop only goes on the diagonal," write something like "warranted as a game rule of...", and then name or describe whose game it is. Institutions have games. For example, "The Pope is infallible" is either unwarranted because he can make mistakes, or warranted "as a game rule of Catholicism only."

22. *Economic claims* may well be myths about free markets, free trade, the benefits of corporate rule and its effects on people and the environment. Such myths should be found unwarranted and hard facts, economic and social statistics which contradict them should be given to show they are unwarranted.

When doing exercises, always include in answers either the word "definitely" or "probably""true" or "definitely" or "probably" "warranted" or "unwarranted" or "false" for each problem statement or basic reason. Then explain the judgment in one or two sentences. It is one's explanation that shows ability to apply the concepts of critical evaluation, not just the words "true," "false," "warranted" or "unwarranted."

The student should now do Excercise 24 on Evaluating Unsupported Claims.

INDEX

BIBLIOGRAPHY

Arguelles, J. (1987) *The Mayan factor: the path beyond technology.* Santa Fe, NM.: Bear & Company.

Alston, W. (1985) "Concepts of epistemic justification." In Moser, P.K. & vander Nat, A. (Eds.) (1995) *Human knowledge: classical and contemporary approaches.* New York: Oxford University Press. 321-340.

Andersen, K. (1997) "The Age of Unreason." *The New Yorker.* (March 2.)

Bachman, S. (ed.) (1989) *Preach Liberty: Selections from the Bible for Progressives,* New York: Four Walls Eight Windows.

Baergen, R. (1995) *Contemporary epistemology.* Orlando, Fl: Harcourt Brace and Company.

Baron, R. J. (1987) *The cerebral computer: an introduction to the computational structure of the human brain.* Hillsdale, New Jersey: Lawrence Erlbaum Associates, Publishers.

Basil, R. (ed.) (1988) *Not necessarily the New Age: critical essays.* Buffalo, New York: Prometheus Books.

Begley, S. (1997) "Seek and ye shall find." *Newsweek,* (June 9)

Ben-Yehuda, N. (1981) "Problems in Approaches to the European Witch - Craze." *Journal for the Scientific Study of Religion,* 20.

Berlitz, C. (1974) *The Bermuda triangle.* Garden City, New York: Doubleday & Company.

Bettinson, H. (1947) *Documents of the christian church.* New York: Oxford University Press.

Bishin, W. R. & Stone, C. D. (1972) *Law, language and ethics.* Mineola, New York: The Foundation Press.

Bonjour, L. (1985) *The structure of empirical knowledge.* Cambridge, MA: Harvard University Press.

"Briefly..." (1988), *U.S.A. Today.* Sec. 1 p. 2. (April 28.)

Brenner, L. (1997) "What people earn." *Parade Magazine.* (June 22.) 4-7.

Caplow, T. (1976) *How to run any organization.* Hinsdale, IL.: The Dryden Press.

Capra, F. (1977) *The Tao of physics.* New York: Bantam Books.

Carson, R. (1962) *Silent spring.* Boston: Houghton Mifflin.

Charen, M. "Weird world: gender feminism." (1994) *The Titusville Herald*. Titusville, PA. (June 1.)

Choate, P. & Walter, S. (1981) *America in ruins: beyond the public works pork barrel.* Washington: The Council of State Planning Agencies.

Copi, I. (1961) *Introduction to Logic.* (2nd. Ed.) New York: MacMillan Publishing Company.

Cornell, G. "*Isolated in anguish, they find others to share the pain.*" (1992) *Erie Times News*. Erie, PA. (November 7) p. 8A.

Cowley, F. (1991) *Metaphysical Delusion.* Buffalo, New York: Prometheus Books.

Condon, E. (1969) *Scientific study of unidentified flying objects.* New York: Bantam Books.

Daniels, T. *Millenial prophecy report.* The Millennium Watch Institute, P.O. Box 34201, Philadelphia, PA. 19101. Various issues.

Davidson, D. and Harman, G. (1975) *The Logic of grammar.* Encino, CA.: Dickenson Publishing Company.

Davis, T. (1993) *Philosophy, an introduction through original fiction, discussion and readings.* (3rd. ed.) New York: MCGraw-Hill.

Descartes, R. (1641) *Meditations on first philosophy.* The Library of Liberal Arts, New York: Howard W. Sams & Co. Inc. (1960.)

Diamond, H & M. (1985) *Fit for Life.* New York: Warner Books.

Double, R. *Beginning philosophy.* New York: Oxford university Press. Forthcoming.

Double, R. (1991) *The non reality of free will.* New York: Oxford University Press.

Doyle, R. P. (1994) *Atlas of contemporary America.* New York: Facts on File.

Drosnin, M. (1997) *The Bible code.* New York: Simon and Schuster.

Earthworks Group. (1989) *50 Simple things you can do to save the earth.* Berkeley, CA.

Earle, W. (1992) *Introduction to philosophy.* New York: McGraw-Hill.

Edwards, P. (1996) *Reincarnation: a critical examination.* Bufalo, New York: Prometheus Books.

Emery, C. E. (1997) "What? I don't remember that! tabloid predictions miss again." *Skeptical Inquirer,* Vol. 21, No. 1. p .8-9.

Falk, R. (1979) "Comparative Protection of Human rights in Capitalist and Socialist third world countries." In Falk, R. Kim, S. & Mendlovitz, S. *Toward a just world order.* Boulder, CO.: Westview Press. (1982) 405-431.

F.C. (1995) *Industrial society and its' future.* (The Unabomer Manifesto.)   Berkeley, CA.: Jolly Roger Press.

Feigl, H. & Sellars, W. (1949) *Readings in philosophical analysis.* New York, Appleton - Century - Crofts, Inc.

Folbre, N. & The Center for Popular Economics. (1995) *The new field guide to the U. S. economy.* New York: The New Press.

Fraser, S (1995) *The Bell curve wars.* Glenview, IL.: HarperCollins.

Freud, S. (1913). *The interpretation of dreams.* New York: Modern Library. (1950.)

"Gates tops Forbes' list of billionaires." (1997) Associated Press. *Erie Times News,* Erie Pa. July 14. p. 8A.

Gettier, E. "Is justified true belief knowledge?" In Moser, P.K. & vander Nat, A. (Eds.) (1995) *Human knowledge: classical and contemporary approaches.* New York: Oxford University Press. 273-274.

Giere, R. (1991) *Understanding scientific reasoning.* (3rd. ed.) Fort Worth, TX.: Holt, Rinehart and Winston.

Gilovich, T. (1991) *How we know what isn't so, the fallibility of human reason in everyday life.* New York: The Free Press.

"Girl, 6, stood in front of train 'to become an angel'." (1993, June 6) *Erie Times News.* p. A2.

Goldman, A. (1967) "A Causal theory of knowing." In Pojman, L. P. *The Theory of Knowledge.* (1993) Belmont, CA.: Wadsworth Publishing Company. p. 137-145.

Gough, J. W. ed. (1966) *Locke's Second Treatise of Government.* New York: Barnes and Noble.

Govier, T. *A Practical Study of Argument.* (1988) (2nd. ed.) Belmont, CA.: Wadsworth Publishing Company.

Grant, A. and Burrell, W. (1992) *The patriotic consumer: how to buy American.* Kansas City, MO.: Andrews & McMeel.

Grice, P. (1975) "The logic of conversation." In Davidson, D. and Harman, G. (1975) *The Logic of grammar.* p. 64-75. Encino, CA.: Dickenson Publishing Company.

Gross, P.R. & Levitt, N., (1994) *Higher superstition: the academic left and Its quarrels with science.* Baltimore, MD.: Johns Hopkins University Press.

Gup, T. (1996) "The Mother Jones 400." *Mother Jones* magazine. (March -April.) 38-59.

Harnack, A. (1957) *Outlines of the history of dogma.* Boston, MA.: Beacon Hill Press.

Haugeland, J. (1985) *Artificial intelligence, the very idea,* Cambridge, MA.: The M.I.T. Press.

Haught, J. A. (1995) *Holy hatred: religious conflicts of the 90's.* Buffalo, NY: Prometheus Books.

Hawken, P. (1997) "Natural Capitalism." *Mother Jones* magazine. (March - April.)

Hempel, C. G. (1942) "The Function of General Laws in History." In Feigl, H. & Sellars, W. *Readings in philosophical analysis.* (1949) New York, Appleton - Century - Crofts, Inc. 449-471.

Hines, T. (1988) *Pseudoscience and the paranormal: a critical examination of the evidence.* Buffalo: Prometheus Books.

Hubbard, L. R. (1950) *Dianetics, The modern science of mental health.* Los Angeles, CA.: Bridge Publications, Inc. 1985 edition.

Huber, P. (1991) *Galileo's revenge.* New York: BasicBooks, Inc.

Humanist Manifesto 1 and *Humanist Manifesto 2* . (1933, 1973) Amherst, NY.: The American Humanist Association.

Hyman, R .(1996) "Evaluation of the military's twenty year program of psychic spying." *Skeptical Inquirer.* Vol. 20, No. 2. (March-April) p. 21-26.

The Impact of homophobia and other social biases on AIDS. (1997, February) San Francisco, CA: Public Media Center.

Inbau, F. , Reid, J. and Buckley, W. (1986) *Criminal interrogation and confessions.* Baltimore, MD: Williams and Wikins.

"Job creation for the disabled, key goal of act, hasn't happened." (1993) AP. *Erie Times News.* (August 20.)

Kahane, H. (1992) *Logic and contemporary rhetoric: the use of reason in everyday life.* (6th. ed.) Belmont, CA: Wadsworth Publishing Company.

Katz, L. (1987) *Bad acts and guilty minds.* Chicago, IL: University of Chicago Press.

Keating, Jr., J. C. (1997) "Chiropractic: science and antiscience and pseudoscience side by side." *Skeptical Inquirer.* Vol. 21, No. 4. (July/August.)

Kenny, A. (1978) *Free will and responsibility.* London: Routledge & Kegan Paul.

Klass, P. (1996 January-February) "That's entertainment! TV's UFO coverup." *The Skeptical Inquirer.* 20, #6. p. 29-31.

Klass, P. (1988) *UFO abductions: a dangerous game.* Buffalo, New York: Prometheus Books.

Koernke, M. *America in Peril 1* [video] (1995) Adrian, MI.: Proclaim Liberty Ministry.

Koff, S. (1988a) "Changing strategy, scientology now steps right up to controversy." *St. Petersburg Times.* (December 22.)

Koff, S. (1988b) "Dozens of groups operate under the auspices of church of Scientology." *St. Petersburg Times.* (December 22.)

Koff, S. (1988c) "Xemu's cruel response to overpopulated world." *St. Petersburg Times.* (December 22.)

Korten, D. C. (1995) *When corporations rule the world.* West Hartford, CT: Kumarian Press.

Krassner, P. (1986) "Brief notes," *The Realist,* No. 102, pp. 2.

Krauss, L. (1995) *The Physics of star trek.* New York: BasicBooks.

Kuhn, T. (1957) *The Copernican revolution.* Cambridge, MA.: Harvard University Press.

Kusche, L. D. (1975) *The Bermuda triangle mystery - solved.* New York: Harper & Row Publishers.

L. Ron Hubbard: a profile. (1995) The L. Ron Hubbard Personal Public Relations Office International. Los Angeles, CA.

Law Enforcement Investigations. FM 19-20 (29 April 1977) Washington, D.C.: Headquarters, Department of the Army.

Lehrer, K. & Paxson, T. (1969) "Knowledge: undefeated justified true belief." *Journal of Philosophy.* 66, 225-237.

"Loch Ness monster myth good for $42 million." (1990) *AP - Erie Morning News* Sec. 1, p. 1 (May 29.)

MacDougall, C. D. (1983) *Superstition and the press.* Buffalo, New York: Prometheus Books.

MacLaine, S. (1986) *Out on a limb.* Toronto, Canada: Bantam Books.

Magner, C. (1995) *Chiropractic: the victim's perspective.* Buffalo, New York: Prometheus Press.

Martindale, D. (1996) "When It's the Viewers Who Are in the Twilight Zone", *A&E Magazine,* May, pp. 26-28.

Marty, M. "You get to teach and study religion." *Academe.* (1996 November-December.) pp. 14-17.

McMenamin, R. W. (1986) Clergy malpractice. Buffalo, New York: William S. Hein Company.

Melton, J. G. "A History of the New Age Movement." In Basil, R. *Not Necessarily the New Age.* (1988) Buffalo, New York: Prometheus Books.

Menchu', R. (1983) *I, Rigoberta Menchú: an indian woman in Guatemala.* (Ed. Borgos-Debray, E.) Ann Wright (tr.) New York: Verso

Minsky, M. (1988) *The society of mind.* Portland, OR.: Touchstone Books.

Modde, P. J. (1985) *Chiropractic malpractice.* Columbia, MD: Hanrow Press.

Moore, N.B. & Parker, R. (1991) *Critical thinking.* Palo Alto, CA: Mayfield Publishing Company.

Moser, P.K. & vander Nat, A. (Eds.) (1995) *Human knowledge: classical and contemporary approaches.* New York: Oxford University Press.

Mumford, M; Rose, A. and Goslin, D. "CIA Concludes no value to program." *Skeptical Inquirer.* Vol. 20, No. 2. (March-April) p. 27.

"Muslim cleric gets 7 years in French exorcism death." (1997) *AP- Erie Times News* (June 7) p. 4A.

Nader, R. (1996) "Acceptance Speech." (for Presidential nomination) Green Party USA, PO Box 100, Blodgett Mills, N.Y.

National Science Board. (1996) *Science and Engineeering Indicators.* Washington, D.C.: U.S. Governement Printing Office.

Nickell, J. (1982-3) "The Nazca drawings revisited: creation of a full sized duplicate." *Skeptical Inquirer* 7 (N0.3) 36-44.

Nickell, J. (1989) *The Magic detectives.* Buffalo, New York: Prometheus Books.

Nickell, J. (1996) "Sleuthing a Psychic Sleuth." *Skeptical Inquirer.* (Jan. - Feb. 1996.)

Niebuhr, G. (1993), "Offerings of aid on the front lines." *Erie Times News.* Sec. S, p.1. (November 14)

"Notice of 1997 Annual Meeting," (1997) Bartlesville, OK.: Phillips Petroleum Company.

"Notice of 1997 Annual Meeting and Proxy Statement." (1997) Armonk, New York: International Business Machines Corporation.

Nuland, S. (1995) *How we die: reflections on life's final chapter.* New York: Random House.

Oberg, J. (1979-80) "Astronaut 'UFO' sightings." *Skeptical Inquirer*, 3, # 1, 39-46.

O'Reilly, D. (1997, March 1). "Luke John: A Miracle in Their Midst" *Erie Times News.* (1997 March 1) p. 7A.

Parenti, M. (1986) *Inventing reality: the politics of the mass media.* New York: St. Martin's Press.

Paul, R. *Critical thinking: what every person needs to survive in a rapidly changing world.* (ed.) Binker, A. Sonoma State Universty, Rohnert Park, CA.: Center for Critical Thinking and Moral Critique.

Paulos, J.A. (1988) *Innumeracy: mathematical illiteracy and its consequences*, New York: Random House, Inc.

Penrose, R. (1989) *The Emperor's new mind: concerning computers, minds, and the laws of physics.* New York: Oxford University Press.

Persinger, M. (1990) "The Tectonic Strain Theory as an Explanation for UFO Phenomena." *Journal of UFO Studies*, 2, 105-37.)

Pollock, J. (1986) *Contemporary theories of knowledge.* Totowa, N. J.

Pollock, J. "The Gettier problem." In Moser, P.K. & vander Nat, A. (Eds.) (1995) *Human knowledge: classical and contemporary approaches.* New York: Oxford University Press. 276-284.

Radner, D. and Radner, M. (1982) *Science and unreason.* Belmont, CA: Wadsworth Publishing Company.

Rand, A. *Philosophy, who needs it?* (1982) New York: Bobbs-Merrill and Company. p. 74.

Randi, J. (1980). *Flim-Flam!* New York: Lippincott and Crowell.

Randi, J. (1995) *An encyclopedia of claims, frauds and hoaxes of the occult and supernatural.* Buffalo, New York: Prometheus books.

Rapping, E. (1993) "Sex, commercials and rock and roll," *The Progressive.* p. 37. (July).

Rawls, J. (1971) *Theory of Justice.* Cambridge, MA: Belknap Press of Harvard University.

"Religion beating sports at the gate" (1994) *Erie Times News.* (April 23).

Rescher, N. (1976) *Plausible reasoning.* Assen-Amsterdam: Van Gorcum.

Rhine, J. & Pratt, J. (1962) *Parapsychology: frontier science of the mind.* Oxford: Blackwell.

Robbins, R. H. (1959) *The Encyclopedia of witchcraft and demonology.* New York: Crown Publishers.

Robertson, P. (1991) *The New world order.* Dallas, TX.: Word Publications.

Rothman, M. A. (1988) *A Physicist's guide to skepticism.* Buffalo, New York: Prometheus Books.

Ruchlis, H. (1991) *How do you know it's true?* Buffalo, New York: Prometheus Books.

Russell, B. (1961) *Why I am not a Christian.* New York: Oxford University Press.

Ryle, G. (1949) *The concept of mind.* New York: Barnes and Noble.

Sagan, C. (1995). *The Demon-haunted world: science as a candle in the dark.* New York: Random House.

Schick, T. & Vaughn, L. (1995) *How to think about weird things.* Mountainview, CA. Mayfield Publishing Company.

Schumacher, E. F. (1960) *Small is beautiful: economics as if people mattered.* New York: Harper & Row.

Sifakis, C. (1996) *The Big book of hoaxes.* New York: Paradox Press.

Shermer, M. (1993) "The Unlikeliest Cult in history." *Skeptic Magazine.* (Vol 2, No. 2.)

Shermer, M. (1993) "Proving the Holocaust" *Skeptic Magazine.* (Vol 2, #4)

Shultz, T. (1976) *The Fringes of reason.* New York: Harmony Books.

Sloan, A. (1996) "The Hit men." *Newsweek.* (February 26.) p. 44-48.

Smith, K. (1995) *Ken's guide to the bible.* New York, NY.: Blast Books.

"Special interest influence in the 1996 elections." (1996) Washington, D.C.: Common Cause.

Stalker, D. & Glymour, C. (eds.) (1985) *Examining holistic medicine.* Buffalo, New York: Prometheus Books.

Stenger, V.J. (1990) *Physics and psychics: the search for a world beyond the senses.* Buffalo, New York: Prometheus Books.

Stenger, V. J. (1995) *The unconscious quantum: metaphysics in modern physics and cosmology.* Buffalo, New York: Prometheus Books.

Stine, G. H. (1994) *Mind machines you can build.* Pinelas, FL.: Top of the Mountain Press.

Stokes, T. (Jan. - Feb. 1996) "How to make an alien for autopsy" *The Skeptical Inquirer.* 20, No. 1 21-23.

Strieber, W. *Communion.* (1987) New York: Morrow.

SubGenius Foundation. (1983) *The Book of the SubGenius.* New York: Simon & Schuster.

"A Sucker's born ... forty-thousand gullible internet users fall for a scam as old as the pyramids." (1996) Netline. p. 19. *Internet Underground Magazine.* April.

Swords, M. (1987, May) "Communion: A Readers' Guide." MUFON UFO Journal.

Targ, R. & Puthoff, H. (1977) *Mind reach.* New York: Delacorte Press.

Thomas, S. N. (1978) *The formal mechanics of mind.* Ithaca, NY: Cornell University Press.

Thomas, S.N. (1991) *Argument evaluation.* Tampa, Fl: Worthington Publishing Company.

Thomas, S. N. (1986) *Practical reasoning in natural language,* 3rd. Ed., Chap. 4. Toronto: Prentice-Hall.

Thomas, S. N. (1990) *How to keep your vcr alive.* Tampa, Fl: Worthington Publishing Company.

Thompson, B. E. (1992) *An introduction to the syllogism and the logic of the proportional quantifiers.* New York: Peter Lang.

Thompson, L. "Ultimatum." (1994) In Parfrey, A. *Cult rapture.* (1995) Portland, OR.: Feral House. 318-320.

"Vanishing Jobs." (1996) [Video] REKO, PO Box 40005, Joplin, Mo.: *U.S. Awareness Productions.*

Von Daniken, E. (1970) *Chariots of the gods?* New York; Putnam.

Walton, D. (1996) *Argumentation schemes for presumptive reasoning.* Mahwah, NJ: Lawrence Erlbaum Associates, Inc.

Warraq, I. (1995) *Why I am not a Muslim.* Buffalo, New York: Prometheus Books.

Wason, P. (1972) *The psychology of reasoning.* Cambridge, MA.: Harvard University Press.

Weinberg, S. (ed.) (1994) *Ramtha.* Ranier, WA. : Sovereignty.

Wells, J. T. (1996) *Report to the Nation.* Austin, TX.: Association of Certified Fraud Examiners.

Wells, J. T., Bradford, N.S., Geis, G., Kramer, W.M., Ratley, J.D. & Robertson, J. (1994) *Fraud Examiners Manual.* (2nd. ed., rev.) Austin, TX.: Association of Certified Fraud Examiners.

White, M. (Speaker) (1996) "The Rhetoric of intolerance: An open letter-video to Pat Robertson." [video] Laguna beach, CA.: "Video" P.O. Box 4467.

Wiseman, R. (1997) *Deception & self-deception: investigating psychics.* Buffalo, New York: Prometheus Books.

White, A. D. (1896) *A History of the warfare of science with theology in christendom.* Buffalo, New York: Prometheus Books. 1993.

White, R. J. et. al. (1996) "The Isolation and transplantation of the brain, an historical perspective with emphasis on the surgical solution." *Neurological Research*, Vol. 18, No. 3, 194-208.

Wilson, K. D. (1992) *Cause of death,* Cincinnatti, Ohio: Writer's Digest Books.

"Woman dies from injuries in exorcism." (1996) Associated Press, *Titusville Herald,* (July 6.)

"Woman who feared cancer kills children, then herself." A.P (1993, June 19.) *Erie Times News.* p. A5.

Zepenzauer, M. & Naimen, A. (1996) *Take the rich off welfare.* Tucson, AZ: Odonian Press.

EXERCISES

EXERCISE 1A: INDICATOR SORTING

Use the Table of Indicators in Chapter 1 to circle the correct letter or blacken the correct alternative of a multiple choice form. If you find no match, ask yourself whether the phrase means the same as "because" or "so". If a word or phrase has uses both as an indicator and in other ways, treat it as an indicator.

		REASON	CONCLUSION	CONNECTIVE	SIGNAL	NONE
1.	thus	A	B	C	D	E
2.	may be deduced from	A	B	C	D	E
3.	argue that	A	B	C	D	E
4.	if	A	B	C	D	E
5.	because	A	B	C	D	E
6.	therefore	A	B	C	D	E
7.	that's why	A	B	C	D	E
8.	additionally	A	B	C	D	E
9.	consequently	A	B	C	D	E
10.	not	A	B	C	D	E
11.	implies that	A	B	C	D	E
12.	follows from	A	B	C	D	E
13.	as shown by	A	B	C	D	E
14.	for	A	B	C	D	E
15.	so	A	B	C	D	E
16.	it	A	B	C	D	E
17.	owing to	A	B	C	D	E
18.	must	A	B	C	D	E
19.	since	A	B	C	D	E
20.	suggests that	A	B	C	D	E
21.	and	A	B	C	D	E
22.	it follows that	A	B	C	D	E
23.	since	A	B	C	D	E
24.	that	A	B	C	D	E
25.	however	A	B	C	D	E
26.	for the reason that	A	B	C	D	E
27.	for this reason	A	B	C	D	E
28.	If..., then...	A	B	C	D	E
29.	suppose that	A	B	C	D	E
30.	cannot	A	B	C	D	E
31.	inasmuch as	A	B	C	D	E
32.	surely	A	B	C	D	E
33.	necessarily	A	B	C	D	E

EXERCISE 1B: INDICATOR SORTING

Use the Table of Indicators in Chapter 1 to circle the correct letter or blacken the correct alternative of a multiple choice form. If you find no match, ask yourself whether the phrase means the same as "because" or "so". If a word or phrase has uses both as an indicator and in other ways, treat it as an indicator.

		REASON	CONCLUSION	CONNECTIVE	SIGNAL	NONE
1.	if follows that	A	B	C	D	E
2.	seeing as	A	B	C	D	E
3.	or	A	B	C	D	E
4.	whence	A	B	C	D	E
5.	as	A	B	C	D	E
6.	assuming that	A	B	C	D	E
7.	then	A	B	C	D	E
8.	because	A	B	C	D	E
9.	should	A	B	C	D	E
10.	for the reason that	A	B	C	D	E
11.	know that	A	B	C	D	E
12.	follows from	A	B	C	D	E
13.	thus	A	B	C	D	E
14.	necessarily	A	B	C	D	E
15.	so	A	B	C	D	E
16.	for	A	B	C	D	E
17.	entails that	A	B	C	D	E
18.	firstly	A	B	C	D	E
19.	since	A	B	C	D	E
20.	implies that	A	B	C	D	E
21.	from	A	B	C	D	E
22.	that	A	B	C	D	E
23.	on account of	A	B	C	D	E
24.	we can derive that	A	B	C	D	E
25.	nevertheless	A	B	C	D	E
26.	if	A	B	C	D	E
27.	guess that	A	B	C	D	E
28.	and	A	B	C	D	E
29.	for this reason	A	B	C	D	E
30.	being as	A	B	C	D	E
31.	that's why	A	B	C	D	E
32.	I think that	A	B	C	D	E
33.	therefore	A	B	C	D	E

EXERCISE 2A: MAKING ARROW DIAGRAMS FOR THE SIMPLEST POSSIBLE REASONING DISCOURSES

In each discourse, underline the one inference indicator and label it "R" or "C." Put angle brackets around each statement. Number each statement: the first, 1, the second 2, just above its' left bracket. Make an arrow diagram of the reasoning to the right of it. Put the number of an indicated reason above the arrow and the **R** number of an indicated conclusion below the arrow. In some cases it may be necessary to make minor ↓ changes and add words to a participial phrase or imperative to make it express a complete declarative claim **C** or delete "that" before a claim as shown in Chapter 1, Section 3. If you are using a multiple choice form and the diagram is 1—>2, blacken the "A" alternative. If it is 2—>1, blacken "B."

PROBLEMS

1. Guns with checkered grips can be picked up by the grip, since the checkering makes it impossible to get useful prints from this area.

2. I still have checks left, so I can't be overdrawn.

3.   It must have been a heck of a Mosh Pit, because I got two flesh wounds and didn't even notice it.

4. I know you can't read fast, that's why I'm typing really slowly.

5. For testing purposes, do not use a VCR tape with important material on it, because the tape may get damaged.

6. The record club tapes are excellent; consequently I'll keep them.

7. She's sleeping now, owing to partying late last night.

8.   He's spent all his money. Hence He'll soon lose interest in the Amusement Park.

9. Assuming that it snows for another two days, we'll be stranded here for at least one month.

10. There are fresh tracks, which proves that someone was here a short while ago.

11. All glass fragments at the alleged point of entry were found outside. This suggests a fight inside in which they fell outward, not a break -in and struggle inside.

12. Take the flashlight, as it will soon be dark.

13. His second in command has just surrendered. Therefore the general has lost his contact with the outside world.

14. They haven't paid this bill in 90 days; accordingly I'm turning it over to Legbreak's Bill Collection Service.

15. Moses could not have been the author of the "5 Books of Moses", for his death and burial are described in one of them.

EXERCISE 2A

16. The tape will not run in a VHS machine correctly if there is a bright light shining on it with the cabinet top removed, because a bright light will activate the photosensor that normally tells the machine when the tape reached its end.

R
↓
C

17. His giving her an expensive diamond implies that he still loves her.

18. Since the main road is blocked, we'll try the alternate route.

19. She's sad because of his being away so much.

20. At the scene of the hit and run, make tire casts right after one another equaling the circumference of the tire, about 5 - 8 feet, for this increases the probability of of matching the tire track.

21. You shouldn't eat that pie, since the cat sat on it.

22. The sound track from Starlight Express has some super songs. Thus you ought to buy it.

23. I've got her gift covered, as I've got an extra gift certificate.

24. You can't keep stringing us along. You see that you should choose one of us and let the other go.

25. Newton's and Einstein's theories of gravity are inconsistent, but both are scientific theories. What makes a theory scientific, then, is not absolute truth, but testability and the method by which it was constructed.

EX 2A-W. On a lined piece of paper write in pen (or type or word process) 5 original examples of these simplest reasoning discourses. Each sentence must have a subject and verb in agreement. For originality, make up examples about subjects familiar to you. Circle indicators, bracket, number and diagram your examples.

EXERCISE 2B: MAKING ARROW DIAGRAMS FOR THE SIMPLEST POSSIBLE REASONING DISCOURSES

In each discourse underline the one inference indicator and label it "R" or "C." Put angle brackets around each statement. Number each statement: the first, 1, the second 2, just above its' left bracket. Make an arrow diagram of the reasoning to the right of it. Put the number of an indicated reason above the arrow and the number of an indicated conclusion below the arrow. In some cases it may be necessary to make minor changes and add words to a participial phrase or imperative to make it express a complete declarative claim or delete "that" before a claim as shown in Chapter 1, Section 3. If you are using a multiple choice form and the diagram is 1—>2, blacken the "A" alternative. If it is 2—>1, blacken "B."

R
↓
C

PROBLEMS

1. The bill is twice as big as usual, seeing that you ate twice as much as usual.

2. When you stop working out, all that steroid muscle turns to blubber, which is why you've got to keep at it.

3. The new, experimental football has solid yellow lines around the seams, for this increases its' visibility.

4. You've got to kiss a lot of frogs before one turns into a Prince, so you ought to go out with him.

5. That rule doesn't apply, inasmuch as he was already out of bounds.

6. The underside of the car shouldn't be too bad, being that it was undercoated when it was new.

7. Technicians hate to answer the question whether you can watch one channel while recording another, because they are afraid you will expect them to explain, in slow detail over the 'phone how to make all the connections.

8. The flash was 5 seconds before the sound which means that the storm center is 15 miles away.

9. Supposing that there is life on Mars, there must be water there.

10. Things are solid and impenetrable not because matter is compact, but because electrons of different things repel each other. Hint: 3 sentences should be bracketed and numbered, but only 2 diagramed.

11. Check the body carefully for saliva and semen, because 80% of the population are secretors whose body fluids permit accurate blood typing.

12. The complainant has not proved his case; accordingly, I am instructing the jury to bring in a verdict of "Not Guilty".

13. The game was called because of rain.

14. The impossibility of this construction suggests that the theory on which it is based is false.

15. They took seats in the back row, since they wanted to make out.

16. There was a Rave that evening, so we went to it.

R
↓
C

17. Do not become impatient while observing whether the VCR loads the tape correctly, because it is normal for the tape in a VCR to move very slowly.

18. That there is a massive body out there follows from there being a large disturbance in the orbits of the planets.

19. The circular cracks in the glass caused by the bullet to the lower right stop where they contact the cracks made by the hole in the upper left. The bullet which went to the upper left, therefore, was fired first .

20. Everybody ate it which implies that they found it very tasty.

21. We shouldn't have to pay that insurance claim, as it was on fire when he lay down on it.

22. Speech ought not to be a required college course, on the ground that it is included in grade school English.

23. I think I recall that it is red, which would entail that it isn't transparent.

24. The wounds are very jagged, which leads me to believe that they were inflicted by an animal.

25. The cheese is spoiled, as indicated by the mold on it.

EX 2B-W. On a lined piece of paper write in pen (or type or word process) 5 original examples of these simplest reasoning discourses. Each sentence must have a subject and verb in agreement. For originality, make up examples about subjects familiar to you. Circle indicators, bracket, number and diagram your examples.

EXERCISE 3A: DIAGRAMING CONDENSED FORMS

Numbers in the problems stand for statements. Underline each indicator and write "R" or "C" above the words. Make a diagram of the indicated reasoning by placing the numbers for the indicated reason above, and drawing arrows down to the numbers for the conclusions. One point may be awarded for each correct underlining, arrow or + where indicated.

Examples: 1. <u>Because</u>[r] 1 , 2

$$1 \\ \downarrow \\ 2$$

2. 3 , <u>because</u>[R] 4

$$4 \\ \downarrow \\ 3$$

1. 1 implies that 2.

2. 3, seeing that 4.

3. 5 follows from 6.

4. 1 is entailed by 2.

5. 3. It follows that 4.

6. 5, being as 6.

7. Since 1, 2.

8. 3 inasmuch as 4.

9. 5 demonstrates that 6.

10. 1, for 2.

11. 3. Consequently 4.

12. 5, as shown by 6.

13. 1. thus 2.

14. Since 3, 4.

15. 5, whence 6.

16. 1, accordingly 2.

Note: Sections 2.1, 2.2 and 2.3 will help with 17-20.

17. Since 3, and since 4, we conclude that 5. ("and" = +) (4 pts.)

18. Since 3 and 4, consequently 5, hence 6. (6 pts.)

19. 1 may be deduced from 2 and 3. (3 pts.)

20. 4, so since 5, 6. (4 + 5) (4 pts.)

EXERCISE 3B: DIAGRAMING CONDENSED FORMS

Numbers in the problems stand for statements. Underline each indicator and write "R" or "C" above the words. Make a diagram of the indicated reasoning by placing the numbers for the indicated reasons above, and drawing arrows down to the numbers for the conclusions. One point may be awarded for each correct underlining, arrow or + where indicated.

Examples: 1. <u>Because</u>^R 1 , 2   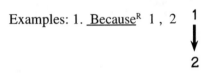   2. 3 , <u>because</u>^R 4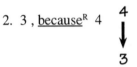

1. 1, since 2.   2. 3, inasmuch as 4.

3. 5 suggests that 6.   4. 1 follows from 2.

5. 3. for the reason that 4   6. 5 may be deduced from 6.

7. 1, assuming that 2   8. 3, for 4.

9. 5 demonstrates that 6.   10. 1, whence 2.

11. 3. Accordingly, 4.   12. 5 indicates that 6.

13. 1. So 2.   14. 3, because of 4.

15. 5. Therefore 6.   16. 1, consequently 2.

Note: Sections 2.1, 2.2 and 2.3 will help with 17-20.

17. Because 3 and because 4, 5. ("and" = +) (4 pts.)

18. 6, as 5, since 3 and 4. ("and" = +) (6 pts.)

19. 1 in view of the fact that 2 and 3. (3 pts.)

20. 4, thus because 5, 6. (4 + 5) (4 pts.)

EXERCISE 4A: DEVELOPING YOUR SENSE OF EVIDENCE

Do each of the following by means of the So/Because test in Chapter 1, Section 5. Read each pair of sentences twice, once with "so" and once with "because" between them. You can assume that a pronoun in one statement refers to a noun in another. But don't assume the truth of any other statement not written. Don't read a lot into the statements given. Where at least one reading makes sense and it is at least moderately strong reasoning, underline the letter "s" or "b" for the word "so" or "because", which makes the strongest reasoning, bracket and number the statements and draw an Arrow Diagram of the discourse to the right of it. Where it does not make sense either way, make "x"'s above both "s" and "b", do not bracket and number the statements. Write "No Reasoning" after the passage, and make no diagram. Where it makes sense with either "so" or "because", underline both and diagram it as an argument rather than an explanation.

The first statement, assuming it were true, could raise the probability that the second was true (R) lower the probability that the second was true (L) or have no effect on the probability that the second was true (N). The second could independently have any of these effects R, L or N on the first. If either raises the probability of the other significantly, it is a good reason for the other. So for each pair, also consider whether each raises, lowers or has no effect on the other and circle R, L or N in the forms "1 R L N 2?" and "2 R L N 1?"

PROBLEMS

1. One of them is very short.   The other is quite tall.
       1 R L N 2 ?   2 R L N 1 ?

2. You've done a poor job in many ways.   You're fired.
       1 R L N 2 ?   2 R L N 1 ?

3. The car was right there.   The fire hydrant was newly painted.
       1 R L N 2 ?   2 R L N 1 ?

4. She's very good looking.   I'd like to meet her.
       1 R L N 2 ?   2 R L N 1 ?

5. Use the secret weapon now.   We're losing and need it.
       1 R L N 2 ?   2 R L N 1 ?

6. He is 4' 10" tall.   He is very hungry.
       1 R L N 2 ?   2 R L N 1 ?

7. He's been missing for two days.   He is very hungry.
       1 R L N 2 ?   2 R L N 1 ?

8. The Virgin will forgive them.   They made a sincere confession.
       1 R L N 2 ?   2 R L N 1 ?

9. This must be a counterfeit $50.   The front and back are the same size.
       1 R L N 2 ?   2 R L N 1 ?

10. You shouldn't eat it.   It's still wiggling.
    1 R L N 2 ?   2 R L N 1 ?

11. A hard-driven helmet to the chest can break ribs.   Spearing an opponent with your helmet is illegal.
    1 R L N 2 ?   2 R L N 1 ?

12. I've been ripped off.   This pack has 10 cards and only 8 envelopes.
    1 R L N 2 ?   2 R L N 1 ?

13. I don't suffer from stress.   I'm a stress carrier.
    1 R L N 2 ?   2 R L N 1 ?

14. It was a blue, contemporary ranch style house.   The wall paper was old - fashioned.
    1 R L N 2 ?   2 R L N 1 ?

15. I ate 6 chocolate bars last Tuesday.   Today my face looks like a pepperoni pizza.
    1 R L N 2 ?   2 R L N 1 ?

16. Never eat anything bigger than your head.   It might stick in your throat.
    1 R L N 2 ?   2 R L N 1 ?

17. Don't try to buy a chic new dress at" Buttons and Bows".   All the transvestites shop there and clean out the nice stuff as soon as it gets in.
    1 R L N 2 ?   2 R L N 1 ?

18. The only entrances are a couple narrow mountain passes.   The government can easily block overland smuggling.
    1 R L N 2 ?   2 R L N 1 ?

19. Do the killing with a shotgun.   The pellets can't be linked to the gun by ballistics.
    1 R L N 2 ?   2 R L N 1 ?

20. Stop doing this dumb exercise and turn on the TV.   It's time for the "Soap"s to start.
    1 R L N 2 ?   2 R L N 1 ?

EXERCISE 4B: DEVELOPING YOUR SENSE OF EVIDENCE

Do each of the following by means of the So/Because test in Chapter 1, Section 5. Read each pair of sentences twice, once with "so" and once with "because" between them. You can assume that a pronoun in one statement refers to a noun in another. But don't assume the truth of any other statement not written. Don't read a lot into the statements given. Where at least one reading makes sense and it is at least moderately strong reasoning, underline the letter "s" or "b" for the word, "so" or "because", which makes the strongest reasoning, bracket and number the statements and draw an Arrow Diagram of the discourse to the right of it. Where it does not make sense either way, make "x"'s above both "s" and "b", do not bracket and number the statements. Write "No Reasoning" after the passage, and make no diagram. Where it makes sense with either "so" or "because", underline both but diagram it as an argument rather than an explanation.

If you are not sure whether one statement is a reason for another ask yourself this question "Does" SAY the proposed reason "give me any reason to believe" SAY THE PROPOSED CONCLUSION? Alternatively, you might ask "If I didn't believe" SAY THE PROPOSED CONCLUSION, "Would I tend to be persuaded or convinced by being told that" SAY THE PROPOSED REASON ?

PROBLEMS

1. I'm an honest guy.   Nobody trusts me.

2. You won't enjoy the game this year.   Both teams are terrible.

3. It's unfair to think men will try to have sex with anything that moves.   Movement's not essential.

4. Fu dogs are inexpensive and interesting.   I collect them.

5. The waves were very rough.   We didn't go surfing.

6. Wait here.   I'll go kill the baby.

7. There was a large, talkative crowd.   The buildings were freshly painted.

8. I've just had a bad scare.   I'll have a double Martini.

9. He told a dirty joke.   She glared at him.

10. I do expect you to do that.   It's your job.

11. These colored stripes are drawn on the bill.   This must be a counterfeit $50.

12. It's a point of principle.   I must stay here.

13. No one in Pennsylvania dies of old age. The law requires a specific cause of death on death certificates.

14. The sand was very fine.   It was a dull yellowish color.

15. The stirrup revolutionized warfare in Europe.   It made mounted shock combat (knight's jousting) possible.

16. I was arrested.   I was "mooning" cars from an overpass.

17. I'm not wearing any underwear.   Somebody stole it all when I left the laundromat for a minute.

18. The house is finally finished.   Now we can rent it.

19. He's not your best friend.   He's a serial murderer and you're his next victim.

20. No obvious accidental means of ignition was found for the fire.   It's likely that arson was the cause.

EXERCISE 5A: DEVELOPING YOUR SENSE OF EVIDENCE

In some cases below one statement is a Basic Reason (BR) supporting an Intermediate Conclusion (IC) which supports the third as a Final Conclusion (FC). In others only two of the statements are related as evidence and conclusion. In still others none of the statements are so related. Do these problems as explained in Chapter 2, Section 1.

Problems

FINAL DIAGRAM

_____ 1 < We should turn back.>

↓

_____ 2 < The light is failing.>

↓

_____ 3 < We won't be able to see the trail soon.>

Forms: Read, check S or B: 1 S/B 2 , 1 S/B 3 , 2 S/B 3 ?
Arrow diagrams based on reading:

_____ 4 < The flags flapped wildly in the breeze.>

↓

_____ 5 < He was wearing a royal blue tunic.>

↓

_____ 6 < The sun shown brightly.>

Forms: Read, check S or B: 4 S/B 5 , 4 S/B 6 , 5 S/B 6 ?
Arrow diagrams based on reading:

_____ 7 < you should throw them out.>

↓

_____ 8 < They stink to high heaven.>

↓

_____ 9 < The cat barfed on your old shoes.>

Forms: Read, check S or B: 7 S/B 8 , 7 S/B 9 , 8 S/B 9 ?
Arrow diagrams based on reading:

_____ 10 < It is a large, older home.>

↓

_____ 11 < No one has lived there for years.>

↓

_____ 12 < The place is haunted.>

Forms: Read, check S or B: 10 S/B 11 , 10 S/B 12 , 11 S/B 12 ?
Arrow diagrams based on reading:

Final Diagram

_____ 13 < He has a fine record.>

↓

_____ 14 < Let's nominate him.>

↓

_____ 15 < People will vote for him.>

Forms: Read, check S or B: 13 S/B 14 , 13 S/B 15 , 14 S/B 15 ?
Arrow diagrams based on reading:

_____ 16 < The reactor core will melt down in 20 minutes.>

↓

_____ 17 < Sixty thousand people downwind will be irradiated.>

↓

_____ 18 <We've had a Loss of Coolant Accident uncovering the core.>

Forms: Read, check S or B: 16 S/B 17 , 16 S/B 18 , 17 S/B 18 ?
Arrow diagrams based on reading:

_____ 19 < Turn on Central Processing Unit and VDT.>

↓

_____ 20 < Boot the DOS in the 3.5" drive.>

↓

_____ 21 < Type DIR to get a directory.>

Forms: Read, check S or B: 19 S/B 20 , 19 S/B 21 , 20 S/B 21 ?
Arrow diagrams based on reading:

EXERCISE 5A

_____ 22 <I'm not going to the dance.>

↓

_____ 23 <I haven't a thing to wear>

↓

_____ 24 <People would gossip about me.>

Forms: Read, check S or B: 22 S/B 23, 22 S/B 24,23 S/B 24?
Arrow diagrams based on reading:

FINAL DIAGRAM

_____ 25 <It then appears reddish brown.>

↓

_____ 26 <It is extremely toxic.>

↓

_____ 27 <It becomes visible at a magnification of 60, 000x.>

Forms: Read, check S or B: 25 S/B 26, 25 S/B 27, 26 S/B 27?
Arrow diagrams based on reading:

_____ 28 <I've got to get an "A" in this course.>

↓

_____ 29 <I want to graduate this semester.>

↓

_____ 30 <I've got to get an over-all 2.0 average.>

Forms: Read, check S or B: 28 S/B 29, 28 S/B 30, 29 S/B 30?
Arrow diagrams based on reading:

_____ 31 <The couch and love seat are brick red.>

↓

_____ 32 <The carpet is forest green.>

↓

_____ 33 <The walls are white.>
Forms: Read, check S or B: 31 S/B 32, 31 S/B 33, 32 S/B 33?
Arrow diagrams based on reading:

EX5A-W: On a lined piece of paper write in pen (or type or word process) three original examples of serial reasoning (at least 9 statements). For originality, write about subjects you know about.

EXERCISE 5B: DEVELOPING A SENSE OF EVIDENCE AND CONNECTING PARTIAL DIAGRAMS

In some cases below one statement is a Basic Reason (BR) supporting an Intermediate Conclusion (IC) which supports the third as a Final Conclusion (FC). In others only two of the statements are related as evidence and conclusion. In still others none of the statements are so related. Do these problems as explained in Chapter 2, Section 1.

Problems

FINAL DIAGRAM

_____ 1 <We're going to win.>

_____ 2 <The ball went through the goal posts.>

_____ 3 <We're 3 points ahead with only 15 seconds to play.>

Forms: Read, check S or B: 1 S/B 2, 1 S/B 3, 2 S/B 3?
Arrow diagrams based on reading:

_____ 4 <Soybean futures are up 10%.>

_____ 5 <Corn is up 15%.>

_____ 6 <Winter wheat is off 5 points.>

Forms: Read, check S or B: 4 S/B 5, 4 S/B 6, 5 S/B 6?
Arrow diagrams based on reading:

_____ 7 <Martin Luther King's birthday is a holiday in 46 states.>

_____ 8 <It is not a holiday in Arizona.>

_____ 9 <Its' governor was a racist.>

Forms: Read, check S or B: 7 S/B 8, 7 S/B 9, 8 S/B 9?
Arrow diagrams based on reading:

EXERCISE 5B

FINAL DIAGRAM

_____ 10 <The refrigeration system has broken down.>

↓

_____ 11 <The harvested organs will be ruined in 6 hours.>

↓

_____ 12 <The power has failed.>

Forms: Read, check S or B: 10 S/B 11, 10 S/B 12, 11 S/B 12?
Arrow diagrams based on reading:

_____ 13 <The water was an incredible blue.>

↓

_____ 14 <The sand sparkled in the sun.>

↓

_____ 15 <The breeze blew gently.>

Forms: Read, check S or B: 13 S/B 14, 13 S/B 15, 14 S/B 15?
Arrow diagrams based on reading:

_____ 16 <They are out to kill us.>

↓

_____ 17 <We have to keep moving.>

↓

_____ 18 <We didn't even know them.>

Forms: Read, check S or B: 16 S/B 17, 16 S/B 18, 17 S/B 18?
Arrow diagrams based on reading:

_____ 19 <He fell 15,000 feet.>

↓

_____ 20 <He must have died instantly on impact.>

↓

_____ 21 <The parachute didn't open.>

Forms: Read, check S or B: 19 S/B 20, 19 S/B 21, 20 S/B 21?
Arrow diagrams based on reading:

FINAL DIAGRAM

_____ 22 <Giant corporations have tremendous influence on government.>

↓

_____ 23 <The Coast Guard approved Exxon's first slow, cheap,
        weak efforts to stop the flow.>

↓

_____ 24 <The oil slick got way out of control.>

Forms: Read, check S or B: 22 S/B 23, 22 S/B 24, 23 S/B 24?
Arrow diagrams based on reading:

_____ 25 <The headache went away shortly thereafter.>

↓

_____ 26 <She took aspirin.>

↓

_____ 27 <She had a low - blood pressure headache.>

Forms: Read, check S or B: 25 S/B, 25 S/B 27, 26 S/B 27?
Arrow diagrams based on reading:

_____ 28 <The opposing attorney was excellent.>

↓

_____ 29 <But the hearing went OK anyway.>

↓

_____ 30 <We'll do alright in the settlement phase.>

Forms: Read, check S or B: 28 S/B 29, 28 S/B 30, 29 S/B 30?
Arrow diagrams based on reading:

_____ 31 <I can't think of any more examples.>

↓

_____ 32 <I'm real tired.>

↓

_____ 33 <I'm going to quit.>

Forms: Read, check S or B: 31 S/B 32, 31 S/B 33, 32 S/B 33?
Arrow diagrams based on reading:

EX5B-W: On a lined piece of paper write in pen (or type or word process) three original examples of serial reasoning (at least 9 statements). For originality, write about subjects you know about.

EXERCISE 6A: CONNECTING PARTIAL DIAGRAMS

The following problems represent reasoning with 3 or more statements connected by inference indicators and sometimes connectives. Do them like the examples 1 through 6 in Chapter 2, Section 3. Be careful not to underline connective words or to draw arrows between the statements they connect. Underline indicators (1 point each). Write a partial diagram of each pair of statements. Then connect the partial diagrams into a complete arrow diagram. 1 pt. for each correct part of the complete diagrams, but no points if you don't write the correct partial diagram first, (at least 2 partials per problem).

Problems:

1. 1 and also 2, therefore 3. LINKED

2. Since 1 ; 2 and also 3 . DIVERGENT

3. 1. Additionally 2 , hence 3.   CONVERGENT

4. 1. Consequently 2 and besides which 3.   DIVERGENT

5. 1 as indicated by 2 , which follows from 3.

6. 1. That's why 2 and also 3. DIVERGENT

7. 1. Accordingly 2 , which bears out the point that 3 .

8. 1   on the grounds that 2 , because 3.

9. Since 3 , and since 4, it follows that 5.   LINKED

10. Since 3 and 4, consequently 5, hence 6 .   LINKED, then SERIAL

11. 1 may be deduced from 2 and 3. LINKED

ANGLE BRACKET, <...>, NUMBER AND DIAGRAM: Each indicator should be underlined separately. 12 and 13 have different completed diagrams. Treat 12 as an argument. 13 and 14, a Categorical Syllogism and a Conditional Argument, are traditional DEDUCTIVE arguments. ALWAYS put only ONE set of brackets around the WHOLE <If—then—.> statement.

12. He has a fever and spotty skin, so since he has the measles, you had better give him some aspirin.

13. All men are mortal, thus because Socrates is a man, Socrates is mortal.

14. If I can remember a large number of details, then I can do mistake - proof work on these exercises. I can do mistake - proof work on these exercises, for I can remember a large number of details.

EXERCISE 6B: CONNECTING PARTIAL DIAGRAMS

The following problems represent reasoning with 3 or more statements connected by inference indicators and sometimes connectives. Do them like the examples 1 through 6 in Chapter 2, Section 3. Be careful not to underline connective words or to draw arrows between the statements they connect. Underline indicators (1 point each). Write a partial diagram of each pair of statements. Then connect the partial diagrams into a complete arrow diagram. 1 pt. for each correct part of the complete diagrams, but no points if you don't write the correct partial diagrams first, (at least 2 partials per problem).

Problems:

1. 1 because 2 , as 3

2. 1 , for 2 and 3.   LINKED

3. 1. Consequently 2 , and 3.   DIVERGENT

4. 1. Also 2. Hence 3.   CONVERGENT

5. 1 which may be derived from 2 , which is entailed by 3.

6. 1. Therefore 2 and also 3.   DIVERGENT

7. 1 implies 2 , which suggests that 3 .

8. 1 as 2, since 3.

9. Being as 3 and 4, you see that 5.   LINKED

10. Supposing that 4 and 5, it follows that 6, so 7.   LINKED, then SERIAL

11. 1, on the assumptions that 2 and 3. LINKED

ANGLE BRACKET, <...>, NUMBER AND DIAGRAM: Each indicator should be underlined separately. 12 and 13 have different completed diagrams. Treat 12 as an argument. 13 and 14, a Categorical Syllogism and a Conditional Argument, are traditional DEDUCTIVE arguments. ALWAYS put only ONE set of brackets around the WHOLE <If—then—.> statement.

12. She won three very different events, thus because she is a very versatile athlete, we should give her a try-out for the Olympics.

13. All quadriplegics are physically nearly helpless without assistive technology, so since Jeff is a quadriplegic without assistive technology, he is nearly physically helpless too.

14. The next set of exercises should be easier. If they are easier, then I'll finish them quicker. So I should finish the next set of exercises quicker.

EXERCISE 7A: DIAGRAMING THE 4 BASIC ARGUMENT STRUCTURES

Each of these discourses is best analyzed as either Serial, Linked, Convergent or Divergent. There are 4 of each. Do them by the methods of Chapter Two, Sections Two and Three. Make partial diagrams under the problems and a final diagram to the right. Write the letters S, L, C, D and keep track of the numbers of cases of the 4 types of argument so you can decide which is which in difficult cases by a process of elimination.

PROBLEMS:

1. That's outgoing mail, and all outgoing mail is to be presorted, so sort it please.

2. The printer won't even print its' own self-test, so the problem must be in the printer itself, which implies that we won't get the job done before quitting time today.

3. I don't have any homework tonight. Mom sent me an extra $10.00. We should party tonight.

4. I've had two six-packs of beer already. There's a time out for an injury on the field. Now's the time to go to the john.

5. Visibility for star gazing will be great tonight because of a super - cold high pressure system moving in, so I'd better check out the furnace fuel oil supply also.

6. If there are faint fingerprints on the glass, then you will need good back lighting to get a good photo of them. There are faint fingerprints on the glass. So you will need good back lighting to get a good photo of them.

7. She ought to be promoted, because she's very reliable; as she got all that work done on time.

8. She's planning to cook a big dinner. I'd better get some cash for shopping. Also, I'd better pick up a bottle of Pepto-Bismol.

9. Nobody likes you because you are a loser, and people don't like losers.

10. Neutron activation analysis shows powder burns on his hand. His shoe tread fits prints at the scene of the crime. He is, therefore, a pretty good suspect. Hint: this is a typical inductive argument.

11. He has measles. His skin is spotty. Better put him to bed.

12. I just got a new car, so I guess I'll have a better social life now, but I'll also have more bills.

13. We'd be better off under a Republican administration. Besides, Dole has a better grip of foreign affairs than Clinton, so we should vote for Dole.

14. The dump leaks toxic stuff, so since it's dangerous, it ought to be closed.

15. We need an experienced man at that position. He's just been cut from the team and could be hired cheap, so let's make him an offer.

16. They've accepted our offer, so I'll be able to pay off my debts. Also, our business is likely to get new clients.

EX7A-W: On a lined piece of paper write in pen (or type or word process) 1 original example of each or the 4 types of arguments: serial, linked, convergent and divergent. Underline indicators, bracket, number and diagram your examples.

EXERCISE 7B: DIAGRAMING THE 4 BASIC ARGUMENT STRUCTURES

Each of these discourses is best analyzed as either Serial, Linked, Convergent or Divergent. There are 4 of each. Do them by the methods of Chapter Two, Sections Two and Three. Make partial diagrams under the problems and a final diagram to the right. Write the letters S, L, C, D and keep track of the numbers of cases of the 4 types of argument so you can decide which is which in difficult cases by a process of elimination.

Problems:

1. Papparazi's promises delivery in 30 minutes, so their delivery boys have to drive too fast, which is why several families have filed large wrongful death suits against them when their sons were killed trying to delivery a lousy pizza.

2. Music is a combination of sounds pleasing to the human ear and Heavy Metal is not pleasing to the human ear, so it's not music!

3. Smoking offends a lot of people. Besides, it is not good for my health, so I should quit.

4. I've been away from school about a week, so I'd better visit my girlfriend and also call my profs. to get the assignments I missed.

5. I don't like that guy very much. Also, I get a little car sick sometimes. So I won't go to the concert in his car.

6. Plant some trees or a garden. It's healthy exercise and it combats oxygen depletion in the atmosphere

7. Somebody's been in these woods before, because this line of pines is pretty straight, and straight lines of trees aren't produced naturally.

8. We should switch to sattelite dish. My brother says the reception is great. Also, it's cheaper in the long run.

9. You've wasted more material than the value of what you made and sold. Your appearance and behavior have cost us several customers. You're fired!

10. Paper suspected of bearing latent prints is best developed with chemical, because paper acts as a blotter when touched. Therefore, the latent prints will not rub off as they do on a nonporus surface.

11. There are no blood stains, so the victim must have been shot in the head elsewhere, because dead bodies don't bleed.

12. It is a strong material, and we need strength at this point. That's why we use it.

13. It's going to rain and then freeze, so I'd better get the studded tires on the car. But there's no sense in risking the trip to the ski resort.

14. The hands are badly charred, so call the police surgeon to amputate the fingers, so they can be sent to the lab for possible fingerprint identification.

15. The mid - winter thaw is coming, which means that all the potholes will get larger and the viruses will be reactivated.

16. The diet and exercise industry holds up a beauty ideal of a body so slim practically nobody looks like that, for they just want to make the most sales, as this gives them maximum profits.

EX7B-W: On a lined piece of paper write in pen (or type or word process) 1 original example of each or the 4 types of arguments: serial, linked, convergent and divergent. Underline indicators, bracket, number and diagram your examples.

EXERCISE 7C: LONGER PASSAGES FOR DIAGRAMING

Diagram the following longer discourses. Because they deal with technological or philosophical material, you will have to go to a dictionary and look up the meanings of some words. In later passages you may also have to look very hard for the main subjects and verbs and sometimes to put parentheses inside of parentheses to mark off whole claims contained inside other claims.

1. Since fluorescence examination to determine if two fragments of glass could have come from the same object requires glass to be absolutely clean, to preclude fluorescent reaction from contaminants, it must be washed in acetone, or similar solvent, and in water. Therefore caution should be exercised in that this exercise is not performed until after other examinations for fingerprints, surface debris and so forth have been completed.

2. Unplugging a malfunctioning VCR for about 10 minutes sometimes enables it to start working properly again, because the trouble was caused by a power surge causing bad data to be stored in its little computer, and unplugging for 10 minutes or more may allow the bad data to disappear out of its memory.

3. Modern crime lab techniques are highly scientific in nature and require the use of a variety of sophisticated equipment. It follows, therefore, that testimony in this field may be presented only by a qualified examiner testifying as an expert witness as defined in the manual for Courts - Martial. It also follows that the examiner must be able to qualify before the court to give expert testimony in the field of firearms identification.

4. Since the main cause of dirty or worn [VCR] heads is the material from which the tapes are made, the brand of tape you use can make a big difference in the life expectancy of the heads. Off brand bargain - basement video cassettes are usually no bargain in reality, because the money saved in the purchase price is lost many times over in the time and expense involved in extra head cleaning or even replacement.

5. Collection and laboratory analysis of glass fragments at a burglary scene may be worthwhile, for in the commission of a burglary the perpetrator may break a window or glass door and particles of glass which can be matched may stick to a suspect's gloves, pocket or trouser cuff.

6. Clean cut holes on the outside indicate that three shots were fired from outside into the room. However, because there is a clean cut hole on the inside with a greater diameter on the outside, we may conclude that at least one shot was fired from the inside outward.

7.   Since the pulses recorded on the top track of the tape determine, among other things, when the electronic circuitry inside the VCR switches back and forth between one video head and another, as well as the exact position of the rotating video heads at any given instant, the distance along the tape between the cylinder and the audio/control head is another critical adjustment.

       Since small variations in this distance from one VCR to another are inevitable, all VCR's have a front panel "customer tracking control" to enable the user to advance or delay these pulses to compensate for small variations in distance so as to get the best picture when playing back tapes recorded on other machines.

       This is why the tracking control sometimes must be adjusted to eliminate horizontal stripes or bands that look like scratches, or scratch lines in the picture, when you play a rented tape or a tape originally recorded on someone else's machine.

8. In sandy or loamy soils, the particles frequently lack cohesion, and the footprint is, therefore, fragile. Thus the impression should be strengthened with plastic spray or shellac. Hair spray makes a good substitute, if others are not immediately available, but because direct application could destroy details, the spray should be directed against a baffle, so a fine mist will settle gently into the footprint.

EXERCISE 7C

9.   Since I have a clear and distinct idea of myself in so far as I am only a thinking and not an extended being, and since I have a distinct idea of a body in so far as it is only an extended being which does not think, it is certain that this "I" , that is to say, my soul, by virtue of which I am what I am, is entirely distinct from my body and therefore can exist without it.

      ... there is a great difference between the mind and the body, in that the body, by its nature, is always divisible and the mind is completely indivisible. For, in reality, when I consider the mind, myself in so far as I am only a thinking being, I cannot distinguish any parts. I recognize and conceive quite clearly that I am a thing which is absolutely unitary and entire. And although the whole mind seems united with the whole body, nevertheless when a foot or arm or some other part is amputated I recognize that nothing has been lost to my mind on that account.

      - Rene Descartes (1596 - 1650).

9.   But, Descartes, it still remains to be explained, how that union or intermingling [of mind and body] is to be found in you, if you are incorporeal, unextended and indivisible. For if you are not greater than a point, how can you be united with the entire body, which is of great magnitude? How can you be united even with the brain, or even any part of it, since any part of it has some extension? If you are wholly without parts, how can you mix with its tiny parts? For there is no mixture unless each of the things to be mixed has parts that can mix with one another. - Pierre Gassendi (1592 - 1655)

10. Something exists in the understanding than which nothing greater can be conceived. That being, than which nothing greater can be conceived cannot exist in the understanding alone. For suppose it exists in the understanding alone: then it can be conceived to exist in reality, which is greater. Hence there is no doubt that there exists a being than which nothing greater can be conceived, and it exists both in the understanding and in reality... and this being thou art, O Lord, our God. -The Ontological Argument, Anselm of Canterbury (1033 - 1109).

11. In nature there are things which can be or not be, since they are found to be generated and to disintegrate, and consequently, they are possible to be and not to be. But it is impossible for such things to exist always, for that which is possible to not be at some time is not. Therefore, if everything is possible to not be, then at sometime before now there could have been nothing in existence. But if this were true, then even now there would be nothing in existence, because that which does not exist only comes into existence by something already existing. Therefore, if at one time there was nothing in existence, it would have been impossible for anything to have begun to exist. Thus, even now nothing would have been in existence. But things do exist now. Therefore not all beings are merely possible. So there must exist something whose existence is necessary, and this being is what we mean by "God".

    -The Cosmological Argument Thomas Aquinas (1224- 1274).

12. The universe looks and operates in many ways like a machine, for example, a watch. A watch has parts which have regular shapes, the parts are not all of the same material, the parts move in regular motions. The same can be said about the planets and stars of the universe. If somebody was walking in an empty field and stubbed his toe on a rock, he might think it was always there. But if he stepped on a watch, he couldn't say it was always there, because it seems obviously designed. Design requires the existence of a designer. Since the universe is obviously designed also, we must conclude that it, too, has a designer (God). - The Design Argument William Paley (1743-1805)

13. Some people are born healthy, some ill, and some retarded or even terribly deformed. Some are born to wealth and long, comfortable lives, others to poverty, pain, disease and death within a year. So life is not fair. If there exists a merciful and just God, then life is fair. So there does not exist a merciful and just God.

EXERCISE 7C

14. AN ESSAY CONCERNING THE TRUE ORIGINAL, EXTENT AND END OF CIVIL GOVERNMENT
Chapter 1

It having been shewn in the foregoing discourse:

1. That Adam had not, either by natural right of fatherhood or by positive donation from God, any such authority over his children, or dominion over the world, as is pretended.

2. That if he had, his heirs yet had no right to it.

3. That if his heirs, there being no law of nature nor positive law of God that determines which is the right heir in all cases that may arise, the right of succession, and consequently of bearing rule, could not have been certainly determined.

4. That if even that had been determined, yet the knowledge of which is the eldest line of Adam's posterity, being so long since utterly lost, that in the races of mankind and families of the world there remains not to one above another the least pretense to be the eldest house, and to have the right of inheritance.

All these premises having, as I think, been clearly made out. it is impossible that the rulers now on earth should make any benefit, or derive any the least shadow of authority from that which is held to be the foundation of all power, Adam's private dominion and paternal jurisdiction; so that he that will not give just occasion to think that all government in the world is the product only of force and violence, and that men live together by no other rules but that of beasts, where the strongest carries it, and so lay a foundation for perpetual disorder and mischief, tumult, sedition, and rebellion (things that the followers of that hypothesis so loudly cry out against), must of necessity find out another rise of government, another original of political power, and another way of designing and knowing the persons that have it, than what Sir Robert Filmer hath taught us. (John Locke)

15. ANTIMONY OF PURE REASON[1]: Third Conflict of Transcendental Ideas

Thesis

Causality according to the laws of nature, is not the only causality operating to originate the phenomena of the world. A causality of freedom is also necessary to account fully for these phenomena.

Proof

Let it be supposed, that there is no other kind of causality than that according to the laws of nature. Consequently, everything that happens presupposes a previous condition, which it follows with absolute certainty, in conformity with a rule. But this previous condition must itself be something that has happened (that has arisen in time, as it did not exist before), for if it has always been in existence, its consequence or effect would not thus originate for the first time, but would likewise have always existed. The causality, therefore, of a cause, whereby something happens, is itself a thing that has happened. Now this again presupposes, in conformity with the law of nature, a previous condition and its causality, and this another anterior to the former, and so on. If, then, everything happens solely in accordance with the laws of nature, there cannot be any real first beginning of things, but only a subaltern or comparative beginning. There cannot, therefore, be a completeness of series on the side of the causes which originate the one from the other. But the law of nature is, that nothing can happen without a sufficient a priori determined cause. The proposition, therefore— if all causality is possible only in accordance with the laws of nature— is, when stated in this unlimited and general manner, self-contradictory. It follows that this cannot be the only kind of causality.

Thesis

From what has been said, it follows that a causality must be admitted, by means of which something happens, without its cause being determined according to necessary laws by some other cause preceding. That is to say, there must exist an absolute spontaneity of cause, which of itself originates a series of phenomena which proceeds according to natural laws— consequently transcendental freedom, without which even in the course of nature the succession of phenomena on the side of causes is never complete.

Antithesis

There is no such thing as freedom but everything in the world happens solely according to the laws of nature.

Proof

Granted, that there does exist freedom in the transcendental sense, as a peculiar kind of causality, operating to produce events in the world — a faculty, that is to say, of originating a state, and consequently a series of consequences from that state. In this case, not only the series originated by this spontaneity, but the determination of this spontaneity itself to the production of the series, that is to say, the causality itself must have an absolute commencement, such, that nothing can precede to determine this action according to unvarying laws. But every beginning of action presupposes in the acting cause a state of inaction; and a dynamically primal beginning of action presupposes a state, which has no connection — as regard causality— with the preceding state of the cause—which does not, that is, in any wise result from it. Transcendental freedom is therefore opposed to the natural law of cause and effect, and such a conjunction of successive states in effective causes is destructive of the possibility of unity in experience, and for that reason not to be found in experience—is consequently a mere fiction of thought.

We have, therefore, nothing but nature to which we must look for connection and order is cosmical events. Freedom —independence of the laws of nature — is certainly a deliverance from restraint, but it is also a relinquishing of the guidance of law and rule. For it cannot be alleged, that, instead of the laws of nature, laws of freedom may be introduced into the causality of the course of nature. For, if freedom were determined according to laws, it would be no longer freedom, but merely nature. Nature, therefore, and transcendental freedom are distinguishable as conformity to law and lawlessness. The former imposes upon understanding the difficulty of seeking the origin of evens ever higher and higher in the series of causes, inasmuch as causality is always conditioned thereby; while it compensates this labor by the guarantee of a unity complete and in conformity with law. The latter, on the contrary, holds out tot he understanding the promise of a point of rest in the chain of causes, by conducting it to an unconditioned causality, which professes to have the power of spontaneous origination, but which, it its own utter blindness, deprives it of the guidance of rules, by which alone a completely connected experience is possible.

1. Reprinted from <u>Great Books of the Western World,</u> copyright 1952, 1990, Encyclopedia Britannica, Inc.

EXERCISE 8A: DISTINGUISHING CLAIMS FROM REASONING

Use the table in Chapter Three, Section Two to draw a straight, evenly dark line through the whole of those of the following sentences which represent misuses of the evaluation adjectives of critical thinking (or mark "A" on a multiple choice form for those that make sense and "B" for those that should be crossed out.) Locate the noun at the end on the Statements side or the Reasoning side. Then look down to see whether that the adjective in front of it does or does not apply to that type of noun.

1. That's a deductive assertion.

2. That's a false proof.

3. That's a valid explanation.

4. That's a proven claim.

5. That's a deductive explanation.

6. That's a weak proposition.

7. That's a deductive statement.

8. That's a weak statement.

9. That's a valid proposition.

10. That's an invalid argument.

11. That's a true deduction.

12. That's a valid proof.

13. That's a true statement.

14. That's a warranted argument.

15. That's an inductive claim.

16. That's a true induction.

17. That's a strong argument.

18. That's a valid deduction.

19. That's a false argument.

20. That's a true argument.

21. That's an inductive argument.

22. That's a sound argument.

23. That's a strong statement.

24. That's a valid statement.

25. That's a unwarranted assertion.

26. That's an unproven argument.

27. That's an unsound conclusion.

28. That's a false conclusion.

29. That's an unwarranted truth.

30. That's a sound reason.

31. That's a warranted proof.

32. That's a deductive proof.

33. That's a strong induction.

EXERCISE 8B: DISTINGUISHING CLAIMS FROM REASONING

Use the table in Chapter Three, Section Two to draw a straight, evenly dark line through the whole of those of the following sentences that represent misuses of the evaluation adjectives of critical thinking (or mark "A" on a multiple choice form for those that make sense and "B" for those that should be crossed out.) Locate the noun at the end on the Statements side or the Reasoning side. Then look down to see whether that the adjective in front of it does or does not apply to that type of noun.

1. That's a true argument.

2. That's a deductive argument

3. That's a false assumption.

4. That's an invalid truth.

5. That's a strong argument.

6. That's a nil claim.

7. That's a sound reason.

8. That's a warranted truth.

9. That's an inductive conclusion.

10. That's a moderate argument.

11. That's an unproven demonstration.

12. That's a false argument.

13. That's a true statement.

14. That's a weak explanation.

15. That's an deductive assertion.

16. That's a proven truth.

17. That's a weak falsehood.

18. That's a moderate statement.

19. That's deductive reasoning

20. That's a valid reason.

21. That's an inductive proposition.

22. That's false reasoning.

23. That's invalid reasoning.

24. That's a valid claim.

25. That's a warranted demonstration.

26. That's a false assertion.

27. That's an unsound argument.

28. That's a weak conclusion.

29. That's unwarranted reasoning.

30. That's an valid truth.

31. That's a moderate reason.

32. That's an inductive argument.

33. That's a weak proof.

EXERCISE 9A: EVALUATING THE DEGREE OF SUPPORT REASONS GIVE TO A CONCLUSION

Diagram each problem. Then judge the degree of support each reason or set of reasons gives to its conclusion and write one of the degree of support phrases, "Deductively Valid", "Strong", "Moderate", "Weak", or "Nil" beside each arrow in the argument. The Magic Question of Chapter Four, Section Two is formulated right after each problem. Where the answer to it is "Yes", provide an explanation of how the reason(s) could all be true and the conclusion false. You may do this by answering the specific question or by the Inconsistency or Logical Analogy methods of Chapter Four, Section Four.

Points will be awarded for each correct judgment of degree of support and explanation. Emphasis is on getting the correct degree of support and an explanation of how the reasons can be true and the conclusion false in cases of less than deductive validity. However, if you don't even get the argument diagramed correctly, your answer will be worthless, so you must diagram the discourse correctly to get credit.

PROBLEMS

1. The bag is completely filled with stones, so it must be very heavy. (Can it be that the bag is completely filled with stones and yet it is NOT very heavy? How?)

2. He said that he will never take another drink. So he won't get drunk any more. (Can it be that he said that he will never take another drink and yet he does get drunk another time? How?)

3. He will never take another drink. So he won't get drunk any more. (Can it be that he will never take another drink and yet he does get drunk another time? How?)

4. This glass is exactly half full, so it is exactly half empty. (Can it be that this glass is exactly half full and yet that it is not exactly half empty? How?)

5. I don't even know him, so he's not a friend of mine. (Can it be that I don't even know him and yet he is a friend of mine? How?)

6. I have a super strong impression that this chick in my class likes me, so when I ask her for a date, she'll say "yes". (Can it be that I have a super strong impression that this chick in my class likes me and yet when I ask her for a date, she will not say "yes"? How?)

7. It has been snowing off and on for three days, so final exams will probably be postponed. (Can it be that It has been snowing off and on for three days, and yet final exams will probably not be postponed? How?)

8. If the disk drive is bad, then it won't boot the program. Aha! It does boot the program. So the drive isn't bad. (Can it be that If the disk drive is bad, then it won't boot the program and It does boot the program, and yet the drive is bad?)

9. If the unit is getting less than 135 volts, it won't work. It is getting less, so it won't work. (Can it be that If the unit is getting less than 135 volts, it won't work and It is getting less, and yet it will work?)

10. She drives a very expensive foreign car, so her dad must make a pile of money, so I guess dad must be a very good stock broker. (Can it be that She drives a very expensive foreign car and yet her dad does not make a pile of money? And can it be that her dad makes a pile of money and yet her dad is not a very good stock broker?)

EX 9A-W: Arguing Opposite viewpoints. Write 6 brief arguments, one for each of the following conclusions. Make each argument as strong as possible. Circle, bracket, number, diagram, and evaluate each of your arguments.

11a. Abortion is murder.

11b. Abortion is a woman's right to choose.

12a. Concealable handguns ought to be prohibited by law.

12b. Everyone ought to be required to own a handgun.

13a. Recording companies should be required to put warning labels on recordings with possibly offensive language in them.

13b. Recording companies should not be required to put warning labels on recordings with possibly offensive language in them.

EXERCISE 9B: EVALUATING THE DEGREE OF SUPPORT REASONS GIVE TO CONCLUSIONS

Diagram each problem. Then judge the degree of support each reason or set of reasons gives to its conclusion and write one of the degree of support phrases, "Deductively Valid", "Strong", "Moderate", "Weak", or "Nil" beside each arrow in the argument. The Magic Question of Chapter Four, Section Two is formulated right after each problem. Where the answer to it is "Yes", provide an explanation of how the reason(s) could all be true and the conclusion false. You may do this by answering the specific question or by the Inconsistency or Logical Analogy methods of Chapter Four, Section Four.

Points will be awarded for each correct judgment of degree of support and explanation. Emphasis is on getting the correct degree of support and an explanation of how the reasons can be true and the conclusion false in cases of less than deductive validity. However, if you don't even get the argument diagramed correctly, your answer will be worthless, so you must diagram the discourse correctly to get credit.

1. Jack had sex with Tina and now she is pregnant, so he ought to marry her. (Can it be that Jack had sex with Tina and now she is pregnant, and yet he ought not to marry her? How?)

2. I lost my keys over there in the alley, but I'm looking for them over here under the lamppost because the light is better. (Can it be that I lost my keys over there in the alley and the light is better under the lamppost and yet I'm not looking for them under the lamppost? How?)

3. Hillary Clinton is a man, so he is a male. (Can it be that Hillary Clinton is a man, and yet he is not a male? How?)

4. The burden of proof is on the maker of a claim to prove it. For this reason, persons are considered innocent until proven guilty. (Can it be that the burden of proof is on the maker of a claim to prove it and yet persons are not considered innocent until proven guilty?)

5. The snow is up to his waist, so it must be 3 feet deep. (Can it be that The snow is up to his waist, and yet it is not 3 feet deep? How?)

6. I was born in 1940, so I am not the young man who was your friend on the USS Coral Sea in 1956. (Can it be that I was born in 1940, and yet I am the young man who was your friend on the USS Coral Sea in 1956? How?)

7. I know that 729 will win the Daily Number Lottery today, so 729 will win the Daily Number Lottery today. (Can it be true that I know that 729 will win the Daily Number Lottery today, and yet 729 will not win the Daily Number Lottery today? How?)

8. I hope that 729 will win the Daily Number Lottery today, so 729 will win the Daily Number Lottery today. (Can it be true that I hope that 729 will win the Daily Number Lottery today, and yet 729 will not win the Daily Number Lottery today? How?)

9. Causes are events and Free Will isn't an event, so Free Will can't be the cause of actions. (Can it be true that causes are events and Free Will isn't an event, and yet Free Will is the cause of actions?)

10. You are out of Budweiser, so you are out of beer, so you better drive down to the grocery store and buy some more. (Can it be that You are out of Budweiser, and yet you are not out of beer? How? Can it be that you are out of beer, and yet you better not drive down to the grocery store and buy some more. How?)

EX 9B-W Arguing Opposite viewpoints. Write 6 brief arguments, one for each of the following conclusions. Make each argument as strong as possible. Circle, bracket, number, diagram, and evaluate each of your arguments.

11a. There should be required minimum prison sentences for drug trafficking crimes.

11b. No, Judges should have the power to set punishments for drug trafficking crimes.

12a. Any sex a woman has after firmly saying "no" is rape.

12b. Some sex a woman has to be "talked into" is not rape.

13a. Public colleges should admit any in-state high school graduate, even those who graduated in the fourth lowest quintile (20%) or the bottom quintile of their graduating classes.

13b. High school graduates who graduate in the fourth or bottom quintile should have to pay for private college until their grades show that tax financed colleges should admit them.

EXERCISE 9C: EVALUATING THE DEGREE OF SUPPORT REASONS GIVE TO A CONCLUSION

Diagram each problem. Then judge the degree of support each reason or set of reasons gives to its conclusion and write one of the degree of support phrases, "Deductively Valid", "Strong", "Moderate", "Weak", or "Nil" beside each arrow in the argument. The Magic Question of Chapter Four, Section Two is formulated right after each problem. Where the answer to it is "Yes", provide an explanation of how the reason(s) could all be true and the conclusion false. You may do this by answering the specific question or by the Inconsistency or Logical Analogy methods of Chapter Four, Section Four.

Points will be awarded for each correct judgment of degree of support and explanation. Emphasis is on getting the correct degree of support and an explanation of how the reasons can be true and the conclusion false in cases of less than deductive validity. However, if you don't even get the argument diagramed correctly, your answer will be worthless, so you must diagram the discourse correctly to get credit.

PROBLEMS

1. Forrest Gump to his banker: I still have checks left, so I can't be overdrawn. (Can it be that I still have checks left and yet I can be overdrawn? How?)

2. I still have more money in my account than the total of my uncashed checks, any automatic withdrawals, and bank fees, so I can't be overdrawn. (Can it be that I still have more money in my account than the total of my uncashed checks, any automatic withdrawals, and bank fees, and yet I can be overdrawn?)

3. No human athlete has ever jumped more than 27 feet in the running broad jump, so no human athlete will ever jump more than 30 feet. (Can it be that no human athlete has ever jumped more than 27 feet in the running broad jump and yet that some human athlete will jump more than 30 feet?)

4. No human athlete ever observed has jumped more than 27 feet in the running broad jump and we have observed all jumps of all human athletes who ever will jump in the running broad jump, so none of them will ever jump over 30 feet. (Can it be that no human athlete ever observed has jumped more than 27 feet in the running broad jump and we have observed all jumps of all human athletes who ever will jump in the running broad jump, and yet that one of them will jump over 30 feet?)

5. Forrest Gump's letter to his mother : I know you can't read fast Momma, that's why I'm typing very slowly. (Can it be that I know you can't read fast, and yet I'm not typing very slowly?)

6. You are out of beer, so you are out of Budweiser beer. (Can it be that You are out of beer, and yet you are not out of Budweiser beer? How?)

7. I can hear music coming from the basement, so the TV must be on down there. (Can it be that I can hear music coming from the basement, and yet the TV is not on down there? How?)

8. The cocaine sampled in this seized shipment, at least in 93 of the 100 bags seized, was 100% pure. We conclude that the whole shipment was pure cocaine. (Can it be that the cocaine sampled in this seized shipment, at least in 93 of the 100 bags seized, was 100% pure and yet that less than the whole shipment was pure cocaine?)

9. The dogs are getting very excited, so we must be getting close to the suspect. (Can it be that the dogs are getting very excited, and yet we are not getting close to the suspect? How?)

10. There are 5 people in that professional band and that is one more than we can afford to pay, so you had better get another band. (Can it be that there are 5 people in that professional band and that is one more than we can afford to pay and yet you had better not get another band?)

EX. 9C-W Arguing Opposite viewpoints. Write 6 brief arguments, one for each of the following conclusions. Make each argument as strong as possible. Circle, bracket, number, diagram, and evaluate each of your arguments.

11a. School administrators should have a right without getting a warrant to have any student, his or her locker or room searched and to confiscate any prohibited things found.

11b. School administrators should not have a right without getting a warrant to search any student, his or her locker or room and to confiscate any prohibited things found.

12a. Traditional one - man, one - woman legal marriages ought to have legal advantages over other types of family structures.

12b. Traditional one - man, one - woman legal marriages ought not to have legal advantages over other types of family structures.

13a. U.S. companies having legal freedom to open and close plants anywhere in the world is in the best interest of the American people.

13b. U.S. companies having legal freedom to open and close plants anywhere in the world is not in the best interest of the American people.

EXERCISE 10:   SEMANTIC CLARIFICATION

In each of the following discourses there is an ambiguous word or phrase. Use the method of semantic clarification in Chapter Five to translate the statement which is ambiguous so that the different senses of the ambiguous word or phrase are made clear. If an inference is drawn, diagram it by writing out the reason, drawing a line under it, an arrow down and writing out the conclusion translated if necessary. Put the correct degree of support word, "Nil", "Weak", etc., beside the arrow. Hint: first read carefully and ask yourself: "Exactly what word or phrase is ambiguous here, and what two phrases can I most economically use to express these different senses?"

1. Person A says: "Stiff opposition is expected to funeral director's plans for casketless funerals." Person B replies: "I disagree. How would you know? Those kind of customers are notoriously the silent, uncomplaining type."

2. A militia man says: "I named my new rifle 'Bill Clinton.' So I should not be arrested for threatening the President when I say 'I'm going to shoot Bill Clinton.'"

3. Improbable events happen every day. But what happens every day is a very probable event. So improbable events are very probable events.

4. All seaplanes are boats and boats are permitted to go within 100 yards of the beach, so seaplanes are permitted to go within 100 yards of the beach.

5. No human being can presume to decide who deserves to live or to die. Euthanasia ("Mercy killing") consists of a human being deciding that another deserves to die. So no human being can presume to commit euthanasia.

6. Mary's conception of Jesus was immaculate and "immaculate" means "clean of sex", so sex must be dirty.

7. The more you study, the more you know. The more you know, the more you forget. The more you forget, the less you know. But anything which causes you to know less is contrary to the aims of education. So studying is contrary to the aims of education.

8. Person A says: "When they got married, a five year friendship ended at the altar." Person B replies: "I guess they should never have gotten married."

9. Person A says: "The newspaper says the defendant's speech ended in a long sentence." Person B says: "Do you really think anybody counted the words?"

10. A woman isn't pregnant until the fertilized egg has attached itself to her uterine wall or somewhere else. So RU 486 is really a contraceptive, not an "abortion pill."

EXERCISE 11A: TRANSLATION INTO CATEGORICAL FORM

For each of the following, eliminate the negation phrase by identifying the type of statement it applies to and using the Square of Opposition diagonals to rewrite the statement as its contradictory. Example: It is false that almost all F are G. "Almost all F are G" is a B type. The table says the negation of a B is a G type. Write "Many F are not G."

1. It is false that most F are G. = _____
2. It is not the case that many F are G. = _____
3. It is not true that no F are G. = _____
4. It is false that Few F are G. = _____
5. Not Many F are not G. = _____

Singular subjects frequently translate into universal quantifications. Examples: "Whales are mammals" = "All whales are mammals" "Bats *aren't* birds" = "*No* bats are birds." But "Bats flew in my window" = "*Some* bats flew in my window." Articles: "A," "An," "This," "That," "These," "Those S are P" translate into "All S are P." If the verb is followed by "not," make it negative. Proper names and abstract nouns require creation of a plural *unit class*, a class with only one member. Insert a parameter into the subject and make the verb plural. Examples: "Socrates is mortal" = "All *persons who are* Socrates are mortals." "Socrates is *not* mortal" = "*No* persons who are Socrates are mortals." "That lake is *not* polluted" = "No *lakes which are that* lake are polluted lakes." "Violence is never justified" = "No violent acts re justified acts." Sometimes a parameter required is abstract and you have to ask "What does subject F come in, acts, principles, instances, cases, pieces, items?" Force the following standard form:
Standard Quantifier (plural noun phrase) are (plural noun phrase.)

1. Pigs are cloven-hoofed animals. = _____
2. There are deer in the field. = _____
3. This pen is leaky. = _____
4. Music is a combination of sounds. = _____
5. Newton unifed the laws of Galileo and Kepler. = _____
6. I am not a great self-promoter. = _____
7. Knowledge is power. = _____
8. Bloody clothes were found at the scene. = _____
9. Truth is beautiful. = _____
10. George Washington was the first U.S. President. = _____

Sophomoric generalizations are unquantified ones. The student has to decide for him or herself how many F's they are true of. Remember that predicates of affirmatives are minimally distributed, i.e., "Some F are G" = "Some F are *some* G" and that subcontrariess like I and O can both be true. For example, "Women are less intelligent than men" is probably true only as meaning "Some women are less intelligent than some men" and can be true at the same time as "Some men are less intelligent than some women" is also true.

For each of the following, supply the *maximum* quantifier that you think allows the statement to be true.

1. <u>Swans are white.</u> =   <u>Swans are white.</u>

2. <u>Men expect their wives to be virgins.</u> =   <u>Men expect their wives to be virgins.</u>

3. <u>People who fall for cults are stupid.</u> =   <u>People who fall for cults are stupid.</u>

4. <u>Asians are smarter than Caucasians.</u> =   <u>Asians are smarter than Caucasians.</u>

5. <u>Atheists are immoral or amoral.</u> =   <u>Atheists are immoral or amoral.</u>

6. <u>Native Americans are alcoholics.</u> =   <u>Native Americans are alcoholics.</u>

7. <u>Plane triangles have 180 degrees.</u> =   <u>Plane triangles have 180 degrees.</u>

8. <u>Whites are stronger than Blacks.</u> =   <u>Whites are stronger than Blacks.</u>

9. <u>Religions say humans are sinful.</u> =   <u>Religions say humans are sinful.</u>

EXERCISE IIB: TRANSLATION INTO CATEGORICAL FORM

Translate each of the following into standard form. First, decide whether it is (and write after it) "affirmative" or "negative." Second, decide whether it is (and write) "universal," "predominant," "majority," "common," or "particular." Third, write the appropriate quantifier to start: "All," "No," "Almost all," "Few," "Most," "Many," or "Some." Fourth, find the subject/verb break and put parenthesis around the subjects and predicate, leaving out quantifiers. Fifth, where necessary, insert "are," a parameter and "that," to make predicates into noun phrases. Sixth, rewrite any statement with a singular subject as a Universal with a unit class subject. Examples: "Socrates is mortal" = *"All people who are Socrates are mortal people."* "Justice is never unfair" = *" No acts of justice are unfair acts."* Seventh, get rid of any negation like "It is false that ..." by translating the following statement into its contradictory. Standard form: Standard quantifier, subject noun phrase, "are," possibley "not" and predicate noun phrase.

1. Quite a few students went to the game.

2. Not many of the students became disruptive.

3. When you walk through a storm hold your head up high.

4. A lot of men died.

5. Wherever you go, there you are.

6. Once in a while, guys like you get a break.

7. If it's a Volvo, it's the safest car a medium amount of money can buy.

8. People who are not aggressive self-promoters are rarely successful.

9. Disease among the colonists is extremely widespread.

10. Just a few friends will be coming over tonight.

11. It's true that most of the people invited did not show up.

12. If the Philistine smite thee, smite him hip and thigh.

13. Only those who memorize translation tips will pass.

14. Not only a few gamblers have lost money in Las Vegas.

15. These roses are wilting.

16. Except for those who do not study, no one will fail this next test.

17. Scarcely a day goes by that I do not think of her.

18. The only fortifications on the western salient are stockade fences.

19. None but the king governs by divine right.

20. Gangsta rap is quite frequently profane.

21. Wise are they who prepare for the future. Hint: What state of being is mentioned ? (that's the predicate!) Who is said to be this way? (subject)

22. Whites always have long noses like a dog's snout.

23. Justice is always fair.

24. The book you seek is on the desk.

25. Whenever you hear the bell, you start salivating.

26. Any friend of John's is a friend of mine.

27. All persons are welcome who have struggled against injustice.

28. Every one of the ten men in the patrol was killed.

29. Less than five people in a thousand have HIV.

30. Twisted Sister did a lot of good numbers.

31. It is false that "police psychics" have ever provided specific clues which solved cases.

32. Ben Franklin participated in debunking Mesmer's theory of "animal Magnetism."

33. Inheritance of acquired characteristics is totally mythical.

34. When the Rapture comes, you'll know it.

35. Several students stayed after the lecture.

EXERCISE 11C: CONVERSION

For each write the valid converse, or write "no valid converse."

1. No R are F

2. Many G are not A

3. Some S are not J

4. Almost all non J are L

5. Some non M are non Z

6. No R are non G

7. Few T are G

8. Most non Q are not W

9. Some non A are not J

10. Some A are non J

11. Few T are non G

12. Almost all F are H

13. No non W are M

14. No M are non W

15. Some Z are non I

16. Many Y are M

17. Most P are not T

18. No T are non J

19. All R are L

20. Some non Q are L

EXERCISE IID: CONTRAPOSITION

For each write the valid contrapositive, or "no valid contrapositive."

1. Some non P are non J _____

2. Some non P are not non J _____

3. Many F are not A _____

4. Almost all G are N _____

5. All G are non N _____

6. All non N are non G _____

7. Most N are not G _____

8. Many G are U _____

9. All U are P _____

10. All non P are non U _____

11. Many R are not non Q _____

12. Some R are not non Q _____

13. Few T are B _____

14. Some non T are not non B _____

15. Some B are not T _____

16. Almost all M are I _____

17. Most L are B _____

18. Some non B are not no L _____

19. Almost all T are J _____

20. Few D are E _____

EXERCISE 11E: OBVERSION

For each write the obverse.

1. Most F are non E

2. No G are E

3. Almost all non A are non B

4. Some X are not non Z

5. Many non L are not non M

6. Some P are T

7. Some non P are non T

8. Some T are P

9. Some non T are non P

10. Few A are B

11. Few A are non B

12. Many F are non G

13. Most H are not non I

14. Most I are non H

15. Most H are I

16. Most non H are I

17. No G are D

18. Almost all S are F

19. Few J are non K

20. Few non K are J

EXERCISE 12A: DETERMINING THE VALIDITY OR INVALIDITY OF SYLLOGISMS

Do these problems by the method of Extended Syllogistic Logic in Chapter Six. Make a linked arrow diagram to be sure of getting the right conclusion first, translate into standard form, make a cross hatch and show rules satisfied or violated. Watch out for complements that need to be reduced. Remove unnecessary words and sentences.

1. All the basketball players on my team are people contracted to sports shoe advertisers and not just a few players on my team are All-stars, thus some people contracted to sports shoe advertisers are All-stars.

2. Only hard workers get A's in logic. Jill gets A's in logic, so Jill is a hard worker.

3. Only hard workers get A's in logic. Jill is a hard worker, so Jill gets A's in logic.

4. Many spiders are poisonous. On the other hand, many spiders appear to be completely harmless. It naturally follows that many things that appear to be completely harmless are actually poisonous.

5. Unfortunately, a few predators that eat human beings are members of an endangered species. So since almost no Siberian tigers are predators that eat human beings, some Siberian tigers are not members of an endangered species.

6. Only very big contributors can get access to the top politicians and you aren't a very big contributor, so you can't get access to the top politicians.

7. Few insane persons are confined to mental hospitals so, since most people confined to mental hospitals are violent paranoids, some violent paranoids are not sane people.

8.   If you are thinking about manufacturing for the American market, remember that women who wear petites are short, and most American women are not short, so many of them don't wear wear petites.

9. Many addicts will end up dead in some alley, because no addicts voluntarily check into methadone clinics, and few people who voluntarily check into methadone clinics end up dead in some alley.

10. Almost all natural skin condoms are very expensive and many of them present a danger of AIDS virus getting through, so some expensive prophylactics present a danger of AIDS virus getting through them.

11. No people in this car are claustrophobic, for not one claustrophobic likes to take long car rides and everybody in this car is a person who likes to take long car rides.

12. Many "drink till you puke" parties are well attended and most fraternity parties are "drink till you puke" events, so some fraternity parties are well attended.

13. Some gullible suckers are not students at this school, because quite a lot of students at this school are critical thinkers and no critical thinkers are gullible suckers.

EXERCISE 12A

14. All staff meetings called by Foster are very unpleasant and nerve - wracking. Jack said that yesterday's staff meeting was pleasant and relaxed, so Foster must not have called yesterday's staff meeting.

15. It is false that any wimps are Assistant Principals, since no wimps are macho dudes and every Assistant Principal is a macho dude.

16. Some geniuses are Hispanic. Thus some of the Hispanic are very talented, because all geniuses are very talented.

17. All Top 40 songs are heavily promoted and some lousy lyrics are Top 40 songs, so some lousy lyrics are heavily promoted.

18. Almost all people who rationalize are self - deceivers, thus because all self deceivers are wishful thinkers, many rationalizers are wishful thinkers.

19. Almost all untreated sewage effluent is dangerous and no dangerous material is acceptable fertilizer, so most untreated sewage effluent is not acceptable fertilizer.

20. Very few candidates discuss the real issues, but a few elected officials discuss the real issues, so some elected officials are not candidates.

21. Most politicians are con artists and all con artists are non-violent thieves, so many politicians are non-violent thieves.

22. No right-brain dominated people do well at logic. Thus because many artists are right brain dominated people, some artists do not do well at logic.

23. Most home improvement repair is a pain in the fanny, but some of it is work necessary to keeping the value of a home, so some work necessary to keeping the value of a home is a pain in the fanny.

24. Some kids who get too easy access to guns are ruined for life. This is because some kids who get too easy access to guns become teenage murderers and all teenage murderers are ruined for life.

25. Many who pray are self - deceivers and all wishful thinkers are self deceivers; accordingly many who pray are wishful thinkers.

26. Few grizzly bears are still in hibernation on Ground Hog's Day. Hence a lot of grizzly bears are animals who live in Yellowstone Park, for few of the animals who live in Yellowstone Park are still in hibernation on Ground Hog's Day.

27. Almost all of the carnivores that live in the Serengetti are scavengers. This is true on the grounds that quite a few of the carnivores that live in the Serengetti are jackals, and all jackals are scavengers.

EXERCISE 12A

28. It is clear that no dolphins are friendly to humans, because almost all dolphins are animals that live in the ocean, and many animals that live in the ocean are not friendly to humans.

29. Only those events that have happened are events that anyone has seen. No future events are events that have happened, so no future events are events anyone has seen.

30. Most owls are birds that hunt at night. Quite a few birds that eat mice are owls, so many birds that eat mice are birds that hunt at night.

31. Almost all true feminists are politically correct, and only women can be politically correct, so not just a few women are feminists.

32. Almost all concert pianists are Scotch drinkers and not many Scotch drinkers fail to have a taste for the good life. Accordingly, many concert pianists have a taste for the good life.

33. Some jobs aren't well paid and no jobs are guarantees of a high income, so some guarantees of a high income are not well paid.

34. The Bible forbids capital punishment, because one of the commandments in the Bible is not to kill, and capital punishment is killing.

35. Some men over 45 are not men trained in guerrilla warfare, for almost all active Rangers are men trained in guerrilla warfare and no active Rangers are men over 45.

36. Most people who live in trailers are unsafe in a tornado, hence some young families are unsafe in a tornado, because many people who live in trailers are young families.

37. Most gill nets are pretty good at killing dolphins and many nets used by commercial fishermen are gill nets, so many of their nets are good at killing dolphins.

38. No experiences which can be produced by electrical stimulation of the brain in a lab. are experiences which need to be explained by real UFO abductions. Many UFO abduction experiences are ones that can be explained by ESB, so some of these experiences are not ones which need to be explained by real UFO abductions.

39. All suckers are people who will be more frequently taken for love, money or something of value sometime, and no critical thinkers are people who will be more frequently taken for love, money or something of value sometime, so no critical thinkers are suckers.

40. Nowhere in the USA is it safe to buy Crack on the street, but some Detroit neighborhoods are places where it is safe to buy crack on the street, so some Detroit neighborhoods must not even be in the USA.

EXERCISE 12B: REDUCTION, MISSING ASSUMPTIONS AND CONCLUSIONS

For any of the following which are not validly reducible to a 3 - term syllogism, write "not reducible." For any which can be reduced but which cannot make a valid syllogism, write "not valid." For enthymemes, supply the missing reason or conclusion according to the Principle of Charity (Ch. 6.11.) Use the suggested key letters. Make a cross hatch for each reducible problem to show validity or invalidity.

1.   All True Christians are humble people.
   <u>Many churchgoers are proud people.</u>
   So
   T= True Christians, P=proud people, C=churchgoers

2.   All intoxicated people are undependable people.
   <u>All alcoholics are intoxicated people.</u>
   So all dependable people are non alcoholics.
   I= intoxicated people, A= alcoholics, D=dependable people

3.   All enthymemes are incomplete arguments.

   _____

   So few arguments on this test are complete arguments.
   E=enthymemes, C= complete arguments, T= arguments on this test

4.   No rude people are good sales people.

   _____

   So most of our employees are polite people.
   E= our employees, G= good sales people , P= polite people

EXERCISE 12B

5.　　No typical subteen girl's rooms are neat.
　　　<u>All my daughter's rooms are messy.</u>
　　　So all my daughter's rooms are typical subteen girl's rooms.
　　　T =typical subteen girl's rooms, D = my daughter's rooms, M = messy rooms

6.　　Few non V are W.

　　　_____

　　　Many non X are not W.

7.　　Almost all J are N.
　　　<u>Many non J are M.</u>
　　　So

8.　　No B are C.

　　　_____

　　　Few A are B.

9.　　Many D are not E.
　　　<u>Almost all D are F</u>
　　　So

10.　　All non B are non S.
　　　　<u>Some non M are non S.</u>
　　　　So some non M are non B!

EXERCISE 13A: DETERMINING THE FORMS OF CONDITIONAL ARGUMENTS

Do each of the following problems by the methods of Chapter Seven. Use brackets and numbering as usual. Then put parentheses around the simple component statement and answer the questions below the problems. The first one is done for you as an example

I.   If you registered and paid in advance, then there will be a seat for you in the class, so you will not lose your seat in the class, because you registered and paid in advance.

A. What should be labeled P? P= You registered and paid in advance.

B. What should be labeled Q? Q= There will be a seat for you in the class.

C. ^{1} <If (you registered and paid in advance), then (there will be a seat for you in the class) > is symbolized as <If P, then Q >

D. ^{2} <you will not lose your seat in the class> is symbolized as Q

E. ^{3} <you registered and paid in advance.> is symbolized as P

F. Write here the form of this argument: <If P, then Q> + <P>

$$\downarrow$$

Q

G. The name of this form of argument is: Affirming the Antecedent

H. Is this form of argument valid or invalid? valid

2   If foreign workers are taking too many German jobs,   then   the Neo-Nazi's will make a strong comeback.   There will be a strong comeback of Neo-Nazism, so foreign workers are taking too many German jobs.

A. What should be labeled P? P= _____

B. What should be labeled Q? Q= _____

C. ^{1} <If foreign workers take too many German jobs, then the Neo-Nazi's will make a strong comeback.> is symbolized as _____

D. ^{2} <There will be a strong comeback of Neo-Nazism.> is symbolized as _____

E. ^{3} < Foreign workers take too many German jobs.> is symbolized as _____

F. Write here the form of this argument: _____

$$\downarrow$$

_____

G. The name of this form of argument is: _____

H. Is this form of argument valid or invalid? _____

3. If the football game runs overtime, then I won't get to watch the Simpsons. But I will get to watch the Simpsons, so the football game won't run overtime.

A.   What should be labeled P? P= _____

B.   What should be labeled Q? Q= _____

C.   ¹ <If the football game runs overtime, then I won't get to watch the Simpsons.>

     is symbolized as _____

D.   ² < I will get to watch the Simpsons> is symbolized as _____

E.   ³ <The football game won't run overtime.> is symbolized as _____

F.   Write here the form of this argument: _____

$$\downarrow$$

_____

G.   The name of this form of argument is: _____

H.   Is this form of argument valid or invalid? _____

4. If we can save him, then he hasn't lost too much blood. But he has lost too much blood, so we can't save him.

A.   What should be labeled P? P= _____

B.   What should be labeled Q? Q= _____

C.   ¹<Ifwe can save him, then he hasn't lost too much blood.>

     is symbolized as _____

D.   ² < He has lost too much blood> is symbolized as _____

E.   ³ < We can't save him.> is symbolized as _____

F.   Write here the form of this argument: _____

$$\downarrow$$

_____

G.   The name of this form of argument is: _____

H. Is this form of argument valid or invalid? _____

EXERCISE 13A

5.   If there's a shell in the chamber, then taking the magazine out of the gun doesn't make it harmless. Taking the magazine out in this case does make it harmless, so there's no shell in the chamber.

A.   What should be labeled P? P= _____

B.   What should be labeled Q? Q= _____

C. ^{1} <If there's a shell in the chamber, then taking the magazine out of the gun doesn't make it harmless.>

is symbolized as _____

D. ^{2} <Taking the magazine out in this case does make it harmless>

is symbolized as _____

E. ^{3} < There's no shell in the chamber.> is symbolized as _____

F.   Write here the form of this argument: _____

$$\downarrow$$

_____

G.   The name of this form of argument is: _____

H.   Is this form of argument valid or invalid? _____

6.   If the president of the Ryka athletic shoe company is a woman and a feminist, then she'll have trouble getting loans for expansion of her company. The president does have trouble getting loans to expand her company, so the president must be a woman and a feminist.

A.   What should be labeled P? P= _____

B.   What should be labeled Q? Q= _____

C. ^{1} <If the president of the Ryka athletic shoe company is a woman and a feminist, then she'll have trouble

getting loans for expansion of her company .> is symbolized as _____

D. ^{2} <The president does have trouble getting loans to expand her company.>

is symbolized as _____

E. ^{3} <The president must be a woman and a feminist.> is symbolized as _____

F.   Write here the form of this argument: _____

$$\downarrow$$

_____

G.   The name of this form of argument is: _____

H.   Is this form of argument valid or invalid? _____

7.   If the light hitting the prism is ordinary sunlight, then it will split into the spectrum. But this light does not split into the spectrum,   so it is not ordinary sunlight.

A.   What should be labeled P? P= _____

B.   What should be labeled Q? Q= _____

C.   [1] <If the light hitting the prism is ordinary sunlight, then it will split into the spectrum.>

is symbolized as _____

D.   [2] <This light does not split into the spectrum.> is symbolized as _____

E.   [3] <it is not ordinary sunlight.> is symbolized as _____

F.   Write here the form of this argument: _____

$$\downarrow$$

_____

G.   The name of this form of argument is: _____

H.   Is this form of argument valid or invalid? _____

8   The speed of water increases as it pours out, if   the rapids through which it pours gets narrower. The rapids narrow up ahead, so we better be prepared for the speed of the water to increase rapidly.

A.   What should be labeled P? P= _____

B.   What should be labeled Q? Q= _____

C.   [1] <If the rapids through which water pours get narrower, then the speed of water increases as it pours

out.> is symbolized as _____

D.   [2] <The rapids narrow up ahead.> is symbolized as _____

E.   [3] <we better be prepared for the speed of the water to increase rapidly.>

is symbolized as _____

F.   Write here the form of this argument: _____

$$\downarrow$$

_____

G.   The name of this form of argument is: _____

H.   Is this form of argument valid or invalid? _____

EXERCISE 13A

9. If the red warning light comes on, then you have 30 seconds to evacuate before the computer seals the containment with you inside.   But you don't have 30 seconds before the computer seals the containment with you inside,   so the red warning light did not come on.

A. What should be labeled P? P= _____

B. What should be labeled Q? Q= _____

C. [1] <If the red warning light comes on, then you have 30 seconds to evacuate before the computer seals the containment with you inside.> is symbolized as _____

D. [2] < You don't have 30 seconds before the computer seals the containment with you inside.> is symbolized as _____

E. [3] <The red warning light does not come on.> is symbolized as _____

F. Write here the form of this argument: _____

$$\downarrow$$

_____

G. The name of this form of argument is: _____

H. Is this form of argument valid or invalid? _____

10. If the leak in the hull is unrepairable, then the ship will sink. The leak is repairable, so the ship will not sink.

A. What should be labeled P? P= _____

B. What should be labeled Q? Q= _____

C. [1] <If the leak in the hull is unrepairable, then the ship will sink.>

    is symbolized as _____

D. [2] <The leak is repairable.> is symbolized as _____

E. [3] <The ship will not sink.> is symbolized as _____

F. Write here the form of this argument: _____

$$\downarrow$$

_____

G. The name of this form of argument is: _____

H. Is this form of argument valid or invalid? _____

EXERCISE 13B: DETERMINING THE FORMS OF CONDITIONAL ARGUMENTS

Do each of the following problems by the methods of Chapter Seven. Use brackets and numbering as usual. Then put parentheses around the simple component statements and answer the questions below the problems. The first one is done for you as an example.

1.   If I go to the basement, I'll be able to work uninterrupted. But I won't get to work uninterrupted, because I won't go to the basement.

A.   What should be labeled P? P= <u>I go to the basement.</u>

B.   What should be labeled Q? Q= <u>I'll be able to work uninterrupted.</u>

C.   ¹<If I go to the basement, I'll be able to work uninterrupted> is symbolized as <u><If P, then Q></u>

D.   ²<I won't get to work uninterrupted> is symbolized as <u>NOT -Q</u>

E.   ³<I won't go to the basement.> is symbolized as <u>NOT -P</u>

F.   Write here the form of this argument: <u><If P, then Q> + <NOT -P></u>

↓

<u>NOT -Q</u>

G.   The name of this form of argument is: <u>Denying the Antecedent.</u>

H.   Is this form of argument valid or invalid? <u>invalid</u>

2.   If Sam is out driving the convertible, then he hasn't gotten done the work I asked him to do. I see that he hasn't got it done, so he must be out driving the convertible

A.   What should be labeled P? P= _____

B.   What should be labeled Q? Q= _____

C.   ¹<If Sam is out driving the convertible, then he hasn't gotten done the work I asked him to do.> is

symbolized as _____

D.   ²<I see that he hasn't got it done.> is symbolized as _____

E.   ³<He must be out driving the convertible.> is symbolized as _____

F.   Write here the form of this argument: _____

↓

_____

G.   The name of this form of argument is: _____

H.   Is this form of argument valid or invalid? _____

3. If the words "mind", "soul" and "spirit" don't serve to explain or predict anything accurately,   then people will eventually stop using them. But people won't ever stop using them, so they must serve to accurately explain or predict something.

A. What should be labeled P? P= _____

B. What should be labeled Q? Q= _____

C. ¹<If(the words "mind", "soul" and "spirit" don't serve to explain or predict anything accurately) , then (people will eventually stop using them.).> is symbolized as

    _____

D· ² <people won't ever stop using them.> is symbolized as _____

E. ³ <they must serve to accurately explain or predict something..> is symbolized as _____

F. Write here the form of this argument: _____

$$\downarrow$$

_____

G. The name of this form of argument is: _____

H. Is this form of argument valid or invalid? _____

4. If Joe is a dealer, then he will take the Fifth Amendment when testifying. He will take the Fifth Amendment, so Joe is a drug dealer.

A. What should be labeled P? P= _____

B. What should be labeled Q? Q= _____

C. ¹<If(Joe is a dealer) , then (he will take the Fifth Amendment when testifying.)>

    is symbolized as _____

D· ² <He will take the Fifth Amendment.> is symbolized as _____

E. ³ <Joe is a drug dealer.> is symbolized as _____

F. Write here the form of this argument: _____

$$\downarrow$$

_____

G. The name of this form of argument is: _____

H. Is this form of argument valid or invalid? _____

EXERCISE 13B

5. If Nike's or Reeboks are made by foreign workers paid so little they end up working 60 hours and almost starving, then you ought not to buy them no matter how "cool" they look. That's the truth, so you ought not to buy them.

A. What should be labeled P? P= _____

B. What should be labeled Q? Q= _____

C. [1]<If(Nike's or Reeboks are made by foreign workers paid so little they end up working 60 hours and

almost starving) , then (you ought not to buy them no matter how "cool" they look.)>

is symbolized as _____

D [2] <That's the truth.> is symbolized as _____

E. [3] <you ought not to buy them.> is symbolized as _____

F. Write here the form of this argument: _____

$$\downarrow$$

_____

G.   The name of this form of argument is: _____

H. Is this form of argument valid or invalid? _____

6. If he doesn't stop groping her, she'll scream. She will scream. So he does stop groping her.

A. What should be labeled P? P= _____

B. What should be labeled Q? Q= _____

C.   [1]<If(he don't stop groping her), then (she'll scream.)> is symbolized as_D [2] <She will scream.>

is symbolized as _____

E. [3] <He does stop groping her.> is symbolized as _____

F. Write here the form of this argument: _____

$$\downarrow$$

_____

G. Not a named standard form. Write out the Magic Question:_____

H. Is this form of argument valid or invalid? _____

EXERCISE 13B

7.   You can't go on the trip unless you raise $300. You haven't raised $300, so you can't go on the trip.
     Hint: translate the "unless" statement into a conditional statement.

A.   What should be labeled P? P= _____

B.   What should be labeled Q? Q= _____

C.   ¹<If(you do not raise $300), then (You can't go on the trip.)>

     is symbolized as _____

D·   ² <You haven't raised $300> is symbolized as _____

E.   ³ < you can't go on the trip> is symbolized as _____

F.   Write here the form of this argument: _____

$$\downarrow$$

_____

G.   The name of this form of argument is: _____

H.   Is this form of argument valid or invalid? _____

8.   If you depress the accelerator pedal, then the car accelerates. So if you don't depress the accelerator
     pedal, then it doesn't accelerate.

A.   What should be labeled P? P= _____

B.   What should be labeled Q? Q= _____

C.   ¹<If(you depress the accelerator pedal), then (the car accelerates.)>

     is symbolized as _____

D·   ² <if (you don't depress the accelerator pedal), then (it doesn't accelerate).>

     is symbolized as _____

E.   Write here the form of this argument: _____

$$\downarrow$$

_____

F.   The name of this form of argument is: _____

G.   Is this form of argument valid or invalid? _____

EXERCISE 13B

9. If our top suspect has an air-tight alibi, then either the number two suspect is guilty or the number three one is guilty. The top one has an air-tight alibi. So either number two or number three is guilty. But number two can't be guilty for other reasons. So suspect number three is the guilty party. Hint: You need to use 3 letters for statements and two rules here.

A. What should be labeled P? P= _____

B. What should be labeled Q? Q= _____

C. What should be labeled R? R= _____

D. ^{1}<If(our top suspect has an air-tight alibi) , then (either the number two suspect is guilty or the number three one is guilty)> is symbolized as _____

E. ^{2} <The top one has an air-tight alibi.> is symbolized as _____

F. ^{3} <Either number two or number three is guilty.> is symbolized as _____

G. ^{4} < Number two can't be guilty for other reasons.> is symbolized as _____

H. Write here the form of this argument: _____

$$\downarrow$$

_____

I. The names of these forms of argument are: _____

J. Is this compound form of argument valid or invalid? _____

10. If we have a capitalist economic system,   then we have the capacity to produce much more value than our workers get in wages to buy the value back. We do have a capitalist system. So we have the capacity to produce much more value than our workers get in wages to buy the value back. If we have the capacity to produce much more value than our workers get in wages to buy the value back, then we get stagnation: permanent recession with very slow or no job growth. So we get stagnation: permanent recession with very slow or no job growth.

A. What should be labeled P? P=_____

B. What should be labeled Q? Q= _____

C. ¹<If(we have a capitalist economic system) , then (we have the capacity to produce much more value than our workers get in wages to buy the value back.)>

   is symbolized as _____

D. ² <We do have a capitalist system.>is symbolized as _____

E. ³< We have the capacity to produce much more value than our workers get in wages to buy the

   value back> is symbolized as _____

F. ³ <If (we have the capacity to produce much more value than our workers get in wages to buy the

   value back), then (we get stagnation: permanent recession with very slow or no job growth.)> is

   symbolized as   _____

G. ⁴ < we get stagnation: permanent recession with very slow or no job growth.>

   is symbolized as _____

H. Write here the form of the 1st argument: _____

↓

_____

I. The name of this form of argument is: _____

J. Is this form of argument valid or invalid?_____

K. Write here the form of the 2nd. argument: _____

↓

_____

L. The name of this form of argument is:_____

M. Is this form of argument valid or invalid?_____

EXERCISE 14:   DEDUCING MISSING CONCLUSIONS IN CONDITIONAL ARGUMENTS

For each of the following, fill in the answers to the questions below in order to find which form of conditional argument it is. After symbolizing and finding the form, write the conclusion. Number 1 is done.

1.   Apparently the watchdog didn't bark enough to wake the people in the house. And if the watchdog didn't bark enough to wake the people in the house, then he probably knew the intruder. So...

A.   What should be labeled P? P= <u>the watchdog didn't bark enough to wake the people in the house.</u>

B.   What should be labeled Q? Q= <u>he probably knew the intruder.</u>

C.   ¹ <The watchdog didn't bark enough to wake the people in the house.> is symbolized as <u>P</u>

D·   ² <If the watchdog didn't bark enough to wake the people in the house, then he probably knew the intruder.> is symbolized as <u><If P then Q></u>

E.   Write here the form of this argument: <u><If P then Q> + <P></u>

$$\downarrow$$

<u>Q (missing)</u>

F. The name of this form of argument is: <u>Affirming the Antecedent</u>

G. Write the conclusion, Q, here: <u>He probably knew the intruder.</u>

2   Mr. James, 75, has been started on 50mg. Zoloft™ and complains of feeling hot. If an elderly patient complains of feeling hot after 50 mg. Zoloft™, then he should be watched for hyperthermia, so...

A.   What should be labeled P? P= _____

B.   What should be labeled Q? Q= _____

C.   ¹ <Mr. James, 75, has been started on 50mg. Zoloft? and complains of feeling hot.>

is symbolized as _____

D·   ² <If an elderly patient complains of feeling hot after 50 mg. Zoloft?, then he should be watched for

hyperthermia .> is symbolized as _____

E.   Write here the form of this argument: _____

$$\downarrow$$

_____

F.   The name of this form of argument is: _____

G·   Write the specific conclusion, (Q), applied to James: _____

3. If that computer error message meant "Document Damage", then the file could not have been reconstructed. But we have reconstructed the file, so...

A. What should be labeled P? P= _____

B. What should be labeled Q? Q= _____

C. [1] <If that computer error message meant "Document Damage", then the file could not have been

reconstructed.> is symbolized as _____

D. [2] <We have reconstructed the file> is symbolized as _____

E. Write here the form of this argument: _____

$$\downarrow$$

_____

F. The name of this form of argument is: _____

G. Write the conclusion, NOT-P, here: _____

4. To pass inspection, a car must have intact motor mounts. Your car has broken motor mounts, so...

A. What should be labeled P? P= _____

B. What should be labeled Q? Q= _____

C. Translate [1] <To pass inspection, a car must have intact motor mounts.> into a conditional

"If _____, then _____"

D. [1]<> is symbolized as _____

E. [2] <Your car has broken motor mounts> is symbolized as _____

F. Write here the form of this argument: _____

$$\downarrow$$

_____

G. The name of this form of argument is: _____

H. Write the conclusion, NOT-P, here: _____

EXERCISE 14

5. If the suspect called in sick before 8 am. E.S.T. April 19, then he is probably not the Unabomber. He called in about 7:50 am., so...

A. What should be labeled P? P= _____

B. What should be labeled Q? Q= _____

C. [1] <If the suspect called in sick before 8 am. E.S.T. April 19, then he is probably not the Unabomber.>

    is symbolized as _____

D. [2] < He called in about 7:50 am.> is symbolized as _____

E. Write here the form of this argument: _____

$$\downarrow$$

_____

F. The name of this form of argument is: _____

G. Write the conclusion, Q, here: _____

6. If the carpet was any sort of dark color, then a spatter of dried blood might go unnoticed. The carpet is a dark, mottled brown. That's why...

A. What should be labeled P? P= _____

B. What should be labeled Q? Q= _____

C. [1] <If the carpet was any sort of dark color, then a spatter of dried blood might go unnoticed.>

    is symbolized as _____

D. [2] < The carpet is a dark, mottled brown.> is symbolized as _____

E. Write here the form of this argument: _____

$$\downarrow$$

_____

F. The name of this form of argument is: _____

G. Write the conclusion, Q, here: _____

EXERCISE 14

7. If the hurricane comes ashore at Miami, then it will be a national disaster. So if... (Hint: This one is of the form called "Transposition".)

A. What should be labeled P? P= _____

B. What should be labeled Q? Q= _____

C. [1] <If the hurricane comes ashore at Miami, then it will be a national disaster.>

is symbolized as _____

D. Write here the form of this argument: _____

$$\downarrow$$

_____

E. Write the conclusion here: _____

8. The speed of water increases as it pours out, if the opening through which it pours gets narrower. The opening narrows up ahead, so ...

A. What should be labeled P? P= _____

B. What should be labeled Q? Q= _____

C. [1] <If the opening through which [water] pours gets narrower, then the speed of water increases as it

pours out.> is symbolized as: _____

D. [2] <The opening narrows up ahead.> is symbolized as: _____

E. Write here the form of this argument: _____

$$\downarrow$$

_____

F. The name of this form of argument is: _____

G. Write the conclusion, Q, here: _____

EXERCISE 14

9. If the amount of dark matter in the universe is greater than that of visible matter, then the universe will eventually collapse again. The universe will always expand, so...

A. What should be labeled P? P= _____

B. What should be labeled Q? Q= _____

C. [1] <If the amount of dark matter in the universe is greater than that of visible matter, then the universe

will eventually collapse again. .> is symbolized as: _____

D. [2] <The universe will always expand> is symbolized as: _____

E. Write here the form of this argument: _____

$$\downarrow$$

_____

F. The name of this form of argument is: _____

G. Write the conclusion, NOT-P, here: _____

10. If the leak in the hull is repairable, then the ship will not sink. The leak can be fixed, so the ship will not go down.

A. What should be labeled P? P= _____

B. What should be labeled Q? Q= _____

C. [1] <If the leak in the hull is repairable, then the ship will not sink> is symbolized as:

_____

D. [2] <The leak can be fixed.> is symbolized as: _____

E. Write here the form of this argument: _____

$$\downarrow$$

F. The name of this form of argument is: _____

G. Write the conclusion, Q, here: _____

EXERCISE 15:   SUPPLYING MISSING ASSUMPTIONS IN CONDITIONAL ARGUMENTS

For each of the following, fill in the answers to the questions below in order to find which form of conditional argument it is. After you have symbolized and found the form you should be able to write the missing reason. The first one is done for you.

1.   This piano will need a heating rod installed, because If a piano is going to be installed in a damp room, then it needs to have a heating rod installed, and because...

A.   What should be labeled P? P= _A piano is going to be installed in a damp room._

B.   What should be labeled Q? Q= _It needs to have a heating rod._

C.   [1] <This piano will need a heating rod installed.> is symbolized as: _Q_

D.   [2] <If a piano is going to be installed in a damp room, then it needs to have a heating rod installed,> is symbolized as: _<If P, then Q>_

E.   Write here the form of this argument: _<If P, then Q> + **P (missing)**_

$$\downarrow$$

_Q_

F.   The name of this form of argument is: _Affirming the Antecedent_

G.   Write the mising reason, P, here:_____

2   You can't have a rabbit, because rabbits are dirty, disgusting animals, and ...

A.   What should be labeled P? P= _____

B.   What should be labeled Q? Q= _____

C.   [1] <You can't have a rabbit> is symbolized as: _____

D.   [2] <rabbits are dirty, disgusting animals> is symbolized as:_____

E.   Write here the form of this argument: _____

$$\downarrow$$

_____

F. The name of this form of argument is: _____

G. Write the missing reason, <If P, then Q>, here: _____

3. It is a flywheel-based mechanical tredmill, so it should be cheaper and last longer than a motorized one because...

A. What should be labeled P? P= _____

B. What should be labeled Q? Q= _____

C. [1] <It is a flywheel based mechanical tredmill> is symbolized as: _____

D. [2] <It should be cheaper and last longer than a motorized one>

   is symbolized as: _____

E. Write here the form of this argument: _____

$$\downarrow$$

$$\underline{\qquad}$$

F. The name of this form of argument is: _____

G. Write the missing reason, <If P, then Q> , here: _____

4. If Anita Hill was telling the truth, then Clarence Thomas was guilty of sexual harrassment. So he was guilty of sexual harrassment, because...

A. What should be labeled P? P= _____

B. What should be labeled Q? Q= _____

C. [1] < If Anita Hill was telling the truth, then Clarence Thomas was guilty of sexual harrassment.> is

   symbolized as: _____

D. [2] < He was guilty of sexual harrassment.> is symbolized as:_____

E. Write here the form of this argument: _____

$$\downarrow$$

$$\underline{\qquad}$$

F. The name of this form of argument is: _____

G. Write the missing reason, P, here _____

EXERCISE 15

5. If we came down under heavy tree cover, then the G.P.S. (Global Positioning System) Locator would not work, so we did not come down under heavy cloud cover, since...

A. What should be labeled P? P= _____

B. What should be labeled Q? Q= _____

C. ¹ < If we came down under heavy tree cover, then the G.P.S. (Global Positioning System) Locator would not work> is symbolized as: _____

D· ² < we did not come down under heavy cloud cover> is symbolized as _____

E. Write here the form of this argument: _____

↓

_____

F. The name of this form of argument is: _____

G. Write the missing reason, NOT-Q , here: _____

6. If I go to work at a job I can get, I'll make less money than my welfare benefits which themselves leave us in poverty. So I won't got to work at a job I can get, because...

A. What should be labeled P? P= _____

B. What should be labeled Q? Q= _____

C. ¹ < If I go to work at a job I can get, I'll make less money than my welfare benefits which themselves leave us in poverty> is symbolized as: _____

D. ² < I won't got to work at a job I can get> is symbolized as: _____

E. Write here the form of this argument: _____

↓

_____

F. The name of this form of argument is: _____

G. Write the missing reason, NOT-Q, here: _____

EXERCISE 15

7.   If somebody cut your bangs too short, then you look dumb, so you look dumb, because, Girl,....

A.   What should be labeled P? P= _____

B.   What should be labeled Q? Q= _____

C.   ¹ <If somebody cut your bangs too short, then you look dumb.>

       is symbolized as: _____

D·   ² <You look dumb.> is symbolized as: _____

E.   Write here the form of this argument: _____

$$\downarrow$$

_____

F.   The name of this form of argument is: _____

G.   Write the missing reason, P, here: _____

8.   If 8 is not a prime number, then it is a composite number, so it must be a composite number, because...

A.   What should be labeled P? P= _____

B.   What should be labeled Q? Q= _____

C.   ¹ <If 8 is not a prime number, then it is a composite number.>

       is symbolized as: _____

D·   ² <It must be a composite number.> is symbolized as: _____

E.   Write here the form of this argument: _____

$$\downarrow$$

_____

F.   The name of this form of argument is: _____

G.   Write the missing reason, P , here: _____

EXERCISE 15

9. Your grades went down a half a letter, because you got a Mohican style hair cut and...

A. What should be labeled P? P= _____

B. What should be labeled Q? Q= _____

C. [1] <Your grades went down a half a letter.> is symbolized as: _____

D. [2] <You got a Mohican style hair cut.> is symbolized as: _____

E. Write here the form of this argument: _____

$$\downarrow$$

_____

F. The name of this form of argument is: _____

G. Write the missing reason, If P, then Q, here: _____

10. If the water leak is entering between the tiles and the floor, then either the seal is cracked or there is a hairline crack in the pipe immediately below. There is a hairline crack in the pipe below, because..., and because... (Hint: This involves 3 statements, P, Q, R and 2 steps of inference. The first "because" is a conditional, the second is Disjunctive Syllogism.)

A. What should be labeled P? P= _____

B. What should be labeled Q? Q= _____

C. What should be labeled R? R= _____

D. [1] < If the water leak is entering between the tiles and the floor, then either the seal is cracked or there is a hairline crack in the pipe immediately below.>

is symbolized as: _____

E. [2] <There is a hairline crack in the pipe below> is symbolized as: _____

F. Write here the form of the conditional argument: _____

$$\downarrow$$

_____

G. The name of this form of argument is: _____

H. Write the first missing reason, P, here: _____

I. Now we have as a conclusion "Either the seal is cracked or there is a hairline crack in the pipe immediately below." Write the reason, according to the form of Disjunctive Syllogism, which we need to conclude R. _____

_____

J. Symbolize this missing reason: _____

EXERCISE 16:   *MODERATE TO FALLACIOUS ARGUMENTS*

For each of the passages follow the methods of Chapter Eight. Number and angle bracket the reasons and conclusions. Make an arrow diagram of the passage. To find the type of argument, *work by process of elimination.* Cross out the names of the argument types that clearly don't seem to you to be involved in the passage. *Don't just guess!* Review the definitions, forms, and examples if necessary. Judge whether the argument is moderate, weak or a fallacy.

GROUP 1: Each of the following is best analyzed as one of these forms: Appeal to Authority, Two Wrongs Make a Right, Argument from Ignorance, Slippery Slope, and Argument from Force.

1. People have been claiming for years that there is some large, unusual sea creature in Loch Ness, but none of them has ever produced a single piece of decisive evidence that this is true, so their claims must be *false.*

DIAGRAM:
Process of elimination: It is *not*: Authority, Two Wrongs, Ignorance, Slope, Force.

This is MOST LIKE the form or example of:_____

_____
Final Answer: Name of Form: _____

Answers to Test Questions for this form:_____

_____

_____

This argument is (circle one) Moderate   Weak   Fallacious

Explain your choice _____

_____

2.   Blacks and women have been discriminated against. But if you are going to have affirmative action for them, you should have it for other groups of people who have been discriminated against. So you should have it not only for gays and the handicapped, Epileptics, poor people, ugly people, sex workers and fat people have all been discriminated against. Where will affirmative action end?

DIAGRAM:
Process of elimination: It is *not*: Authority, Two Wrongs, Ignorance, Slope, Force.

This is MOST LIKE the form or example of:_____

_____
Final Answer: Name of Form: _____

Answers to Test Questions for this form:_____

_____

_____

This argument is (circle one) Moderate   Weak   Fallacious

Explain your choice_____

_____

EXERCISE 16

3. I wouldn't be overly concerned about 50,000 Cubans being diagnosed with optic neuritis because they can't get proper nutrition owing to the United States embargo. After all, when the Castro government took over Cuba, it stole casinos, brothels and other American property and never paid the owners back.

DIAGRAM:

Process of elimination: It is *not*: Authority, Two Wrongs, Ignorance, Slope, Force.

This is MOST LIKE the form or example of: _____

_____

Final Answer: Name of form: _____

Answers to Test Questions for this form: _____

_____

_____

This argument is (circle one) Moderate   Weak   Fallacious

Explain your choice _____

_____

_____

4. Now you want to let these college dorms be coed floor by floor. What's next? - room by room? Why not boy and girl in the same room? How about providing condoms so they can have "responsible sex"? How about welfare for the little bastards that happen "by accident"? Just tell me this: have you got cures for all the cases of herpes, the cervical cancer that increases with sexual activity, the cases of clap, syphilis and AIDS that will result from coed dorms?

DIAGRAM:

Process of elimination: It is *not*: Authority, Two Wrongs, Ignorance, Slope, Force.

This is MOST LIKE the form or example of: _____

_____

Final Answer: Name of form: _____

Answers to Test Questions for this form: _____

_____

_____

This argument is (circle one) Moderate   Weak   Fallacious

Explain your choice _____

_____

_____

EXERCISE 16

GROUP 2: Each of the following is best analyzed as Argument Against the Man, Hasty Generalization, Ignoring Qualifications, Questionable Analogy, Questionable Cause, or Ambiguity.

5. An uncorrupt big city mayor is about as rare as a round square. So you are as likely to run into the one as the other.

DIAGRAM:

Process of elimination: It is *not*: Argument Against the Man, Hasty Generalization, Questionable Analogy, Questionable Cause, or Ambiguity.

This is MOST LIKE the form or example of: _____

Final Answer: Name of form: _____

Answers to Test Questions for this form: _____

_____

This argument is (circle one) Moderate   Weak   Fallacious

Explain your choice _____

_____

6. Watching violent TV results in increased violence by the watching audience. Look at the US, in which we have teenagers watching more hours of more violent TV than anywhere else in the world, and we also have the highest rate of homicide by teenagers anywhere in the world.

DIAGRAM:

Process of elimination: It is *not*: Argument Against the Man, Hasty Generalization, Questionable Analogy, Questionable Cause, or Ambiguity.

This is MOST LIKE the form or example of: _____

Final Answer: Name of form: _____

Answers to Test Questions for this form: _____

_____

This argument is (circle one) Moderate   Weak   Fallacious

Explain your choice _____

_____

EXERCISE 16

7. Men are all alike. They all want the same thing and only that! This is the third time this month I went to a singles bar, and the third time I've been propositioned!

DIAGRAM:

Process of elimination: It is NOT: Argument Against the Man, Hasty Generalization, Questionable Analogy, Questionable Cause, or Ambiguity.

This is MOST LIKE the form or example of:_____

_____

Final Answer: Name of form: _____

Answers to Test Questions for this form:_____

_____

_____

This argument is (circle one) Moderate   Weak   Fallacious
Explain your choice _____

_____

_____

8. People have an absolute human right to marry whomever they want to. Therefore in a free society with separation of church and state they should have a civil right to marry someone of their own sex.

DIAGRAM:

Process of elimination: It is NOT: Argument Against the Man, Hasty generalization, Questionable Analogy, Questionable Cause, or Ambiguity.

This is MOST LIKE the form or example of:_____

_____

Final Answer: Name of form: _____

Answers to Test Questions for this form:_____

_____

_____

This argument is (circle one) Moderate   Weak   Fallacious

Explain your choice _____

_____

_____

EXERCISE 16

9. "You've got to play to win." Advertising slogan of the PA lottery. (Hint: First draw the conclusion.)

DIAGRAM:

Process of elimination: It is *not*: Argument Against the Man, Hasty generalization, Questionable Analogy, Questionable Cause, or Ambiguity.

This is MOST LIKE the form or example of: _____

Final Answer: Name of form: _____

Answers to Test Questions for this form: _____

_____

_____

This argument is (circle one) Moderate   Weak   Fallacious

Explain your choice _____

_____

_____

10. Mary's conception of Jesus was immaculate and "immaculate" means clean of sex, so sex must be dirty.

DIAGRAM:

Process of elimination: It is NOT: Argument Against the Man, Hasty generalization, Questionable Analogy, Questionable Cause, or Ambiguity.

This is MOST LIKE the form or example of: _____

Final Answer: Name of form: _____

Answers to Test Questions for this form: _____

_____

_____

This argument is (circle one) Moderate   Weak   Fallacious

Explain your choice _____

_____

_____

GROUP 3: Each of the following is best analyzed as one these forms: Straw Man, False Dilemma, Begging the Question, Inconsistency or Irrelevant Reason.

11. "Chiropractic is not a treatment for ear infections. Chiropractors free the spine from spinal nerve stress (also called vertebral subluxations or spinal lesions) by using spinal adjustments. And yet a chiropractic spinal adjustment is one of the best things that could happen to a child (or adult) suffering from ear infection."   Ear Infections, pamphlet, Koren Publications, Inc. Tedd Koren, D.C. 1991

DIAGRAM:

Process of elimination: It is NOT: Straw Man, False Dilemma, Begging the Question, or Inconsistency.

This is MOST LIKE the form or example of: _____

Final Answer: Name of form: _____

Answers to Test Questions for this form: _____

_____

_____

This argument is (circle one) Moderate   Weak   Fallacious

Explain your choice _____

_____

_____

12. The Environmental Protection Agency ought to be abolished.   Those nuts even want to prohibit outdoor barbecues!

DIAGRAM:

Process of elimination: It is NOT: Straw Man, False Dilemma, Begging the Question, or Inconsistency.

This is MOST LIKE the form or example of: _____

Final Answer: Name of form: _____

Answers to Test Questions for this form: _____

_____

This argument is (circle one) Moderate   Weak   Fallacious

Explain your choice _____

_____

_____

EXERCISES 16

13. Guns don't kill people, People kill people. (slogan of the National Rifle Association) (Hint: draw the conclusion first.)

DIAGRAM:

Process of elimination: It is NOT Straw Man, False Dilemma, Begging the Question, Inconsistency.

This is MOST LIKE the form or example of: _____

Final Answer: Name of form: _____

Answers to Test Questions for this form: _____

_____

_____

This argument is (circle one) Moderate   Weak   Fallacious

Explain your choice _____

_____

_____

14. I won't do that, because it is simply not right. I know it is not right because my conscience tells me so. My conscience tells me so because it's wrong to do that!

DIAGRAM:

Process of elimination: It is NOT: Straw Man, False Dilemma, Begging the Question, Inconsistency.

This is MOST LIKE the form or example of: _____

Final Answer: Name of form: _____

Answers to Test Questions for this form: _____

_____

_____

This argument is (circle one) Moderate   Weak   Fallacious

Explain your choice _____

_____

_____

EXERCISE 16

15. Because a woman can become pregnant only 1 or 2 days a month, but can catch or transmit diseases 365 days a year,   condoms must be much less effective in preventing disease than in preventing pregnancy.

DIAGRAM:

Process of elimination: It is NOT: Straw Man, False Dilemma, Begging the Question, Inconsistency.

This is MOST LIKE the form or example of:_____

_____

Final Answer: Name of form: _____

Answers to Test Questions for this form:_____

_____

_____

This argument is (circle one) Moderate   Weak   Fallacious

Explain your choice _____

_____

_____

EXERCISE 17:   STATISTICAL PROBLEMS
CONSISTENT OR INCONSISTENT SUPPORT?

Read each of the following pairs of passages each consisting of a statistical claim (SC) and a conclusion (C) drawn from it. Then resolve the problem presented by the two passages following the method Chapter 9, Section 3. Select that one of the following possibilities which best characterizes the relation between the passages. To do this you will have to judge whether the two statistical claims are consistent or inconsistent, then judge which of the statistical claims gives the higher degree of support for its conclusion and write the letter of the correct alternative (A, B, C, D or E) immediately after the last word of passage II.

A   The statistical claims in the two passages are inconsistent, so that one must be true and the other false. Therefore at least one of the two arguments is unsound.

B   The statistical claims in the two passages are not inconsistent and the degree of support that the SC in I gives to its conclusion is higher than the degree of support that the SC in II gives to its conclusion.

C   The SC's in the two positions are not inconsistent and the degree of support that the SC in II gives to its' conclusion is higher than the degree of support that the SC in I gives to its' conclusion.

D   The SC's are not inconsistent and provide about the same amount of support for their conclusions.

E   The conclusions are too ambiguous or vague or the statistics are at cross purposes, so the issue is not really resolved by the information given.

Problem 1. I. As of 1969, a total of 26.4 million Americans, in 50 states, of 412 distinct occupations, owned common stock. Therefore we have in this country a "People's Capitalism" with very widespread participation in ownership and control of profit producing property.

II. A controlling interest in a corporation is as little as 6% of its widely held stock and by 1969 99 families owned nearly 12% of the common stock of the 232 largest industrial corporations. So "People's Capitalism" is a laugh - most profit producing property in the US is owned and controlled by a very few very rich people.

Problem 2. I. Of 2213 heroin addicts examined 70.4% had used marijuana before their addiction. Therefore the use of marijuana leads to the use of heroin.

II. There are, at most, only 3.3 heroin addicts in the country for every 100 pot smokers. Therefore marijuana is not a stepping stone to heroin for 96.7% of its smokers.

Problem 3. I. The incidence of sex crimes in Copenhagen has dropped 26% since the Danes legalized publication of pornography. So pornography does not lead to more sex crimes.

II. In a cleverly designed experiment, 100 adult male subjects were kept in waiting rooms containing pornographic magazines, given a brief, irrelevant psychological test, and released into a dead end alley where a woman unmistakably dressed and made up as a prostitute was standing on the corner at the mouth of the alley they had to exit by. The woman was a "plant" and was instructed to make no overt contact other than to look at the subject with an indifferent air. Then it was done with a control group of 100 adult males with no pornographic magazines in the waiting room. Results indicate that 18% more of the subjects exposed to the pornographic magazines made sexual overtures to the woman. Since solicitation to commit prostitution is a crime, we can certainly conclude that pornography does lead to an increase in sex crime.

EXERCISE 17

Problem 4. I. The voting rate in urban areas is lower than in other areas. So urban areas have less than their share of influence in presidential balloting.

II. 70% of the American public lives in urban areas. Electoral votes are apportioned to states according to their populations. So highly populated areas have an overly large influence in presidential balloting voting rates.

Problem 5. I. The cumulative average for all students at this school is 2.2 on a 4.0 basis, while for those involved in varsity sports, it is 2.4. So being in varsity sports helps your grades.

II. 19% of students in this school are on academic probation. But 21% of those students involved in varsity sports are on probation. Therefore being on a varsity sports team hurts your grades.

EXERCISE 18:   PSEUDO EXPLANATIONS
"THE DEVIL MADE ME DO IT"

Find in a news story an example of pseudo explanation of events which seems to have one or more alternative, more probable explanations. Stories involving excuses for criminal activity are now and then of this sort. For example, a Pastor Rossi was accused of beating his wife and leaving her near death in an out of the way place. He contended, and she finally supported him in claiming that a demon who looked just like him did it.

Bring the story to class with a write-up containing a neutral description of the event, the pseudo explanation given, your criticism or it and what you think is (are) more likely alternative explanation(s.) (Write at least 200 words in clear, grammatically correct sentences.)

EXERCISE 19:   JURY RESEARCH AND LEGAL JUSTIFICATION
PICKING A SURE-FIRE WINNER?

Something called "jury research" is gaining popularity among defense attorneys in particular for cases in which defendants have the means to pay for it. It was used, for example, in the Simpson murder case. Research the subject of jury research in your state with respect to the number and types of challenges allowed in seating a jury. Find or develop your own arguments pro and con on the subject. Write a 500 word essay defining and giving examples of jury research. Summarize the arguments for and against it in its effect on the justification of jury verdicts.

EXERCISE 20:   MINDS AND COMPUTERS
CAN COMPUTERS THINK?

Alan Turing developed the mathematical theory of computing. In a 1953 paper called "Computing Machinery and Intelligence," in a journal of philosophy named *Mind,* he argued that computers would eventually be able to think. Turing's paper began an long controversy in philosophy still going on today. Read Turing's original paper and writings supporting and arguing against this thesis. Writers arguing for this are Herbert Simon, Douglas Hofstadter, Marvin Minsky, Roger Shank and John Haugeland (*Artificial Intelligence, The Very Idea*.) Writers arguing against it include John Lucas, Hubert Drefus, John Searle, and Roger Penrose (*The Emperor's New Mind.*)

Write a philosophical paper summarizing arguments on both sides. What implications would it have for the nature of the human mind if a computer could be programmed to behave with competence indistinguishable from a human mind? (1,000 words.)

EXERCISE 21:   CONTROVERSIAL RELIGIOUS BELIEFS

Numerous Christian denominations have specific beliefs on subjects such as the nature of God, Christ, the Holy Spirit, sin, redemption, salvation, retribution, healing, Armageddon and other theological topics.

Find the controversial beliefs on one or more of these topics held by one of the following denominations: Christian Science, Theosophy, the Jehova's Witnesses, Mormonism, The Way International, Unity, the People's Temple, the Branch Davidians or the Unification church. Write a short essay, at least 300 words, stating the controversial belief(s) and the arguments, if any, the denomination gives for them. Cite your references for these beliefs and arguments.

Usually there is some testimonial in writing by some former member of such a denomination critical of the beliefs and practices of the denomination. Find one such, quote from it and provide a bibliographical reference to it.

EXERCISE 22:   MINOR PSEUDOSCIENCES AND PARANORMAL CLAIMS

Almost all of the following topics are among many found in the index to James Randi's *Encyclopedia of Claims, Frauds and Hoaxes of the Occult and the Supernatural* (St. Martin's Press.) Look one up in Randi's book or some other skeptical source and also a report of it in a source favorable to the existence of the phenomenon.

Write a brief report (at least 300 words) describing the alleged phenomenon, the report given of its occurrence and why it is improbable that it ever occurs. If possible, explain how the favorable reporter might have been deceived into making the claim he or she makes or give an explanation you think is the most probable for the claims made in the report.

The List: Akashic records, Appollonius of Tyana, Bed of Nails, bilocation, Edgar Cayce, clairaudience - clairvoyance, demons, divination, dermo-optical perception, dowsing, ectoplasm, exorcism, false memory syndrome, fakirs, Gnosticism, the Great White Brotherhood, Greatraks the Stroker, Hellstroemism (muscle-reading), Holocaust Revisionism, Peter Hurkos, The Illuminati, jaduwallah, the Jupiter Effect, Kabala, Koot Hoomi, Lemuria, lycanthropy, macumba, Malleus Malleficarum, the Masonic Order, necromancy, Necronomicon, numerology, obeah, orgone, philosopher's stone, phrenology, plant perception, psychic surgery, psychometry, qi or "qi gong," Rosicrucians, scarab, scrying, seance, Seth (Channeled entity), shaman, spondylotherapy, the Templars, Theosophy, voodoo, World Ice theory, Yggdrasil, yin and yang.

EXERCISE 23:   CHECKING AND INTERPRETING STATISTICS

Pick one of the statistical or other claims in Chapter 15 on a subject of interest to you. Attempt to check its' accuracy by consulting any source cited in the text. Go beyond that reference to any original source. See if you can find any source which makes a claim inconsistent with the one you pick. For example, this author once saw the claim that it takes 100 times more energy to melt down and recycle metal cans than to just throw them away, mine more metal and make new cans. (Conservative and fringe publications are a frequent source of such claims inconsistent with what you have read in Chapter 15.) Decide what you think is the fact on the matter. Consider and write out alternative interpretations or explanations for the fact. Write this up as a paper, including an argument for your view as to what the fact really is or your interpretation of the fact.

EXERCISE 24A: ON JUDGING UNSUPPORTED STATEMENTS

Evaluate each statement as definitely or probably true or unwarranted. Apply concepts summarized in Appendix II. Start with "This statement is definitely (or probably) true" or "...unwarranted." Then apply one of the concepts correctly in explanation of the answer. No credit will be given for just the words "definitely true", "probably true", or "unwarranted." Write several complete, grammatically correct sentences for each. Where there are quotes, judge only what is in the quotes. Pay special attention to words in *italics*.

1. As he took his last breath, I saw his Spirit float up out of his body.
2. We're having cadavers for lunch on Thursday.
3. The Einsteinian constant is not a constant, is not a center. - J. Derrida
4. Derrida's observation relates to the invariance of the Einstein field equation under nonlinear space-time diffeomorphisms. - Alan Sokal
5. I was in the 4th. Battalion at the time last year when it was overrun and absolutely, totally wiped out - everyone was killed.
6. Americans fear speaking before a group more than they fear sickness or death.
7. After being with you, no other woman will ever do.
8. This statement, #8, is false.
9. I feel the presence of Jesus in my life.
10. Skiing is like sex: you don't have to be good at it to enjoy it.
11. The Statue of Liberty is located in the harbor of New York City.

12. Now, you can make $100 per week working in your own home stuffing envelopes.
13. Most people find being murdered painful.
14. Some unidentified flying objects are piloted or guided by intelligent aliens.
15. Said Wednesday: "There was a huge fight in the local bar last Saturday and a guy was knifed and killed, only it's been hushed up."
16. The *average* American family receives an income of $29, 272 per year.
17. Cats that stay indoors probably live an average of several years longer than those that go out.
18. If we have sex now, it will deepen our commitment to each other after marriage.
19. Jobs in American manufacturing have increased under global free trade.
20. I feel the presence of Jesus in my life *telling me that abortion is murder.*
21. These size 19 footprints must have been made by Bigfoot.
22. Most of the leaders of the French Revolution were eventually decaffeinated.
23. Femininity is sweetness, passivity, nurturance.
24. When I weep, it brings tears to my eyes.
25. Advertising smoking as in any way desirable is morally wrong.

EXERCISE 24B: ON JUDGING UNSUPPORTED STATEMENTS

Evaluate each statement as definitely or probably true or unwarranted. Apply concepts summarized in Appendix II. Start with "This statement is definitely (or probably) true" or "...unwarranted." Then apply one of the concepts correctly in explanation of the answer. No credit will be given for just the words "definitely true", "probably true", or"unwarranted." Write severalcomplete, grammatically correct sentences for each. Where there are quotes, judge only what is in the quotes. Pay special attention to words in *italics*.

1.   Edgar Cayce could fall asleep on a book and in the morning, without having read it, he would know its contents.
2.   The Absolute reveals itself in the structures of consciousness.
3.   To me, dogs noses look like electrical outlets.
4.   Life before domestication/agriculture was largely one of leisure, intimacy with nature, *sensual wisdom,* sexual equality and health. - by F.C.
5.   Somewhere in the world today, a ruthless billionaire hunts for his fugitive clone.
6.   Plane crashes always *come in threes.*
7.   "I did't inhale" - said by Bill Clinton about smoking marijuana.
8. " Students [should realize] that program completion expectations may vary from initial expectations." Edinboro University Catalog. Paraphrase!
9.   A large majority of us are more intelligent and less prejudiced than *average.*
10. 5,000 new people a day in the United States try cocaine.
11. Functioning Iraqi soldiers were involuntarily interred in trenches by US forces. Paraphrase!
12. The sex was so good I thought my hair was going to catch fire.
13. Primitive humans did not engage in cannibalism.
14. The Yucatan peninsula has *the same* sort of climate as the Baja Peninsula.
15. Most adults like sex.
16. You can get rich buying real estate with little or no money down.
17. Cats that stay indoors live an average of 3 years, *7 months, 13 days and 3 hrs.* longer than those that go out.
18. There is an amusement park near Cleveland, Ohio.
19. All dodeca*hedrons* are *polygons.* Hint: look up poly*gons* and poly*hedrons.*
20. A 15km. race would be about 18 miles.
21. My *puppy* is 12 years old.
22. Woman has an innate religious impulse toward the transcendent.
23. Mexico had an economic boom after the North American Free Trade Agreement.
24. It is right to put murderers to death.
25. Ideas, like viruses, contain elements that help them reproduce in new hosts.

EXERCISE 24C: JUDGING UNSUPPORTED STATEMENTS

Evaluate each statement as definitely or probably true or unwarranted. Apply concepts summarized in
AppendixII. Start with "This statement is definitely (or probably) true" or "...unwarranted." Then apply
one of the concepts correctly in explanation of the answer. No credit will be given for just the words
"definitely true," "probably true," or "unwarranted." Write several complete, grammatically correct
statements for each. Where there are quotes, judge only what is in the quotes. Pay special attention to words
in *italics*.

1. It's OK to eat these candy bars , so long as I have only a diet soda with them.
2. My mother had no children of any sort at all.
3. Me and Gloria were in the back seat of the car, just rubbin' and buffin'. Paraphrase!
4. This is a no-risk investment which will double your money in just 4 years.
5. The Texas capital punishment law deterred *6,341* murders last month.
6. I confess I worshipped Baphomet, the goat-headed god, while drinking the blood of unbaptized babies.
7. Instructing at our university is challenging because of over-enrollment of students with extreme
    intelligence or motivational deficits. Paraphrase!
8. " Teacher, I saw the 2 problems on this side, but I didn't see the 8 problems on the other side of the
    test." Take the teacher's viewpoint!
9. In a top secret experiment, the U.S. government has kept the severed head of a terrorist alive for over
    two years.
10. I must have had 10 pieces of your exquisite pizza!
11. Growth in the Gross National Product benefits the poor and the environment.
12. America is a Christian nation. - Pat Robertson
13. I swear I saw Elvis at the Country Fair store at 2 am last night.
14. To beat the Raiders, you gotta outscore 'em! - John Madden
15. When I was in the Marines, I single - handedly wiped out a company of the enemy.
16. The Nothing annihilates. (translation of Martin Heidegger's "Das Nicht nichtet.")
17. "I am 110 % innocent (of killing my ex-wife)" - O. j. Simpson.
18. Checkers move only on the diagonal.
19. 94% of college professors are better teachers than the average professor.
20. Most people vomit out of spite.
21. Being is one and motionless.
22. I feel that the Dead Kennedy's music was obscene.
23. Man is a constructive animal, always building structures to outlive him.
24. Government, like a family, should never spend more yearly than its annual income.
25. Dad, I swear, the car was damaged by a meteor!